A Probation Officer

in the

Cauldron of India

We are all alchemists in the laboratory of life;
Each distilling the elixir of experience

The most holy trinosophia
of the Comte de St Germain

Mhaletta Taylor

Other books by Mhaletta Taylor:

Telling Tales - The Art of Mystical Storyteling

Published by R.A. Associates 2006
ISBN 978 0 9535210 3 6

Benjaya's Gifts

Published by Hazelwood Press 1996
ISBN 978 1901 272000

Typeset in Times New Roman

* *Cover photo by Mhaletta*

ISBN 0 9535210 8 7
ISBN 978 0 9535210 8 1

Published by R.A. Associates 2011
Designed and printed in the UK
mail@whitefeather.org.uk

For The Family of Adam House
Sandra : Carmella : Marc : Charlotte
Sommer: Joshua: Amy
Benjaya : Asher
Yasmin : Daisy
& Isla

In thanksgiving: for their inspirational presence in my life and that
the generations yet to come may truly know an ancestor.

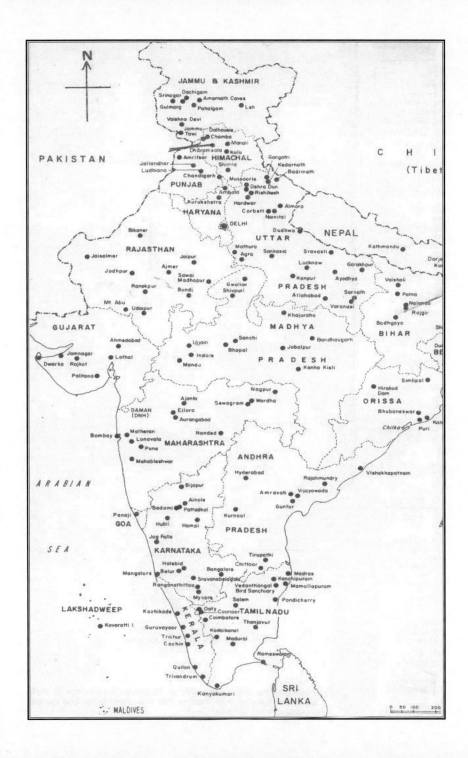

Contents

Cauldron of India

The First Part

The Second Part

The Third Part

Prisoners of the Law

A child, tender in years, grew in a great city where Giant Gates and long-legged walls encircling a secret place, shadowed her path. Day came when filled with daring she asked the question:

> *'Mother, what lies behind the Giant Gates?'*
> *The mother answered, short with busyness, 'People.'*
> *'Why mother? Why do they lie down in there?'*
> *'Because they have not obeyed the letter of the Law.'*

Filled with a wide eyed fear for her own obedience the child fell into a safe silence. She knew her alphabet from A to Zee but no-one had told her which was the letter of the Law, nor for that matter how to obey a letter. So she waited in watchful ignorance until day came when her father stood alone. Risking yet again she asked the question:

> *'Father, what lies behind the Giant Gates?'*
> *'People who have not obeyed the Spirit of the Law'*

answered Father in tone so serious that the child shrank into a pocket of thought. First a letter, then a spirit! This was much worse. She knew her letters but no-one had taught her about spirits.

Seeing her consternation her father in a strangely knowing voice wrapped her mind in words of wonder that stemmed the tide of questions.

> *'They lie there child because they cannot stand the world.*
> *Day will come when you will teach the letter of the Law*
> *and the Spirit of the Law will teach you.'*

A Probation Officer
in the
Cauldron of India

Introduction

Few books are written by Probation Officers because of the sensitive and confidential nature of their work. There are none to my knowledge that transport the reader on a roller coaster from the West Midlands of England into the jails of Delhi and the Punjab, setting a trail that through the ensuing years leads onwards through the heart of Hyderabad and the jungles of Orissa, onto the golden shores of Goa, and beyond to wherever the voice of wisdom calls, whilst revealing the essence of their personal and inner life. This is an autobiographical tale of exploration and endurance, a mystery charged with emotion that crosses the threshold of everyday reality.

A Probation Officer is trained to penetrate to the truth of lives in turmoil, to help turn them around. Transformation is not to them a luxury, but a necessity, if people who have transgressed the Law are to remain free citizens. Transformation is their profession, sometimes referred to as a 'mongrel profession'. Elements of the psychologist, lawyer, teacher, policeman, social worker, confessional priest and most certainly scribe, combine as they search for ways to uphold both the Law and the transgressors. The body of their work takes place behind closed doors and shuttered personal lives. Yet how wide can a door open when India comes knocking? India stepped into my life like a predestined marriage. It felt as if I had made a pledge, a commitment to engage. It is a union that has disrupted my life, enriched it immeasurably, brought status in profession and become synonymous with death; taught me about life of body and spirit, thrown me out sick and whimpering and welcomed me back like a long lost lover. My heart is bound up in her inescapably.

The First Part

The Bare Bones

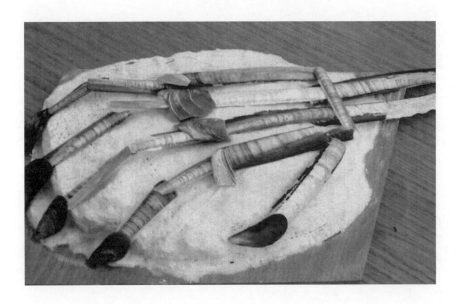

Every country has a tide that ebbs and flows. They are
The Tides of History. Step into that flow and you become
creator as you add a droplet to the cauldron of that nation.

1. The Prophesy

India, land of endless legends newly told
by voices of the prophets of tomorrow
gleaming even now within their faint disguise.

The Coming of the Prophets

Prophecies come in many guises, falling from the pen or delivered to the doorstep, threading into the fabric of an unsuspecting life.

There's a woman on my doorstep, smiling, hesitant.

'I'm trying to find lodging for two Indian men for a month'.

It's 1968 in Clent, a village in the Midlands of England. Options are limited and I am not one either. We had taken down the Guest House sign when we bought the dilapidated Victorian house the previous year, but adverts were still turning up in old accommodation columns. On occasion, it had been necessary to bed down cyclists or late night travellers, but I was not a landlady. I was a housewife taking a rest from teaching to enjoy baby number four in peace. So why did my mind appear to disengage in the moment that it took to say 'yes' without question to an unknown neighbour. 'Yes' is a life changing word if ever there was one

They arrived, a Hindu (who was a Brahmin) and his companion, a Sikh. Travelling from India they were part of a United Nations project designed to study English family life in the 1960's, unbeknown to their subjects. An organisation was placing people strategically around the country and my neighbour was one of the strategists. So they came as flies on the wall of my house on a hilltop, to live for a month in a family of six who, in their innocence were under a microscope, an Eastern microscope.

By the end of their project month we had become friends and the 'strangers' revealed their task. There were neither videos nor photographs, just a dossier of closely written scripts. Fragments and facets of the family's lives in daily transit were mirrored back. Faithfully recorded were mealtimes and menus, clothes for each occasion, choices of television programmes, books, magazines and papers read by each member, amounts and purposes of money changing hands, reported dialogue, even to contents of scribbled notes and messages taken from the communal kitchen blackboard. Performances of domestic tasks were described together with rituals of early morning and bed times, comings and goings with destinations. All was there, giving the effect of the inter-play between parents and their children, three daughters and one son. The painstaking accuracy of the facts was faultless yet as the pages turned to assess them, to interpret behaviour, identify roles and relationships, analyse values, beliefs and attitudes, the family became unrecognisable to itself. They had been viewed through the eyes of India. A mantle of the East overlaid their western identities and it seemed as if the essence of their lives had been expunged by omission.

This was my family. It has an inner life, as all families do, where deep reservoirs of thoughts and dreams lie wrapped in humour, fantasies and fears, charged with intricate emotions, in unseen undercurrents. Without the inner life the picture was wooden, its spirit trapped in a welter of activities. I felt the silent agonies of the children, one struggling with the dragon of dyslexia another withdrawn into a speechless world whose strategies for coping with communication had been interpreted as appropriate gender differences of the shy, subdued female contrasted to the ebullient male, who talked because writing brought confusion and despair. Misinterpretations painted heavy brushstrokes across the family canvass yet how was it possible to reveal these intangible, subtle aspects of lives which rested on two intrinsically different frameworks? It was impossible to unpick all their neat conclusions which left me deeply thoughtful. Though they had not interpreted western culture with any accuracy they proved to know more of my future life by means way beyond my comprehension.

As they unrolled a map of India on the floor I bent to read the unfamiliar names which had no relevance to me or my life. The Brahmin spoke with a serious smile.

'You will go to India, alone, here and here'.

Pointing to the Punjab, his moving finger traces areas in the north. This is so unlikely it is laughable. My hands and life are already full; India is not on my agenda. What is more I set scant store in prophecy so the whole episode drops into the vaults of memory. But India had made her pronouncement and in some secret inner place was waiting patiently to reveal her purpose and the claim she has on me.

The Vocation

I have discovered a vocation. In 1970 the Probation Service had found itself short of officers to meet the courts demands. The landlady life had taken off and we had become a refuge for 'hard to place' people such as battered wives, drifting ex-husbands and lonely youth. Social Services were complimentary, sending us people who needed more than a roof and so the family evolved, each making their contribution in the lives of rather diverse characters, whilst I was learning how to steady lives in turmoil, if only temporarily. By now, ready for a change of career, these experiences landed me a place on the fast track of a one year crash course to become a fully fledged Probation Officer.

Our three youngest children were all now at school and Sandra, the eldest, who had completed training as a Hotel receptionist had volunteered to act as mother for a year and deal with any guests who found their way to our door. The plan worked and I began a period of intensive study in a wide variety of unexplored fields; social welfare, psychology, sociology, law and court procedures; skills of care, control, assessments of human behaviour - most noticeable being criminal tendencies; report writing and keeping running potted histories of lives in turmoil, trauma counselling and citizens rights. It was mind blowing. After assessments, projects and examinations, we were let loose on clients under the supervision of fieldwork tutors up to their ears in their own enormous workloads. I loved every minute of it. My brain was reeling in masses of new information to be applied in real lives.

So what is a vocation? Something that pulls you in and drives you on. It is beyond choice. It is something that is waiting for you to recognise and then commit to whole heartedly. It is a compulsion to take a particular path. Well, I had recognised it and so was compelled to get on with it and discover its effect upon my life. Unfortunately my local Probation Committee in my Home County of Worcester and Hereford were uninterested in my calling and my A grades and I was treated in interview to a remarkable display of prejudice that made my blood boil. I was asked 'How many children did you say you have? Don't you think your place is at home with them?' Very shady shades of the 1970's that needed lightening up but I was not to be the one to do it. Without offer of a post I was forced to apply further afield.

The West Midlands Probation Service is the second largest in the country covering the urban conurbations around Birmingham, England's second city. It was my birthplace and I knew it well, not all its alleyways but I knew the *energy* of it. I could have had a bushel of children, was welcomed unreservedly and posted to Smethwick. Six miles out of the city centre, Smethwick is a suburban area of six square miles. Densely populated and multi-cultural, it had become home during the last twenty years or so to over 5,000 Sikhs with family origins mainly in the Punjab, Northern India. Some called it 'Little India'. Suddenly I could understand why I had been rudely rejected in my home area. I was not required to be travelling the leafy lanes. Something else was afoot. Now I was the one on India's doorstep!

The Teachers

After a period of sampling the gamut of work on all fronts I requested permission to specialise in Asian cultures. My request for the £4 fee for evening studies in Punjabi was rejected so I paid up and bought more than I had bargained for. Precipitated into a world where language revealed the heart of a strangely familiar culture, it was not long before I was drawing most of the cases of Smethwick residents of Asian origins coming before the courts. We met in prisons, pubs, the Gudwara, shops, the Probation Office and courts but most often within the circle of the family in times of crisis, struggle and adversity. My husband, Derek, who enjoyed both the food and the company, sometimes joined me in the evenings, and Smethwick became a part of our social lives where he played darts and I learnt to score in Punjabi. The pub served as an informal advice centre and I became known as *The Teacher.* There were many opportunities for service, at the least to act as a guide through the process of the law and the intricacies of both the systems and society but, mindful of my family's experience, I sought always for those willing to teach me of their customs, traditions, language, philosophy of life, family roles and rituals and so much more in an effort to represent them fairly in the sentencing reports that were an essential aspect of my work. There were people to be identified willing to train as interpreter/ volunteers, pre-school groups to be set up to prepare non-English speaking children for school, and family conflicts in which to mediate, a difficult position to hold.

Sometimes, not always, they let me in to glimpse behind the curtains of their inner lives. There was no doubt about it; India was making an indelible mark on my life. It was always there, something intangible, fascinating and mysterious. It was there in the faces of the Gurus smiling benevolently down amongst the photographs of relatives standing silently on the shelves but still a living part of their extended families. It was there emanating from the reflections of the waters surrounding the glistening Golden Temple of Amritsar. And it was there in Airline travel posters and the calendars of festivals. The needs of the people left behind were always at the forefront of their minds and often they shared their concerns and the complications of lives spanning both miles and cultures.

The certainty that India was a marker point on my life journey grew in tandem with the developing work. I felt that a time would come when I would be absorbed into the source of the cultures and families in the country with which I had come to feel so involved. Yet for five years, financial pressures and family priorities blocked the way, and the gates of opportunity did not open. Suddenly I saw a way and simply knew it was the road that had to be walked, that **would** be walked. Everything to this point seemed to have been a preparation for what was ahead.

A Prophecy Fulfilled

At this time the Commission for Racial Equality was inviting applications for twelve bursaries given annually to professionals working in communities with a high settlement of residents of Asian or Afro-Caribbean origins. I was amongst 365 entrants that year submitting their work for examination of serious intent and made it through to the interview stage. By this time I was sensing a driving force at work in me so substantial that I had no doubt it would transmit itself to others, overcoming all odds. In a state of elation before the interview I had my pass-port photograph taken. This state seemed to be nothing at all to do with ego, of believing myself to be the most deserving or best candidate, but more like auditioning for a part that had been written for me.

It felt as if a map of the Punjab was imprinted on my mind as I answered questions of geographical locations, rolling my tongue around the village names where the other halves of 'my families' lived. I returned home buoyant, filled with anticipation. The inner confidence in the outcome in no way diminished the feeling of amazement when the plan worked out so smoothly and swiftly. I was allocated Airline tickets to Delhi; a daily living allowance of £10 per day for 45 days; and a book of rail tickets.

The Punjabis were delighted and excited. Men in prison drew maps of their villages, loving messages were taped, friends, colleagues, clients, shopkeepers, all offered contacts and addresses and wrote to relatives to ensure that I received a real Punjabi welcome. But this was not to be a holiday. It was a working tour. The Probation Service gave me a clear brief. I was to extend my understanding of Asian value systems, religions, cultures and historical background and relate this to family dynamics; study offenders, the nature and background to their crimes including the effects of environment, culture and domestic influences. Making contact with Probation and Prison colleagues and the legal and penal systems was my responsibility to be sorted out in situ.

That seemed sufficient given the time scale! Understand; study, learn, and contact, key words that were given. I held others. How these things would be accomplished was supposed to be my choice and to a degree I could make plans, but there was always that elusive force that I sensed would propel me towards people, places and situations that had their place on an even wider agenda. India is not an academic exercise. I knew that I would be moving alone into highly risky territory; that this was an initiatory, life changing, predestined journey.

I had begun to believe in prophecy.

2. The Fire is Lit

Before a curtain rises the stage vibrates with darkness
Then, on that stage a cauldron stands alone, a silhouette, until the fire is lit.

Journal of an Untrodden Road

Journals are different from diaries. They contain more than dates, doings and destinations. They take life to its extremities. It took 55 days, my first ever journey on Indian soil, then reality as I had known it ended. This journey took place from 16th October to 10th December 1977. Every day I gathered information and wrote in an effort to meet my commitments to the Probation Service. The outer life provided the experiences to which mind, emotions, body, and spirit struggled to respond. This is the story of that struggle and of the force that would not let me go. India is my cauldron. Had I known it would I have stepped in? I doubt it. Could I have avoided her? I do not think so. She had been waiting to consume me.

Sunday 16th October 1977

Fog shrouds my disappearing world. Euphoria has been replaced by an inexpressible sadness and a sense of foreboding. Derek, twenty two years a husband and Charlotte, ten years a daughter, stand motionless as my reluctant feet step aboard the train. Then they are swallowed by the fog. Something in me is also disappearing. I am letting go of home and family and of myself. The confident self image is no more than a mirage.

It's no better in the plane. British Airways have me strapped between a deaf German and a Bangladeshi man who deals with my seat levers and the interminable trays. The German asks me to repeat all the announcements into his hairy ear. Even this small effort is unbearable. I'm questioning how an immigrant might feel pulling up the roots of a lifetime. This is a limbo state of apprehension laced with loss. That's all I know. Sleep is the antidote I need. Aches of mind and body have slipped away by the time I wake to see a sun-ball of fire suspended outside my window and Delhi rising to meet us.

Monday 17th October

It's 7am. Everyone is in a hurry to pass through immigration but I am not as I step into a fast moving flow of Indians calling to their families 'mammagi', 'pappagi'.

'Why are you not at the white counter?' A brusque official reprimand. My British passport is opened and expressions change. As a Probation Officer I am an employee of the Home Office which is stamped on my passport. They are calling out 'British Government' in tones that draw attention from porters to airport manager.

'Who meets you, Madame?'   I give a name.

'Where is this man?' I wish I knew.

A search is made inside and out as the new arrivals trickle away in the grasp of relatives. No one arrives for me. Loneliness is one thing, public abandonment is another! Arrangements had been made through the manager of a Birmingham Hotel for a magistrate to collect and transport me to the International Punjabi House from where I would be assisted in making contacts with agencies and the British Embassy in Delhi. The Airport Manager assists me in making a phone call to the magistrate's home. No reply. I try the Punjabi House.

'No, reservation made, Madame. Punjabi House full'.

The interested audience shrugs its shoulders, heads rolling side to side. Nobody of any interest will be arriving and they turn their attention elsewhere. Its up to me to make my own moves and kick start my mind into gear.

Two carpet bags, sewn by prisoners wanting a bit of themselves to reach Indian soil, are glued to my hands as I cash my first traveller's cheque and make for the doorway. My ace is one emergency address in Delhi. Most Punjabis in Smethwick are from the north, not the capital city. On a sudden impulse on the evening before leaving I had telephoned the home of an uncle of our court interpreter who I knew had relatives in Delhi. He had given me the name of his brother assuring me I could call on him if in any difficulties. It is a straight choice between tracing this unknown man who had never heard of me or finding a hotel. As the task is to sample Indian family life the hunt is on for Uncle Pritam Singh.

Taxi drivers converge on me from every angle trying to prise the handles of my bags from between my whiter than white knuckles. They win, my bags are wrenched away and I plunge after them into a taxi, thinking only of escape. I give the address which seems to be understood and we are away amongst scrawny cows, tattered makeshift shelters until making a sweeping turn into a housing estate on the outskirts, we arrive.

My knocks bring no reply. I try again and again until a servant boy appears. My Punjabi stretches just far enough to ask 'Pritam Singh live here?' He nods, opens the door and I walk in, aware of how vulnerable and exposed I had been feeling, needing more than anything to be inside and hardly caring whose house it is. The boy leads me into a bedroom, points to a bed and disappears. I sit self-consciously on the edge, waiting until he re-appears and gestures to me to follow him. It's like a silent movie. We trek down the street and into another house. Still no one to be seen. The boy hands me a telephone receiver and there is a voice the other end. Wonder of wonders it is Uncle Pritam Singh! I explain to him the details of my arrival, my tenuous connection to his brother, my purpose for being in Delhi and my predicament.

'Now there are no problems, my house is yours' he replies without hesitation.

Ramu, the servant boy, has been instructed to cook a meal, arrange a bath and fetch a scooter when I want to go into Delhi. Uncle Pritam's wife has gone to the Punjab to a wedding but will be returning in the evening. We return to 'my' house. A relieved tiredness is floating over me now that I can relax with a secure roof sorted out. I definitely do not want to explore Delhi yet and play with a greasy chapatti sipping Ramu's offering of a cup of tea. Soon another servant appears washing the veranda floor. The sun looks so inviting that I wander to the front porch which is a mistake. Ramu takes this as a sign that I am ready for a scooter. Nipping out past me he jumps on his bicycle calling 'scooter' over his shoulder as he pedals away. I call 'na, na,..later' but he has gone. I have not yet had a wash and am neither mentally nor physically ready to face Delhi. I could of course dismiss the scooter when it arrives, give him some money to go away perhaps, but this might cause loss of face for Ramu who has done well in caring for me so far. I decide I will have to go for an outing, but where to? The heat is building up so I change to some cooler clothes and open my address book at the sparse notations for Delhi. Although I had written letters to several agencies I had received only one rather vague reply suggesting I contact the Institute for Social Defence, however, I decide I would feel more confident at the moment making the required courtesy call on the British Embassy.

The scooter arrives. It is a dodgem car with a canvas roof, with room for the driver in front and two passengers in the rear. He has never heard of the British Embassy and I have no road name. Stalemate. I try three other addresses of social welfare organisations. He shakes his head with what I interpret as a 'no' kind of shake. Is it my pronunciation that is foxing him perhaps? I show him the address in writing. Wrong again. He does not read English. With only one card left to play I ask for *Institute for Social Defence.* He looks delighted. We are off.

The Institute is located in a rambling block of government buildings of peeling paint-work and seedy appearance set in the middle of dusty fields. Inside is a maze of corridors with dark doorways. Following arrows advertising the Defence Institute I reach an office. Faces surround me breaking into smiles, then voices are raised and more people come running.

'Come, come. It is Mrs. Taylor. Madame is here!'

It is as if they have been waiting for me. I find it puzzling. To my surprise I learn that the Indian Government have instructed this department to give me every assistance, care for my well being, and accommodation and arrange a full programme of activities including visits to institutions and prisons, the only trouble being that no one had shared that information with me. I could have been on a train to the Punjab by now!

I had visited the Indian High Commission in London for a delightful afternoon of instructive conversation and was told the Indian Government would be informed of my arrival and the purpose of my visit. I had received a letter of confirmation that this had been done but no-one had led me to believe I would be of interest to anyone at Government level nor that I would receive any official help. Getting **into** prisons I had seen as something of a challenge!

A file bearing my name is placed in front of me containing all the letters I had written to various agencies in Delhi during the previous months. I ask if there is another file marked 'copy replies'. There is not because there have been no replies. There is an expectation that the British Embassy would have met me at the airport and delivered me to the Institute. Frantic telephone calls had been passing to and fro between them with embarrassing questions being asked, both sides seemingly mortified that I was already lost. I understand why they are glad to see me.

It is my turn to contribute to the picture explaining my choice to live with Indian families, which proves unpopular, and that it is my intention to find the addresses in my notebook which proves laughable. I even produce a photocopy of an Army map of villages in the Punjab as no official maps appear to exist, which raises eyebrows. They are impressed so far and concede that I am a 'competent lady' yet I can sense their unease and that there is going to be a challenge. There is. I am asked to go over my plans in detail with official Number Three. Then I am passed to official Number Two to repeat the performance. At last I graduate to meet with the Director of the Institute, Doctor Hira Singh, an imposing Sikh with a hot-line to Government ministers and to all connections in the Social Defence System which include the Prisons. He impresses me as a man of integrity, compassion and warmth and I know that whatever advice he gives I would be well advised to consider carefully.

We spend the whole morning making arrangements for the next two days. He asks whether there is anyone I want him to contact. I reply 'whoever is in charge of the prisons in the Punjab'. A telegram is despatched immediately requesting the Inspector General of

Punjab Prisons to come from Chandigarh to Delhi on 20th October which I am told is a national holiday. Between the business discussions and constant shrill ring of the telephone I am introduced to the story behind the festival of good triumphing over evil.

There is a hitch. I am being introduced all along the line as 'Chief Probation Officer of England' and am not coping well with this fraudulent title. I understand that status is extremely important in the hierarchical structure in India and I want to be on the correct rung of the ladder and not masquerading as a bogus dignitary, so I explain carefully. I am a probation officer with a very small 'p' working in the field. The Director corrects me.

'Madame, in our eyes you have been selected by your country to be honoured for the work that you do in helping Asian immigrants and therefore in India you will be honoured even more so and given every facility to assist this valuable work on your return.' It feels good. I can't remember ever having been honoured before so I submit thankfully now that my position of abandoned isolation of a few hours ago has been reversed by a series of very ad hoc decisions on my part!

Transport is arranged to take me to lunch then to Thomas Cooks to collect my railway tickets ordered by their London Office and on to the British Embassy. Lachmi is selected to escort me and teach me the tricks of the trade in travelling, how to haggle, and not be cheated and where to eat. I learn fast as it is all essential practical information. Cooks office is in the Imperial Hotel where we have a delicious light lunch but Thomas Cooks do not have my rail tickets which is a blow. I am told it is not their practice to take orders from England and reservations can be made only when the exact train time is known. This will add to cost and inconvenience but I let it go, as there seems no alternative. Touring the centre of Delhi I become orientated to the layout discovering where the two main thorough-fares the Raj Path (Kings Path) and the Jan Path (Peoples Path) intersect and see the India Gate Hotel where I was told I had been booked to stay. I still feel much more interested in meeting Uncle Pritam and his family.

Lachmi leaves me at the British Embassy which is about the opposite of the Institute. The building is palatial, intricately decorated. The waving Union Jack gives me a patriotic twinge. My expectations are that I will be given tea and advice from the experts. The tea is forthcoming but I am totally unprepared to be received by the Second Secretary for immigration and the Second Consul who sit facing me and then suggest that I ask questions. About what? This is a double bind situation as I have little idea of what I most need to know so I take a different tack and put forward problems that reach me in Smethwick, asking how they would deal with them in Delhi. This turns into a fascinating conversation as I learn of the daily quota of immigrants, the numbers and priorities, the checks and proofs needed and am taken behind the scenes to talk with investigating officers and see the thousands of files with samples of applications. It is a good lesson to see the process that I know causes such frustration from the other side. Then it is time for the Second Consul to entertain me with anecdotes of his duties, delicate negotiations and, with emphasis, searches for British visitors reported missing. He gives me the definite impression that I will undoubtedly need his services if I continue with my plans to travel alone into the Punjab villages. They are both clear that Dr. Hira Singh, in whom everyone has complete confidence, has been briefed to assist me and their responsibility is now at an end unless I ask for it. There is nothing I need to ask for and so I leave.

Now I can confidently hire a scooter, give clear instructions and am returned safely to Haus Khas where Uncle Pritam, a tall, good looking businessman in his late thirties greets me. He is warm, welcoming and interested to talk but time is short, he has to go to give his evening lecture class on Radio Technology and then collect his wife from the station. He invites me to accompany him and so it is an immediate turn-a-round as we speed back into Delhi in his old black car.

Pritam lectures from six until eight so I try window shopping in Connaught Circus, a ridiculous nerve wracking idea. Darkness falls suddenly. There seem to be so many men about or is it that there are so few women and none of those alone except for me and beggars. The streets are a circular maze and not well lit and whenever I stop, men approach making rather odd suggestions. Some I do not understand some want me to go with them to unspecified locations; some want me to buy postcards. Beggar women clutching babies press me to buy wilting bunches of wild flowers. I have been severely warned not to give money as I would run the risk of being deluged, besides it is against the law so I make my way to Uncle Pritam's office, find a stool in a corridor and fall asleep sitting up. Eight o'clock on the dot he wakes me suggesting a stroll to a cafe where we can sit and talk. He has so many questions of life in England and news of his relatives but we soon transcend the personal as he is deeply interested in the changing nature of women's roles and how it affects families when women work. It is fascinating to have this man's views of the position of women in India. His wife does not work and he would not wish her to do so.

At last it is time to go to Delhi railway station to meet Sheshi, and the children. Everywhere in the streets are people bedding down for the night on the pavement. Uncle Pritam describes them as 'street people' who work at any menial task to scrape rupees together for food. They have no possessions other than the clothes they wear, scraps of blanket or sacking covers and tin cans for cooking. As we step out of the car we are into an intermesh of legs and bodies. This is the first impact of the massive poverty and unemployment problems which Pritam had outlined for me so graphically.

Uncle Pritam passes money to buy platform tickets explaining that as 'a white' I can walk to the head of the long, straggling queue without waiting. I argue this is not at all in my code of practice and he argues in turn that if I stand in line I will be fetched out of it by a railway official. So I do it, with reluctance, and am served immediately without comment. Already I dislike intensely being singled out by colour even when it is for preferential treatment. Left alone on the platform as Pritam goes to buy magazines I feel uneasy. A fight breaks out between a smartly dressed man and a railway official whilst poor looking people with bright yellow ointment spread over sores slide closer on the bench on both sides. When they see Pritam returning they melt away and I sigh with relief taking a deep breath at the mere thought of travelling alone. Then his lovely wife is with us, sari flowing, smiling with surprise at the sight of me but taking in her stride the information that I am her guest. Shaloo, their eight year old daughter, is excited and Kiki the baby boy is shyly peering at me. It is my first day in India and on a grimy railway station I feel that I am accepted into a family.

Our meeting is worthy of a celebration and so we go for a meal to an outdoor area where chickens are being cooked in clay ovens. The meal is delicious, the baby is sick and we all need our beds. At home there are two bedrooms, each with a double bed. The room with bathroom attached is given to me whilst they insist they will all be sleeping together. I invite Shaloo to share my bed but she is not allowed as a guest must have privacy. The bed is a solid wooden base with a thin mattress. I think of the platform sleepers and count my blessings as I set about writing up the events of the day, and noting unanswerable questions that have been stirring.

How can it be that the failure of one connection leads me to a perfect home? Why did the scooter man know only the way to the one place I needed to reach? Is the force that I sensed impelling me towards India influencing my movements? Who is the decision maker here? How long is a day in India? Time has been elongated. The night is punctured by strange noises that I later learn was the 'jokeda', hired by the residents to walk the streets banging his stick to keep unwelcome visitors away. At least I now do not come into that category. I am on the inside.

Tuesday 18th October

My first waking day in India is to be my first visit to a prison. Covering the blotchy patches where mosquitoes had feasted in the night with a long sleeved cotton dress, I join the family for breakfast of halois (semolina) and a banana. Pritam and Sheshi are amazed that their guest is going to the notorious Tihar Jail and hope I will recount the day's adventures in the evening. My escort from the Institute who arrives by taxi is Mr. Sal, a courteous bespectacled gentleman who takes his duties seriously answering my first batch of questions whilst we drive through the city until we draw up in front of the forbidding wooden gates of the jail just before nine o'clock. Prisoners who are being moved off in trucks to the courts shuffle out as the gates open, each handcuffed to a long length of chain linking a dozen men together. The end of the chain is grasped by a police officer, dressed in khaki drill. Mr. Sal informs me that police, prison officers and soldiers all wear similar khaki uniforms and can be told apart by their insignia, some differences in style and in type and colour of turbans.

We are taken straight to the Superintendent's office where he is waiting behind an ornate polished table. Two other men are present and we are introduced to each other as 'distinguished visitors'. I am to spend the day in the company of a professor, Head of Criminology and Corrective Administration from the Tata Institute of Social Sciences, Bombay and the Inspector General of Prisons, Tamil Nadu State in the far south. The Superintendent, the equivalent of our Prison Governor, is in overall charge of the jail and has put his whole day at the disposal of his guests. I could not have arrived on a more convenient day and there are smiles all round.

We are treated to a lengthy speech of introduction to India's complex judicial system for my benefit, from the time when India was declared to be a Sovereign Democratic Republic on 26th January 1950. Laws often derive from time-honoured customs or religious injunctions and therefore differ widely in the 22 States and 9 Union territories. What we learn in Tihar Jail is not necessarily practice in other State Prisons, hence the reason for the other two visitors who are here to compare prison regimes in their respective States. I am viewed as a bonus to be questioned later. In the Punjab many progressive and reformatory moves have been made since State Ministers had sampled the prisons from the inside during the Emergency. We all begin copious note-taking as levels of life in Tihar are outlined. I find it fascinating.

There are two categories of prisoners, *undertrials* (those awaiting trial or sentence) and *convicted.* The undertrials are under judicial custody and appear in court every 12 to 15 days, wear their own clothes and can receive food from outside. There are two classes of prisoner. 'B' stands for Better class and 'C' for Common prisoner. The court makes the decision as to the class in which a prisoner will serve his sentence. A 'B' class prisoner is one who is ranked of high education, social status or income, foreigners usually being included. 'B' class prisoners are entitled to better quality clothing, a wooden bed with clean sheets; personal items such as books and writing materials. They have their own cooking facilities with meat in their diet and better quality chapattis. There are two thousand prisoners in Tihar out of which forty are 'B' class. Of the fifty females only two are 'B' class. If a woman has no responsible person to take care of her children they remain with her in jail but there is no educational provision here or additional facilities for them. The common prisoner sleeps on the concrete floor on a blanket. Security is no risk as there had been only one escape during the last thirty years! In exchange for this eye-opening information I was asked to reciprocate with the classification system in British prisons setting the tone of the day for informative exchanges.

Details of regulations follow relating to visits (known as interviews); earnings; coupon schemes; and health problems, a big consideration as prisoners often arrive in a poor condition. Now we are in the rhythm each one reflects on the differences in their respective systems, all of which accounts for the first two hours. For the next three hours we tour the jail moving from the well ventilated office across miniature deserts of impacted orange dust into the prisoners' quarters where the air is heavy and motionless.

It is obvious that we will be taken first to meet with 'B' class as even inside a certain protocol must be observed. All speak English and certainly have their quotas of white sheets and meat but little else. The common theme is how prison dulls the intellect as there is so little stimulation of any sort other than conversation with each other. Guests are always a welcome bonus, especially unusual ones such as me! In this category are some of Delhi's more notorious criminals who are introduced with proper social ritual, details of their crimes being recounted. One 'B' class is a distinguished eye specialist who had hired assassins to murder his wife as he was in love with his secretary. The assassins had done their part but were quickly arrested together with the doctor and his secretary. It seems to me that there was then a class distinction even in sentencing as the hired assassins had been sentenced to death (by hanging) whereas the doctor and his lover were given life sentences meaning that there will come a time when they will both be released for a happy B Class ending. I am taken alone to meet the doctor's mistress. Prison life had taken a heavy toll of her, the life in her eyes all but extinguished, face impassive, I felt she was hardly aware of either my presence or her own.

Crossing another sandy compound edged by long brick sheds, open fronted except for thick iron bars, we see the juveniles. On concrete floors the little prisoners crouch; some in groups, mostly wearing loin-cloths or tattered clothing. There is excreta on the floor and the stench in the noon-day sun is high. Many I am told are child murderers, run-aways mostly who had been caught raiding with dacoits, the bandit groups. Others are possibly innocent of any serious crime but having been caught with an outlaw group all share the same fate. Their only activity is wrestling with each other. They were totally silent, their eyes following us, but protocol does not allow them to initiate any contact with those in authority. They could only respond if spoken to. My heart was too heavy to know where to begin with words, all my well learnt phrases seem trite and inappropriate in this setting.

The twenty foreigners, sharing a big dormitory with beds are Americans, Canadians and Germans. The contrast from the silence of the juveniles is overwhelming. Words flow that are full of feeling, eyes connect, hands touch on shoulders, there is rapport and an eagerness to connect for these brief moments. The striking difference here is the ingenuity and creativity expended in making this communal room homely. There is an array of snapshots, badges and bits of flags, decorated bed boards, pieces of string with a miscellany of dangling objects, drawings and cartoons on scraps of paper. Why is this? Are the foreigners expressing a need for outward expression of a personal identity? Did the Indian prisoners live more internally than externally? Or did they not have any of these tiny material symbols available to them? Even with the 'B' class prisoners there had been no visible signs of this sort of creativity. Then I had it. It reminded me of a child's bedroom, a microcosmic reflection of western society, reproducing their image of home in their familiar way. Questions are asked in familiar idioms and easy humour that hold the emotions in check.

'What are you doing in this hotel?'

'Just sampling the bed bugs. What are you sampling?'

'You, at the moment.'

'Do you want to take a free sample back with you?'

There were two main categories of offences for which they were being held, one to do with illegal entry and the other a charge of 'cheating', an offence which covers a variety of con tricks including passing dud cheques. There was a tangible sense of all being in a similar boat but eyes told more than words. I am acutely aware that contact with a white woman evoked deep feelings. How I would have liked to stay with them longer but they were all telling me about Mary and asking if I would go and see her.

Mary, a Canadian girl, is the only female foreigner. She has been here eighteen months waiting trial on murder charges. The 'common' females, some with children, are in a prison within the prison, having a small central walled courtyard of their own. They drift about like lost pieces of humanity. Passing through a gate in this courtyard we reach a row of cells and strip of ground belonging to the one 'B' class prisoner. Mary is dressed in a white dress with long sleeves, and full skirt, belted around her tiny waist. She is very thin, her elfin shaped face framed by long dark plaits. She is about thirty years old yet looks like a teenager. A visitor from the outside world is exciting and she wants to show and tell me everything starting with a blocked sewer pipe at the rear of her cell, fronted by inevitable thick black bars in which a gate is left permanently open. She is allowed to mix with the 'C' class women and their children and has set herself the task of teaching them English. She talks expressively with graceful gestures of the heat, the bedbugs, and of her life in a small Canadian town where she worked as a librarian and where she met and fell in love with an Indian traveller. They set out on an exciting tour of East Asia and then travelled through India but she became progressively unhappy at his rootless drifting lifestyle and his treatment of her when she was left alone for long periods of time. An unforgettable day came when they were both arrested and charged with a series of nine murders, which she discovered had taken place in the locations where they had been staying, since when she has continued to protest her innocence of complicity in the crimes. Her parents have spent thousands of dollars on legal fees in attempts at bail but always there are more lawyers waiting with outstretched hands. Her fingers dug into my arm, as she played out her need to hold on to something. She was holding to a faint thread of hope of eventual release. As she gripped me I could feel the fear that gripped her and yet her eyes were clear and steady and I did not sense it was fear born of guilt. The others had gone in a different direction whilst I spent time with Mary. As we reconvened over a late lunch with prison officers we exchanged impressions and when we took our leave I was sorry to have to decline invitations to visit jails in Bombay and Madras.

Next stop is to return to the Institute to take tea with Dr. Hira Singh. I am not at all fond of tea and am finding it difficult to respond to the numerous cups pressed on me at short intervals so I ask whether I might have half a cup to be sociable. It is courteously explained that this is not possible as a guest could not possibly be served half measures, however, if a guest wished to leave half that would be perfectly acceptable. I submit to receiving the full cup and place it on the floor just underneath my chair. When I come to retrieve it I find it half empty. What magic is this? It is a magic rat scuttling away happily full. Even the rats are co-operating!

I admit the day has had a tremendous impact. The information is easy, I know I can write this down and process it but what to do with the emotions? A little gentle domesticity is what I need. Soon I am home in Haus Khas. A young doctor is visiting as the baby Kiki has a stomach germ. He is interested in politics and in particular the sterilisation programme which is causing a stir. I had been well briefed on a week's crash course at Farnham Castle Overseas Briefing Centre before leaving so could respond intelligently, the meeting passed off well and I at last earned a bed rest!

Bed resting is a pleasurable time, when women and children lie chatting in the afternoon. Sheshi considers it essential that I learn the different materials used for saris advising me to buy only pure silk or chiffon. She displays each sari in her wardrobe recounting who had given it and on what occasion, many being for weddings and other celebrations. Each has matching bangles. Then for fun they dress me in a striped sari with scarlet bangles and daughter Shaloo escorts me out to post a letter home. But the lessons do not let up. Everyone I have met so far seems to be intent upon giving information, ensuring that I am shown the ropes, testing my own knowledge and drawing out whatever I have of interest for them. This eight year old is not going to be outdone and teaches me Punjabi phrases as we walk. She knows it is essential to be able to instruct scooter drivers. I must learn the routes I want to travel from my map of Delhi and tell drivers to go left, right or straight ahead. In that way I will not be taken for a ride around the long route or worse! I am wondering if my brain can process any more today. She makes me practice and we lurch hand in hand to the left and right by-passing a mixed collection of wandering pigs. I ask Shaloo what the pigs are doing wandering about without a minder.

'They are street pigs. No-one cares about them.'

'And the cows too?'

'Street-cows, no-one care about them or the dogs either.'

'Do you think anyone cares about the street-people?'

'No, no-one cares about things on the street.'

A child's words, people are 'things on the street'. I have the feeling that there is not enough caring to spare on a wider scale and yet I am receiving care in abundance.

Later I walk out again, for a stroll with Sheshi. It is only 6pm but it is cooler and growing dusk. A rat runs across the road in front of us and is stepped on by a man who takes no notice of the rats screams. Sheshi laughs, it is a commonplace event and I am left with the problem of caring for the rats as well! Women are out and about chatting in social groups and I am introduced at the local shops and restaurant. I discover Sheshi has relatives in Katarpur in the Punjab and people named in my notebook that I plan to visit are her friends!

Is there any time for journal writing yet? No. Pritam is home and dinner is waiting. He has cancelled his lecture tonight as he is intent upon hearing every detail of my visit to Tihar and other activities of my day. So the talking begins again and they are spell bound by anecdotes of the prisoners they have read about. It was good to recount the day as it brought details back to mind. All I then have to do is write them down in my journal, which at 10.30pm I am at last free to open whilst turning over in my mind plans for my next move. It is Tuesday. I must leave Delhi soon and head out to the Punjab but

Delhi is proving to be invaluable and it is hard yet to contemplate leaving. So I give myself a pep talk and write a letter to a family in Ambala to say that I will be arriving on Saturday on the *Flying Mail Train* and ask if someone will meet me at the station. I have sheaves of statistics on Indian Crime from the Prison which I open at random. The page is headed 'Murder by Juveniles'. They are not just figures on the page now that I have seen those faces squatting in their cages.

And what of tonight's questions? Is it mere co-incidence that the visits of the two men coincided with my own and the Superintendent was free the whole day? Is there a limit on the amount of information the mind can process and retain or is it limitless when the mind does not believe otherwise? And why do I feel this immense pull towards trapped human beings?

Wednesday 19th October

A fried egg is a good beginning to the day and Mr. Sal, my escort yet again, bows in late. Taxis are in short supply so he has had to resort to hiring a scooter. He is most apologetic. We are heading for the Head Office of the Delhi Probation Service on the far side of the city, which allows for sight seeing of the River Jammu, Ghandi's ashes and Nehru's Park and places of interest as we pass. Old Delhi is a mass of small ancient buildings, houses, shops, sheds and people pressing their way through traffic. Gates shut at a railway crossing but only cars and scooters stop, everyone and everything else pours over the barriers, cyclists with bicycles on their shoulders, animals being whacked across. We witness drivers in a crash jump out and engage in a fight. It's been a wild ride and I feel shaken to the marrow.

We are only a few minutes late but a women of some obvious importance is striding about. No name is given. She informs me that today is a holiday and she is here at work because of my visit and asks what I want to do. It is a sharp greeting. Mr. Sal quietly tells me she is the Chief Probation Officer. I know Dr. Singh has liaised with her to arrange a few useful visits so tell her I'm will be happy to engage in whatever plans she has made. Despite the continuing chilly atmosphere the whistle stop tour paints a valuable background picture of the size of social problems in which Probation Officers are heavily engaged. It begins with a visit to an institution for 350 homeless or neglected children. They do not have to go to school if they show no interest or aptitude and instead are taught trades such as weaving, welding, or barbering. It seemed incongruous to see rows of tiny children learning to be barbers who can hardly reach the heads of their customers. But then they hardly seem like children with their tired eyes and solemn faces, old with the hurts of living. It is a Probation Officer's task to recommend disposal to the court between Institutional Care or return home. Many children run away from home for a variety of reasons and will be likely to have stolen… or worse, in order to survive. A musical marching display had been hastily arranged and then it was on to a Beggar's Home with 945 beggars in residence and they were the lucky ones - just the tip of the iceberg. Although begging is outlawed, as with many of India's laws it is unenforceable. Collecting all the beggars from the streets and making provision for their welfare would, I am told, merely increase the numbers of beggars. It is only those who come to the notice of the police for committing some offence other than begging that brings them before the court where they are classified into diseased; physically disabled; rehabilitable and returnees. Probation Officers are also the detectives trying to locate families and preparing reports for the courts in which the questions are listed in Hindi to which answers must be written in English! I read some of the answers which are heart-rending. So often they detail the hardships of women deserted by their husbands with no means left of supporting their children. Probation Officers are scarce and their workloads impossible.

Visit number three is officially entitled an 'Observation Home for Boys' but is known locally as 'The Children's Prison'. It caters for 254 boys from aged six to sixteen. We tour the classrooms in the usual eerie silence. The rooms are bare empty shells. The children sit on the floor for lessons and jump to attention at our arrival. The boys sleep in an equally bare oblong room, on small rush mats placed immaculately in rows. There are no personal possessions anywhere to be seen and no chance to talk with any children. I am whisked away into the taxi for the last visit to a Children's Court where I meet people as hungry to talk to me as I am to talk with them. Three Honorary Magistrates join me to discuss the work of the Probation Service in the courts. They speak of the plight of the 'little ones' and we watch them passing from room to room, such tiny scraps of children, even toddlers being moved about by formidable looking police, always in silence. There is a barrier to communication forged by status, authority and age which I find myself resenting and wondering whether anyone ever listens to these children? Efforts had been made to set up Probation Hostels but they remained empty as no-one would go in because of the stigma attached to offending. I was asked to speak of our system of Children's Homes and they thought the idea of small family units interesting but unworkable. These large communal homes were the cheapest method of care and containment for such large numbers.

Our visit over I thank them formally and make it known I would now like to make my own way into Delhi as I have some personal business to attend to. Not acceptable. We end with a compromise.

Mr. Sal will escort me into the centre of Delhi and I will meet him later in the afternoon and return to the Institute with him to report on the outcome of the morning's programme. He has great misgivings about leaving me alone and it is obvious there will be repercussions for him if he loses me. I look at my watch. Is it possible that this tour has taken only four hours! My personal business is that I just want to be left alone to discover a few things for myself such as buying stamps. Finding a Post Office I join the jostling crowd. An Official leaps from behind the counter, gesturing that I must follow him through a hatchway and wait beside him behind the counter without a word being spoken. When someone has placed a chair at the side of a desk I realise it is time to make my request for stamps. He checks the stamps and change twice very loudly while making an exhibition of the transaction. It seems to me that whatever happens there must be no cause for complaint.

The Imperial Hotel is nearby so I call in thinking I will test ordering a snack lunch. As I walk through the doors a young man beams with recognition calling out 'Mrs Taylor, Mrs. Taylor!' A young clerk from Thomas Cooks begins profuse and abject apologies. I had been given wrong information; no-one had known where to contact me to rectify their disgraceful error. All persons had been mortified, and had been alerted to watch out case of my return to the hotel. There had been train tickets booked by London just as I had said. A large package of them awaited me in the office which would take me all over the Punjab. This was great news. We laughed together about the coincidence of my return and he was bursting with pride to be the one to bow me into the office. It was short lived. Not knowing that the clerk had given the game away by admitting their error, a senior clerk took a different approach assuring me I was totally at fault and accusing me of giving false information! Oh dear. I ask if he will kindly explain in detail where my error lay. Guessing his job was at stake if I was to make a complaint, we call a truce, I sign numerous sheets of paper and leave with my prize tickets.

There is no time left for lunch as I want to book a coach ticket to Agra for £5 complete with meals and guide. What a great time I have had! I enjoy it so much when I am in control of my own transactions. I await Mr. Sal at the appointed place. He arrives late flushed from his own exertions but with relief flooding his face when he sees me and we return to make our report of the morning to Dr. Singh. But why is Mr. Sal making his report in Hindi? I find this rather off-putting. Are there matters being discussed that I am not meant to hear? Then I give my report, in English. When asked my opinion of the Chief Probation Officer I was honest in my appreciation of the organization of the programme but do not mince my words about her waspish manners which make a few people catch their breath.

Dr. Singh now comes clean. He tells me that he has been given responsibility for my welfare and my programme of activities by the Ministry of Home Affairs at the request of the Indian High Commission in London. He is concerned by many aspects of my plans, especially my desire for independent travel. This is serious stuff. Now that I have train tickets in my pocket I feel invincible and burning with independence but I choose my words carefully and explain. To be chaperoned in the Punjab by an official from Delhi would mean being saddled with trappings of status that would set me apart from the families with whom I intended to be living and would inhibit communication. He in turn stresses my vulnerability and asks whether I will reconsider the situation the following day when I have had the opportunity of meeting Mr. K.C. Shenmar, Inspector General of Punjab Prisons. I agree to defer final decisions hoping that I am not being inflexibly foolish but, a cavalcade from Delhi into the villages is the last thing I want and Mr.Sal likes to hold a tight rein.

I am beginning to regard Haus Khas as my sanctuary. Sheshi now has a bad throat and has it bandaged and Pritam who already suffers from a weak chest is feeling unwell. I take Shaloo off to play and show her all my clothes. She is particularly interested in my 'swimming dress' as she calls it. Shaloo has never been swimming. Dinner is a simple affair of dhal and vegetables. I am famished, as I haven't eaten since breakfast. The family retire early and I am left to reflect on another elongated day, to wonder at the unexpected retrieval of my tickets; to wonder even more what on earth I am going to say to the Inspector General. I know I was riled by the Chief Probation Officer's bristling resentment and still feel the discomfort of my less than charitable report. I'd better be careful that the honouring doesn't go to my head. The unknown General's holiday is next on the list to be disrupted!

Thursday 20th October

It seems a good idea to stoke up on breakfast while I have the chance as days seem to surge on past mealtimes. Fried bread stuffed with scrambled egg and onions followed by jam sandwiches and bananas makes a good starter. My meeting with the Inspector General is scheduled for 2.30pm so at last I have a free morning to visit the hairdressers escorted by Shaloo. It is a magical journey as I see India through a child's eyes, her walk to school, the homes of relatives and friends with anecdotes about the occupants, her special flower bushes and we even have to stop to look into a cow's eyes.

It is 1.30pm when we arrive home. Sheshi is concerned that I make a big impact on the Inspector General and suggests she should dress me in a shimmering silk green sari - with matching bangles of course!

With every hair in place I admire myself and hope that I will come across as impressive as I think I look.

This self admiration society is rapidly demolished as I go steadily frantic having chosen a manic scooter driver who it seems is out to extract a month's wages from my ride. He scoots madly every which way ignoring instructions for left or right turns (so much for my lessons) until I am totally disorientated. I shout *'rukjow'* (stop) loudly when passing some men in khaki, unable to tell whether they are police or soldiers. He obeys! I ask them to please instruct my driver to take me straight to the Institute for Social Defence. They convey the message. He is obviously poor, very thin and I guess of a low caste. I have frightened him and shame mingles in now amongst anger and distress. I look dishevelled and what is worse am late! My soldiers explain he knows it is a holiday and that the Institute is closed today but did not want to lose my custom so gave me a nice ride. I then ask my interpreters to tell him that I am meeting the Inspector General of Prisons at the Institute and that he will be growing impatient as I am now late. The man's fear now matches my desperation. We take off again, arriving at the Institute to find padlocked gates pulled across the entrance. The driver turns in triumph and then crumples. A large official car with curtains drawn sweeps around the corner and an official leaps out holding open the door, bowing, as he informs us that he has been waiting to drive Mrs. Taylor all of the 100 yards to the back door entrance where the Inspector General is waiting. The scooter driver knows I have a decision to make. He is owed about a quarter of what is on the clock if that, but then he has given me some valuable lessons so he gets a fair handful of change and is happy to escape unscathed.

Dr. Hira Singh and the Inspector General (commonly known as the I.G.) are standing lined up waiting to receive me. The I.G. is also an imposing figure of a man of heavy build, dark skinned, and without turban. He opens the conversation in a formal and direct way by announcing that he is requesting a change in my programme. I guess that he has been primed that I am likely to be difficult on this point but I want to hit the right note of courtesy without leaving myself open to being browbeaten by rank or masculine authority. I ask if he will kindly give me his suggestions to consider. He does. They are pretty good! He tells me there is a religious festival at Amritsar, the religious centre of Sikhism, celebrating the 400th anniversary of the foundation of the Golden Temple and that to attend it will be the envy of every Sikh in the world. He offers to take me there by car to be the guest of his family for four days. A visit to the Golden Temple was already on my agenda but as I had no contact address in that area this is a true gift from heaven. I rearrange the programme. To tie me down he has the clerk type up the rearranged schedule of dates. We agree a few other changes to include staying with people who he considers will be helpful to me and I give him a list of addresses of my families with roughly the dates on which I hope to reach them. Here comes the crunch. He insists on providing an escort throughout the Punjab. I firmly decline. Dr. Singh comes to the rescue. He can see that I have given way substantially and knows this is my sticking point. 'Leave her to her work within the families' he says quietly.

But the I.G. has yet another tempting suggestion. As the Inspector General of Prisons he is also the Head of the Probation Service for the Punjab. Miss Keith, his Chief Welfare Officer is also an experienced Probation Officer. He would like to instruct her to be at my service and assist me in accordance with my needs. It would be ungracious to refuse; anyway Miss Keith sounds exactly what I might need. We are all well satisfied.

The I.G. takes me out to tea to meet with some of his relatives at their home in Delhi. It is homely and comfortable and I enjoy the company of these friendly outgoing people. His daughter Sheshi is also visiting. She is twenty-one and a medical student training to be a doctor. They are all making up a party to go to Agra next day and invite me to accompany them and dispense with my coach ticket. It is very tempting but I have the feeling this will be my one and only day alone to experience India through the eyes of a tourist. They understand.

We pile into their car and as they have no idea of the way to Haus Khas I direct the driver from my map giving instructions in Punjabi. They thump me on the back to show their appreciation at this entertainment. Poor Sheshi is past wondering who will be arriving at her home next but as always she takes it all in her stride. Shaloo is waiting to welcome me and suggests some entertainment. Tonight she dances for me wearing her one hundred and fifty brass bells on ankles and wrists. She is a member of a dancing team and of course the opportunity to teach me cannot possibly be wasted. I am not a competent pupil and cannot perform the foot movements fast enough so I do some graceful arm waving instead. We play clapping games and I teach her some songs but have to give in when she starts to teach me to sing in Hindi.

Pritam returns home having visited the doctor where there appears to be a financial pecking order. Waiting time is determined by whether one pays ten, five or two rupees. Pritam had paid five rupees. He goes to bed exhausted whilst I, revitalised by the dancing lesson, set the pen to work marvelling how everything is falling into place.

3. Stepping into the Tide

Friday 21st October 1977

The family pile into the car to take me to the Lodi Hotel for the coach to Agra. It is dilapidated and not air conditioned as advertised. Allocated a seat alone I welcome a breather from communicating and sit in happy isolation for a spell of recuperation. Hopes are shattered when our guide, an old Hindu, a scholarly man with horn rimmed glasses and a walking stick, sits beside me smelling of stale tobacco. He is the only person on a non-smoking bus to smoke to the annoyance of passengers, especially me and, as he assures us that rules do not apply to him, we are all condemned to a day of thickening air. He did not introduce himself so I named him R.G. (rude guide). R.G. determined to give good value for money, booms out general information backed by statistics, adding snippets often unintentionally funny. There are only three white faces on the bus, myself and two French boys, but R.G. treats everyone as foreigners. He speaks in English like a guidebook enunciating clearly.

'India ranks second in the world estimated population 597.9 million; density 177 per square kilometre; average life span fifty years', then in an added aside 'I am, as you might expect, above average!' India is mainly an agricultural country, 80% of people living in villages. R.G. is of course not a villager as he hastens to point out. He is delighted to see me take out my notebook, waiting while I jot down facts and quips.

We travel through the southern corner of Haryana State then the road disappears for the next six miles due to flooding during the monsoon. The driver carries on guessing where the road should have been. Agra is 128 miles from Delhi. They are long miles. I peer out of the filthy windows. We are now in Uttar Pradesh passing villages of mud huts where everyone seems to be doing everything conceivable in brown brackish pools. Breakfast is a welcome break then, wandering towards the sound of music I discover a scraggy brown bear swaying at the end of a long chain. It is not for me. From then on I doze and R.G's words of wisdom no longer penetrate. We pass through an imposing red stone gateway and I buy a post-card to discover that we have stopped at the impressive mausoleum, tomb of Akbar the Great, a conqueror with dreams of a great unified empire.

It is mid-morning and the coach has become a greenhouse, nevertheless history lessons begin in readiness for the Taj Mahal where we are to be let loose to explore alone. My thin cotton skirt is sticking to my legs as I step out at Agra gasping for air into a swarm of beggar children clamouring for bakshish.

Once inside the grounds the hawking ceases and there it stands, my well worn poster brought to life. Built by Shah Jehan in the Golden Age of Mogul architecture the Taj Mahal is said to have been built to the design of ancient diagrams of the Garden of Paradise. A living love story carved in white marble, The Taj commemorates the love of the Shah for his second wife, Mumtaz-i-Mahal, who died in 1630 giving birth to their fifteenth child. Twenty thousand skilled craftsmen from all over the world laboured on this enduring work of art for seventeen years. Now I am here, not to delve deeply into history but to bring to life the poster that has hovered behind my desk for five years, placed to deliberately face those who come to sit in front of me so they can rest their eyes on it and see less of me and my threatening pen!

It's mid-day. The approach at the sides of the shimmering oblong pools gives me time to take in the long view. Through half closed eyes the white marble does not appear to me to be solid, just a shimmering mass of energy. My sturdy sandals look out of place amongst the rows of flimsy footwear. The marble burns the soles of my feet as a swelling throng of bodies, carry me in towards the tombs. The tomb of Mumtaz is in the centre. Shah Jehan originally planned to build a black Taj as his mausoleum on the opposite side of the River linking it to the Taj by a bridge. As he was imprisoned by one of his sons it never came to fruition and he was entombed next to his wife in what is described as an 'off-centre afterthought', the only asymmetrical element in the entire design, a filigree of precious stones and marbled latticework. Outside, the four famous minarets tower gracefully over the sandstone mosques designed to slant so that if they ever tumbled they would fall outward away from the precious Taj.

The Restaurant is an anti-climax and I'm only too glad to pass on the hotly spiced food and trundle on in the heat box to Agra Fort, a vast structure, its walled circumference measuring a mile and a half. It is here that Akbar was imprisoned by his son and, rather than do a round, I choose to stand at one of the slit windows drinking in the timeless vista of the Taj in the changing light.

Somewhere on the long road home we have a puncture and are asked to alight. Thankful for the cool evening air we stand talking in groups. One old lady bent double and draped in a grubby sari shuffles to squat by the road. I try out a few words of Punjabi asking if she has enjoyed the day. Her face lights up. She grabs my arm, pats it, and waves to a man who joins us. He is her son, a Gujerati, settled in USA who has returned to bring his ninety year old mother from the other side of India for this visit to the Taj. We talk of immigration, of those he calls 'the lucky ones' who have built new lives in other countries and of the plight of many that remain behind.

The puncture is mended but we have lost travelling time and it is growing late. R.G. reprimands the two young Frenchmen for 'necking and pecking' with two Indian girls, in his eyes the ultimate bad behaviour in public. There has been a man sitting at the side of the driver throughout the journey who I discover is a guard. I ask R.G. what he is likely to be guarding us from which leads to a recounting of horror happenings on his coaches. The guard carries rope and on a recent trip had to tie up a tourist and throw him from the coach sixty miles from Delhi for pulling a knife. I decide to behave myself and go to sleep. But then a row breaks out. A girl expects to miss her train because of the delay. Voices become strident and people take sides but R.G. maintains a policy of 'no responsibility' and I am relieved when we enter the suburbs.

It is 9.30pm and moonless. There are no taxis or scooters around and I had not taken note of my location as I had arrived by car. Where on earth is House Khas? I go inside the hotel and locate a scooter driver who had called in for some change. I have made a mess of it. He is a demon who takes off into unknown regions in pitch darkness then suddenly swoops off the road into bush lined tracks in unlit College grounds. I dare not wait to discover his next move as he is clearly up to no good and is no longer pretending to find the way, so I lunge forward and thump him hard between the shoulder blades, beating again and again as his back arches. I've given him a shock, myself a flood of adrenalin, and have realised how easy it is to become violently aggressive! We career across the path and my Punjabi lessons come to the rescue.

'Inspector General Prisons meri sehali hai. Jail jana', loosely translatable as 'the Inspector General of Prisons is my friend. You go to jail'. I always feel it is better to take the initiative at the optimum point and that was as close to optimum as I wanted to get! He took the message, swung around and exited the gates. By immense luck I recognised a landmark from my walk with Shaloo. We were close enough to home for me to direct every move left, right and centre until we arrived at the sleeping household. I decided how much to pay him as he was no longer speaking to me, which seemed fair enough. Sheshi answered my knocking and after whispered apologies for my lateness I decide that my first day as a tourist will be my last. So what else can I be?

Saturday 22nd October

Shaloo comes in to tell me we are going out to breakfast then to the Q'utb Minar before I catch my train. Can I be ready immediately? I simply haven't learnt yet how to put a stop to the extras that keep being squeezed in, probably because I don't want to miss a trick. Instant decisions now have to be made of what to take and what to leave. I have a pile of literature from the Institute that I had wanted to sort. It's all quite a hassle.

The Q'utb Minar is one of Delhi's famous monuments. It is a tower, 71.3 metres high, built originally to serve as a place for the call to prayer for the nearby mosque. I decline to climb the hundreds of stairs, instead playing the game of hugging the rusted pillar made of an unknown metal. There is a story that if a person standing with their back to the pillar can encircle it with their arms and make their fingers touch, then they are not a bastard. My arms are short of the mark and it makes a good laughing finale.

My ticket allows me to choose any seat on this train. I choose a comfortable corner and find the parting with Uncle Pritam and his family to be quite a break. The journey takes four hours and the ride is uneventful. Stations seem to be clearly marked so I cannot mistake Ambala. I jump off with excitement, ready to greet my new hosts. It will be easy for them to identify me as the only white faced passenger. No one greets me. Oh no, not again! This could be serious as I know of only this one family in Ambala. Of course it could be they have not received my letter. The disappointment is substantial and the address unintelligible to me.

There are no scooters or taxis, only cycle rickshaws and no-one wants to take me aboard. At last I find a volunteer and my luggage is wedged in behind me. As we set off a man who has been watching me intently follows on his bicycle riding closely behind and making no attempt to overtake, although the road is wide and my heavy rickshaw slow. Imagination begins to work overtime. Are they working as a team with the bicycle rearguard intending to snatch my luggage? I turn round and squat on my seat facing backwards, putting my hands through the handles of my bag and stare at him with what I hope is a daring scowl. I have been well warned about travelling alone and my nerves are paying the cost. We roll on mile after mile but he makes no move. I have no way of knowing whether I am being taken in the right direction or whether my first big venture north will be my last. When we sight habitation the bicycle whizzes by and is gone.

My rickshaw man finds the house with ease. It is in the centre of a bazaar, baronial doors set into a high wall. There is excitement at my arrival. My letter had been received and the train had been met at Ambala City, the local station. I had alighted at the outlying station of Ambala Cant. My mistake. My apology. Sidargi is a retired factory inspector, a handsome bearded and turbaned Sikh. I called him Sidargi from the beginning, the title of respect for a true practicing Sikh. He is the uncle of a social worker colleague. His wife is a teacher and they have a daughter Bulbul also a trained teacher not yet employed. Relatives have been invited to the welcome party and it is difficult to know who is who as neighbours and friends pour into the courtyard. I am surrounded by smiling faces, relief overtaking anxieties. My practised greeting *'Sat Sri Akal'* (God is Truth) delights everyone and as soon as I am refreshed the plan is to walk through the bazaar on a social promenade. Bulbul and her friends are in charge surrounded by neighbours and groups of children. It is quite an entourage. This family is obviously well known and highly regarded. I try to do them justice stopping to speak to elderly ladies or anyone my escorts think I should meet. Shop goods are poor quality by western standards and there is nothing of interest to buy but I thought it impolite not to make a purchase so I asked Bulbul and friends to help me choose a sari. I had no idea this would be such a treat for them. They explain that they will not wear a sari themselves until they are married. All Punjabi women wear the *salwar chemise,* the blouse top with baggy pants.

The salesmen sit cross legged on their floor/counter patiently displaying mountains of material lengths. It is a riot of colour. The girls sort and feel expertly, each with a different idea of what would suit me, agreeing on a length of pure silk in burgundy embroidered with silver thread. The sari is one six foot length heavily decorated at one end to form the pelu which is draped over the shoulder. An extra piece of material at the opposite end is cut off to make an under blouse. We visit the tailors and I am measured with much discussion about cut and style. I defer to the experts, decisions are taken and the garment will be ready next day.

All activities take place in the courtyard. It is there we eat and then I am shown to Bulbul's bedroom, one of a number of brick rooms opening off the courtyard. Falling into bed, I write a letter home, complete the day's journaling, only to find I am not alone. Tiny mice are tumbling through holes in the windowsill six inches above my bed, slithering across the cover and diving onto the floor. I am not happy. Even with the covers over my head I can hear them scratching and scampering but I tell myself it could become worse as I move into the villages and I had better toughen up.

Sunday 23rd October

During breakfast the Professor of Zoology from the local college arrives with his family and offers an invitation to their home that evening. At least I know the protocol and am able to reply that Sidargi will decide as to where I eat, as I am his guest. Sidargi is pleased and gives his permission. Bulbul and two friends are escorts for the morning's outing to Ambala Cant for a surprise visit delivering gifts and messages I had brought from the headmistress of a Smethwick school, a former visiting bursar who had stayed with a Hindu family. We travel by bus and find it easily. It is a substantial house, home to the four families of the brothers Kapoor, all with the initials P.C. There is excitement and delight to know they are so well remembered. We are plied with refreshments while the Sikh girls and the Hindu women exchange conversation. The obligatory round reveals seven rooms leading off the downstairs courtyard and upstairs each brother and wife has a private bedroom with huge double bed, the children all sleeping communally. Though I would have enjoyed a stay in this large family I remember their previous guest telling me she was not expected to go out and had bought some knitting wool to keep occupied. I had not come to India to knit!

Strolling back through a shopping area I am able to buy a map of the Punjab but once again villages are not marked. How *do* I find addresses? The girls suggest a café treat of ice creams where conversation is sparked by seeing a boy and girl sitting together. They disapprove of young people of marriageable age being seen together in public. Narange has just agreed to marry and had given her father a list of requirements. He must of course be a Sikh, preferably a Sidargi, six feet tall and an engineer. She asked what I though of 'foreigners' as husbands and I discover she is referring to Sikhs living anywhere outside India. So we talk of whether they think they might enjoy a foreign lifestyle and I am questioned on habits of drinking, smoking, courting, cosmetics, leisure and finance.

Outside Sidargi's household is a tandoori oven. A woman squats beside it and customers bring large maize chapattis to be cooked by her. She flips them inside and they stick to the clay sides. When they are done she flips them out again and they fall onto the dusty ground where people are standing. Their owner collects them and shakes off the dust. A lady with her face partially covered joins the group. She is a leper. Parts of her toes and fingers have gone and the scarf reveals a hole where her nose should be. She sees me watching her and holds my gaze. I move towards her and greet her as sister with *'Sat Sri Akal, panji'*. I feel she understands that I am acknowledging her suffering. She bends and touches my feet in a sign of respect. I feel she is acknowledging my journey.

I cannot eat. Emotion has surfaced and I beg to be excused to rest before the next round of visits that I know are to come. An hour later, when I emerge, it is as if I have been away for a week. Neighbours are waiting to escort me next door where a ramshackle exterior houses shiny Formica furniture and show cases filled with displays of plastic toys used as ornamentation. The children are dressed in frilly party clothes and perform nursery rhymes in English. The tour includes the roof. People wave from their courtyards and no-one appears to mind being viewed from above.

A visit to a second neighbour replicates the first, then I learn the two sets of neighbours jointly own a sweet factory, my next port of call. It is an astonishing sight.

Men crouching in intense heat stir black cauldrons of melting sugar. Others dip in giant ladles dripping the contents onto cooling trays, expertly making designs and shapes. It is my idea of purgatory. The girls tell me I can return home while they go and collect my sari and sewing. A blessed half an hour for private time with Sidargi and his wife and the girls return high with excitement as they spirit me away to see if I look the part in pure burgundy and silver silk. They are so pleased that it is time for another parade next door where the older ladies put the finishing touches, re-arranging pleats, a skilful task.

Dressed, looking ready for a ball, I am placed in the courtyard now buzzing with children and more neighbours who are watching a film on television. Activity never ceases, the only difference is it is now on screen. One moment the villain is murdering a child then we switch to pathos as the murderer tends his dying wife before leaping up to dance and sing. It draws me into this roller coaster of emotive entertainment but in the middle I find it is time to leave for the Zoologist party.

We stroll to the outskirts of town. Bulbul is to remain, Sidargi and his wife accompany us to the gates then turn back home. Inside the scene I have just left is repeated as the courtyard is filled with people watching the same film. An empty chair is already in place in centre front row where I enjoy the saga until the evening meal is served. It's a very long film and while the visitors return to their seats I'm treated to an enlightening conversation with the professor. He knows my areas of interest and gives his opinion on the major causes of crime, focusing on land disputes; monetary disagreements such as dowry settlements; political agitation and corruption; sexual harassment or infidelities; and domestic quarrels, all of which can erupt into murder. Much is taking shape in my mind as we are escorted home by the professor and a friend while in the courtyard the film plays on and on. It has been a delightful evening and another full day. Now I really feel that I have stepped into that stream of history, into a culture which becomes more intriguing every day.

I am ready for bed, unaware there is also a long night ahead of me. After a nap I wake with indigestion and as I thump and rub my chest a mosquito army makes a dive bombing attack. In the corner of the courtyard is a cupboard in the wall with a toilet drainage hole now due for a visit. It proves to be the onset of a bout of diarrhoea. A good portion of the night is spent in the cupboard and as I finally drift into oblivion at dawn I can hear Sidargi's deep voice intoning verses from the Granth Sahib (Sikh Holy Book) which also has a little room all to itself.

4.Anatomy of Murder

Monday 24th October

Both ankles are swollen and stomach stirrings persist. It is risky catching the 8.30am train to Patiala but my schedule is so tight I just get on with it. Sidargi, his wife and Bulbul escort me to the train but somewhere along the way Sidargi disappears. When the crowded train pulls in I discover he has been waiting down the line ready to jump aboard the slowing train to secure a seat for me. No wonder, it is crowded with the early morning farm workers and their implements piled on the slatted wooden benches. Relieved to see that I am opposite a toilet I dive in as soon as the train pulls away, find it filthy and begin to heave. It is a journey of survival.

I check and recheck that the sign says 'Patiala'. A young Sikh kindly loads my luggage into a cycle rickshaw and I give instructions to be taken to the Jail. The driver reacts by tuning his legs up a gear whilst turning round to look at his jail hungry passenger, rides straight off the road and I am flung from side to side as we career over the rough grass. It is manic. I have never been so glad to knock on the door of a jail! No questions are asked and I am escorted silently to the Superintendent's office. He is in the grounds doing a round, which gives me time to close my eyes, recompose myself and think of how to avoid doing a round myself. Hitting on the idea of asking for a group discussion with a handful of prisoners, I await events. The Superintendent arrives in regulation khaki. He has received written instructions from the I.G. which he intends to follow to the letter and tells me I am now to inform him of how I can best be accommodated in his prison. I ask for a group discussion and he agrees immediately, despatching an officer to select four men.

They arrive dressed in white kudda cloth, two bare headed and two turbaned. A prison guard is positioned in a far corner and told that we must not be disturbed then the Superintendent leaves us alone. All are 'B' class prisoners and all speak good English, reasons I guess for their selection. One man stands out as leader and I agree with him that we should choose a topic on which to focus our discussion and add that I would be grateful for introductions so that I might know how to address them. All are Sikhs named Singh so we use their forenames of Mohan, Zora, Bhupinder and Amajit. All are serving sentences for murder and are interested in talking about themselves and their situations.

Mohan suggests our title *'The Anatomy of a Punjabi Murderer'*. It suits us all admirably so we begin.

The discussion is orderly and structured. Each speaks in turn and then is open to questions from the group. Some questions are technical and go above my head as they debate the sections of the law under which they had been charged, other questions they ask each other I would not have thought of nor dared to ask even if I had. This idea, born of desperation was inspired and a tremendous learning experience. In essence they analysed the crimes in which they had been implicated, the consequences and effects upon themselves and their future prospects. As I wanted to be fully involved in the discussions I made only brief notes but am finding these volumes of information are easily reclaimed when my pen is in hand.

Mohan Singh, our leader, had been a University lecturer teaching English and Punjabi at Patiala University. He was married but had no children. He had been one of nine men whom it was alleged had conspired together to kill his father-in-law. The prosecution maintained they were not on good terms and that he was an instigator of the plot, which he disputed. Four of the nine arrested had been acquitted. Mohan was found guilty receiving a life sentence, which in India means 14 years. He had lodged an appeal and had now served five years whilst the appeal was still pending. He spoke forcefully about the arbitrary methods of police investigation and the power the police hold. A prisoner can earn maximum remission of two fifths of his sentence but the police cast a final vote as to whether they will accept him back in his home village. A negative response has devastating consequences to a prisoner's morale as the sentence then looms before him to the bitter end. Mohan thought this unethical and unjust.

Zora was a student aged 32 years. He had been studying English at the time of his conviction. Again it was a group offence. All five defendants were convicted and received life sentences. The murder was committed during a sudden quarrel over land. There had been no intent to kill but the victim had died of injuries. Three convicted had been members of one family, Zora, his father and uncle. Zora had now served eight years but his father and uncle had both died in prison. Zora's appeal was also still pending. His mother is blind and is cared for by his surviving brother. He thought it unlikely the police would ever sanction his return to his home village as he had enemies there. His only idea is to make for Saudi Arabia to work and make a fresh start.

Bhupinder Singh, previously a lecturer in Public Administration, told a story of local political struggles for leadership leading to the deaths of two men. Five men were charged with murder and two were convicted receiving life sentences. Four years into sentence he also was awaiting an appeal hearing.

He considered himself fortunate to have visits from both his father and brother.

Lastly, Amjit Singh was an MA student studying Punjabi. He had been accompanying a friend on a visit to another village and had been an eyewitness to his friend's murder. When the killers learnt they had been seen they tracked him down and tried to kill him. He maintains he fired a gun he was carrying for protection and escaped. He was arrested and tried for attempt to murder and was acquitted. Then his enemies came after him again when he was unarmed and he fought for his life, killing an assailant with a brick. He was tried for premeditated murder and was sentenced to life. This was a moving account relived with the latent emotion of these encounters.

So what of their anatomy? Mohan Singh tells me I may write his exact words as he summarises and he leans towards me as I write.

The Anatomy of a Punjabi Murderer

'For centuries the Punjabis have repelled the blows of the invaders from across the frontier. He cannot contemplate surrender. The Punjabi has become drunk with the wine of self-confidence and still imbibes that spirit. He is fierce in his pride. He fights for his honour and for protection of his land and his women. His land is dearer to him even than his religion. It is his security, his means of survival. Most disputes can be traced back to the land. As property continues to be divided between the sons the portions become smaller, yielding less and less, thus every inch becomes precious. Every inch I tell you. And I ask who would spare a man who is guilty of molesting women? I tell you no one!

Many will act together in these things for theirs is a common conscience with a common aim. The State makes its contribution as it is common practice to arrest all those who might have been implicated and some will be convicted to satisfy their poetic justice. The police think themselves to be above the law... they are below it. They turn justice into a travesty.'

The statement is a powerful one.

'Is there a hand of fate?' I ask. 'And if so how do we reconcile fate with justice?'

'As Punjabis we must fight, even if we must fight against fate.'

I was left to contemplate the answer as they are urgent to take me on a round of the jail to meet their friends. First I ask for information about the prison and learn some amusing facts. Central Jail, Patiala was built in 1887 to house prisoners from three neighbouring States, Patiala, Nabha and Jind. As all the State rulers were related to each other, for economic purposes, they pooled resources to build a communal jail. Each State then had its own gate and a portion marked out inside for its own prisoners. Maybe all these fingers in the pie accounted for the four sides being of different lengths giving it a drunken rhomboid appearance. The 18ft high wall holds over a thousand prisoners in place. It has its own hospital and factory buildings in which carpentry, weaving of drill on power looms, carpet weaving sheds, leather work and tent making are major prison industries. Forty-five acres of land are enclosed and a further fifty are attached to enable prisoners to receive training in modern methods of agriculture and poultry farming. All this is geared to rehabilitation on release, the difficulty being getting the release in the first place! Recreation is overseen by the resident Probation Officer (called a Welfare Officer when serving inside a prison), who acts as referee for football, wrestling, kabbadi, tug-of-war and such like, a bit outside my skills range!

The prisoners have a committee known as the panchayat who help with administration, maintaining discipline, distribution of food and counsel and advise prisoners. These are some of the most respected men in the prison. The canteen is well stocked with articles the men can purchase with money earned on a wage earning scheme. The philosophy of the security system is to hold the outer wall secure, allowing maximum freedom inside whilst encouraging regular family contact. The place a man would wish to escape to would be his home and family where he would be swiftly caught. I am told that those without family contact are the most disruptive, difficult to handle and would be the most closely watched.

Mohan spoke to the Prison Officer and the round was agreed. It lasted two hours in the rising heat of late morning. My group were free to wander anywhere within the perimeter amongst men growing crops, doing the washing and cooking and so on, meeting and chatting in groups in what appeared to be a generally relaxed atmosphere. Guards with batons were evident but it lacked the tenseness that is so often prevalent in UK prisons. Despite some shortcomings I felt there was much to be learnt from the Indian prison system.

The Welfare Officer joined our group explaining the rules of furlough and parole. After three years a man may return home for two weeks leave (furlough) every year. He may also apply for parole which is short time release for special purposes such as funerals, house repairs after the monsoons or to harvest his crops, but parole leave is not deducted from his sentence. Reports are compiled by the Prison Superintendent and ratified by the Inspector General. But here comes catch 22 again! The District Magistrates, advised by local Police Chiefs have the last word which is so often 'No!' The phrase is 'refused leave during sentence'. The Welfare officer also shares their frustration as he is in there trying to keep families ticking over year after year.

We passed through the library, an open air theatre, visited factories which were a hive of industry and shook hands with patients in various states of disarray. By-passing the juvenile block, housing city urchins imprisoned for persistent petty offences, we pass through locked gates in a high wall and enter a small, arid airless compound where eight women have been arranged in a straggly line. They look utterly dejected. Each is introduced and her crime briefly stated.

Kashmir, who together with her lover murdered her husband, was serving ten years. Her four year old son is in an orphanage. Maya had murdered her nephew by butchering the child with a knife and slicing his body into pieces, believing she was sacrificing him to a goddess and that if she was well pleased he would come to life again. Gurmez had killed her step mother-in-law and had remained totally silent ever since. Baldev, homeless and impoverished, had killed one of her own children by throwing him down a well as she could not bear to watch him starve. Her two remaining children were with her in prison. She looked emaciated and weary unto death. Surrinder, aged sixteen had been charged with killing her grandmother and Sangitor had been found wandering homeless. I greeted each one in turn and they put their hands together in the ritual greeting but no one attempted to communicate. I felt their isolation was draining the life out of them.

Out of one thousand prisoners only twenty-three were 'B' class and all of these were men. There was a former M.P, councillors, graduates, politicians and those with equivalent high status. Class division is the same in Punjab State. By the time we reach the sleeping barracks I am nauseous and exhausted by the heat. Gently they lay me on a bed. I feel my sandals being slipped off and my ankles being bathed in cool water. Scalding hot tea is brought and I sip it, hoping for a revival. Prisoners gather, sitting, squatting or standing around the bed. I smile at them and tell them in best Punjabi that it is good to be in their company. The Welfare Officer melts away, sensitive to leaving the men on their own ground and I think what an extraordinary situation I am in. There is no question that anyone would wish me any harm. One man tells of his agonising wait for execution, after being sentenced to death for murder and his feelings when, after five years, it was commuted to life imprisonment. When sentences are converted from execution to life there is no remission and the full fourteen years have to be served. He was in his ninth year. These men are my teachers. How strange to feel so valued and at home in such a place. I could happily have stayed on to work in this prison and shared the thought with them. They were most enthusiastic!

Lunch is not on my agenda and I have to disappoint the Superintendent's wife but I have to move on to Naba Jail by bus. My escort is to be Maxwell Robinson who has gone home to prepare himself for the occasion so in the meantime

I am entertained by the District Probation Officer. His office is situated outside the entrance. As prison and probation are a combined service I'm told it is cheaper to use existing prison buildings than rent offices. His duties are heavy to impossible. He is expected to supervise 250 offenders, the requirement being to see them twice per month, once in his office and once on a home visit. He must obtain monthly signatures from a responsible person, such as a village elder, to confirm his probationer's good conduct. This man is unwell, has put in a doctors certificate and been refused sick leave. He is trying to get a post inside a prison but his application has brought only a letter of censure. I commiserate.

Maxwell, the D.P.O's clerk returns. He thinks it important that I understand he is a Christian who leads an English life-style. I am intrigued but in a hurry, so we head for a bus station where he secures the last seat on a bus for me and we head for Nabha Jail. I had heard of the Superintendent of this prison by reputation. He had previously been a Probation officer in the Punjab and had become one of the foremost social reformers in the State. This is Davinder Singh, a majestic Sikh with curly moustache and he was to be my host for the night. He organises tea, gives me a booklet of information, shows me to a soft seat in an airy office and leaves me to rest. The perfect welcome. I scan the pages picking out important pieces ready for the round which must come.

Nabha Open Air Agricultural Jail opened in 1970 on 1004 acres of uncultivated Forest Department land which is gradually being reclaimed. Carefully selected prisoners work in open conditions under minimum watch and ward arrangements. Aims are high; to increase national food production; train prisoners in new methods of agriculture, improve attitudes and equip them to stand on their own legs in open society. Prisoners earn one day's remission for three days work, wages being paid at a flat rate of 50 paisa per day which can be spent or sent home. I have the picture and am impressed. What is more there is no B and C class at Nabha!

A jeep arrives with Davinder Singh in it. He is a flamboyant driver and the round is exhilarating down rutted tracks, up and around the pits and fish tanks, through acres of paddy fields and I'm left in no doubt the chemical process of ridding the soil of saline is working a treat. There are plans for cattle and sheep breeding and a piggery scheme. Davinder Singh is undoubtedly an entrepreneur with a social conscience. I could see men working in the fields but we were never near enough for contact. We bounce out onto a road and speed on to District Jail windswept and laughing after a very different kind of round.

District Jail is a small circular prison mainly occupied by Pakistanis awaiting deportation for illegal border crossings. I was glad to hear this was a courtesy visit only and not a full round but was immediately touched by the plight of the few prisoners I saw. All leapt to their feet as gates opened standing to attention in front of makeshift tents pegged at all angles to the dusty compound. There were women and children, remnants of families, their men probably in another section of the prison. Their clothes were tattered and the children waif-like. They were waiting interminably to be returned to Pakistan, the place they had striven to escape in the hope of a better future and all they had found was a prison tent. I was astonished to see one white face, a German girl caught without correct entry papers. I spoke in the small amount of German I could muster which made her smile and she explained there were plenty of illegal tourists around who were ignored but she had got on the wrong side of the police. I wonder how.

Davinder Singh was itching to spirit me away to his newly built house and I asked him a little about himself on the way. He is a descendant of the Maharaja of Patiala and times have changed dramatically for his family. He had started a dairy farm for the manufacture of *Horlicks* when he realised the great challenge in the field of social reform and had chosen to see how he could influence the corrective system. He is well pleased with Nabha. At home his three daughters are waiting to greet us. All are studying English and are delighted to practice. The house is spacious and richly furnished. As I had been on the move all day my need was to wash and change, however my luggage had not been delivered from Patiala Jail as promised. Feeling grimy and unkempt I join Davinder's brothers and the District Probation Officer at dinner. We work our way through course after course of beautifully prepared food.

Dinner is over, guests have left, the jeep has a flat battery, and the road outside is impassable as a sewer is having attention. Vehicles can neither leave nor arrive and I still have no luggage. The prison is contacted to despatch the luggage as far as it can reach by rickshaw. It arrives. I seize my bags, wash with speed and dive into crisp white sheets to wake only when the door is knocked at 8am and that is late in India.

Tuesday 25th October

It had been my intention to stay in Patiala with the family of a man serving a prison sentence in England. The I.G. had persuaded me that I should first consult Davinder Singh as the address is in a remote area. We discuss it. It is a job for the jeep and he will be my interpreter. As we drive through the town he points out the National Institute for Sport adding that it was once the Maharaja of Patiala's Palace and his ancestral home. It is impressive. Then we try to find Behru.

We are hunting for the family home of Ranjit Singh, currently serving four years imprisonment for an offence of wounding. He had been involved in an affray outside a London public house when visiting friends, had jumped bail and returned for a while to his home village. There he became engaged to a local girl. He returned to England, was arrested immediately and was remanded in custody awaiting sentence. His fiancé arrived, already pregnant, but not yet married. It then became the duty of Ranjit's father and older brother to care for her. She was taken to their rented house in Smethwick where she was kept without being told the whereabouts of her prospective husband. After three months her visa ran out but she did not return.

As Ranjit's offence had been committed in London he was serving his sentence in Wandsworth Prison and communication with his family was difficult. Eventually, affected by the pressure of the situation, he asked for help from the Prison Welfare Department who telephoned and asked me to sort out the situation. It was just as he had explained, plus an added complication. Ranjit had been married previously and divorce papers had to be acquired before a wedding could be arranged. Negotiations with the Home Office followed and an extension of visa was granted in the recognition of the difficulties I was having arranging a wedding at Wandsworth Registry office. We were all working through interpreters and to everyone's relief the wedding eventually took place under escort. The baby was born and was six months old before meeting his father on a never-to be forgotten day when I took Ranjit's elderly father, his wife and baby and numerous carrier bags by train to London. No-one spoke any English. The father folded his Underground ticket double to press it into the automatic ticket machine, trapping himself, baby and bags in the revolving barrier. Mechanics at the station were still trying to extricate him when the clock ticked up the time of our appointment. Making a mad dash by taxi we just had time for them all to face each other briefly before shut down. Husband and wife did little more than smile at each other whilst Ranjit had a few words with his father. At least he held his son for the first time. After that I became an accepted visitor in their home, learning that this family had been split down the middle. The father and two sons, their wives and children had settled in Smethwick whilst the mother, eldest son and his family remained in India. I was now about to visit the Indian half.

Behru is indeed rural. The jeep negotiates winding cart tracks and we stop at a collection of square sandy coloured houses of baked brick decorated with ornamental cow pats. It is a dead end. Our farm is four furlongs away across fields. I have no idea how long a furlong is and decide it is probably better if I do not find out. Davinder asks if I can walk it. I answer 'yes', having no option other than being carried. We are single file. A villager strides ahead, Davinder in the middle and I bring up the rear. I do not have the easy swinging stride of the men and notice that they walk with elbows bent and fingers bunched into fists.

I try it, feeling foolish, but it makes no difference to my progress over the stones and stubble. The Smethwick family children had described this path to me on their one and only visit here, sharing amazement at disturbing sleeping snakes and fetching water from the well. I had never thought to be retracing their steps!

We are greeted with astonishment by Ranjit's sister-in-law. No introduction is made and I initially make the error of believing this person is his mother, as she looked so old. Davinder interprets. Ranjit's mother has gone out to the next village and his brother must be fetched from the fields to go and collect her on the back of his bicycle. So we wait.

The farmhouse, standing in solitary state consists of one brick room containing three beds. The expanse of rough grassland looks, even to my unpractised eye, distinctly infertile. I rest on a bed drinking tea until mother arrives. She is overwhelmed. No one had told her I might be visiting although she had heard much about me through letters from England. She hugs me until I am breathless. All the news that I can give her pours out and is translated at top speed by Davinder Singh. She cries copiously and asks many questions.

'What are English jails like? How is my son's health? And my grandchildren?'
This I knew she would ask and was able to relay the children's loving messages in Punjabi which they had taught me themselves. She wept and I wept at her tears. It was noticeable that she did not ask after her daughter-in-law and I try to imagine for myself the turmoil and distress of a pregnant village girl travelling such a distance to face the confusion and trauma that awaited her. Not such a golden land for her!

Mother tells me that she refuses to live in England. India is her home. The family farm, twenty acres of land, is partly bought with money from England and part rented, but without fertilisers is not likely to yield much produce. They live hand to mouth and have not heard from England for two months. When Ranjit was free to work there was money from England. Now Ranjit is in prison, the father is sick and has retired and the one working son has women and children to keep. She shows me a letter propped on the dusty shelf addressed to Smethwick. It has been there for weeks and they do not have the money to buy a stamp.

I am fitting the picture of these two homes together. The mother looks old and worn out. She is wizened and wrinkled and short of teeth. There are grandchildren here too and I ask about school. School is a long way away, they do not go often, if at all. The only decorations in this room are photos of Smethwick relatives so we take photos for them in colour, a great luxury. Now I can see the I.G.'s wisdom. As well as the communication problem, staying with this family was not an option. There would be too many difficulties for us all and it is too highly charged with emotion. I leave sharing their sadness, hardly noticing the route march back across the fields.

Patiala is a congested town with tightly packed narrow streets filled with cupboard shops. Davinder wants to present me with a momento of my visit and the speciality of Patiala is embroidered slippers. He stops at a shop where my feet are measured and chooses a blue velvet inner shell, which is to be covered with filigree of golden thread. They will be sent on to me. I have no idea to which address.

At home discussion is under way to discover how I can be helped to reach Chandigargh, capital of the Punjab and home of the I.G. A relative arrives, who I am astonished to find is on his way to Chandigargh to buy a tractor. Now there is no problem. He will deliver me. These connections never cease to amaze me yet no-one else shows surprise. The I.G's daughter, Sheshi, who is studying at Patiala Medical College, will accompany us. I discover that apprehension and anticipation are fast being replaced by acceptance of whatever lies ahead.

5. A Sensational Family

Wednesday 25th October

I like both the I.G's house and family immediately. Sheshi is proving delightful and fun, her mother and brothers Surrinder and Mohinder are waiting with a warm welcome. All except the I.G's wife speak fluent English. I feel I have arrived home. Then the I.G. arrives and everything happens. He is dynamic. He slaps everyone with affection, including me and is the immediate focus of attention.

'Any instructions for me, Madame?' he asks.

My request is dealt with immediately. I need to contact a Mr. Perminder Singh, a friend of a wise old gentleman, Mr. Ajit Mangat. One of our first volunteers, Mr. Mangat had played an invaluable role as counsellor and advisor to the Probation Service. We telephone Perminder Singh, whose address I had given for letters from home. He is delighted that I have arrived and am in safe hands, telling me rather reverently that he has a letter in hand for me from Sir Gordon Taylor. I am in a crazy position as my status has now risen about ten notches because of a joke title from Mr. Derek Gordon Taylor, my normal status husband. I try to explain but status is not understood to be a joke-worthy subject. We arrange to meet next day. Half an hour later the letter arrives by hand delivery and is presented on a silver tray. Bet Sir D.G.T. didn't envisage this when he licked the stamp!

Records are played and the young people tempt me to dance. I feel happy, relaxed and more or less well again. The I.G. changes into his wrap around *dhoti*, spreads himself on a couch and we all perform for him like children at a party. It was what I needed, to shed the cares of the world at least for a while. There is no television or piped gas and water is difficult to heat but other than this I am now in a western style interior sharing a bedroom with Sheshi. All rooms are on the ground floor and the doors are always open giving the impression of an open plan. Everyone is free to wander everywhere. I am told to be one of the family which is easy here. Mohinder is going to Southall in December to marry a girl of his family's choice. He has never left India before and is hungry for information about his new country where he intends to live. I am their first ever English guest and there is much to be shared with these warm hospitable people.

Thursday 26th October

There is a daily routine. The I.G's day starts at 6am with reading the daily papers. When he has done so, we are all woken to take tea with him, plan the day and discuss any matters together and make important decisions. The subject in hand is the forthcoming journey to Amritsar.

Breakfast is a delicious omelette and I am fortified for my outing with Perminder Singh. He arrives with his nephew as escort. A visit has been arranged to meet a Dr. Sandu, a wealthy eye specialist. I am told he has just returned from America where he had a heart operation. He knows Britain well but has become so disillusioned by our political arguments about the entry to the UK of Indians with British Passports, that he has now surrendered his own in protest. He talked politics, social education and the problems facing immigrants in Britain. It was a searching debate for early in the morning.

Perminder is an affluent businessman. His home is extensive and spacious. Though he has not seen his old friend Ajit Mangat for many years, their bond remains and each could ask the other for help at any time knowing it would be given. Photograph albums introduce me to the faces of family and friends spread out across the world. The nephew joins us sharing his concerns about how the cost of education limits progress for so many, explaining how college places can be bought and are not always given on merit by entrance examination, then how this practice persists with examination passes being bought. He speaks with feeling of how soul destroying it is for those who work hard and are trying to respond to family pressure to succeed due to financial sacrifices being made, only to be by-passed by those who can afford to buy higher marks.

It is time for sightseeing. Chandigargh, capital of the Punjab, is a beautiful city designed by the late French architect, Le Corbusier, and I am told it is the most novel experiment in architecture and town planning in India. The roads are wide and well surfaced with well built houses divided into forty sectors, each with their own shopping centre. We take a round of the Punjore Gardens. Landscaped into seven tiers of rectangular pools, surrounded by fruit trees and exotic plants with a backdrop of the Himalayas it is like a film set. Perminder is searching for a shop where he can purchase some beer which, to my surprise, I discover is to accompany my lunch! He has an image of English women as smokers, and beer drinkers.

'Madame, I think you are a little unusual' was his response when I tell him that neither is to my taste! Lunch, however, is tasty then the nephew is permitted to drive me home.

Back at the I.G.'s Surrinder, the eldest son, is waiting. He had wanted to join us in the morning but had not thought it polite to ask. It seems we are sharing the same hesitation about doing the right thing. He has a scooter and would like to show me his own special corners of Chandigargh. I must ride side-saddle for the sake of modesty which feels rather insecure but soon am enjoying this whizzing fresh air tour around the local area of Sector 15. Taking the opportunity to order some hand-made shoes for Derek, we find a friendly cobbler who passes us a Mail Order catalogue. He can make anything from the pictures so I indicate slip-on style in suede tan. I had come prepared with an outline of Derek's foot. The cobbler tells me I am mistaken. No foot is this size. It is a normal nine and a half. I reply that this is the true size so he shrugs and puts up the price.

The Rose Gardens are next. Here we walk amongst rivers with rustic bridges, fountains and a magnificent rose bush collection, talking. Surrinder is taking his M.A. in English. He is not yet ready for marriage but knows his wishes will be considered when the time comes. Next we speed on to the Rock Gardens. Created by an engineer it has won many awards for its artistic scenes and models of people and animals made out of old electrical plugs and sockets, broken bangles, crushed glass, plastic containers, stones and broken pottery. It is an ingenious feast of creativity. Darkness falls before I am ready to move on to the skating rink.

One of Surrinder's hobbies is roller-skating so I am introduced to skaters playing tag and other games on wheels. We are in Sector 17 where shops are glass fronted, hence expensive, so drive through to the market in Sector 15 where we purchase vegetables for the evening meal. There are many stops for handshakes, introductions and an invitation to 'do a round' of the University offered by Surrinder's Professor. Reluctantly I have to refuse. The programme is too tight. Dinner is followed by retirement to a quiet corner with the I.G. He has brought a pile of pamphlets on prisons and borstals and we talk business until at 10.30pm I ask if I may be excused to do my writing work, however Mohinder and Sheshi have been waiting for the dancing to begin. They request that I teach them ballroom, rock and twist that they have seen on the films and have all the appropriate music. It is hilarious, ending only as we make up formation dances in a mixture of eastern and western steps and run out of floor space. This uninhibited, spontaneous behaviour which is a part of this culture catches the free spirit in me that rarely find such avenues for escape.

We tape records on my hand recorder in preparation for our holiday in Amritsar as they want lessons to continue, then though it is late, I still write for an hour. They think I am most diligent but in a different way I also enjoy my nightly dances with the pen.

Three dancing partners.
Surrinder, Sheshi and Mohinder

What is it that I am experiencing in the bosom of this family that is a great deal more than a collation of facts? Firstly I feel a sense of belonging and a willingness to be open; to discover more of myself; the enjoyment of receiving and responding; communicating in words and dance, by touch and through music; interest, compassion, service, all generating a vitality that makes itself felt, holding Mrs. I.G. in a gentle cocoon. There is a tacit realisation of the seriousness of her failing health and yet life is carrying her kindly through her suffering. There is too not only a sense of connection to the wider world but of the power this extra-ordinary man exerts far beyond the family enclave. I have wanted to be inside the families, absorbing traditions and cultures in daily living, yet had given little thought to the effect upon me, an outsider, being absorbed into it so swiftly. I find I hardly know myself. Parts of me that have not seen the light of day for many a year are unlocking and my prized independence is taking a shaking as it feels something else cloaking it, claiming it. The family is a group and to be in it is to be part of it. There are issues here of obedience, of responsibility, and of just letting go that are going to be testing. I can sense it coming.

Friday 27th October

We all respond to reveille, piling onto the I.G.'s bed in our nightwear. He is reading notes into my recorder from the morning newspaper about the forthcoming celebrations for the 400th anniversary of the Golden Temple in Amritsar. The phone starts ringing and an elderly Indian man, who has lived in England, calls to pay his respects and to regale me with nostalgic tales of England in the 1940's and to tell me how he hopes to return to die.

The Government car arrives to take I.G. to work. I am to accompany him so I try out a suitable outfit of a sober long skirt and formal long sleeved blouse. He approves. In the centre of Sector 17 is the Headquarters of the Prison and Probation Administration Departments. The most senior staff are introduced personally and the vast room of clerical workers collectively standing silently as we enter, stiffen as we approach. None will speak unless addressed. Two years ago I had been involved in discussions in a Smethwick factory where management were questioning the attitude of their Indian work force. The Director on his rounds was used to smiles, nods and 'Good morning Mr. David', but he felt his 400 workpeople ignored him which he construed as rudeness, held some grievances or that they simply did not like him personally. Whilst I had been able to explain this cultural difference in formalities it was unnerving to experience it in action.

The files are dusty bundles tied with string, in piles upon piles. The I.G has a spacious office with huge polished desk. This is a totally different face of the man I had danced for the previous evening, one these people are unlikely to see. He is like a commander going into battle. Orders are machine gunned out in every direction and no doubt will be carried out with speed and efficiency. He would accept no less.

The Superintendent of Chandigarh Jail arrives and I am spirited away to his prison which houses political agitators, the next planned agitation being at Amritsar, I am not pleased to hear. He tells me there is little organised crime in India. 'You will find no bank robbers here'. On the round a tiny man catches my eye. His clothes envelop him, leaving only a bird-like face and praying hands to show there is a man inside. He looks like a lost soul. He had found his wife was having an affair with the milk vendor so he had killed her, her lover and all his six children. Then he tried to commit suicide but had failed. He had over served his sentence but had nowhere to go and was hoping he could be found a job and somewhere to live. I also meet a man who had killed a Deputy Superintendent and am more aware here that a watchful eye was being kept on our movements. The Superintendent takes pride in the quality of the food. The dahl is thick and rich and he is instigating imaginative rehabilitation schemes.

It certainly seemed to me as if the I.G. inspires men with initiative to be in charge of his prisons.

Returning to the I.G.'s office I find a motley collection of people are awaiting an audience. They arrive singly, stand to attention well back from his desk and are told to state their business. All want help of some kind and many are given a listening ear, advice and a thoughtful word or so, others receive short shrift such as the employee who asked for promotion. The I.G. made it quite clear, in English that made me cringe, that this man had burnt his boats and may as well burn his boots.

The I.G.'s Deputy is named Mr.Gill whose wife is the Director for Social Welfare in Chandigargh. I am taken to meet her and find her charming and businesslike. She is interested in my methods of supervision and requests to see me at work. This is not an easy matter to arrange. All I can do is give a note of where and when I will be with a family in Banga and invite her to join me if she chooses.

Only the I.G, his wife and Sheshi are now in the Amritsar party. We pack and leave for a five hour drive across the Punjab as Amritsar is close to the Pakistan border. Our driver, Gurbax Singh, surmounts all obstacles which are many. We sweep past, even on occasion over, dead dogs and squashed livestock and around crashed lorries hanging drunkenly over ditches. There are bikes, rickshaws, carts, elephants and people. The world is heading for Amritsar!

Amritsar is a fairyland of multi-coloured lights, tinsel and a sea of bobbing turbans. The streets are thick with people. It is only because we are in a government car that we can inch through and make our way to the jail where we are to stay in a house in pitch dark grounds. As there is no electricity, because the lights are consuming it so rapidly, we feel our way around inside. It is eerie. All I find is a bed so I sit on it until dim lamps are brought and we move outside to sit together, a little group of four. Then the I.G. tells me that many years ago he had been Superintendent of this jail and had lived in this very house with his wife and three small children. He excuses himself as, speaking in Punjabi they pull out strands of memory from the distant past.

Later the I.G. tells me that he and his wife came to India from Pakistan in 1947 at the time of the partition when Pakistan became a Muslim country. They lost everything that they owned and were lucky to escape with their lives. The I.G. had served seven years in the army and found employment in the Punjab Prison Service. He rose to the rank of Superintendent and was in charge of several of the Punjab Prisons and also became a trained lawyer. The family had always lived in prison accommodation until they had the house built in Chandigargh. As the only home they have ever owned, it means a great deal to them all. I now see the I.G. as a man who has risen to meet all the challenges that life has offered and feel privileged to have stepped into the heart of this family. He respects me as a professional at the same time treating me as family, a difficult enough blend, whilst I have learnt to appreciate his protection, his wisdom and most certainly his organization on this extraordinary trail

Sheshi asks me to respond to their story with my life history which is a sizeable task and not one I relish as she wants all the more lurid details and is fascinated by the amount of freedom westerners have to make their own mistakes. We talk until 10pm. The I.G. is in consultation with staff. We are hungry but Sheshi, who says she does not dare to intrude, persuades me that I could break in and suggest dinner. I dare, he smiles, seeing straight through Sheshi's strategy and supper is served by prisoners sneaking glances and thinking what, I wonder?

6.Ministers of Fairy Land

Saturday 28th October

Ministers of Punjab State have been invited to evening celebrations at the prison. First they will visit the Golden Temple and then return to the prison where many of them had been imprisoned during the Emergency. This is to be a historical working day for the I.G. He tells me I can assist by making a round as a trial run for the Minister's tour. The grounds are a whirl of activity and the atmosphere is tense with anticipation. The bushes have become webs of wires, linking tiny coloured lights to form an avenue, lighting the way to the enormous striped tent. Unused today, the execution podium sits in the middle of a sandy compound like a miniature bandstand. It has an ornamental domed roof, a platform and open sides. These are the gallows to which I am told the Punjabis go boldly, even after years of harrowing uncertainty. As we pass I am treated to details of the sequence of the execution process, 'paralysis, unconsciousness, bone breaks, heart stops, body hangs for half an hour and is handed over to the relatives'. Short clipped phrases to end longing for life.

We have in hand a booklet "Face-lift to the Punjab Prison Industries 1977" published to coincide with the celebrations. It publicises the developments of new trades to be displayed in an Exhibition. These are our important targets for inspection. Intricate and attractive designs in carpentry, carpet weaving and glass engraving, iron pipe furniture and the prize exhibit of a carved suite inset with rows of tiny bells, displayed not only the artistry but the pride and patience of these craftsmen. This to me was rehabilitation at its best. They are to be sold on the open market bringing revenue into the Prison Service. It is a brisk and business-like round. The District Probation Officer who walks back with me to the bungalow is eager to share his problem of supervising 341 probationers dotted around the largest district in the Punjab. He too wants to transfer inside the prison. It is easy to see why.

Lunch is laid and so are plans for the afternoon. Two men arrive by car and, with Sheshi as escort we are transported to a cinema. The men walk straight past straggling queues and we follow as they indicate our seats. Sheshi tells me that the proprietor is 'daddy's friend'. The men leave without a word having been exchanged between us. Then we are into a Hindi movie, a slow-moving love story in which the heroine is blinded in a car crash and I have a doze. The silent males return, reload us into the car and drive into the city. Every inch of the pavement and roadway is a rainbow of moving bodies, dressed for the occasion. Swords and daggers are well in evidence around the waists of Sikhs who have converged from all corners of India and no doubt beyond. Our driver bleeps the horn relentlessly and is ignored, so he drives slowly and deliberately into the crowd which parts in waves for the few seconds it takes to pass and then joins together again. We are surrounded, faces pressing and peering through the windows. These are not agitators but they are distinctly curious. Gazing back I can see something rolling along in the gutter. It is a turbaned head, on a muscular neck swinging to and fro, causing a limbless trunk to roll, over and over. He is not begging, just rolling to the Golden Temple.

We have to park and walk, barefoot. Water troughs have splashed all over the pavements, hundreds of feet are superimposing their wet imprints on top of each other, its impossible to hold the mind steady. All I can think of is people and feet, some with and some without! Then I see the Temple. Its radiant golden covering forms a shimmering reflection in the rippling lake causing it to move with a life of its own. I am absorbed by it. Unfortunately the crowds are becoming aware of us. I am a curio. Women keep touching me, stroking and feeling my skin and the material of my clothing, talking, trying to get me to speak. I smile and smile but I do not want to engage with them, it is the Temple that transfixes my attention and it is being side- tracked. The men cannot risk any incidents. They motion to us to leave for our next experience, Jallianwalla Bagh.

This would not have been my choice of venue. Though I value each experience I am beginning to find having decisions made without any consultation difficult to handle and this is one of them. A plaque informs me that this square is saturated with the blood of two thousand Indians, massacred by the British at the command of General Dyer in 1919. I am shown the well into which one hundred and twenty people leapt to escape the bullets but nevertheless died. Sheshi graphically describes each aspect of this awful scene. It is a truly fearful place to stand and show myself as English. I do not know how to act. Is there any protocol for this? Should I apologise for the sins of the past because they were committed in the name of my nation? I could only shake my head in sadness; not only because of past unholy acts but that we had moved from a place of the Most Holy to one that felt unholy even today. The staring people I now interpret differently, as if they are glaring at an old enemy. All of this happened so long ago yet whatever it is that brings a chill to the air is still there. I was relieved to leave.

It was good to be moved on for a spot of shopping. I buy a bedcover in multi coloured squares as a memento of this multi-coloured day and we are returned to the cinema for refreshments. There is a message from the I.G. and refreshments are forgotten as we read 'Return to the prison immediately!' We go at top speed.

Beyond the gates the world has exploded into light. The bushes are ablaze, arc lighting from the roof of the marquee is trained on 2,000 prisoners, all dressed in white kudda suits, most with white turbans. Ministers of Punjab State are assembled and speeches are under way. I find it strange that I had been sent out to the cinema up to this point and now, without even a change from cinema clothes, am to make a grand entrance onto the stage! I am the only white face and the only woman present and have no idea what is expected of me or where to sit. Any minute they could call me to make a speech, give prizes or do a somersault! I personally am in the dark. So I choose a position that is not too prominent but where I can see and be seen which is quite easy in this elevated position. The atmosphere is electrified. I can see the guards are not guarding anyone as no-one would dream of leaving or moving. There is absolute stillness, eyes concentrating on the stage. The words being spoken are life changing. They are an announcement of Amnesty Release announced by the Chief Minister, Mr.Parkash Singh Badal:

'All prisoners aged 65 or above and invalids to be released immediately from Punjab prisons without any reference to the police or the district administration. All prisoners who have undergone eight and a half years substantive imprisonment making a total of fourteen years, including remission to be released without any reference about their conduct to the district authorities; and a general remission for all prisoners serving up to six months.'

I understand the immense significance of it all.

To my amazement the silence holds; no clapping or outward show of emotion until permission is given for some prisoners to speak. Elderly white bearded men who I guess are the over 65's stand, hands together at waist height, to make their 'Sat Sri Akal' and bow their head, speaking softy and with great respect. I sense there is a rapport between these who are prisoners now and those who have suffered imprisonment themselves for their political beliefs. Moved beyond words I would have done anything asked of me yet all I had to do was be there, observe and listen.

The band begins to play and I am one of the first to be ushered out. I do not know this man who escorts me to a car and my mind is racing, concerned about the protocol but assuming the I.G. has given instructions about my next move. He hasn't! Gurbax, the I.G's driver sees what is happening, speeds after us and engages in rapid conversation. He insists we wait until the I.G. arrives. We wait. The I.G. arrives and I am driven the hundred yards home by Gurbax. Then the plot unravels. The gentleman who had wanted my company is a local transport chief who is hosting some of the Ministers and had wanted me to 'grace his dining table'. Sheshi explains that her father does not usually socialise because there is such an element of currying favours and also due to his wife's frail health. Tonight however, he has agreed to accompany me to this important dinner party, which, I had not yet heard about and nearly discovered a mite too soon.

We sit on the terrace and talk over the day's events with the I.G asking questions that tax my brain to the limits. I am amazed he chooses this time with so many dignitaries about to learn of our Welfare State, systems of taxation, property laws, loans, mortgages and hire purchase. We have begun on the education system when I insist on time to change my clothes as for once I know where I am going. I am pleased to know that Sheshi and the I.G.'s wife are also invited.

Our hosts have a large house of modern design with luxurious furnishings. The centre-piece in an elegant lounge is a twelve seater dining table shaped like a giant lotus flower with fluted edges. The inner circle rotates and I am shown how food is placed in the centre and twizzled around so that guests can reach all the dishes. As male guests arrive we are ushered into the back living quarters to meet the ladies of this household. A little girl has learnt a welcome speech in English.

'We welcome you. We like you. We love you'. Its my place to answer. Punjabi being the correct language I try out:

'Your house is beautiful. You are my friends. I am happy here.'
Good marks all round! I hear other guests arriving but no more ladies join us and I don't know what the plan is for eating. There are only twelve places at the table. A nagging thought comes to me that if it is so important that I attend, why am I sitting in the back room playing with the children? Part of me is of course itching to be eavesdropping on affairs of state. I soon learn the answer. Dinner is served and my host, the transport chief, comes to take me in to join the men. I ask if any of the other ladies will be joining us. They will not. Thanking him for his invitation and to everyone's astonishment, including my own, I hear myself saying quite firmly that I prefer to eat with the ladies. It is possible that I have deeply offended my host and will cause him to loose face with his guests but something has just pushed me over a cultural line into my western model of protocol. I would not have blamed anyone if I had been transported back to base in a reverse kidnap operation. Host returns to consult with his male guests. Dinner is put on hold. Like the good statesmen that they are they come up with a compromise and host returns. Sheshi and Mrs. I.G. are invited to accompany me in to dinner. I accept to smiles all round and some deep breaths from Sheshi. Now, I decide I will behave like a proper English lady out to dinner without causing

any more embarrassment. Wrong!

The men are all positioned at the tip of their respective flower petals that seem to have grown an extra couple of leaves to accommodate us. There are nods and smiles as the table is swivelled and we all eat with relish. The men talk amongst themselves not addressing the ladies directly which is not surprising, but in a short time I tune in to the obvious, that they are talking about me. Apart from the odd snippets of Punjabi that I can follow, the non verbal signs would be readable in any culture. So I begin to feel ruffled again. It seems so discourteous to be talking about me rather than to me when I know they all speak English, so I wait and listen. They are discussing my age which turns into a guessing game, my lowest score being 25 and the highest 50. The I.G. steps in to settle it with an authoritative 48. I cannot resist it.

'Gentlemen you have aged me by four years. I am just turned 44'. Consternation is an understatement.

'Madame, do you speak Punjabi?'

'A little; I am particularly good at numbers'. I am blessing my darts tuition. Now no-one knows what I have gleaned from their conversations when they could have been discussing other parts of my physiology. Now they are not about to let me off the hook. They want proof of my proficiency.

'Madame, will you speak some lines of Punjabi to us?'

Dinner is forgotten. I had stirred up a hornets nest and it is my responsibility to retrieve a delicate situation. I begin a recitation of some verses of the Adi Granth which I had committed to memory and end with my favourite phrase 'I am glad you are my friends'. There is an uproar of laughter, thumping of the table and I am no longer in a straightjacket playing the part allotted to me. It is easy then to explain that it is an honour to be in their company but that I had felt uncomfortable eating in silence when in my culture it is impolite not to engage in conversation with my host and his friends. We are all eating again and the food tastes even better!

'Madame, is it acceptable if we ask you questions?' I had opened a door and must take the consequences.

'If I know the answers, I will be pleased to reply'.

'Even delicate questions?'

'Yes, if they are of importance to you.'

It was a necessary gamble as I had little idea of what they would consider delicate. So I found out.

'Will you inform us Madam, on the English methods of contraception.' Now this was not as difficult as it might sound as I had been through all of this with the Doctor friend of Uncle Pritam Singh and knew the sterilisation programme was contentious and very much in the news. It was indeed an important question for Ministers to address. All I had to do was select the most appropriate words for a dinner party! I explained that I had been asked this question many times by Sikh wives in Smethwick and would give them the same reply as is given at our Family Planning Clinics. It raised tremendous interest and we debated population control at some length.

A deluge of other questions followed. Of particular interest were male and female roles and relationships, western lifestyles and family life. Some were more personal. I was asked at one point whether my husband gives me presents and if so what, when and why! One question floored me completely when the Minister for Transport asked 'What is the composition of your motorway? That is not my speciality so I hone in on describing the motorway network, and reflect on the cultural differences in village life.

Dinner had long since been cleared away and still we sat. We had reached the subject of religion. I spoke of how the Sikhs had purchased old churches, cinemas and other ready made buildings to set up their Holy Places of worship and of the warm welcome I had always received at the Gurdwaras. It was much harder to answer questions about Christianity so instead I shared my personal interest in the Wisdom inherent in all faiths. We conclude with more verses from the Adi Granth which I repeat, first after them and then with them. Barriers had fallen to the touch. There were requests that I remain in India for a longer stay to join with them again and suggest I could earn a fine living as a professional dinner guest. I had redeemed myself. They all escort us to the waiting car and I embrace them, one by one. We have made our own protocol.

The I.G. is delighted with the outcome of the evening and admitted to his anxieties. Sitting in the darkness on the porch he said that until this night his family had only five members and now it had six. I will never be forgotten in India. There is a depth of feeling expressed here that is so often buried by English reserve. I am learning how to plumb deeper every day.

Sunday 29th October

The Tribune newspaper is passed around at our morning meeting. Amongst all the news of the celebrations there is a big spread about the events at the Prison. I read:

'The pay grades of all jail employees from the I.G. down to the warder will be immediately revised with an upper slab' and I hope that includes the Probation Service. Mrs. I.G. has to attend hospital in Amritsar for tests for her recurring heart trouble.The I.G. takes her so, after guard inspection I have a few hours free for journal writing. I need this spell for clearing my brain.

Servants, who are prisoners, dodge in and out asking if they can do anything, enjoying glimpses of Madame at work so I give them the task of getting bath water organised. It is a delicious experience, if primitive, with two tin drums, one for hot water one for cold and a plastic jug for self mixing. Men with grass switches flick around the floor raising what I thought was dust and then on closer inspection find they are microscopic insects. It's a great morning.

Lunch is rushed as I learn when the I.G. returns that we are all attending

an exhibition. Arriving amongst milling thousands of people we find a reception committee lined up consisting of the Head of Police, Deputy Superintendent of the Prison and his staff, the Faridkot Borstal Boys Band and the organisers of the Exhibition. I was in a short skirt and should have been wearing finery but as usual was unaware that I was centre stage and was also an exhibit. I am to draw attention to the section promoting the prison-made goods. This is a pleasure except for the police who swing their batons thumping people indiscriminately as they cut a swathe through the crowds. Photographers rush in every direction thrusting goods from different stands into my hands and I wonder if I am going to be sold for publicity of some unusual items.

With Sheshi and Mr.and Mrs. Shenmar in an exhibits tent.

Stalls selling plastic goods are drawing attention. Plastic is a new industry in India. I learn the raw material is imported from England but I do not particularly want to promote plastic. It gets ridiculous when I am pushed towards a tractor so I side-step towards a dress display of exquisitely worked Rajasthan mirror-ware. The stall holders are ecstatic when I buy two star items.

Duty is done and I have had a great time. The I.G. and his wife return to base leaving Sheshi to orchestrate an evening programme. She organises a return to the Golden Temple for a firework display. As expected the crowds are dense but it is worth the ride to see the Temple silhouetted against the darkening sky. The crowds become excited as the show begins and heave forwards towards the lake. It is becoming dangerous ground and I vote for a retreat. Sheshi is happy to retreat into a record shop selecting a pile of records she wants to play, a long job as the electricity fails three times. I choose a Neil Diamond for her dancing classes back in Chandigargh. I am tired. It has been hot work this afternoon and I can spy a quiet couple of hours ahead. Quiet hours are not an entry in the programme. The I.G. is waiting to suggest that I may want to change straight away as another dinner party is arranged. I express my concern that I am too tired to be good company, a lame excuse as the I.G. is inexhaustible and his burden of responsibility is a great deal heavier than mine. I change.

The venue is a large nearby farm where two brothers own adjacent farmhouses. They also jointly own the cinema so I am able to thank them for my outing. I am introduced to a doctor and surgeon from the hospital, which the I.G's wife has been attending, and then am shown into the back of the house to be with the women. The host's wife speaks no English but has the good idea of taking us next door to watch the television. The film showing is about Indian freedom fighters. The parts of the English baddies are played by Indian actors. The stereotypes are hilarious. No one can understand what is making me laugh to the point of tears but the laughter is infectious and when Sheshi and I are summoned to dinner we are high and happy without a trace of tiredness. The chapattis are thick and heavy; meat and vegetables are spiced and liberally dosed with chillies none of which I can eat but no-one appears to mind as I stoke up on creamy rice pudding. I do not think the clocks in India work.

7. Heights of Folly

Sunday 30th October

The prison guard parades in front of the house, presentations of photographs of the visit are made and all thanks are given for an unforgettable time. We are on our way back to Chandigargh, give or take a few diversions. Our first stop is a medical college to meet an old friend of the I.G. who, during the I.G.'s reign, was a medic at Patiala Jail. They have much to share so I talk with the daughter of the house who is studying medicine. She tells me a story of a young medical student. Fearful of failing his examinations, he made a bargain with the examiner that he would marry one of his seven daughters without dowry for the promise of a good mark. He passed, married and there was a happy ending as his marriage was a success and he turned out to be a good doctor.

We move into the heart of Hoshiapur territory where the I.G. has relatives who keep his buffaloes. Far from a main road, over rough sandy tracks we enter a small village where we are met with enthusiasm. The most senior citizen greets me, hookah pipe in hand. The I.G. suggests I shake his hand to see what happens and find my fingers being crushed in a vice and he only looks like a puff of wind. Beds are brought out and placed under a tree, children are sent to the fields to pick groundnuts and buffalo milk is brought for our refreshment. I never drink 'neat' milk as my stomach acts like a churn, but protocol and the I.G. insists. Where on earth does the line fall between protocol and common sense? The oldest lady then steps forward and clasps me in her arms in another vice like grip so my welcome is complete. The young boys want to be in on the act and suggest they show me the tube well and give a demonstration, starting a small motor and water gushes out of a standing pipe. This is the village supply that means a great deal to them all and brings standing to the village.

Sheshi stands by the car examining a woman who has a large neck tumour. It is serious and she needs hospital treatment. The woman shrugs. Sheshi tells me she is not likely to go to hospital as it is too far, would cost too much, and someone would have to accompany her and stay with her. Women would not travel alone so it would mean one of the men leaving the fields. There are just too many problems to be overcome. She will not go. She will die in her village. At a Government hospital the diagnosis would be free but an operation or medicine would cost money. There is a fatalism and acceptance, which I find hard to bear and can appreciate even more the enormity of the fight for life.

Taking two of the old people with us we pile back in the car to visit a neighbouring village where the I.G. buys sacks of grain and we sit in a brick shed amongst swarming flies. Buffalo milk, hot and skimmed is brought. Now I am in difficulties. The pressure is on again and nausea is rising.

It is a relief to be on the road to Hoshiapur for a garlanded reception at Government Rest House. The I.G. is wreathed with three hoops of flowers, his wife one, whilst I have two. This Rest House is kept available for visiting Government officials. It has beds with crisp white sheets, spring mattresses and large soft feather pillows. Feeling by now really unwell I sink onto a bed and am in another grip, this time of my own stomach. The cramps are violent but there is a bathroom where I can double up on the western sit-down toilet. The door is being knocked. Madame is required to grace yet another table. It is a nightmare. All I can do is nibble a tomato and listen to the Deputy Superintendent of the Jail. He is a delightful man and I agree to his invitation to use the Rest House as a base when I return to visit families that are in my notebook. That is my last word. Despite my sincere desire to communicate politely I have to rush from the table and just make the bathroom to regurgitate all the milky contents of a stomach in turmoil. 'Home, please' I request on creeping out. Application refused. We are going to another village. Now I'm trying to control both stomach and temper.

At the next stop we are seated directly in the blazing sun. A young man is brought to sit in front of us. He has grown up in this village without schooling, as many of the village children I have seen today, hence can neither read nor write in any language and naturally speaks no English. He is awaiting interview at the British Embassy in Delhi to make application for an entry certificate. His father, settled in England has arranged a match for him. He is betrothed to a beautiful Indian girl who is a clerk in Southall. He shows her photograph with pride whilst his mother watches our reactions. The Holy Book is already in position ready for the leaving ceremony and prayers for his success and safety that will last several days. He is a handsome enough young man, dazed by the golden opportunity that he believes awaits him and ready to take on the role of benefactor to his mother and community by hard work, but his challenges are obvious and formidable. I have met many such young men, including some who have skipped bail and fled to India, only to return again voluntarily to stand trial. They tell me that to serve a prison sentence is bad but to return to their situation in India is to serve a life sentence. I read his application papers and just nod. I admire his courage and he has a hard enough pathway to travel without my shadowy reflections.

At last, we reach the welcoming house in Chandigargh and speak of my future programme. I have train tickets for Simla and this seems to be a good time to go. The I.G. telephones Perminder Singh who arranges to collect me at 6am next day and install me on the train for Kalca, my departure point. They are dubious whether I should go alone and there are offers to accompany me but I feel the need to have a little reflective space, draw breath, and take a rest from protocol. My heels are dug in. It is permitted.

Monday 31st October

I am anxious. The stomach problems have not abated. Perminder Singh, complete with added escort, arrives on schedule. My urgency is for a recommendation of a good hotel in Simla. They agree 'Clarks' is the most suitable place for me. Chandigargh to Kalca is a thirty mile train ride.

I am alone in a first class compartment. A soldier passes the door twice glancing in and then takes the plunge and opens the door. We are both on the way to Simla. He offers his services if he can be of any assistance with the change of train. I thank him politely but the shutters are up today. At Kalca I attract the personal services of a ticket collector with a lifelong ambition to visit England. As many others before him he questions whether I am aware that the British ruled India for a hundred years, adding that they always kept buildings in good repair but the Indians do not bother and I will see proof of this in Simla.

The Simla train has a small first class carriage, four seats on either side. The soldier takes one side and I take the other. People look through the window, and thinking they are looking for seats I move across to sit by the soldier who is proving helpful and reliable. The ticket collector raps on the window with a disapproving face and motions me to move back to my seat. He directs the other passengers elsewhere. The rest of the train is packed solid. People are hanging out of windows and dangling from foot-plates. The soldier tells me it is half the fun of the ride as they jump off when the train chugs around at hairpin bends racing across the loops to leap on again the other side… unless they miss!

My normal self would so much enjoy this entertainment but I do not have a normal self today. The nausea and stomach cramps strike again with added gripes but more than that I find myself slipping down in the seat, unable to stay upright. I make a pillow from a bundle of clothes; lie flat out covered by a towel and tell my escort I am tired. Glad to drift into oblivion I remain in a self-created co-coon for the first two hours of the journey. My solider offers tea. I shake my head. He asks if he may take refreshment. I give my permission not understanding this relationship at all. He encourages me to sit up.

'Madame, this scenery is worth seeing. We are moving high, you should not be missing it'.

I do not care if I am passing the Pearly Gates. The toilet is my only goal when the waves begin and, though I have taken no breakfast even the lining of my stomach seems to be leaving me. It is incongruous on a journey of a lifetime. Wedged up in a corner I can see people are singing and dancing on the track, drinking fizzy drinks and having a high old time. I watch the fantastic ranges of hills sprinkled with tiny houses flashing past and at some isolated halt the soldier leaves, thanking me for my company. I feel wretchedly guilty. I even wonder if he had told people he was my guard to hitch a first class ride, uncharitable thought, but I am a bit loose minded today. All that really matters is that I find the hotel fast.

It is not fast. The journey has taken six hours. Unable to cope with the deluge of porters I step past them all with my overnight bag. Simla is spread out up one side of a steep slope that is part of a bowl shaped hollow. There is a high road and a low road. I take the high road as it is the least congested, stopping every fifty yards or so to rest and drink in the scenery, asking from time to time for 'Clarks Hotel'. As nobody has ever heard of it I change route to the low road. It is lined by dilapidated Government buildings, endless shacks with food bubbling in cauldrons, refuse littering the lower slopes. Police cars and trucks career up the narrow roads horns blaring, forcing me into a dark doorway to avoid extinction. There is no sanctuary from the dust, heat, noise and motion and there is no hotel.

Turning a corner I find myself in the hotel sector on a road that is going uphill again. Many look derelict but I can see they are inhabited when I peer through doorways. Signposts advertise **H & C tap water and carpets**. That is as may be but most have broken windows and no curtains. I cannot comprehend why I am here on a survival course. Then, I spy the magical sign 'Clarks' on a rambling old building. It passes inspection through the windows and I fall in through the back door. A servant takes my bag and encourages me to make the effort to cross the deep pile carpet to reception. They can see I am in a bit of a state and take me straight to a bedroom. The relief is overwhelming when I see a bathroom with bath and hot running water, spring mattress and feather pillows. I could ask for nothing more. It costs 165 rupees a night including all meals, a fortune to so many; an affordable life-saver for me today.

A housekeeper arrives and says she is allocated to look after my every comfort. She brings fresh lemon juice and a sandwich but after hardly a bite I fall into bed and sleep until evening. The atmosphere of the hotel is calming and aesthetic with soft music and dim lights. In the lounge a record spins out 'I'm a little on the lonely side'. True enough. In the candle lit dining room I sit, toying with the courses as they arrive and thinking nostalgically of home, wanting to recover my spirits, my health and strength and continue with my programme. It has been a low day in a high place.

Tuesday 1st November 1977

My digestive system is definitely out of action. The tasters of last night passed straight through with attendant aches and pains, but the most nerve wracking thing is that my arms, legs and neck are smothered in large measles- type spots which itch like mad. When scratched they turn into blotches. They are not bites. Running a bath I lie in it wondering what to do. Getting out I am shaking and shivering. This could be a reaction to the buffalo milk, food poisoning, contaminated water, the possibilities are endless. My programme allows for a stay of only one night but I know it would be stupid to attempt the train journey in this condition. Calling a doctor is the obvious logical course which, inexplicably, I resist. So I opt for a little nourishment from the housekeeper and, with tea and toast in the comfort of my bed, spend the morning writing overdue letters home.

Next move is to test my legs on the balcony. Monkeys are chattering and leaping about on the low roofs but there's a nip in the air that sets my body shivering again. It is afternoon before I make an attempt to take my letters to the post but my legs are like jelly and I get no further than the entrance. Changing direction I creep to reception, book another night and telephone the I.G. to confess my situation. Mrs. I.G. answers the phone. I know she recognises my voice but all she replies is 'Mrs. Taylor'. Certain that she cannot understand my explanations I print a simple message: UNWELL IN SIMLA RETURNING TOMORROW and ask the receptionist to relay it to the households of both Perminder Singh and the I.G. He reaches Perminder Singh who tells him to take good care of me and to arrange transport to the train next day. I leave the receptionist to remake the call to the I.G later believing that Perminder will also put him in the picture so I am doubly covered. Feeling I have achieved something, I go a step further and book a meal for later. A servant, sent to collect me, holds my arm respectfully as I am having such trouble with my legs on the descent downstairs. The meal is delicious, washed down with a glass of fresh pineapple juice but I am low with the disappointment that in my self imposed exile I have missed the best of Simla.

Wednesday 2nd November

After sleeping the clock round with only two bathroom attacks I stand on the balcony taking a look at the long winding road to the station marvelling at how I ever made it up the slope. Then I discover that even taxis do not make it up this gradient and there is a cliff lift, which will have to be negotiated to reach my transport to the mid-day train. It is such folly to have come to this inaccessible place. Missing out on the challenge of breakfast, everything happens in slow motion, including the train journey in reverse, where I watch the day slip past the window from the relative luxury of a Ladies Only, first class compartment.

At 6.30pm the train pulls through the darkness into Kalca. My ticket collector friend spots me and escorts me to the Chandigargh train. It will not be leaving for over an hour and so is unlit with all blinds drawn. I get on and off three times, each time being caught by railway officials who put me firmly back on. Somewhere I hear a Canadian accent and feel my way down the corridor following the sound. Candle-light is flickering across a white face. Should anyone try to fetch me out of here and take me back to a Ladies Only I am now ready to remonstrate. Jim invites me in to dine as if it is his home. I decline the gooey yellow curry, and buy a bunch of bananas that are being dangled through the window. There is plenty of time to exchange adventure stories. He is a doctor of all things! Travelling from his home in Canada to Afghanistan he crossed into India six weeks previously. He tells me that he has taken all possible precautions yet has had five bouts of food poisoning which have had similar symptoms to my own, giving scary pictures of salmonella germs harboured by meat left hanging at room temperature and hookworm that can be caused by walking barefoot. So far his experiences in India have been all bad, from illness, goods stolen, extortionate demands for money, and rough accommodation. He is somewhat envious of my journey 'on the inside' and it does me good to realise what good care is being taken of me, despite this recent demise.

Mary, the Canadian prisoner I had met in Tihar Jail is big news in Canada so I hear of her case from another angle. He tells me the newspapers and magazines are full of her story and have already judged her to be guilty. He is fascinated to hear my inside story. Talking with Jim is my first 'white' conversation for two weeks and there was not a pinch of protocol to be observed. It is my highlight of the day.

9pm at Chandigargh station is neither a good time nor a good place. Women would not be expected to be out and about alone. There is no telephone in sight and darkness stretches out in every direction. It is eight miles to Sector 15. There are no buses but there are a lot of males who approach me with a variety of suggestions. Would I like to go with them (purpose and destination unspecified), would I enjoy a sit in the grass, or would I care to share a taxi? I do not make a selection. There are also a dozen or so scooter rickshaws available but I hesitate to make a choice. Then, I have what I think is an inspiration. A scooter arrives and a well dressed Indian man steps out. I cross and speak to him, asking whether he could recommend this driver to me as trustworthy as I have to make a journey alone and am finding it difficult. He replies that he knows the man and agrees to give him exact instructions to go straight. When I give the address, adding that it is the home of the Inspector General of Prisons that clinches it. We go straight and he asks for only five rupees, the correct fare. I give him a good tip, say a prayer of thanks and, momentarily, feel glad to be home.

The I.G. is angry. The whole household is still awake and I have caused much concern. I have made many mistakes. Obviously I should have consulted the Stationmaster who would have telephoned immediately and transport would have been sent. What is even worse, my messages of the previous day had not reached the I.G either via the receptionist or Perminder Singh. He was the person who should have been contacted direct and by me, regardless of any difficulties on my side. I was out of order, my protocol was all wrong. I try twin tactics of an apology and an explanation. They sound lame. Arrangements had been made for me to meet many people the previous day and people have been disappointed. Wow. This is heavy and is not my idea of a homecoming. I feel myself to be in disgrace. And that is not all. The I.G. has made arrangements for Mohinder's wedding to take place in Southall on Christmas Day. All my family members are to be present. I know this is an honour however I am not a family director on Christmas day or any other. Basic cultural differences are being highlighted here. It seems traitorous to spoil his plans but the truth must out from the beginning and so I tell it the way it is, adding that Christmas Day would be unsuitable for a wedding for many reasons. The I.G. can cope. He will change the day and he will visit my home after the wedding.

A chicken has been cooked for my return but I am past both food and thought. A hot drink and bedcovers is all I ask. Mohinder lies down on the empty bed next to mine.

'Can I talk to you, Auntie?'
He thinks he will want to live in England after his marriage but his father wants him to return to Chandigargh with his bride. What do I think? Can I advise him? We talk it over until midnight.

8. Under the Wings

Thursday 3rd November

It is critical that I find the correct balance between my own welfare, the work I still have to do and the responses expected of me. Diplomacy and strength of mind are called for, as I firmly and carefully explain to the I.G. that I do not feel able to accompany him to work today. He responds that Miss Keith, Chief Welfare Officer of the Punjab has been called to his office and is awaiting me even as we speak. It is imperative that this meeting takes place. She is inviting me to stay in her home in Julluder. I request for her to visit me at the house. It is agreed. Gurbax drives the I.G. to work and returns with Miss Keith.

Miss Keith is a lady of middle years with her greying hair neatly coiled. She is wearing a soft brown sari and she radiates serenity. It is a delight to make arrangements with her in such a co-operative way. We work through my programme and arrange that I will take the Flying Mail from Ludhiana in the late afternoon of 7th November. She will meet me at Jullunder Station and we will work together from her home for the next few days and celebrate Diwali, the Festival of Lights on the 11th. She will take aboard locating the villages I need to visit.

Mr. Perminder Singh, after receiving my phone message from Simla, instead of contacting the I.G. had sent for Captain Gulzara Singh, the brother of our mutual friend Ajit Mangat. I already had the Captain's address in my notebook but it was a little off my visiting route. However, the Captain had made the sixty-mile journey by scooter the previous day, waited until late and then returned to his village with the instruction to return. He is on the way. Everything is escalating. Today is the 3rd and I am committed to be in Banga on the 4th. My host in Banga is an elderly gentleman living alone. He has sent for his daughters to be present during my stay and they have travelled a long distance. Pressure is on to reach Banga as arranged, a Captain is on the way and my walking condition is questionable.

In the first moment of meeting the Captain I know that I have an affinity with this man and that I will step willingly under his wing. He is in his 60's, tall and straight with the body of an athlete, a man so used to loving his God that it spills over. The Captain has strength enough for the two of us. I marvel at these people who reach me by so many different routes. The Captain brings two more letters from my family via Perminder Singh and they are like treasure-trove.

Today Captain Gulzara has travelled by bus and plans for us to return the same way. He understands my condition, accepts my weakness and telephones the I.G. A decision is reached between them that it is preferable to travel by taxi. Permission to leave immediately is given and packing is swift, as I had not even undone my bag from the night before. First stop is at a grocery store to choose whatever food I feel right for me. I do not know what is in the tins, few having writing on in English. When I have settled on a tin of soup, pineapple juice, a loaf of bread and some jam we are away to Katani Kalan. We talk little. There is no pressure to give out information and it is a lovely relaxing drive. All bodes well.

After passing through a small shopping area the road becomes too narrow for a taxi and we have to walk. It is not far but I am struggling. At the end of a twisty passageway is a baronial style building, distempered in powder pink and blue. Street doors open into a lounge that also houses the Captain's orange scooter. A double bed sits comfortably behind a partition and beyond that is a small bedroom that has been prepared for me, complete with brilliant orange embroidered bed sheets, a perfect resting place. There is one snag and it could be a big one. The toilet is through two sets of locked doors, across an alley and is bolted and padlocked. I imagine this operation in the pitch dark and am quaking.

The Captain's wife is shy. She is his second wife and they have a three-year old daughter, Jaswinder. He tells me that his first wife and two daughters are all dead. He has been a sportsman all his life and still keeps physically active. There is nothing I want more than to retreat between the orange sheets. It is permitted. The Captain brings a Harold Robbins novel, a transistor radio, fresh lemon juice and some Mexaform tablets he has had from Canada and assures me they will help my digestive upset. I accept all thankfully and sleep.

On waking I am ready for the round of the house and take a few spoons of soup, then follows a delightful family evening as we journey through his photograph albums and I recognise his Smethwick relatives in some very different outfits! He is the youngest of three brothers and they have all been travellers. He has been to England and North Africa but has chosen to remain in India in control of the collective family land. This he rents out, and with his army pension of 600 rupees per month is reasonably well placed. He tells me that some of his nephews have married English girls who have been brought to visit him. Though he could see they were nice girls he was sure I would understand that naturally the family had been disappointed. My wise old friend, his brother Ajit Mangat, now settled in Wolverhampton was a man of status and influence in Tazmania. I am shown photographs of him with diplomats and at Government receptions. I had not known – he had not told me.

The Captain explains the absence of a television set is because it would be impossible not to share it with those less fortunate and this would have repercussions on his chosen life style. He is a man of peace and regular habits which would be interrupted by the coming and goings of neighbours and friends which would also of course entail the obligation to provide refreshments and safe travel homewards. On top of this the electricity supply is so expensive and unpredictable and worst of all it would make his daughter lazy with her lessons. The Captain is a man who thinks matters through. My torch is at the ready and is used only twice for the journey through the padlocks and bolted doors.

Friday 4th November

Prayers and songs vibrate across the roofs and in through my window at 4am. A loud speaker system unites the whole village in worship. I join them in thought under my embroidered sheets and sleep on. At 8 o'clock I am upright and dare to face the day. We plan our morning. My introduction to Ajit Mangat had been made through his daughter-in-law Rajinder. As part of a Job Creation Programme she had been placed in my office for nineteen weeks and I had learnt a great deal from her that was most useful in my work. Now I learn more of her background. Ajit Mangat had asked Captain Gulzara to select a worthy bride for one of his sons. Rajinder had been chosen as the daughter of an army friend of the Captain. As the mediator, it is important that he should have chosen wisely, and it was a delight to him that I could confirm this to be a happy match and that I knew Rajinder's husband and two children. I had brought gifts from Rajinder for her mother, so a ride in their direction on the orange scooter is to take priority after a visit to the medicine shop.

A chemist-cum-doctor is sitting in the doorway of a little room stocked with pills and potions. He asks for full description of symptoms and diagnoses either salmonella or amoebic dysentery. Without tests he cannot tell which but sees no harm in prescribing for both. He hands me 3x2 pills, which I take in the shop.

What a superb ride this turns out to be along the Sirhind Canal. The Captain tells me 'the ingenious English' constructed it. Tall, slim silver trunked trees stand straight and soldierly along the bank, between them military people are camping and practising building bridges. I am wearing a shorter skirt today, as I feared entanglement in the wheels and the warm breeze fans my legs, arms and face. It is exhilarating and I feel vitality and enthusiasm surging back on the fifteen-mile ride to Rajinder's village. The family home is large and barn-like.

A shy young sister greets us but it is disappointing to find her parents are away, so we leave the presents, rest awhile and ride back by a different route. This has been a good test and I feel able to head off again after lunch on the fifty-mile ride to Banga where Master Grewal and his daughter are expecting me.

We head for the bazaar in Ludhiana and make a rendezvous at a sari shop owned by friends where it is agreed we will meet at 3pm next day but today he is driving me all the way to Banga. These loose arrangements are quite usual where there are neither telephones nor public transport. The last leg of the journey is all farming country, mile after mile of crops and bent brown bodies teasing shoots from rock hard soil. The first person we ask knows Master Grewal, of Tungal Gate. He is a retired schoolmaster and a respected elder but what is more his house carries his name in a huge mosaic decoration.

We arrive to a rousing welcome. I have been eagerly awaited all day. Both daughters and their children have arrived, one travelling from Rajasthan. Master Grewal's elderly sister completes this family reunion. The Master and the Captain take an immediate liking to each other. The Captain gives instructions about my health and that I am to be consulted on everything I want to eat, which is a relief as I do not want to appear rude if preparations have already been made. There is no problem. All they want is to make me feel welcome and have put so many kind thoughts into my comfort. Toilet paper, powder and hair oil are presented and fresh oranges squeezed. The Captain leaves having confirmed I will be deposited at the sari shop next day and plans are all working out perfectly. Then the visitors begin.

The first is a young man who tells me he is the local advocate, assures me he is intelligent and well educated and asks why the British Government is keeping him waiting for his entry permit. His fiancée is a nurse in Birmingham. I tell him I have no idea, as I do not represent the Government in this respect. He finds this difficult to accept believing that I have connections with the Home Office and therefore could bring influence to bear, should I choose. The pressure is mounting as the next visitor also has a visa problem. There is general discussion as to where these hold ups lie. Is it in Delhi or the U.K.? Wanting to be off the hook I suggest we go out for a walk.

It proves a good idea. We stop often for introductions to people who send messages of greeting for me to deliver to Master Grewal's son in Smethwick and are invited in to weaving sheds to watch the hand loom skills. The snake master who is sunning himself in a corner jumps into action with his cobra to amuse us. We call on the village doctor and various shopkeepers, Master Grewal presenting me with eight jangling bracelets just because I was having a close glance at the intricate bead designs. Next we meet the master mason who decorated Mr.Grewal's house and is busy plastering his own. He breaks off immediately to present me with a little book of Guru wisdom and we end up making a round of the neighbours. This is the first walk I have had in five days and it is a real treat.

I had a surprise in my bag for them as I had brought a tape recording from his son, Piara. Family and friends congregate filling the small room to capacity. People crane their necks in the doorway and then the listeners are completely astonished and emotionally overwhelmed at the sound of Piara's strong voice booming out with his 'Sat Sri Akal' greetings to each family member by name, as is customary, followed by personal messages. It is played over several times. I suggest that they then record messages for me to take back. One by one I persuade relatives to speak, a novel experience for them all. The children are a delight, one with a tuneful voice sings a song and our impromptu party ends with a formal speech by Master Grewal to which I respond in a mixture of short textbook Punjabi phrases which sound okay with some extra expression.

Now it is time for the poorer people to be allowed into the house. They want only to see me so they do exactly what they have come for; they stand and stare. I find this disconcerting and encourage some responses by picking up children, admiring jewellery, worn I think especially for this occasion, and try to give a simple greeting to everyone. There are so many it is both a strain and a joy. At last they leave, Master Grewal presents some hydrocortisone cream for the day's insect bites, three rounds of toast and butter, specially bought, and a cup of English tea. It tastes like nectar and I feel so happy to be back in my stride. Nine o'clock is the time to retire in this household. It suits me perfectly and I stay exactly where I am put until further notice.

Saturday 5th November

My eyes open to see Master Grewal's beaming face then, through the open door, the formation of a queue. Sitting up, I slide my legs over the edge of the bed and am thought ready to receive, albeit in my nightdress. These are workers waiting to see me before they set off for the fields. Between inclining my head, with palms together, I sneak a few strokes with the hairbrush. The last man is elderly, wrapped in a piece of blanket, a curled rusty knife clutched at knee level. He cuts the fodder for the cattle. This is hungry work. I order a boiled egg, toast and tea and am served in my bedroom to three lumps of cherry cake, a plate of cream biscuits, an onion omelette, two boiled eggs and two slices of bread dipped in egg and fried. It is a little too much and already they are planning a luncheon party.

'The Tribune' is delivered and by the time I have scanned it the Master returns accompanied by two friends to discuss certain articles on the subject of corruption. It is complimentary to note that the English have always been renowned for their honesty and amazing to discover that police rewards for not accepting bribes cause little comment. The dowry system is aired and although it has been declared illegal tradition dies hard and it is thought dowry traditions will persist for many years yet.

This house is newly built with money sent by the two sons in England. Both are well placed and sufficiently secure to provide for their father's future but would like him to be in England with them. He too has been refused an entry certificate and an appeal is under way. The authorities believe he has other family members to care for him, the cultural argument being that the daughters do not have this responsibility. It is for the sons to make provision.

We decide to go out for a stroll to the Bank. In a narrow alleyway we meet Mrs. Gill, the Director of Social Welfare from Chandigarh determined to accompany me to work today. She has two male escorts, I have three, and so seven of us pile into her car and head out to Mangawal, a village several miles distant. She offers to play interpreter so I prime her with the situation.

These elderly parents we are visiting have four sons and a daughter. They had arranged a match for their daughter with a young man already settled with his parents and brothers in England and have not seen her since she left to marry. Her life in England has not run smoothly. She has four children under the age of five and her husband has served a prison sentence, which is how I met her. After his release a further, less serious, offence followed and he was placed on Probation under the terms of a Suspended Sentence Supervision Order. Neither the husband nor any member of his family speaks much English and they had little conception of what was happening in court or what such an order meant. They only believed that I had rescued the husband and had recommended my services to their friends! The husband's brother, a juvenile, was then also placed under supervision and another relative became involved in a dispute with neighbours and so I had become interwoven into the fabric of this family. Their knowledge of appropriate cultural, social and moral behaviour was limited. Offences had been committed without understanding of their seriousness or the penalties. Taking a teaching role had brought the desired results and I had been privy to the wife's concerns for her elderly parents, also in difficulties.

It is a heart-rending visit. This is a very poor household in the middle of a sun baked village. As Mrs. Gill explains why seven important looking people have descended on her courtyard, the mother bursts into tears and we follow her into a dark interior where we perch on the edge of dusty bed frames. Tragedy has struck this household. Of their four sons, two have left home to seek for work;

a third son and an uncle have been charged with committing a political murder and have served five years in prison. They had been released and re-arrested for the same crime when the authorities decided they had not served enough time after all. The father had broken under the strain and had been taken for psychiatric treatment. He was now able to work again in the fields and, with his only remaining son, supported his wife, two daughters in law and their children.

The father is called from the fields. Bare-footed with horned toe nails, stringy as a beam, his sad small frame is silhouetted in the archway. It is unbelievable that this is the father of the buxom woman in Smethwick with her shining oiled hair, painted nails and bustling energy. He was spent; the breaths left in him must be few. Mrs. Gill speaks with him briefly and his voice bursts out, loud with emotion. Rapidly she interprets. 'The Smethwick people do not know of all our problems. They must not be told. They can do nothing.' They ask for news of their daughter and all members of her family. I give it, careful to omit reference to their son-in-law's imprisonment as I believe they may not have been told of it. Or, maybe I did not tell them to protect myself from their distress. The only joy of their life appears to be the success of their daughter in reaching England and the luxurious life they believe she lives. It is indeed one of riches in comparison to the harsh realities of Mangawal. Searching for joyous news I speak of the betrothal of their daughter's brother-in-law. They did not know of this and it is most unwelcome news. They had been hoping his parents, who had chosen once from their family, would select a bride from amongst their many relatives. Obviously they had not. I could not answer to the name of the bride nor would have done so even if I had known it. These are delicate matters as to what information it is correct to divulge.

So what can I say to give happiness or comfort? I tell them that maybe I will be able to meet their son when in Jullunder jail, stressing that I am not in a position to discuss his sentence. Then I talk of their grandchildren whom they have never seen and I am asked to describe all the electrical items in their daughter's house. There are nods of satisfaction. We do not tape messages, all they want to say is for me to ask them to write more often. It is a great day when a letter arrives from England. A hollow cheeked daughter-in-law has brewed tea, which is sipped soberly then we speak our farewells with the frail old woman clinging in a sad embrace. The men, who had played a silent audience in the background, had been listening intently and filled us in on the murder details. It was a Naxalite killing when a group of would-be assassins entered the home of their intended victim with swords, but in error killed the wrong man who was a house guest. Herein lies a lesson. I was advised 'Take care of who you stay with and do not become involved in any political issues'.

Mrs. Gill reminds me of my promise to speak at her conference on delinquency and we make arrangements for me to be collected from another village location. She has pressing engagements in Amritsar and begs to be excused from returning to Master Grewal's for refreshments. As we had met in the street she had not yet graced his home and it was imperative that she should do so. The Master cannot comply with her request and she capitulates with good grace, giving us the opportunity to talk of drinking rituals. She deplores the amount of time spent taking tea during a working day, and gives a warning that there is status in the length of time a guest remains in your house. If the guest is important, you prolong the pleasure of their company by taking a long time to produce refreshments and serve tea burning hot! Lunch and an after dinner rest offer another gap for more viewers to assemble. I count seventeen women and children pouring in. A spokeswoman has prepared a speech and I ask for an exact translation.

'We are honoured to be allowed to enter the house of the Master to see the memsahib'. He translates my response in which I tell them that I bring many messages and good wishes from people in England. I am certain that he has found just the right expressive phrases to give the most pleasure. Then it is time to leave amongst many invitations to return. I would particularly have liked to be visiting his daughter's home in Rajasthan, which is again a journey too far.

A taxi deposits us at the 'Lovlee Saree Shop' in Ludhiana and Captain Gulzara arrives beaming to find me safe and well and to take me back to yet another of my 'homes'. As I spin away on our faithful scooter it seems that the day has had a dream like quality, a stream of people, many now faceless, have slipped in and out of my life as I have theirs. Tomorrow is Sunday. On Monday I am due to meet Miss Keith of the brown sari at Jullunder station and have yet to meet a doctor in Ludhiana and make a round of the Jail, visit Rajinder's parents and find a village which no one has heard of named Sahauli. How to fit it all in? The Captain says 'It will be done'.

Sunday 6th November

Breakfast in Galoti with Rajinder's parents has been arranged. Her mother, a younger sister and father, a Sidargi with a thick curly beard, make a welcoming trio. We enjoy an omelette feast, play the taped messages and exchange news. At least here it is all good news but we are soon on our way to Sahauli visiting a Gurdwara on the way.

Rama Sahib is a temple created by Sant Isher Singh, surrounded by botanical gardens of tropical flowers. There are vast open air eating spaces where anyone visiting is welcome to a free meal. Sikhs regard the mouth of the poor as the receptacle of the Guru. There are many who bring food to this holy place and countless thousands who benefit. Of interest to me is the free mobile eye surgery unit. Patients are lying in rows on beds, the sightless, those bound after operations and those giving thanks for the recovery of sight. I learn of the quack surgeons who tour the villages offering eye operations for 50 to 100 rupees. In one village alone I am told they have recently 'spoiled' seventeen eye cases, so now rural people arrive in groups to genuine eye camps. There is still much superstition to be overcome. Some believe operations are only successful in certain months, others that an operation can be performed only when the vision is completely lost. Getting correct information to reach villagers is a constant problem. I am told that 30% of people in India need glasses and am seriously advised never to be out without sunglasses.

Captain Gulzara's friend is a resident photographer based here. He has spent all of his time since leaving the army photographing the Sant Isher Singh so it is from him that we hear the Sant Isher's story. When he first arrived there was nothing but jungle that he began to clear. Soon others joined him and this vast holy site sprang up that is used in a practical way for both the spiritual and social welfare of the people. Sant Isher Singh died from a heart attack on a visit to Wolverhampton in 1975. We are invited to enter the house where he had lived to view his carefully preserved belongings and the extensive photograph collection.

We ride on to Sahauli. It is so hard to find. We ask the way many times as we cross forty miles of farming country. At last we find our village on the banks of a canal. We are looking for the mother and fourteen-year old sister of a young man imprisoned for murder. As he was under eighteen when the crime was committed, he was sentenced to be detained at Her Majesty's Pleasure. There is no comparable indeterminate sentence in India and it has been impossible for his mother to understand his situation.

It is a sad story. Raj was ten when he was brought to England by an uncle. Four years later he returned to India to see his sick father, who wanted him to remain to care for his mother and sister. Raj however, persuaded his father to let him return. Within months his father was dead and Raj, receiving letters of recrimination from his mother for deserting them, left his uncle's home in a distraught state, took up with a group of youngsters on the loose which resulting in a death by stabbing when they were all the worse for drink. Having disgraced family and community all extended family cut off contact saying: 'We must cut off the diseased limb to save the tree'. I had been Raj's only life line to the outside world for the last two years. My task here was to persuade the mother to give permission for the branch of the family in England to re-establish contact so that

Raj would have an acceptable home address on release. Raj, an intelligent young man, was urgent to redress the anguish he had caused.

The position in India is dire. Eight acres of land were left on his father's death but he was in partnership with his brother who took his half share plus an additional acre 'by force'. The mother is left with three acres of land she cannot farm and hires labour for which she gives half of the crops in payment, thus she has income from only one and a half acres. Then there is the question of marriage for the daughter. There is no dowry and no male to provide one. I have told the Captain all of this, as it is a delicate situation and I must have accuracy. The time will come when I will be required to write a report giving information pertinent to any consideration of release. They may well be surprised by the content when reading of this 'home visit'.

We ask for the mother by name and are told she is dead. I cannot believe it and we carry on and find her living, but only just, in the poorest circumstances of anyone I have yet visited. Dust lies thick over piles of maize drying in her brick shed, shared with an unsociable goat. Mrs. Kaur is dry as a stick and angry, so angry with her only son, that her anger fuels her whole being. It shows in her eyes, her voice and is no doubt the driving force that keeps her alive. We patiently unpack all the circumstances and it is exactly as Raj has explained. She wants the Queen to release her son. I gently explain that day will come but it is not yet, and tell her I have come a long way to ask for her help. Prison regulations did not allow me to tape a message from Raj and I so much wished this had been possible as this woman is unlikely to live long enough to hear her son's voice again. I ask her to speak to him on the tape recorder. She tries but shakes with tears and emotion. I cannot think of words to comfort her and can only gather her in my arms and pat her as I would a child. Then the words that had been festering in her for so long pour out. Waving her arms she shouts at the machine. The Captain translates. She is ranting at her son, telling him how fed up she is, instructing him to get out of prison, work hard and send money for his sister. The sister takes her turn and is able to speak a gentle greeting. At last we manage to sit together and talk more calmly of how to make the best of this bad situation. I have what I need, permission to contact the Uncle and request him to visit Raj and begin discussion about all aspects of their welfare. Visibly moved by our joint work of the afternoon the Captain ushers me gently away. It is hard to leave them.

At Katani Kalan we stop at the village Post Office. The Captain has arranged a lift for me to Ludhiana next morning so I try to telephone the I.G. or Ludhiana Jail to tell them of my planned arrival but the lines are out of order. So it is home for a last evening with the Captain's family. I hate the thought of moving on. Making and breaking relationships at this rate is becoming emotionally stressful. The Captain comes to my bedside to wish me goodnight and asks me not to leave. He tells me that in this short time I have become as the daughter that he had lost. I hear myself saying the inevitable 'it is necessary to complete my programme 'and I am sick at heart with myself for being so conscientious.

9.Killing Desires

Monday 7th November

My next driver, a neighbour and friend of the Captain, has lived in Smethwick for eleven years, working at the Birmid Foundry. England had been good to him. He had earned promotion and saved money but his wife had found the climate caused a persistent chest complaint, so they had returned to their village bringing items of western comfort with them. Now he is a business man with high status. We move out to the car and of all the words I had rehearsed to say to the Captain only manage 'I am sad to be leaving'. He can find no words either in reply. I am driven away hoping for a speedy arrival at Ludhiana Jail but find myself on the way to the Christian Medical Hospital for the wife's appointment. Valuable time passes as the doctor is located. Always it seems I must contend with the pressure of moving on. I apologise, explain my impatience and am driven straight to jail. I am let in. They have been waiting with impatience much greater than my own. The I.G. had arrived the previous day expecting to see me. Not only was I not in place but no one had received a message as to my whereabouts. There is a tense atmosphere and stern faces register disapproval with the terse question: 'Where have you been?'

I had not made any firm arrangements to arrive at this jail on any given day or time, and I had definitely not been told the I.G. would be visiting. Anyway, by now I am in a waspish mood myself, irritated by my own irritation and the stress of keeping a gamut of emotions under wraps. Matching their forthright manner I make a forthright speech myself that has been brewing for some time.

'Gentlemen, though I appreciate your concern, I am an independent visitor to your country, entirely free to travel without explanation. Your communications systems do not always work efficiently and I have been about my work in the villages as efficiently as I am able. I have not broken any appointments as none were made. Now that I have arrived I am at your disposal this morning. If we are to make a round I am particularly interested in the female wing.' There is a stunned silence. I admit I have gone over the top a bit but I need to be heard and I am. All forces are mobilised. Madame is here and will accompany the Superintendent on his round. The timing is perfect. Today is Monday when prisoners parade with their belongings outside their cells. They sit in rows on the sheltered walkway, holding cards giving all the information about their cases and dates of court appearances in front of their chests.

When our cortege arrives they all stand, display their cards for the Superintendent to read if he chooses, and sit when he passes leaving only those standing who wish to speak. There are several. They are heard courteously, instructions are given for medicines, advances on wages agreed, and family and personal matters are resolved.

Then I had an experience I was not ready for that day, or any other day. We move to the condemned row. There is one man per cell; each cell is open fronted with iron bars, projecting side walls preventing the men from seeing each other. Here within adjacent cells, within sound but not sight of each other, is a father and his two sons, all condemned to death. There had been a killing over a land dispute. They are strong Sikhs, ram rod straight and still vibrant with life. Believing that I can influence the gods of power they entreat me to grant them mercy. The Supreme Court had confirmed their death sentences and now only the President was able to commute death to a life sentence. Would he do it? No one could tell. Helplessness washes over me. I hold the bars and bow my head in a gesture that conveys what is beyond expression in words. What else is there to do? The whole world seems torturously imperfect this morning.

We move on to meet a notorious child kidnapper charged with the abduction of nine children for sale. I was told he would snatch them from the streets and sell them for the sexual pleasures of elderly men. This is a small prison, congested in numbers but beautifully kept. Two hundred and thirty men sleep on stone floors on mats. I am shown the cell where Badel, Chief Minister of the Punjab was imprisoned for a year during the emergency. Although it had its own private compound he must have felt every inch a prisoner.

We take tea and the District Probation Officer, two deputy Superintendents and the female prison officers join us. I am asked to give a talk on British Prisons. It serves me right as I had said I was at their disposal. Piecing together a variety of facts is easy now that I have some idea of the differences in our systems, which gives rise to a lively debate. They are discussing plans to instigate conjugal weekend visiting to help relieve sexual problems and to aid in the continuity of family life. They had identified a crisis point after six to seven year's imprisonment when the strain becomes intolerable. I explain our 'Dear John' letters that can arrive at any moment, announcing the breaking of a relationship or a marriage. They shake their heads in disbelief that wives would dare!

The women's wing, adjacent to the main prison, is of prime interest. Most convicted females in the Punjab are housed here. A gate is set in a high wall and the square courtyard has been cultivated in patches of colourful flowers. Bordering the left side are sleeping dormitories with mats and a small schoolroom. Basic reading and writing is taught by a female teacher who is a member of the prison staff. During the day the women spend most of their time in a large communal room which we enter. They are sitting on the floor; bright sunlight pouring through the bars makes black stripes across their delicate needlework. The information I can gather here will be invaluable in the research and must be recorded meticulously.

A table is brought and placed in the centre of the room. I sit with the female Superintendent and teacher who will interpret. One by one the women are called to the table. All are dressed in white salwar chemise suits, all stand with heads bowed, palms together and speak only when addressed. Life for a female means serving six years; much shorter than for a male. Gradually a picture forms.

❖ 25 of these 30 women prisoners are serving life sentences for murder. One is serving three years, one two years and one only one year. The remaining two are awaiting sentence.

❖ 21 of the 25 lifers had murdered relatives.

9 husbands	2 fathers-in-law	1 step-son	1 son
1 nephew	1 brother-in-law	3 daughters-in-law	3 sisters-in-law

❖ of the remaining four:
1 had murdered her husband's mistress
1 had murdered a house owner for money
2 had murdered children

One woman serving a life sentence for the murder of her husband pronounced herself quite satisfied at the outcome. She had fallen in love with a servant. As he is serving a longer life sentence she will live with his parents and become part of that household on release and await his return, then they will marry. She foresees a happy ending for herself and her four children with the man she loves. The husband of another woman had deserted her and gone to live with a woman in the same village. The shame and distress was so great that she took an axe and killed the other woman whilst she was working in the fields. One woman had received a sentence of three years at her own request after her lover had murdered her husband. She greatly feared reprisals from her husband's family which it seems may not be put into action if she is seen to pay the penalty for her adulterous behaviour. A pathetic inarticulate woman had killed the child of a neighbour as she was barren and had consulted a Sadhu, (a professed holy man), as to how she could conceive a child. He had told her to kill a child by throttling and then she would conceive. She had acted on his advice. The woman serving two years had taken the nine-year old daughter of her sister-in-law to sell to a man for 2,000 rupees. She was convicted on the statement of the girl, who escaped.

The three older women were mothers-in-law who had all killed their sons' wives and were all said to have done so for gain. The death of the daughter-in-law would allow them to possess their dowry and leave them in the position whereby they could arrange another profitable marriage for their sons. This decision to kill, I am told, can be precipitated if the daughter-in-law is not thought to be sufficiently pliant, respectful or hardworking.

A beautiful sixteen-year old girl of a higher social class than the rest kept herself aloof and spoke to no one at all. She was awaiting trial charged with killing her sister-in-law by pouring kerosene over her and setting it alight. She had been in prison for sixteen days and was expecting to be released on bail. The owner of the one year sentence was serving the penalty for making Desiu Sherab - home made wine!

The main reason for killing husbands was their behaviour with other women. Extra marital relationships are against the teachings of the Sikh religion. Others were unhappy with the marriage match in the first place but would have to be treated badly by their husbands with additional factors coming into play before such dramatic retaliation. Methods used were mainly primitive largely featuring fire, water, or farm implements, in other words, whatever was to hand With wells a part of village life it is not difficult to push a victim over the edge. Children are drowned or strangled. Men more commonly use swords and knives. It was explained that women, prior to sentence, are usually silent, denying guilt and remaining apart from other prisoners. After conviction guilt is invariably admitted and the sentence is accepted. The women are said to be easy to contain. They keep busy with their handiwork and lessons and also retain the responsibility of caring for their children. In any event their sentences are invariably shorter than the men, a discrepancy for which I found no explanation.

To mark this occasion the women are willing to dance. The prison staff join in and they perform village dances to music, made by a woman blowing into the mouth of an earthenware jar and tapping the side in changing rhythms. It is an astonishing performance. They swoop around gracefully, miming killing each other in various ways, then lie in their graves with faces covered only to rise again as dancing ghosts. I love to dance and to their surprise join in, adding a few interesting movements of my own which set them dancing faster and more furiously than ever. We whirl around making strange noises, laughing and clapping hands, the differences in our lives and fortunes maybe forgotten for that short while. I am grateful for their co-operation, as I have learnt so much. We have to understand the motives that drive women to kill if we have any hope of preventing such drastic actions and provide the services that may prevent loss of life. Today in particular has shown that this research is vital and valid. My earlier aggravations now seem trivial in the extreme.

A meeting with Simret Karma, the doctor friend of a colleague is my last engagement in Ludhiana. An escort from the prison accompanies me to help find the address. She is not at home so an obliging servant hops in to direct us to the hospital where she works leaving only two hours before I'm due to catch the Flying Mail to Jullunder. We spend the precious time visiting patients, a different kind of round. Malaria has been bad this year, and there are a wide variety of other conditions particularly skin and eye diseases. She talks of the patients' fear of operations and asks many questions about English hospitals. As time runs out Simret rushes out to engage a rickshaw with me calling after her 'automated…it must be automated!' The man insists he is automated. 'Yes, yes, go fast!' As I climb in and wave Simret away he does not start an engine but his spindly legs flash round and round as he tries to pretend he is automated. As soon as we pass a scooter stand I stop him peddling. He looks dismayed. Then my joke of thanksgiving for the day is to give him a bundle of rupees, in the hope that he can *become* automated. He is speechless, and looks as if he has seen an apparition. Perhaps I am one of the resurrected ghosts of the morning! No one ever takes money from me for all this hospitality. Surreptitious gifts are the only way to ease my conscience. I leap into an auto-rickshaw shouting *'jeldi jeldi, jail jana'* which loosely means 'hurry up and go to jail'. It all sounds like a monopoly game but the anxiety is real enough. The District Probation Officer is tapping his toes. The prison carpenter who is to be my escort to Jullunder throws in my luggage and we make it, marginally.

It is a vile journey. The carpenter who has been sent to keep an eye on me sits opposite with a table between us. He takes no action when a man sits beside me and immediately strokes my arm and begins to paw my clothes. He smells of drink and makes loud and lewd suggestions. Other men in the compartment turn and snigger and smirk. It is unpleasant but I am thinking this out carefully knowing how easy it is for fights to break out and the guard to arrive with a rope! The carpenter is useless and avoids my eyes, so I ask the tormentor politely if he will excuse me for a moment and lose myself in another part of the train where I am left unmolested. Just before our destination I return to retrieve my luggage. The luggage is safe but I am not. The antics start with more determination all over again and I have had enough. Speaking in a voice that I hope resembles royalty, I stand up, giving myself a status advantage, tell tormenter loudly that I do not know him, nor do I wish to and insist he takes his unwelcome presence elsewhere. He retreats. The audience smile in satisfaction. At last I have done what was expected of me and they have had good entertainment. I think they should have clapped!

Miss Keith is not on the platform. That is all I need. There is the usual hassle with the porters and I step outside into the night. Thankfully I see her. Her home, in a modern part of the city is spacious. She shows me to a private bedroom with adjoining bathroom. She serves steamed vegetables and her calming influence pervades the whole house. Two letters are waiting from my husband. I am plunging through so many emotional states daily, this is just one more.

10. The Sentence

Tuesday 8th November

What a night! Indigestion has been the problem and I wake at 8 o'clock to find myself propped up with pillows on top of my travelling bag. Over breakfast of porridge I discover this is an all-female household, consisting of Miss Keith, her mother and elderly paralysed grandmother, a niece and her baby, Mitou.

The District Probation Officer arrives and invites us to join him for a reporting session. This sounds too interesting to miss. The Probation Office is one square room and clerk in attendance. Outside is a wooden bench where probationers wait before entering in military style to stand to attention before the desk. The clerk presents their records as they offer their identity card for signing. No probation reports are called for prior to sentence, so little, if anything is known about the offenders when they arrive. The Office only opens on Tuesdays and there is a strict requirement for attendance any two Tuesdays in the month which, for offenders from the villages, is time consuming and costly.

All those I meet are on probation for the distillation of illicit liquor, the first three swearing their innocence complaining of planted evidence, the fourth blaming his landlord. Nothing makes any difference; rules will be applied across the board. Why are there so many offenders on this charge? I am given an article to read from the 'Illustrated Weekly of India' which, whilst not listing drunkenness high on the scale of social problems graphically illustrates the harmful effects of alcohol with illustrations of victims of wood alcohol poisoning. Leprosy patients are featured hiding alcohol in rubber balloons tied to their legs followed by a salutary warning: 'Bootleggers have few scruples. For a quick fermentation they use any rubbish including dead reptiles, rotten fruit, nausager and jaggery crawling with worms. The water is often from the sewage drains.'

I am getting the picture. Illicit distillation is serious and probation officers are in the front line. It is their responsibility to visit the home of any person convicted for this offence and search it for hidden distilleries. The Probation Service in the Punjab is fifteen years old and has remained a low priority in the constant battle for resources in social reform and welfare aid. Fifteen District Probation Officers are expected to supervise 1,545 probationers between them, an impossible task in numbers alone. Added to that they use public transport and are required to submit a travel itinerary before making village visits. A female D.P.O. needs to take an escort, as she should not travel alone.

Miss Keith tells me she walked twelve miles one day to find her probationer out as appointments are not made by letter because of postage costs. We talk all morning exploring the world of Probation from where we both stand.

At home I sit quietly with grandmother who lies, limp as a rag doll on her wooden palisade. Her eyes are bright and she can still smile. I hold her hand while I contemplate a letter that has arrived from my eldest daughter Sandra who is making plans for an April wedding.

The grapevine has been working and we receive a visitor whose relatives had told him to keep a look out for me. He knows I have messages for his family so we are invited to his home for an evening meal. Both the messages and the food are a great success and what is more on our return I find a Swiss roll cooking in a funny round tin oven in my bedroom. It is mouth-watering! There is no pressure to be involved as the family watch a movie and I can write of the vagaries of the Indian Probation system to my hearts content.

Wednesday 9th November

I am looking forward to a morning of meetings at the Courts. We reach a market square full of dilapidated stalls thrown together with bits of wood, nails and string. The stall-holders are the advocates sitting behind their makeshift offices advertising themselves. Some of the counters boast the luxury of a typewriter. Police weave between the stalls, moving prisoners wearing leg fetters in and out of doorways of a long low red brick building. It is unreal, as if I am on a film set.

Back stage we are joined by a Chief Judicial Magistrate. It has been Miss Keith's turn to brief me this morning as she has been trying to raise interest in the Probation Service with scant results. He is clear that probation does not play much of a part in his courtroom explaining that the law specifies that probation cannot be given in certain circumstances, which when considered, leave only distillation of illicit liquor and minor offences of theft. Probation is not seriously regarded as an alternative to prison. He is replaced by a second Magistrate who takes a different tack asking me to ask him questions. So off the cuff I ask: 'Do you find sentencing difficult?' The answer is an emphatic 'No'. He hands me a list of the twelve categories of crime under the Indian Penal Code: murder; culpable homicide; rape; kidnapping and abduction; dacoity; robbery; burglary; theft; rioting; criminal breach of trust; cheating; and counterfeiting. Anything else is considered minor.

The maximum sentence for each category is laid down. This gentleman has no difficulty in selecting the appropriate period of imprisonment or fine, seemingly his only options. His word is final. I ask if there are any areas of difficulty in his work. This brings some vital information. Almost all defendants plead 'not guilty' and, he adds, would be most likely to sack any advocate wanting to throw in the towel. Most cases are therefore contested and by the time cases reach court, evidence has been lost or mislaid or witnesses have vanished. Advocates become artistes in prevaricating and appearing without full facts. All these adjournments mean fatter fees and a better chance of a 'not guilty' outcome for the defendant. This man had little respect for lawyers, having been one adding, 'I almost refused promotion to the bench. I would rather talk nonsense for forty minutes per day than listen to it all day'. Then he motions us to go inside and experience it for ourselves.

The courtroom appears chaotic. The case being heard is the death of a child and the loss of both legs of another in a road accident. There was little sense of dignity and solemnity in the proceedings. There are two advocates for each party but no defendant, who I learn did not want to come so had sent double legal representation. Below people move around talking loudly, above, the magistrate sits on a railed platform watching the four advocates wrangle amongst themselves in English but I cannot catch the drift. A passing court clerk tells us the outcome will be 'inconclusive' as is most frequently the case. We glance in other courtrooms, most in a similar state and I can see how overwhelmingly different our court system must appear with its rules of procedure, traditional etiquette and strict protocol!

Lunch is a welcome break before heading for Jullunder Jail to visit Gurbax Singh from Mangala. We speak with the Superintendent and he explains that Gurbax served five years of a sentence imposed for murder. After his release The Supreme Court reversed their decision and he was returned to jail for 'revision of sentence'. He has been waiting eleven months for a hearing. Gurbax is in limbo land and that is exactly how he looks when he is brought in. Standing stiffly to attention, straggly beard, and turban askew, he is wafer thin and looks both bewildered and apprehensive. He is told who we are and it is left to me to give greetings from his sister and family but he makes no semblance of a response. Miss Keith talks of our visit to Mangawal but the stunned look remains in place and I wonder at his state of mental health. Gurbax is returned and we follow him on a speedy round of buildings where prisoners are hidden behind closed doors. The jail is an old one in the middle of town, the light is fading and another prison day is ending in a twilight world where time is standing still. After the prison Jullunder bazaar looks like a mad fairy grotto.

Thursday 10th November

Spasms of pain in my right hand jerk me awake. I am hot, feverish, and restless and the night is long. Morning brings no joy. I have lost most of the use in my thumb and two fingers on my right hand. Miss Keith suggests it could be a reaction to a mosquito bite. Could it be the onset of malaria? I've taken tablets regularly. This is not a bite kind of pain, the muscles seem to be contracting and it is a pain that is biting deep into the bone. I am worried.

'Can we please send for a doctor?

'No, regrettably, it is Diwali day.'

'Can I make a visit to a doctor?'

'No, it is Diwali day.'

The gentle Miss Keith is quite adamant. No doctor will be found this day. This is the Festival of Lights to celebrate the homecoming of Rama after he has defeated the demon King, Ravana. It is a day of great rejoicing when houses are painted, new clothes bought, stalls of sweets line the roads, visits are exchanged and gifts given. In the evening lights will beam and flicker from every conceivable corner and rooftop, fireworks displays will burst sky high and prayers will pour out of every heart and Gurdwara door. I had so looked forward to this experience; instead I find I have my own demons to defeat.

There is no telephone and no location to go to for help. I worsen. Most of the day I am semi-conscious; tossing on my wooden bed. Miss Keith sits beside me for a while, smiling as she presents my Diwali gift of a ring worked in delicate traces of silver, shaped into a flower. My body rejects all food. The same gnawing pain has begun in my right foot. By the end of the day my first toe is enlarged, throbbing and purple.

The Gurdwara is very near. Miss Keith asks tentatively if I could visit with her, her niece and little Mitou. I want to go, knowing I need the prayers. Something is seriously wrong. Miss Keith helps me dress and our procession moves slowly out into the night, past roofs ablaze with candles. Above us the sky sparkles with falling stars. The Gurdwara is filled with people, faces glowing in the light, prayers rising on all sides. I curl up on the floor and am lost in waves of strangely haunting music, wanting only to be left a while in this uplifting, God-filled place. Yet even this small comfort is denied. Little Mitou is restless. It is late; she needs to be taken home.

We gather for family prayers in the small room set aside for the Adi Granth. Miss Keith reads in a soft lilting voice. Prayers are half-said, half-sung and four women and a child join in the Sat Sri Akal. It is Miss Keith who cares for us all in this household and now I have added to her burden. Feeling a sense of guilt and sadness I retire to my room.

My need is for words of comfort, the prayers have not been enough, perhaps because they were unfamiliar to my western ears. The music helped more to lift my spirits. But who is to give me words or music that will speak to my failing body? Only myself. And so I do the strangest thing. I sing. Taking my tape recorder that has been so full of words of comfort for others, I gently sing a lullaby, songs and hymns of my childhood, and then I talk as if I am speaking to a sick, frightened child. I have a concert in my hand. Now I can play it back to myself, and listen. Over and over again I play the tape. The effect is hypnotic. I know it is my own voice and yet it seems to be floating in the room as if outside myself.

Sleep cannot make its way through the gnawing waves of pain. I know that I must fight it somehow but tonight I cannot. The sounds of my mothering voice mingle with another that weeps with loneliness and despair. I do not want to believe this agony is happening. Pain is a sentence. It imprisons reason.

11. A Dark Diwali

Friday 11th November

My right hand is still safely anchored in the heat of my left armpit when I wake after a doze. The puffiness has subsided enough for me to see that the main swellings are around joints. I can make no comparison to this pain from anything I have ever experienced. All I can think is that something is gnawing at my bones. No breakfast, and no discussion. A doctor is essential. Miss Keith calls a rickshaw. It is a short way only but agonising as every bump in the road jolts hand and foot. The doctor is away.

'There is something wrong with your bones' says an observant nurse.

Jullunder City Hospital has to be the next choice. People are propped against walls, squatting and lying in the dust. Miss Keith weaves her way through to a door marked 'General Medical Officer'. A gentleman sits at a table in a room full of people. Miss Keith moves straight to the table speaking rapidly. In a trice I am seated as he examines my hand and foot and calls out 'Cortisone immediately'. I ask for his diagnosis and he replies confidently 'GOUT!' I am astonished and disbelieving. The medical officer refuses payment and there is nothing left but to go home to breakfast on a boiled egg and cortisone tablet.

We have already made an appointment with Mr. Singh who arrives on cue by car for a visit to his farm and some very delicate discussions. Miss Keith is already primed on the situation. We are about to meet the parents-in-law of a young man who is serving a five-year prison sentence for rape. The circumstances are unusual. Already on probation for an offence of taking and driving away a car, he fled to India to avoid arrest on a further, more serious charge. His large and well-respected family, in ignorance of the full situation, arranged a marriage for him to the only daughter of a wealthy landowner. The marriage took place in India and after waiting ten months for an entry certificate he returned with his wife and baby son. He was arrested and sentenced to five years imprisonment by which time his wife was again pregnant. The position in India remains delicate. He had acted dishonourably and the in-laws are now bitterly opposed to their son-in-law. It had even been intimated that if he ever returned to India his life would be at risk. It was thought that a visit might diffuse the situation. In Smethwick the daughter and her two sons were well looked after by her husband's family. I can give good news about her material circumstances but emotionally she has suffered greatly. I had taken her on a welfare visit to the prison but as I had to remain in the room for security reasons she had not had a private moment with her husband for three years.

So with quite a challenging scenario ahead we drive through a 148 acre farm, around field after field of potatoes, paddy and orchards thick with fruit. Little mud huts of the farm workers are visible in the clearings and I am invited to take a stroll, but it is useless. My legs are not reliable, so I ask to be taken into the shade of the house. I remember arriving at a lovely farmhouse, which Mr. Singh had built himself, and being shown into a cool and graceful lounge. I made it as far as the sofa and gently keeled over. Then I knew no more until I hear in the distance Miss Keith asking if I will take dinner. They thought I had slumped into sleep and had been much too polite to attempt to awaken me. I have never fainted in my life, so what was this unusual sort of collapse and loss of consciousness?

They had used my absence profitably Miss Keith playing out what should have been my part to the letter. Agreement had been reached that their son-in-law would be allowed time to prove himself as a husband, father and wage earner after his release but until he had done so there would be no further contact. They felt heavy responsibility for accepting this young man as a good match and showed us photos of their beautiful smiling daughter, a sad contrast to the unhappy young mother in Smethwick.

On our return Mr. Chandra is waiting to ask if I will repeat my visit to his home to meet more relatives who are urgent to hear the tapes and to entertain me. I agree, needing this light hearted contact. The pain is dulled, maybe by the cortisone or perhaps by these delightful people who perform folk dances and sing, play strange musical instruments and clap to the changing rhythms. Mr. Chandra tells me that he works in a factory from 8am to 10pm but is always refreshed by his family when he comes home. He is a truly happy and warm-hearted man and there is much love in his house. He walks me home slowly with old-world courtesy, and I take to my bed wondering whether I am through the worst.

Saturday 12th November

Waking up has become nerve-wracking, as I have begun to start each day with an inventory of body parts. The hand pain is now a deep throbbing ache, muted perhaps by the cortisone, but it is still loosing power. I can see from my journal how the letters are loosing their firmness and changing shape – rather like me! My right foot now has three fragile, purple headed toes that stick out at an ungainly angle and at any cost must not be touched! So what do we do?

We take a rickshaw to the bazaar to buy toeless sandals. It is a beggar's field day. My feet hardly touch the ground before ragged people press forwards on all sides. A little girl strokes at me with a twitching stump, others prostrate in the dirt, matted hair falling over my feet as they press their blessings onto the angry flesh bringing stinging tears to my eyes. It is harrowing. I cannot move forwards for hands and bodies pleading for alms for the love of God. In desperation we both give a few rupees but that only draws more attention. Miss Keith tells me these are migrants from the south. An emaciated man looking ravaged by illness begs for medicines. He has a prescription in his hand. When Miss Keith offers to take him to the pharmacists to buy his medication they let us through. A Bata shoe shop provides soft open-toed sandals and briefly we brave the bustling alleyways of the bazaar, as today is another festival when sisters give brothers gifts. Miss Keith must make some purchases so I have her negotiate for wedding gifts for my daughter but sadly the joy has gone out of either walking or purchasing today.

Tomorrow afternoon I leave for a stay in a village. I know it is risky but Baripuri is the one place above all others that I would not miss, the toes will just have to come with me. Today I see Miss Keith off to visit her brother and opt for an afternoon of beauty care. Duped by hoardings advertising thick rich potions to transform my hair into shining glory, I have bought a bottle of sweet smelling oil, a ludicrous idea. Every hair is plastered to my head. Washing and rinsing will not move it. I look a fright, feel a fool and stick to my pillow as I try valiantly to sleep.

Sunday 13th November

Miss Keith is a born teacher. Information is given the added dimension of feelings and even the reasons why she thinks and feels as she does. I have so much to learn from her and the enjoyment of her company distracts my mind from body parts. This morning we are on the way to Katarpur, stopping briefly to pay our respects to her relatives. Joginder, the owner of a furniture shop on the main Katarpur road, is the brother-in-law of a teacher friend. This is to be a surprise visit. A powerfully built Sidargi, Joginder is delighted to meet us, serves refreshments and we roam amongst the furniture displays while he drives home to prepare his family for a visit. My friend had told me the shop would be easier to locate than his house. We can see why. The town is a maze of narrow streets and it is impossible to see where one house ends and another begins due to all the added extensions.

It is a tumultuous welcome. There are so many people, none speaking English. Miss Keith does the honours for us both, explaining that I have brought taped messages from their elderly grandmother living in Smethwick. It is many years since she has seen her daughter Manjit. She wants so much to visit but is now too infirm to travel. Emotions erupt at the sound of her voice. The time spent with that dear old lady helping her to understand the mechanics of my tape machine are worthwhile. Recording sessions are followed by refreshments, and overtures pressing me to stay with them begin. Miss Keith thinks them a delightful and highly respectable family so we reorganise my programme to make space for a short stay later.

They feel sure we would enjoy an afternoon drive and choose Kapurthala where I am fascinated to watch the pot makers at work. Even their houses are made out of pots! It is a feast of architecture in fine red brick, an English style town hall and a Mosque which is empty and silent, now unused, but it still holds an atmosphere of stillness and peace. Pedal boats intermingle with fishing boats on a pleasure lake where we take refreshments to end a relaxing family outing.

Joginder drives us back to Jullunder and before I can turn around Bara Singh arrives. A railway worker and a farmer, he sits, ill at ease in the best room. He has enlisted the services of a young English speaking neighbour with a scooter who will transport me to his home in Baripuri while he follows by bus with my luggage. I sense they are hesitant at taking me to the village, as there is serious conversation afoot with Miss Keith. Guessing the content, I join in to reassure them there will be no complaints from me about food, accommodation, toilets or any other matter if I can see my very old and dear friend, known to me as Father Singh. We leave. Miss Keith stands smiling and serene. She has had a therapeutic effect on me. Let us hope I can hold on to it.

12.Father Singh's Lament

Sunday 13th November (continued)

It is an exhilarating breezy ride through the heart of farming country. Houses thin out, spaces between villages grow longer. As we near the village I realise that this is land that I am familiar with on paper, as I had become involved in protracted negotiations for its sale to raise money for Father Singh's return to India. It began when a Sikh lady named Binder Kaur bought an old dilapidated house in Smethwick Her elderly father and her two small sons completed this small family group. Binder's husband was in prison and it was because of this that they had uprooted from a town a distance away to make a fresh start. My help had been needed to assist this family with resettlement. Binder had been a teacher in her village before coming to England nine years previously, but her qualifications were insufficient to allow her to teach, although her English was good and we communicated easily. Her father had a small ex-army pension that was their lifeline. He soon became a familiar figure in the High Street walking his grandsons to school and to prayers at the Gurdwara. Just as they had begun to fashion a new life, Father Singh suffered a stroke that left him speechless and partly paralysed. He made it known that he wanted his wife, who had remained living on their small farm with their son's family to join him. But they had no money, hence the need to sell a piece of Father Singh's farmland. As he was unfit to deal with the notary I became his agent. Papers passed to and fro; passport applications, medical certificates to certify his declining state of health and at the end of protracted negotiations his wife was refused entry. She was not even allowed to visit. Father Singh worsened, Binder needed more help and hospital day care was arranged, but it was heartrending to see him sitting in such a strange environment. Gradually the three of us fashioned a way of communicating with him and were convinced he wanted to be sent home to India to be with his wife and to die on his home soil. It was arranged and Binder was left alone. During the next two years we became firm friends. She would read the Punjab Times to me and explain what lay behind some of the news stories, and used her teaching skills in the women's groups I ran. Her main concern at my visit was that they had no toilet facilities at all. 'So what do you do? I asked her. 'We go into the crops'. So she taught me Punjabi for 'I need to go to the crops' then she added that in an emergency it is possible, by careful balance, to crouch on the edge of the roof. I am hoping there will be no emergencies.

After two years in India, I know that Father Singh is still alive. My mind is a jumble of memories as I approach to sample the life Binder left and to which she knows she will never return. This village is built on flat terrain in the midst of a vast expanse of farmland. I know there are no shops, doctors, public transport, cars or telephones, just a Gurdwara, a school and few houses and am uneasy at the thought of being so cut off for the next three days. It seems a long time.

We enter a door in a long high wall. It opens onto a courtyard. Bara's wife Gurdev and his two daughters aged fifteen and ten are waiting to greet me. The courtyard, with a central water pump is the focus of the household. Small brick rooms open off on either side. My first question is about Father Singh's welfare. The two elders live in a brick room built one floor above, overlooking the courtyard. It is reached by a flight of twisting stone steps. Father Singh never comes down and is cared for by his wife. I ask to pay my respects immediately.

He is there, sitting on the edge of the bed, legs dangling, shoes unlaced, spotless white nylon shirt, his turban a little askew. He is the same dear old gentleman that I had talked and walked with so many times. He still cannot speak but he does not need to. His eyes brim with tears of recognition at the sight of me. All I can do is to kneel and put my head on his knees and his now almost useless hand moves to touch my hair in blessing. We are both so moved by our reconnection that I had barely noticed the old lady who is Binder's mother. I address her as 'Matagi' with great respect and she envelops me in her strong arms. We are both weeping.

Matagi speaks no English. Father Singh speaks no words at all except to intone 'Aho... Aho... Aho' like a mantra over and over as he rocks gently, silent tears pouring down his face. No-one moves to wipe them. In halting Punjabi I tell them that I have brought the voices of the daughter and grandsons. I point to my mouth as I speak and wonder if they understand my meaning. The others, who have all remained respectfully outside, join us, but feelings are still too strong to engage in any social chat. To have made the journey says it all.

Bara arrives with my luggage his expression registering his relief that I am safely installed. I follow my luggage as it is carried ceremoniously up stone steps on the opposite side of the courtyard to a small brick room on the rooftop. There are two webbing beds with covers in place and I can make out they are telling me this is Binder's old bedroom. On the wall is a photo of her beautiful fresh face taken with her graduation class. Sukdev, the only son of the family, a strong young man of sixteen, arrives out of the fields as dusk falls. Dusk is, I know, the time of the ritual walk to the crops with the water cans and I pick up the rather embarrassed signals from the women, intimating that I understand where we are going and why!

Four females and one water-can take the stroll down the narrow alley, past the bullock sheds and out into the acres of sugar cane. They select an appropriate field and we part company to choose our private cover. I have custody of the water can. It is full. Am I meant to use it all? If not how do I contact someone to pass it on? It is a tricky procedure, balancing myself amongst the furrows, scooping up my long skirt to do a one handed juggling act. Perhaps I should have practised! I compromise and use half of the water but is seems no-one else is interested. We meander back through waving fronds to a supper of lentil soup, eaten together in a recess off the courtyard, where they have thoughtfully placed a small stool for me.

An English speaking young neighbour has remained to supper and works hard to interpret my answers to the teeming questions as I search for simple descriptive words.   At last I am taken to what I had thought was to be my room, only to discover that the two girls will be sleeping in the other single bed, probably because it is their room anyway. I am happy. This is where I came to India to be, with people whose lives have interwoven with my own.

Monday 14th November

The day begins with the walk to the sugar cane at first light. I swing the can. There is good easy laughter, no embarrassment now. A fire of corn cobs and dung is burning between bricks on the floor of the kitchen. An iron pan of ghee is wedged over the flame. There is no interpreter around so I indicate that fried tomato would be good for breakfast and wander outside while it is cooked. Kuljit, the youngest is not going to school today. It is more important to remain at home to entertain me. She shows me her English lesson book but some phrases are too pedantic, giving it a stilted sound as Kuljit reads to me. So I read them back to her and she immediately picks up the difference in pronunciation and phrasing, becoming absorbed in our ad hoc lesson.

Wandering back into the kitchen I find the pan still in place over the fire with Gurdev stirring a pool of brown glue-like substance that was once a tomato. Maybe it would have been impolite to call me, or perhaps I was expected to tell her when it was done. But then all cooking here seems to be a constant stirring, mixing and blending until ingredients are unrecognisable. Slices of the white loaf that I had brought with me are also cooked to crunchy nut-brown. I spread the red-brown substance and pretend that I am trying a new dish. Bubbling on the back of the fire is the tea with milk long since added to the pot and I watch as a lump of sugar beet and spices are added, not my kind of delicate brew! So I content myself with washing my hair at the pump watching the sweeping and cleaning as the morning routine unfolds. Then Kuldip arrives.

Kuldip is the sister of my translator of yesterday, a young woman of strong character. She presents her credentials. She is eighteen years old, studying at College in Hoshiapur taking MA finals in British, European and Indian history. I am impressed. She tells me her marks are good and she expects to pass all examinations. She is certainly not shy and her English is impeccable. Suddenly questions have answers; plans and programmes are made. She will accompany us on a walk and it is preferable to go in the morning because of the afternoon heat. Usually much work is done in the morning gathering vegetables for the days meals, collecting fuel, washing and feeding the bullocks but today had been declared a holiday so all five women could be together.

We go laughing towards the fields visiting the bullock sheds on the way. All bullocks look alike to me but I do the honours, admiring each one and stroking various places to show willing. In the fields we wander along rutted tracks between sugar cane, brinjels and mustard. Men are at work with crude instruments breaking up the parched earth. From time to time we stop and sit to chat. There are gasps of surprise as I describe my village of three thousand people with its seven public houses, restaurants, stables for hiring horses and spacious car parks so people can come to stroll the hills eating giant ice creams! I wonder if anything could be more satisfying than sitting in the heart of the Punjab in the company of these villagers exploring each other worlds, by foot or in words. We have cemented our little group by this outing and wander home willingly to engage together in a cooking session. Vegetables are waiting to be peeled and diced into minute pieces. I wonder if this cooking method came about through having to conserve fuel. The diced vegetables plop into a big pot of water, then out comes the spice box, little compartments filled with pungent powders. It is frustrating as I find the smells so inviting but my digestive system rebels against anything hot and spicy so I have my own little pot of plain boiled vegetables bubbling separately. I cannot believe my eyes when they are reverently taken off the fire and before I can make a move are liberally spiked with spices. Perhaps they could not believe I could enjoy such a tasteless offering. Who knows? But my dinner has now gone in the same direction as my breakfast and my appetite is rising!

It is time for us to join the elders and play the tape. As I climb the stone steps a sudden biting pain shoots from the right knee jarring me to a standstill. I hope this isn't a foretaste of more trouble. I sit next to Father Singh who is in his usual position; bolt upright, nothing to support his back, legs dangling lifelessly. He is not crying today. I am surprised and sad to hear that village children throw stones at his window and call rude things as I know how he loves children. I switch on the tape and Binder's voice breaks the silence.

'Sat Sri Akal, Mammagi; Sat Sri Akal Pappagi; …..' Each member of the family receives their personal greeting. Then she begins to talk and is it more than Father Singh can stand. He breaks into loud wracking sobs. Matagi is shaking her head to and fro; Father Singh's hands are fluttering with agitation. We cannot continue, the emotional impact is too great. I put the tape aside, hold his trembling hands and talk softly to him. Maybe it is just the sound of my voice that soothes him. He too once had a soft, gentle voice in the days when we sat speaking in English together and I sense he has a good measure of understanding of what I say. So I talk on, telling him of his daughter's success in finding work in the jewellery trade, of his grandson's progress at school and gave good wishes from his old friends at the Sikh Temple. His 'aho, aho, aho' holds a different note as if it is acknowledging me. It had been too sudden to bring those voices back into the room. It is kinder to help his mind travel back to shared times before we move on. I tell Mataji we will play the tape later. She understands.

Sharing something visual is easier. Photographs of my home and family start up a buzz of questions and Father Singh makes a gesture towards the face of my youngest daughter who had, on occasion, played with his grandsons. He remembers. Sensing that I would like to be alone with the elders they drift away and the afternoon moves gently on as Mataji gestures to me to take a rest on her bed where Father Singh can see me. Realising I am tired, mentally and physically I take this quiet moment to lift my skirt to survey the knee. An angry red blotch is spreading around my kneecap. I can hide it under my skirt but not from my mind.

Kuldip comes quietly in to sit beside Mataji who wants her to convey something to me. It is a delicate matter. She wants me to carry back the family's regrets to her daughter that the match they had arranged had not turned out as well as they had hoped. They do not want to speak of it on tape; I must do so privately only in her hearing. I agree to be the messenger. Then there is a chance to ask Kuldip a question that had been puzzling me. I explain that in other villages, neighbours, friends and relatives would all be visiting and pressing to see and speak to me. Here this had not happened today and though I was relieved I wondered why there is this difference. Kuldip knows the answer. She explains:

'This is a good and respectable family, but neither important nor rich, yet a lady from the British Government has come to stay. She chooses to be with them, even with no sanitation and to share their meagre food. It is mysterious to them why she has not come with car, with cook, supplies and servants and stayed at the very best accommodation the village could provide, with reception by the Panchayat or village elders. Because you do not behave as they expect they do not know how to behave. The expected order of things has been changed.'

This is what the I.G. had been asking of me, to travel with a retinue, as he knew what would be expected in the villages as well as being thoughtful of my comfort. My adamant refusal had been, in part, because I believed the greatest learning experience would lie in being closer to the people I had come to meet, but that was not the whole of it. There is something else more subtle, that I am unable to explain to him, to myself or in this village. It is a sense that my feet are moving on a marked path. I am where I must be. So I answer simply: 'I am meant to be here. Tomorrow let us walk into the village.'

And what of Bara, who holds this family together? After the women have made their nightly walk to the crops we find the men are at home and we sit to a cosy meal together in the firelight. It is Bara's turn to lead the conversation in halting English that I did not know he could speak until now. He wants me to talk of England, of our welfare systems, of provision for old age, and of labour saving equipment. My imitation of a vacuum cleaner, washing machine and the like make for such laughter that those behind the courtyard walls must wonder what on earth we are up to. I have great respect for this man Bara who cycles thirteen miles to work as a railway clerk at Jullunder Station and after his return farms his land until dark. He meets all his responsibilities and does all that can be expected of him and more. Beneath his turban his hair is grey and I am not surprised.

Tuesday 15th November

The bedcover feels heavy. I go to kick it off and sharp pains shoot from my knee. I am sweating. Fumbling for my torch I creep outside onto the rooftop and shine a light onto my knee. It is red, puffy and swollen. It is the same process in action as began in the thumb and toe. I hold onto the doorjamb and press my head against the cool bricks. My brain is not functioning yet, it is flooded with the shock of this next problem to be faced. There is no immediate medical help available here and I have no more cortisone. Would it be best to say nothing at all and keep the knee well hidden? In two days I will be in Chandigarh and can request help there. The onset has been just as sudden as the last bout, which deteriorated fast with only one day's delay in medication. This must not ruin my last day here so I decide to take a gamble and try mind over matter.

Sleep is fragmented with worrying thoughts floating to the surface. Up early I make it down to the pump before others appear, to bathe the knee in cool water. There has been another development since my torchlight survey. It is now purplish in colour, nodules have begun to form and it is stiffening. Tying a thin cotton scarf around it, I creep back to the roof and decide on strategy. The girls are happy to join me for an omelette breakfast on the roof. Huge green parrots swoop across the courtyard looking for pickings, and the day's work begins below. I explain to Kudlip that I have to give a lecture next day and need time to think it through. It is understood. I can sit on the rooftop and think.

It is the day to give presents, which causes surprise and excitement. Some are from Binder, others I had brought myself. We visit Father Singh and present him with a pair of socks, there are toilet articles and felt tip pens for Kuljit, a great luxury as even the teacher does not have any! The main present is for Gurdev, my hostess. It is a salwar chemise made by Binder, beautifully stitched in diamond patterns. She was amazed by it. The present giving is a good distraction that had lifted my spirits so I accept the women's suggestion of a stroll into the village. Inquisitive faces peer out of doorways and recesses as we pass. Sometimes there are smiles and greetings. Our first stop is at the Gudwara. The building is crumbling in places yet still it holds the same peaceful ambience that pervades all Sikh places of worship. Their encouragement carries me up the stone stairs to the rooftop. Now I can see that this small village is an oasis set in the midst of fields on all sides. How strange it is that we do not know such places exist one minute and then, suddenly, it is possible to feel their pulse and become a part of them for a while. I want to be able to sit on this rooftop and write and write, painting word pictures of these living stories instead of scribbling hasty lines in corners which do no-one justice. One day I promise myself I will find my rooftop somewhere.

We move on to the school which is no more than open verandas lining the sides of a grassy area, no chairs or desks, no visual aids, just a space sheltered from the sun in which to sit with slate on knee and make one's mark. I find it hard to change tempo from my introspective thoughts when the Headmaster and teachers appear from a corner of the quadrangle, but find them so hungry for an exchange that they soon engage my interest. They remember Binder well and are keen to have news of her. Primary education from age six to eleven is free and compulsory but no sanctions have been built in to ensure attendance. They are interested in our system of Education Welfare Officers and smile as they consider how none of our sanctions could be applied in their circumstances. The courts are too backlogged already; no one could afford to pay a fine; the children are needed in the fields; how are they supposed to travel such distances? Who would remove a child from family and where could they be taken? Their need is not for sanctions but resources of more than slate and chalk and opportunities for learning beyond the eleven-year-old watershed. More teachers are being trained and schools built but it is an enormous task to make comprehensive educational provision. There are ninety-nine Universities in India but the route to reach one is paved with rupees beyond the means of most villagers.

The pupils who had been taken out on a visit had heard of our arrival.

We meet them in the lane, dressed in blue cotton uniforms, and suddenly it is bedlam. One picks up a handful of dried leaves and throws them in the air, then they all began to follow suit. Leaves are sticking to our clothes and hair, covering us in dry dust. It seems to be good-natured fun but is the signal for us to go home and wash.

The afternoon brings out visitors. It seems we had broken the ice by our walk and neighbours and children arrive. No men join us and it is most informal. They sit on wooden beds or squat in the courtyard, children playing chasing, jumping and singing, older girls caring for the babies. A peddler passes up the alley and is invited into the courtyard to display his bales of cotton cloth. One woman buys a length of material. A sewing machine is brought out, and the cloth is spread on the floor with a suit laid on top as a cutting guide. I am amazed at the teamwork as all hands become involved in the creation of a new garment, except mine. It is too uncomfortable to be trying to bend the knee so I opt to entertain the children with the never failing tape recorder. The afternoon is crowned by a visit from village elders who, after touching both my head and feet enjoy the ritual Punjabi exchanges which is all I can muster.

Mataji had not been with us; always she is by the side of Father Singh. While others are preparing an evening meal it seems the right time to visit. It is good to take a quiet space to talk once again to Father Singh and then I show Matagi the knee, telling her that the others do not know of my problem. She takes some liquid from the cupboard, pours a dose and I drink it down under her eagle eye. It is firewater! She lays me on the bed and massages my knee with oil; her strong bony fingers probing and pressing, then gently covering me she sits beside me until suppertime.

This is my last evening with the family and the tapes are still unplayed. We eat together talking over the day's events with the men, then join with the elders for the last time. Father Singh is prepared. He clamps his mouth firmly shut. Then Binder and her two sons speak, the children's piping voices crossing the room as clearly as if they were with us. All send their loving greetings adding the small details that no one else could give. Tonight it is a delight and the few trickling tears are of laughter and pleasure, mingled with the sadness of the distance between them. I have completed the task.

Now there is a surprise for me. It is Gurdev who shyly presents an exquisitely hand woven bed cover. It is a heavy tapestry, ablaze with a geometrical design in an array of autumn colours. This I know must be a family heirloom, likely to have formed part of the bride's dowry. It overwhelms me.

Sleep comes easily but stomach pains waken me in the night. It is time for the unthinkable. Silently I creep to the edge of the roof where I improvise a makeshift toilet. Then, not wanting to return to the darkness of my room, I opt to sit under the night sky.

Wednesday 16th November

Goodbyes are awful. Dear Father Singh sits immobile on the edge of his bed, legs still dangling, laces undone; small things become important at memorable moments such as this. Kneeling beside him his helpless hands are wet with my tears. He too is weeping 'his acho…acho' is a lament, a dirge. Matagi wrings her hands, praying for my safe return. Added to the emotional pain of parting is the physical pain of my knee. It is swollen on every side, a miniature football; in places the swellings are hard and knobbly. It feels as if something alien to my body is boring into my kneecap. Somehow I leave them, knowing it will be the last time I will ever see Father Singh or most likely any of them again.

Inching backwards down the steep steps I am gathered into the arms of an old woman. She has a daughter in England and must send her love through me. Repeatedly she touches me, head and feet, head and feet. So many people are gathered in the courtyard, pressing small gifts of fruit and sweets into my hands for the journey. And the family? No one has gone to school or work this day. How can loving kindness be so unbearable? In two days it has become so easy to be enveloped by the spirit of this family. How then would it be for Binder if she returned only to have to tear herself away from this upsurge of unbridled love?

A car arrives with three officers from the Social Welfare Board, all men. The alley is too narrow for the car to reach the house. They carry my luggage and I walk with Mataji, to the accompaniment of Sat Sri Akal, cries and wails, past all the neighbours in doorways, a blur of faces. The bullocks call; they are left untended this morning. I am settled with care on the back seat and hands press on the windows. Barupuri is India, the India I came to see but then I did not know that no one just *sees* India, she makes you feel depths of feelings which have never before been reached.

13. Crippling News

Wednesday 16th November (continued)

My escorts see my distress and ask if it will help if we stop for tea. I ask for oranges. They stop and buy two bags full. It is as if I have been cut off from the world and am returning through the old familiar scenes. It is important to have help now fast or I will end up as immobile as Father Singh.

Huge banners across the gateway advertise CONFERENCE ON JUVENILE DELINQUENCY. It is being held at Panchayat Bevan, a modern conference centre with its own accommodation. What a joy to see Miss Keith waiting on the step. She tells me she has ordered a special dinner of potatoes and steamed vegetables and asks if I would like it served privately in my room. This is exactly what I need. A social worker joins us and we three eat quietly together. I spy a double bed with relief, hoping that I will be in it alone. Then I try to speak a little of my time in the village but they know only too well how it is.

The programme lists that I will be speaking on Juvenile Delinquency in England and the work of the Probation Service. The hall is filled to capacity with agency workers, teachers, police and social workers. It is a subject which is easy for me to explore in such good company. They are amazed at the vast number of vehicle related offences. T.A.D.A. (take and drive away) is a whole new concept in crime as they say most of the cars in India are owned by Government or the rich and it would be more than any life would be worth to be found tampering with them. In this way we learn from each other more of the relationship between crime, culture and the environment and the evening provides more useful research material. There were many questions on the causes of delinquency in western society and they put forward perceptive views on family breakdown and pressure of materialistic values. It is good afterwards to be able to mingle and talk informally over tea but I know my next responsibility is to telephone the I.G. to let him know of my arrival and to enlist his help in finding a doctor.

The I.G. is in his office. He is displeased that I have elected to stay overnight at the Centre. I explain that I have work to do here and need more time for conversation but that the problem of my knee is urgent. A car will be sent. The car arrives and he is in it. His wife is in Chandigarh General Hospital having tests and treatment. We are to visit her and at the same time take medical advice for my condition. The only item in a colourless side room is the bed. A group of friends are visiting and the elderly house servant squats on the floor. The doctor is called and everyone present examines the knee with interest, chatting to each other, making comments and giving their opinions. The doctor's verdict is given in English.

'This condition is serious and must be seen by specialist. Specialist is away. His return is Saturday. Blood tests are necessary. You remain for three days'.

Another dilemma, or is it? All the Probation Officers in the Punjab are at this moment on their way to Hoshiapur to hear my lecture there tomorrow. I confer with the I.G. and we agree. I am not free to enter hospital for three days at this very moment. The tests will not take place... yet. My sore and runny eyes can be treated immediately and he gives a prescription for eye drops. We return the servant home for the night and collect my prescription but the I.G.'s conscience is bothering him. I am his responsibility and therefore my care must come first. He knows of a bone specialist living locally. I am more than willing to see him. We speed off to his house. He is away. We are both so frustrated.

At the Centre, a small group have planned a select supper party in my room and are waiting for me to reappear. There is one probation officer, two social workers and a teacher who works in a residential home for children. They are my colleagues and we have so much to share. As the night wears on they begin to speak of their personal problems. Two are unmarried and we explore social attitudes towards single females, especially those following a professional career. It is the situation of Selima, a married woman with four children that I found the most disturbing. Her husband had managed to reach England twelve years previously where he had promised to make a home for the family but he had neither sent money nor sent for them to join him. He had visited once during this time, appeared to be in good health and had money in his pocket. All these years she has been dependent upon the charity of her own family, and had struggled to train as a social worker to earn the keep for them all. They live in one room. All the possessions they own can be packed into a cardboard box. The strength of her feelings could be felt as her words etched a picture of her fight to withstand injustice.

'Madame, which way to go? Where is this man's life? Where is my life?' We pieced together the scraps of information that she had gleaned of his life in England and his last known address. My interest is sincere. I had met a number of husbands who had told me of their wives in India and of the formidable challenge of re-establishing family life in another country and culture. Many promises had been made and broken but there were questions to be asked and answered, if I could find him. I assured her I would look.

The teacher's story was one so often repeated in India. Her father had died when she was thirteen years old and, as the eldest she had worked to help her brother and sister to obtain a good education and both were now well established abroad. She had remained at home to care for her aged mother. So many stories of suffering and sacrifice, this is just one more. Selima bathes my eyes. Willing hands shake up the bedcovers, wedge my pulsing knee between two pillows and sleep comes swiftly.

Thursday 17th November

Despite all precautions I wake up in a real mess. Yellow pus is oozing from both eyes, and I am sweating with pain that localises in the knee but seems to be sending heat waves around my body. A fire within is stoking up for trouble.

All my companions of the previous night arrive and set about their self imposed task of caring for me. Warm water and cotton wool is brought and my eyes are bathed. They open just enough but are sore and bloodshot. Buckets of hot and cold water arrive. After my knee is bathed and covered with a warm towel, breakfast is served. It is 7 o'clock. The I.G.'s staff car is to collect me at 7.45 precisely for the long journey to Hoshiapur. Each one embraces me and Miss Keith reminds me we will be meeting again but I wonder. Nothing seems certain now.

Mohinder is coming with us and sits by the driver, the I.G. sits beside me on the back seat but I make a poor travelling companion. Words for the day's lecture float to the surface and are lost in a feverish sleep. Hoshiapur looms before us too soon. I step out of the car hidden behind dark sunglasses, but am swaying. I know that I am really ill and feel it is only a question of time before I collapse. The Prison Superintendent greets us. We had met before and he sees immediately how my condition has deteriorated. The probation officers are all gathered in the lecture hall but he insists that I am taken straight to Hoshiapur Hospital, telling the I.G. that the head man has trained in England and is his friend. His recommendation is faultless. I am not consulted, simply taken, and I no longer care. Two cars and five men escort me to the hospital.

The good doctor receives us all immediately. My escorts sit on a row of chairs provided and I lift up my skirts to show the knee. There are gasps, partly at its unsightly appearance but I think also at the whiteness of the leg against the purple bulging knee and my willingness to exhibit both. I am well past caring about the niceties of protocol. What else would I be expected to do – describe it? The good doctor has no doubt about my disease. He has substantial reservations about me travelling and lecturing in this condition.

'Madame, it is arthritis; Rheumatoid arthritis.'

It is as if I had really known it all along. There is no resistance to his diagnosis, no arguments, no emotional outburst, no words. I had seen the gnarling of joints many years before when working for a while in a geriatric ward, feeding the patients whose joints were too knotted to grasp a cup or spoon.

'Yes, I fear it is progressive and crippling'.

The doctor reads my unspoken question. How progressive and crippling I can consider later. At this moment it simply feels important to return to deliver my lecture and then to find a way of remaining mobile for the next twenty-five days. They seem an eternity.

The doctor is telling me how modern medicine can control the onset. Then he holds out a handful of packets of tablets, some form of steroids, but all I see is the picture on the front of a skeleton hand twisted into an obscene shape with nodule encrusted joints. It will take some time before the tablets take effect but they should ease the pain. He examines my eyes. Yes, the drops are correct, I am to continue and they will improve in maybe a week or so. Enough! There is really no more to be said. None of the men have spoken, not even the I.G.

We return to the hall where my audience appears to have waited patiently. I wonder if they have been told where we have been. There is a formal presentation as the Officers form into rows. Newspaper reporters are present taking copious notes. It is strange how easy it is to slip into gear. It is as if the professional part takes over, divorcing itself from the personal and physical.

The Probation Officers call themselves 'the Rat Catchers'. They tell me they are neither well liked nor highly regarded by anyone. I talk on for an hour explaining the structure of our Service, the tasks of the officers and how we set about fulfilling them. The inevitable barrage of questions follows. Does the Government buy us cars? Why do we need them when we have buses and good walk-along roads? What are welfare benefits? The questions range wider and wider. It had to end to the disappointment of us all.

I had stood throughout, leaning on a lectern. Now I have to be helped into a chair as my knee has set and will not bend. The Superintendent is the man who had offered me accommodation and help to reach a village is his area. I had plans laid to meet with the family of a woman I had helped to leave her husband and make an independent life in a council flat with her two small sons. She really had no choice as her life was at risk. Her husband was an alcoholic and violent and had sawn her arms with a wood saw. She had jagged scars to prove it. She had no relatives in England and her husband's family would not support her decision to leave her husband although they were aware of his deranged state. It would have been such a joy for her to receive news of her family yet I did not dare set out again on another village journey in this condition. It seems prudent to return to Chandigarh.

Now I learn that the I.G. has responded to requests from the Superintendents and Deputies of the Punjab Prisons and committed me to give a repeat of my performance at Luhiana on Saturday. Let us hope there is some speech left in me!

Mohinder's cousin has arrived. His family live in the district and they are hoping to welcome me to their home. The I.G. realises this is not wise. Unable to eat, I take some pills from the skeleton hand packet and sleep all the way back to Chandigarh. The rest is a blank.

14. The Red Carpet

Friday 18th November

Being alone in the house is a luxury. The men have left, and the servant is with Mrs. I.G. at the hospital. It is short-lived. The I.G. returns filled with bustle and excitement. He has been told his wife can return home today. I am asked to prepare a welcome for her, something to show my pleasure at her return. Before my mind engages I hear myself offering to arrange the evening meal, English style. He roars with laughter. Accepted! Surrinder returns ready to help create a party atmosphere. All I want is some private thinking time, now I have put my head into a noose where I have to think of food, not my forte at all.

'Let's go to the market, Auntie'. It seems a good idea to get it over with. The fish are enormous. Slices are carved off by request and diced into minuscule pieces. Before the chopper descends I rescue some large slices. My imagination is blunted today and all I can rise to is the thought of fish and chips, well at least it is a real English dish. Finding flour to make a crispy batter is a challenge. Surrinder says they would never have any reason to buy white flour but we turn up a bag of something flour-like. There are potatoes at home, so that is it, I can forget the technicalities of cooking without gas or electricity until later.

Mohinder has returned home. All three men had been unhappy at leaving me alone. It does not seem that aloneness is understood as a chosen option but Mohinder is delightful company. He does not talk with such animation as his brother; his speech has just the trace of a stammer. Surrinder is an English student with an expressive way with words but Mohinder thinks awhile, searching for the right phrase, then, when he finds it, it is exactly right. So I agree to his suggestion of a round by scooter and find myself glad of his presence on what might have been a sad day if thoughts had strayed to my physical future.

We return to the Rock Gardens for a daylight viewing, try a museum and art gallery but trudging around long galleries is a bad idea, so we end up at a Coffee House and talk. It is my turn to ask questions. I learn of his life, his friends and his feelings about his forthcoming marriage. He answers all my questions thoughtfully. His father knows his fiancé's family who live in Southall. Their only meeting had been for half an hour at the Airport. He thinks she is a very nice person who will be a very nice wife. I think she is a very lucky person and say so. How strange it all seems as a way to decide upon one's life partner, but I know it can work out well. When we return, Mrs. I.G. is lying on her bed moaning with the pain in her head. She struggles to sit, clasps me in her arms and we pat each other on the back.

The servant peels the potatoes and I just rescue them from being chopped into shreds. Chip shapes are unknown to her. Egg batter is mixed to an admiring audience, fish dipped, ghee melted and 'frying tonight' is under way. Mostly I am masterminding events as the servant juggles the pans over the kerosene burner. Knives, forks and plates replace bowls and spoons and everyone enters the spirit of the English eating game. It all looks festive but no one knows what they have to do. We assemble, the I.G. standing to attention, opens with some stirring words

'It is the highlight of our lives to be served by a great English lady cooking the fish dinner.' I keep a straight face but then Surrinder begins to quote from English poets while the fish resting in the kitchen cools by the minute. Mohinder holds his hands over his mouth and catches my eye. He is not tempted to contribute and at last I get to the serious business of explaining how the knife in the right hand cuts the food into small portions, which is lifted carefully on the fork. It begins to sound silly, even to me, and as I dissolve into overdue laughter they all follow suit. The servant helps me to carry in two salvers, one of fish and the other of chips to gasps of admiration (or is it horror) and everyone dutifully follows my instructions. What is a feast for me proves to be a starter course for them. Bowls of curds, dhal and the usual mound of chapattis follow as they begin their proper meal. What I had done was to help create an atmosphere of celebration for them and for me. The fish and chip supper has served its purpose and I am strangely happy.

Saturday 19th November

I know it is Saturday on waking but cannot *see* Saturday or anything else. My eyelids will not lift, neither will my spirits. It is lecturing day in Ludhiana. They can see me not seeing them and know that Auntie is in trouble. Mohinder guides me to the bathroom and sponges my eyes over the basin until red-rimmed slits appear. I am shivering with an inner coldness that persists, even when I pull on a long sleeved velvet top with hood. The driver arrives and I am whisked away with the I.G. sitting beside me in the back seat, shaded from the ever-present sun by looped green curtains. I am totally uncommunicative and lie back with a cotton scarf tied around my eyes bandit style. I have told the boys I will be back early. The I.G. has told them we will be visiting villages in the afternoon. Who will prove right I wonder?

At 11am we reach Ludhiana. This is incredible! People line the village square perched on every vantage point. How did they know we were arriving and who do they think we are? A marquee has been erected in the grounds of the prison and No! – I can hardly believe it –an actual red carpet stretches from the point where our car stops as far as my half-mast eyes can see, inside the marquee. I feel hysterical inside. I had just woken after wallowing in an orgy of self pity when all these people had been working and waiting to see those worthy of such preparations. Sun-glasses must go on to protect the slits and to hide the shame of weakness.

Edging the red carpet a guard of honour stand to attention, immaculate in khaki uniforms, perfectly wound turbans and moustaches glistening. A queenly walk is called for, measured steps along the red carpet, smiles and nods, as photographers have their field day.

Inside the tent, around a horse-shoe of desks sit the Superintendents and other invitees, each one to be named and presented on my way to the lectern.

This is the moment when the driving force that powers the words, takes over. I cannot believe my own ears when a strong voice, enunciating clearly, speaking slowly yet with authority makes its presence felt. That is it. It has been happening gradually and I have not given credence to it. Even though my physical body is loosing power, words seem to have a life of their own and the ability to project a stream of intelligent vitality. What is the subject focus for today? It no longer matters unduly. Whatever is needed will be said.

It is over. I am led out by the ever attentive Miss Keith to the applause of these worthy men. The experience has been both exhilarating and exhausting. The I.G. can see I am flagging. We will go straight home. Miles speed by and I can think only of rest and quietness to engage with this maelstrom of thoughts of the dying body and the living words.

Nods of greeting are enough. I retire straight to bed. No sooner have I fallen into what I consider to be a well-deserved sleep, than visitors arrive. I am raised to greet them feeling like Lazarus. These are the delightful relatives of the I.G. who I had met in Delhi. Uncleji is small, plump and jolly. He is to act as head cook for our evening meal. Sheshi arrives home to hugging and thumping. A photographer has been hired with freedom to follow us around the house catching us in all manner of poses and activities. He even photographs the empty dinner plates to show we have enjoyed Uncleji's cooking! The young ones keep changing their clothes for fun and I am swept along from one group to another. At last the photographer leaves and the dancing begins, working up into a crescendo of noise and movement as I gyrate my remaining moveable parts with some trepidation but it is Uncleji in his dhoti who takes the prize for dancer of the evening.

Sheshi creeps in beside me but tonight but we are both too tired for words of any kind. Sleep brings respite from the lurking ghoulish thoughts of future tomorrows.

15. The Prodigal Son

Sunday 20th November

It is Sheshi who bathes my eyes this morning, stuck fast again. It is a scary feeling not to see the light on waking. Even scarier are the pains in my hands and wrists. Sheshi is studying medicine. She is both interested and concerned and phones a doctor friend for advice. He recommends aspirin in large doses. My luggage has to be sorted as there is opportunity for Mohinder to leave my growing bags of gifts in Delhi for my collection later. Today I am moving on again; more strangers, more effort and I am anxious. The telephone rings. It is to tell me that Joginder Singh's wife is sick and he cannot collect me for village visiting today. He will come for me tomorrow. I feel only relief.

It is as pleasant as a summer Sunday at home, sitting in the garden watching the children playing, learning the Indian version of card games. Later under the shady trees of the Rose Gardens, we sit on the crisp dry grass and sing while Uncleji's sons tap rhythmic accompaniments on my purse and notebook, slapping and flicking. I am astonished at the sounds my belongings can make in such imaginative hands. A round to the roller skating rink completes a perfect, relaxing day before we return for a mashed potato and tuna supper, concocted to my simple recipe. There is so much happy laughter it is a joy not to have missed today.

The mood swings as the dancing begins to Sheshi's records: 'Breaking up is hard to do' and Rod Stewart's 'I'm leaving on a jet plane' and an edge of sadness touches us all. Mohinder is the one who senses the inner loneliness that I suddenly feel and suggests we sit in the moonlit garden and talk awhile. It is two o'clock before sleep claims us.

Monday 21st November

At 4am the household is alive again, everyone as fresh as daisies. Uncleji and family are leaving and naturally must say their goodbyes in person. I had suggested that they might whisper in my ear but they must have thought I was joking. After fond farewells at my bedside, I turn my face into the pillow. Half an hour later it is the turn of Mohinder and the I.G. to pay their respects before leaving for Delhi to collect the I.G.'s entry certificates for Mohinder's December wedding. There are a few more fleeting dozes between having my luggage collected and being brought the newspapers and at six o'clock bed tea. It is a fragmented start to the day, which does not improve. The I.G. has left instructions. When I rise and bathe Surrinder will attend to my breakfast and Mr Kotish the Assistant I.G. of Prisons, is to arrange transport to the villages if Joginder Singh does not arrive. The I.G. leaves nothing to chance, perhaps that is why he is an I.G.

All instructions are followed, Surrinder takes his mother to hospital and I fall asleep, pen in hand. At two o'clock I wake to discover Joginder had not arrived as planned at 12.30. We need the time to find the way to these often hidden corners and with dusk falling around 6pm and tracks that peter out to nowhere, we need our hours of daylight. Worried by the delay, I decide to test the I.G's contingency plan. Mr. Kotish is detected somewhere other than his office. My call is inconvenient. 'I will arrange for your journey tomorrow' is his short response and I can think of no other option but to sit and wait.

At 3.30 Joginder arrives in his car, plus Miss Keith and Mitou, a driver, his wife and two daughters who have all been making a round of visits and taking refreshments while my anxieties were building up. I am not too okay about this and wonder if it shows when, in the same breath of greeting them, I remind them of the time constraints of our visits to the villages. There is consternation. We leave in haste but do not go 'straight'.

Joginder's wife, Manjit has a sore rash covering her back, side and legs. Next stop is Miss Keith's house for creams. When we reload I realise that both village visits will not be possible before dark. One must be postponed but we should be able to make it to Nangal Kalan. I am squeezed in the back with three women plus Mitou, leaving the two men and younger daughter in the front. I am in the worst possible position for travelling, unable to move my limbs, tense and nervous as Mitou clambers over laps, restlessly bumping my knee sending shock waves around my body. We stop for medicines, nuts, sugar cane and pineapple juice, many times asking our way, but cannot locate the village. I press them onwards and before we know it we are enveloped in a grey blanket, as dusk seems to drop out of the sky. We cannot find Kalan. We must find it. I dare not return without making this visit. I gave a promise over a plastic topped table in the prison visiting room, heads bent, talking like conspirators, drawing a map while sharp eyed officers watch curiously at the intensity of our conversation.

Davinder Singh is serving a life sentence for murder. Now aged twenty-three he has been inside for nearly three years. Maybe he struck the blow that killed a man and may be he did not. He agrees he was there with a relative when there was a fight and a man was knifed. Both pleaded innocent and both are serving life sentences.

Davinder came to England aged fourteen after a parting promise to his parents that he would return within five years. Never having seen a white person before he left his village, he was overwhelmed by the freedom and material pleasures of the west, and five years passed quickly, too quickly. Overrunning his return by only a few months he found himself no longer free to make the choice. Whatever else haunts him he finds no peace in the knowledge that he betrayed his parent's trust. In his eyes his parents, in their mid-fifties, are already old and still work the land, living out a nightmare of waiting. I am to explain our prison system to them, ensure them of his good health, his love for them and his determination to return. 'Lifers' sentences are reviewed after four years. There are so many factors to take into account that no one person can foretell the outcome, but in this case a realistic guess would be that he would serve six to seven years. It is reasonable to give hope along these lines.

Then it happens. Looming up out of the darkness is a house built right in the middle of the roadway as it tries to enter Nangal Kalan. I have it scrawled on my map. There is a way round it. We have to find the tube well at the other end of the village. Two young men have seen our headlights. Two more bodies pile in to direct us down rutted narrow streets and bring us to a stop outside huge gates, securely padlocked and bolted like a fortress. Our banging and thumping echoes in the stillness. It is 6.30pm. All households are in bed and the village is in total darkness, not even a candle flickers. Inside there is scuffling, as bolts are drawn and Davinder's father stands impassively, showing not a trace of surprise although he could not possibly have known we would descend that night.

I uncurl from the back seat, pass the bullock sheds, and there is Davinder's mother who, without hesitation, takes me in her arms. Everyone is tumbling out of the car to take refreshments. Everyone talks at once. It is chaotic. Davinder's father is yet another who has served in the British army and speaks some English, though he is a little shy and his English rusty. I take him aside and encourage him to communicate, as there is some serious talking to be done. As soon as Miss Keith and the mother join us we can unravel the stories from both sides. Theirs is vitally important to me.

The second man, imprisoned on the same charge, is a relative of Davinder's mother and the family has inside information on the circumstances that broke out into violence. Whichever of these two had struck the blow that killed a man, it would be a disgrace to the whole family, and yet they tell me that they are greatly relieved they do not carry the higher portion of guilt, as their son was neither the instigator nor the holder of the knife. This matches my own information gained from other sources. How long Davinder will serve in prison is critical for them. It is their responsibility to arrange a good marriage, they have a girl in mind and the farm will be theirs to run one day. They want to hear about life in a British jail. I can honestly tell them that their son is safe. He is well liked and respected and he sticks to his motto 'keep fit; eat well; co-operate; live in the present for the future; and pray often'. His prowess at sports has been useful as he has been allocated to the gym to assist in the physical training regime, a job that suits him well. Although he had made an application for a chapatti pan it had been refused, so he had improvised by making weird shaped chapattis in a pan with curled edges. It is these small cameos that bring their son back into their lives as the young vibrant person that they knew him to be. They are now fortified in the knowledge their son is strong in spirit and will return as soon as he is able.

This is good and fertile farmland that must be worked to keep it productive. To help with the work they had taken a boy into their home, a distant relative whose father had gone abroad and left him. Davinder had told me 'he's only a kid, just another mouth to feed. He goes to school but is not very bright. He is supposed to be there to help my parents, but I don't think he's much use.' I had wondered whether Davinder envied, even maybe resented this boy, thinking he may be usurped by him. But the boy is here, squatting in a corner, silently amazed at this invasion and making no move to be part of it. In contrast to Davinder's maturity and fine physique, this boy is puny and underdeveloped. He is no usurper.

Their parting gift is a tasselled tablecloth. All I have given is words and yet they too have had a value beyond price. I leave feeling so very sorry that I cannot stay in this village for a while with these good people and explore the places marked by squiggly lines on the map. At least we had found them. That has to be enough.

We have talked late, yet still we see work going on in the fields. Red-gold flames from bonfires pierce the darkness silhouetting the carts being loaded ready for the grain market next day. I am in a quiet mood as we drive on through wild desolate terrain, reflecting on the sadness, which overshadows the lives of generations. How far the ripples of crime can reach. It is 9.30pm before we reach Jullunder. Miss Keith invites everyone in and prepares a meal. I eat, but my leg has not weathered the journey well and there is agreement that I would best be served by staying in my old familiar bedroom. Joginder will return to collect me tomorrow. I am grateful. It is a bad night of mosquitoes and nightmares as I dream my home and all my furniture has been sold while I have been away.

16.A Temple Exit

22nd November Tuesday

There are decisions to be made so I lie awake trying to make them, but first must take stock of a few home truths. My eyes have been running now for a week. Small everyday chores of hygiene are becoming increasingly difficult, such as bending down to sponge the dust grained feet and pulsating toes. Turning taps, pressing toothpaste tubes, brushing my hair have become operations needing thoughtful innovations or direct help. My hands feel leaden, as if they are hung with heavy weights, just lifting them to head height requires strength and willpower, only to find that the hairbrush slides ineffectively across the slippery hair. This loss of power and pressure is a strange and unpleasant sensation but it is the increasing heaviness that I fear could eventually immobilise me.

Today is my last day of the tour in India, which I plan to spend in Katapur. A plane ticket to Kashmir is burning a hole in my wallet but dare I use it? My prize to myself is meant to be a week's holiday, maybe on a houseboat, to enjoy the beauty of Shrinagar whilst reflecting on the material I have gathered and how best to present it on return. I have no connections in Kashmir and it seems madness to set off into the unknown in this worsening state. There are seventeen days left before lift off. I must decide how best to use them. There has to be something more than survival. The question is, is it Pakistan? At least I have an address in Lahore, the uncle and aunt of a colleague who had told me he would alert them to the possibility of a visit, if I made it that far. The Muslims of Pakistan are another cultural world that could be usefully explored and enjoyed. I have convinced myself. Pakistan it is to be and Joginder, I have no doubt, will give me the information I need as to how to cross the border. It has been a thoughtful start to the day, now all I have to do is hold myself together.

Over breakfast the new plan is tested on Miss Keith. It passes. She makes the suggestion of a visit to a hospital in Lahore, which makes sense. Joginder arrives and Miss Keith explains my situation. He responds with practical concern. We will go straight to his shop to use the telephone and make note of trains across the border. Miss Keith and Mitou will spend the day at his home and be returned in the evening. It works out. There is a train at 8.15am next day from Amritsar. Heads together, they plan the most perfect exit for me that they could devise. We are to set out at 4am to visit the Golden Temple at dawn to see the sun rise over the lake. I pray sincerely that my body will respond. The sluggish heaviness is still taking hold. I can feel it. One day I may wake to find I cannot move – please let it not be tomorrow.

Many people have gathered at Joginder's home. The first reception committee is of the males and takes place in the best lounge. No-one is able to speak English and Miss Keith has much to tell them. As they listen intently to her recounting our adventures, I feel my mind slipping and then the body follows suit. Unable to hold it upright, I hear myself muttering that I need to lie down. Retiring in a roomful of people is not behaviour that I approve of at all, but the world recedes and I slip down into the darkness. Taking my 'doze' in their stride, they are still talking when I am woken by a buzzing horse fly. They do not know this is not a natural nap, but I know. This is some devilish process at work that they can do nothing about even if they knew, so best not draw attention to it. I sit up ready for the entry of the ladies.

Miss Keith holds the floor and I sit, uncomfortable with being the object of conversation yet not involved. They ask if I would like a chair outside in the sun but I do not dare accept for fear of slipping off it so I suggest a gentle stroll as a means of ensuring I stay upright. Four people are selected to escort me to the nearby Gurdwara, where I make a ridiculous spectacle of myself in my efforts to pay my respects to the Holy Book. I cannot kneel, as my knee does not bend, so I prostrate myself and then cannot get up, as my wrists will not support my weight. Hands haul me to my feet and guide me up to the roof. The reward is a magnificent view of Katapur, worth every creaking moment. I drink it all in and my embarrassment dissipates as we move at my snail's pace through the bazaar until I tell them it is enough.

Everything has been cooked to Miss Keith's instructions and food fortifies me sufficiently to make a round of the house. Various family units share a tall old house in which possessions are stacked, walls to ceiling. Joginder shares a tiny room with his wife and daughters. They show me pictures of their baby son who 'took sick and died' speaking of him with ease as a member of their family whose joyful presence has left them with loving memories. The loss had been great, as he was their only son.

Miss Keith is escorted back home. The young people, who have been waiting for me to be left unguarded, descend as soon as the adults leave. Now every detail of my dress and contents of my bag need to be examined and discussed. I understand how interesting this is for them and am in a patient mood. They are learning English at school and are keen to test it. In exchange I offer to test my Punjabi, creating the laughter that always lightens the pressure of communication.

We move on to family photographs next, mine and theirs. Bit by bit I am able to fit together the pieces of an amazing jigsaw. The elders of this household are the grandparents who have six sons and five daughters. All six sons remain living in the family home, three with their wives. The three younger sons, still at school, are a part of this group, hence are the uncles of some of the others. Joginder is the eldest son, a responsible position, as he will become head of the household on the death of his father. Unmarried daughters also still live at home.

We are now to be entertained with television. They suggest I lie on the couch with as many as can get on either side. It is very homely. More people bring in chairs; sit on the floor and latecomers crane their necks in the doorway as a Hindi movie plays out its dramas. I need sleep, but at 10.30pm everyone moves out to a laden supper table covered in flies. Even brushing a hand to and fro doesn't move them; they simply sit on the hand! All I can manage is a slice of bread and jam before my public ablutions in the courtyard. My clumsiness is noticeable. At last I reach the divan. Spring based, yellow velvet cover, easy to snuggle down in this inviting cosy corner. But not for long! It is of course, entirely incorrect to leave me alone and a young lady is to be my night companion, however she too has a companion and they sit together chatting the night away. People... people... how I need them so and yet ache for space and silence.

Wednesday 23rd November

There is a shower! At 4am I am led into a brick windowless cubicle. Water spurts from a pipe high in the wall. It is beyond my reach and the force is so great that it hits the opposite wall, falling in ice cold cascades. It would knock me sideways to stand under it so I catch some trickles in a tin jug and splash my face without enthusiasm.

There are eight in today's party, in one car. Meeting a procession carrying candles and waving flags seems oddly mysterious in the half-light. After that I see very little on the two hour drive as I am cold and huddle in my corner with a shawl around my face. Familiar now with the procedure at the entrance to the Golden Temple I slip off my sandals but am unprepared for the shock waves of pain as my swollen soles step onto the cold marble. The pain which shoots up my leg meets the pain forking downwards from the knee as I struggle to unlock it after two hours in a bent position. My nails dig into my palms as I feel the blood draining from my face. They are laughing. It is not meant unkindly. They see only the reaction to the coldness on soft white western feet. There are only a few hundred people entering the grounds. The atmosphere is quiet and calm, a perfect place to start the day, *any* day. But this is also an ending and an exit. Surely I can do no more work in India. My body tells me it must be so.

The way ahead is hazardous. A strip of roughly woven coconut matting surrounds the lake. On either side is the freezing cold marble. I step onto the matting but my soles protest so urgently that it has to be the marble. I can see that men are bathing, dipping down under the water around the edge of the lake. There is an area allocated for females screened off from public view. Our females all intend to bathe and invite me to join them. I understand it would be a great honour to bathe in this holy water and yet I cannot do it. They tell me my white body would look lovely against the brown of the water. In good physical shape and the heat of the day I could have been persuaded, but not now. It is too early in the day and too late for my body. I find a corner and watch the women's ritual. Manjit is the only one who does not fully immerse herself. Her skin complaint is severe and she kneels, splashing water over the sore reddened patches. The tank is only cleaned out every fifty years, just once in anyone's lifetime yet so many who are sick and diseased come daily to bathe hoping for a cure or easement from pain.

We meet up with the men. Joginder has been bathing and his beard is free flowing. I watch carefully as he rewinds it and places it back in the fine hairnet which anchors it firmly under his chin. The main temple (the Harimandir) rises from an island in the centre of the sacred pool. Due to the queue to enter and time spent bathing there is no time to cross the two hundred foot marble causeway. In a way I am glad. My need now is to be placed on a train and sent packing! Where did the dawn go? I never did see the sun rise over the lake.

Joginder purchases a ticket for me in a private upper class compartment, with a sleeping berth and toilet. He changes currency, provides tea and cakes, and when I am installed passes nuts, fruit, newspapers and magazines and a ring to remember them by through the widow. They think of everything!

17. A Tasselled World

Thursday 24th November

I am alone again, heading for an unfamiliar country. The emotional exhaustion even greater than the day I left home, twenty three days and a lifetime ago. I know there is no one ahead preparing a welcome and feel fatalistically tired. What will be will be. Why should I doubt? At every step along this journey there have been people who have upheld me. But that was India. What will Pakistan offer, I wonder?

It's an hour's ride to Akari, the border post, where passengers all alight to fill in forms. Officials head for my carriage. Keeping me separate from the crowd they courteously examine my luggage, passport, and tape recorder. As soon as they deduce that I am on government business the station master calls for action stations. Railway police wearing laceless pumps and carrying antiquated rifles quickly form a dishevelled guard of honour for a photograph session. The Customs Officer steps forward in shorts, carrying a well pressed uniform and the crowd wait passively while he dresses to perfection before their eyes. My escort returns me to the carriage leaving me with a luggage porter. I can see it will take a long time to process all the other passengers so I decide to use this available help in re-packing my bulging bags. He folds expertly and with a great deal more patience than I have had lately. A 'surplus to requirements' pile grows on the seat. I indicate that I would like him to be the recipient and pay him handsomely for his services. He sits down on the seat staring at the goods, the money and me. I tell him I would like him to take the items home to his family and they disappear under his tatty tunic. It has been a good border crossing.

Hearing raised voices I look along the platform to see three white faces. Three Canadians who are being reprimanded by the officials for 'bad habits' cannot understand what they have done wrong. As I watch it is made abundantly clear. They are taken to stand in front of a trough where they would have been expected to expectorate and are shown how to do it! Using handkerchiefs are 'bad habits'. They are suitably apologetic. I think of my nearly empty carton of paper handkerchiefs and the number of times I have blown the dust out of my nose and wonder how many people I have offended. What else have I done that is seen as 'bad habits'? It is a sobering thought.

At Lahore I almost slip out swiftly until when asked to declare how much money I am carrying I answer 'two hundred rupees'. He tells me the ration is twenty. I remain unruffled and tell him that had I known of this restriction I would not have made this error but he must deal with me according to regulations. He says he does not wish to offend or cause any inconvenience, and waves me through. I have committed my first offence in Pakistan and must learn the ropes quickly. There is no I.G. to bail me out here.

My luggage is in place in a scooter but the driver cannot understand my instructions. An English-speaking student comes to my rescue and asks if he can be of service. I show him my address in New Muslim Town, which is exactly where he tells me he is heading. So the magic is still working, helpers are in position. I have an escort. Both the student and Lahore are a delight as he points out landmarks and the town looks most inviting.

New Muslim Town is an architect designed estate in the 'highly expensive' bracket. My luggage is heaved out onto the pavement in front of an extensive bungalow and a servant appears at the gate. The student asks if it is the home of Mr. and Mrs. Q. my prospective hosts. It is, but they are not at home. This is a national holiday and they will be away until Saturday. What a bombshell! It is only Wednesday. I will have to find a hotel. Wrong! The student and the servant, deep in conversation in Urdu, have other ideas. The servant will accompany me to where the family is spending their holiday. It will be a five-hour journey by bus. This, I am certain, would be far too great an imposition in any culture and on my fast failing body. I decline this solution. Resolution number two is put forward. The servant's son is a neighbour's houseboy and feels sure that family would like to have me as a houseguest. I am astonished and dubious but people are gathering around us and I do not want to be at the centre of a crowd. Out of nowhere the servant's son appears, takes in the situation, speeds across the road and around the back of an equally large and imposing bungalow. Minutes later he reappears in the front doorway smiling hugely and beckons me in. His father is pleased, the student is pleased, the scooterman is pleased with his payment and I enter a stranger's house.

My hostess is as warm and welcoming as if she had been waiting for me. Having no common language, her smiles and her comfortable chair are all that I need. Over refreshments of tea and biscuits, I interpret her graphic mimes to mean that I am welcome to stay in her home.

My bedroom is just like a Hollywood movie set. The décor is red and gold with a four poster bed in pride of place. The canopy is lavishly decorated with golden tinsel and the bed cover is encrusted with embroidery worked with golden thread. I stand at the bedside in utter amazement. My hostess, Jasmail, has sent for two young relatives who speak English. Standing in the golden bower I introduce myself and explain my predicament. The young man replies 'This is your home'. It is exactly as it had been on arrival at Uncle Pritam's in Delhi, even to the same words. I learn that Jasmail does not know the Q. family but this is not important, as she is delighted to have the opportunity to share her home with me. I feel overcome with their kindness, relief and fatigue. They reflect that I am looking exhausted and recommend bed rest. Turning back the ornate coverlet they tuck it around me as I sink into softness. The last thing I hear is English music coming from a tape recorder placed beside my bed.

It is dusk when I awake to a golden tinsel and tasselled world. They are there, thinking for me, suggesting I might like to bathe. I agree. It is a real bath with taps! My excitement is short-lived. While I have slept in state, my body has taken a lurch for the worse. The fiery pain encircles my wrists. Any twisting movement sends the shock waves shooting into fingers and up to the elbows. The taps do not move. I call for help and the delicious water gives some moments of respite but dressing is an ordeal. Maybe it is worth it as I am complimented by my appearance when I emerge, but that only goes to show what a sight I must have looked on arrival.

The four of us sit together sharing information and talking politics. Mrs.J's husband is a bank manager in Duboi. They consider themselves to be amongst the richer families in Pakistan. They have three huge televisions, the kitchen is like a modern show home and deep pile red carpets stretch across the vast expanses of floor. How glad I am to be on the red carpet this time! The two young people are brother and sister; both engaged to be married and are keen to talk about their prospective partners and to give their political views. They see themselves as pioneers of a young generation fighting for recognition but say the generation gap is huge.

The young people leave and I discover Jasmail has a baby, Jimmy, who is brought to join us as we lie together on a big double bed watching western programmes. Wonder Dog and Bionic Woman are interspersed with Indian dancing and singing, quite a feat of integration! Supper of spicy chops and rice is served which I decline in favour of toast and dried apricots. The Q. family servant arrives with a message. The family has been contacted. They will return on Friday, until then every care is to be taken of me and arrangements will be made to send a doctor to visit me.

Bed is a haven and it seems a crime to have nightmares in such a place but I dream that my family have left home and I do not know where they have gone. In reality it is the reverse. I am the one who has left and even I do not know where I am all of the time.

Friday 25th November

At least there is time on waking to make myself respectable before breakfast of a fried egg and a decoratively iced birthday cake, which has to be by-passed. The doctor is due at 10am, but does not appear. To fill in waiting time I wedge my elbows on a cushion to write a few letters and catch up with my journal. Somehow I convey to Jasmail that I need to visit a hospital for tests and more medication as mine has almost run out. She instructs a male servant to accompany me to the United Christian Hospital in Lahore and I am pleased to have taken a positive step.

The hospital is a large modern building with a reception office. I ask to see a bone specialist, am given the name of Dr. Chandra and am directed to his rooms. He is not present but I am told I may visit him at his home behind the hospital. We trail together across the hospital grounds, the servant insistent on carrying my handbag, and make it to the right house. He is there, a small man with a neat moustache. He will attend me at 3 o'clock precisely in his rooms. We trail back again. People are already crowding into the waiting area and I notice that they buy tickets as they arrive, so I step up to the desk and buy a ticket. I am given no choice. My ticket is fifty rupees allowing me to be dealt with first. The doctor is half an hour late. No-one speaks to me at all nor do they seem surprised when I am led in first.

Mr.Chandra listens intently, asking relevant questions. Tests are essential. X-rays will be taken to see if there has been bone damage, then blood and urine. There will be five tests in all and I am to return in five days for results. FIVE DAYS! Five precious days to be spent waiting for a verdict. He gives me a ticket for a prescription, the X-ray department costs out the prices from a printed list and I am sent creeping down the corridor to pay my dues of another fifty eight rupees. The tiredness is coming now in swathes. Pathology costs their tests at 117rupees. I do not have enough money. It is a holiday and banks are shut. I must have the tests and ask firmly for the Head Cashier. He is sent for. I offer to deposit a traveller's cheque with him. He smiles and tells me to pay next week when I collect the results. We return to Pathology, the servant sitting beside me, for the blood siphoning, but luckily I am allowed to produce urine in private. Next as I am subjected to tests on various other parts I realise that the servant knew the time would come when I wouldn't be able to hold onto my handbag. He was right; there were moments that I could hardly hold onto my sanity. He fetches my prescription and organises our return, proving himself invaluable.

Jasmail produces two older children who jiggle baby Jimmy and as they all pile into the T.V bed for their evening's entertainment I call it a day, an interminable day that will last until next Tuesday.

Friday 25th November

The effect of the pills is disheartening. There is bulging swelling behind the knee and contractions are pulling my fingers inwards. My toes are ugly, knobbly and deeply purpled. I feel trapped, restless and pig-headed. I just have to get out! I know perfectly well that I feel this way because I want to escape from this disaster invading me, to get out of this body before it disintegrates further, but as I have no choice in the matter I just have to go out of the door. Jasmail simply has me followed by two servants who take the initiative. The woman takes my left hand, while the boy removes my handbag. I am discovering to my cost that walking today is worse than yesterday. Pressure of stepping forward on the right foot causes spasms of pain to fan out from the bulbous knee.

It turns out that my escorts are the wife and son of the servant/gardener of the Q. family, who had been so helpful to me on arrival. Seeing that I am not really going anywhere they ask if I would like to step over the road to see where they live. It is a brick built room, about the size of a garage, at the side of the bungalow, packed solid with beds, pots and utensils. I am shown how they bring out the beds at night to sleep on the veranda. They have six children, the eldest is my escort, aged fourteen. Then they showed me something I had not expected to see. Guiding me to the window of the bungalow they point to a letter separately placed on a table holding a pile of post. It is addressed to me. A link from home is the anti-dote I need and a miracle in itself. However did Derek know to send a letter here when I should by rights be in Kashmir? Whatever the content may reveal, its appearance is enough to quell the morning's agitation. They guide me safely home and back to bed.

The news on waking is that the Q. family is home. Servants help me to pack and troop with me over the road. As I come face to face with my hosts I realise that they have not the faintest notion of who I am. No relation has informed them that they are to receive a guest. There is nothing to commend me to them whatsoever. How many times have I opened my own front door to people nearing the end of their tether, bruised and battered, physically and mentally? Now, I am one of *them*, unable to sell myself because my image is unpresentable, unable to articulate my need, dependent on others perceiving it, as so many had. I just stand there, beaten by weakness and self-pity. My speech is disjointed, incoherent. I have information stored, which I know could prove my identity and my connection to their relative but in my confusion I cannot reach it. What is more it is likely that this is my fault as I have arrived a week earlier than intended. They tell me it is of no consequence and I am welcome to share their home. It is of great consequence to me and if I had been fit enough I would have retreated at that moment. But I am reaching rock bottom and it is easier to let myself be led into a spacious airy room and helped into another double bed, its snow-white pillow soon soaked with scalding tears. The Q. family are struggling to piece together my fragments of information. They do not recognise the name I had given of the man I say is their nephew. While I sleep they realise I have given them a western derivative of his name. Of course they know who he is, his instruction to care for me is unnecessary.

Mrs.Q. is one of the most beautiful women I have ever seen and her two daughters are replicas of her mother. They have a list of social engagements during the next four days. I am welcome to accompany them. My clothes are crumpled, not to mention my face and body. It would be ridiculous to attempt to hold my own in a social round but they do not appreciate the handicap of this insidious disease. I am beginning to have nauseating thoughts, creating macabre images of what is happening inside me, beginning to create a fantasy 'what if' scenario. What if this is not arthritis but something else even more sinister? Imagination is having a field day.

This evening I am to accompany the family to a wedding eve celebration at the home of the bride. I cannot find the words to express my reservations about moving out of my newly found bed. Mrs.Q. replies that it is understandable that I am tired and must rest. She will lend me suitable clothes and we will go. I rest. Mrs.Q. brings in a selection of clothes and suggests a silk salwar chemise in soft rose pink. The effort of arranging unfamiliar clothes is unbearable, particularly lifting legs to get into trousers. I prop myself against a wardrobe, hands shaking with the effort, the hairbrush slips from my grasp, I cannot bend to pick it up, the room is swaying – or is it me? I am a liability to take anywhere. Why ever do they want to bother?

The evening swirls around me and I know I am behaving strangely, feeling as if I am partly anaesthetised. By now I realise I am amongst some of Pakistan's most influential and wealthy families. Mrs.Q. tells the assembly of my unseemly arrival and after their good-natured laughter important matters take their attention. In my right mind all of this would be fascinating. In my disassociated state it is an ordeal. Weddings draw together old friends and distant relatives from all parts of Pakistan. Loving reunions take place, memories are recalled and news given. I am a bystander, an observer too tired to observe.

We move on to the bride's house. It is sumptuous. A canopy covers a courtyard, encircled by fairy lights. I am led to a pile of red velvet cushions. Unable to sink down gracefully, I arrange my pink pantalooned legs in an ungainly pose. The bride's friends make a group one side of the room and the groom's on the other. Each group sings in turn accompanied by pulsating drum beats. When food is served in the marquee I prop myself against a tent pole and take a few spoons of rice. A few guests stop and speak but my weak responses do not engage them and they move on. Then the rituals begin. The bride arrives, veiled and swathed in yellow chiffon with golden trimmings. Money is waved around her head before being presented, pinches of sweet stuffs are placed in her mouth and photographers bustle to catch every moment. There is more singing and the same ceremony for the groom. These are vibrant young people who seem very pleased to be joining together. It is a feast for the eyes and the heart amongst these rich, powerful and beautiful people yet all I can think of is oblivion. We return home by car. Mrs.Q. is indefatigable and goes out again to a party. I stumble to the bedroom, find I am unable to undo the zip at the back of my chemise or turn on the taps or spread the heavy quilt. Hunching unwashed under a lump of quilt in Mrs.Q's silken clothes, I move into the horrors of the night.

18.Jeopardy

Saturday 26th November

I am scared. My right leg has sort of curled up backwards. It seems to have been pulled up by something contracting at the back of the knee. I can only reach the floor with the tip of my big toe. The ankles have begun the bulbous swellings and my wrists are setting, stiff and unturnable. I have to return to hospital. How can I wait to discover what will corkscrew between now and Tuesday?

Mrs.Q comes to call on me for breakfast and supports me as I slide one legged along the polished hallway. Trying to control my pulsating anxiety, I pronounce firmly and politely that it is essential I get to hospital. Mr.Q. is leaving for work right away in the car. There is no transport available. Mrs. Q's firmness and politeness is equal to my own as she regrets it is not at all possible to arrange such a journey. Brooding in my room, the feeling of being trapped overtakes me again. There is something about this word that is getting to me. How often have I tried to ease men through the suffering of the shock of their loss of freedom, which can affect mind, body and even the spirit to survive. This seems to be what is happening to me. I am losing my freedom of thought, mobility and actions. My body is encasing me in the limitations the pain imposes; mind is turning inwards and the walls, even with their tassels and drapes may as well be those of a fortress. Depression, self-pity, guilt and fear, all immobilisers, are paralysing me, not just a random germ. I have to control whatever is controllable.

The telephone, a lifeline if I can master it, is in the lounge and Mrs.Q is taking refreshments with her friends. Nodding my respects I pick up the telephone, find the number of the hospital, make the call and ask for Dr. Chandra. He is too busy to take calls. The ladies are making ready to leave. I ask if they will kindly deposit me at the hospital. They agree without discussion as to why. I want only to be deposited at the gate thinking that it might be a good idea to be admitted if they will take me. But just on this short journey my leg has drawn up still further. Unable to walk I am propped up against a fence, undignified and embarrassing to us all. Mrs.Q goes into the hospital to ask the way to Dr. Chandra's consulting room. I am conscious of the ladies waiting in the car in the heat of the morning. She returns to support me to his door. Holding their illnesses, swarms of people wait with dejected resignation for a non-existent doctor. He has gone home with a sore throat. No one else can help me, as I am his patient. Mrs.Q. has no suggestions to make. She knows the system. That is how it is. I will not accept it has to be so. In my book Saturday must become Tuesday or by then I could be deformed in both legs, or anywhere else! The doctor's patients will sit, waiting for his return today, tomorrow, sometime. I do not even hesitate. I know where the doctor lives and Mrs.Q. supports me as I direct the way.

He is there. He has an English wife. No doubt he understands the stubborn nature of the English when the chips are right down. He smiles and is compassionate. Mrs.Q. may leave me in his care and is asked to return to collect me later in the day. He takes me straight into the hospital. I do not notice whether he has a sore throat.

Results of the tests must be obtained immediately. The system works. They have already been completed and arrive to order. Firstly we sit and study the X-rays together. Negative! No bone damage. The relief is inexpressible. At least I have bones intact. Next comes the acidity test for gout. Negative again. Two out of two! So the first diagnosis in Jullunder City Hospital was wrong. The blood tests are positive and there is no contest. It is arthritis, positively arthritis, and I have had a relapse. I agree that I feel that I have. He prescribes large doses of steroids, which he tells me are forty times stronger than the tablets I have been taking. My case is severe and acute. He wishes to admit me to hospital forthwith. I am being offered help that I sorely need yet find I cannot accept it for fear of the unknown, unfamiliar and unacceptable. But what's more I have this urgent impulse today to be in control of my own destiny. There are no words to explain the churning inside me as I shake my head wordlessly.

Dr. Chandra is a bone specialist and as my bones are intact he suggests that what I now need is a physician. I agree and a physician is found. This good man takes me into his office and again we go over all the results of the tests together, he examines me physically, taking time and care, then talks gently and knowledgeably about the different types of arthritic conditions and the way they manifest.

'Arthritis is a disease of the joints, when morbid changes occur in the joint membrane surrounding the joint tissues, cartilage and bones, resulting in deformity and limitation of movements of the affected joints and muscular wasting. The symptoms of different types are similar. The onset is usually acute and is associated with a rise in temperature. Several joints are affected; they swell and are painful at night. The joints most commonly affected in order of frequency are hands and feet, ankles, knees, jaw and neck.'

I log the 'jaw and neck' with apprehension. There is more to come. From his professional observations the physician believes this is not rheumatoid arthritis but **acute polyarthritis.** 'Acute' means sudden onset and 'poly', multiple, affecting a number of joints. He cannot specify the cause other than the possibility of a rogue germ lodging in my system. My lurid descriptions of bowel activity interest him as he weighs up whether it could be a cause; a catalyst or a red herring. Nothing is exactly certain in medicine, says my honest doctor, confessing that much is conjecture yet adding thoughtfully that always there is hope. Polyarthritis has a chance of being reversible. It may take a long time, but it is beatable..... well sometimes. Fortified with a dose of hope, I am ready to learn the basics of how to cope. He draws up a programme for me of how to administer my own drugs on a sliding reduction scale. Rest is imperative to avoid the risk of a germ circulating around my system.

'I have to return to Delhi, should I begin to travel there straight away?'

'No. It is not wise to travel such a way.'

'Is another relapse likely?'

'This disease is unpredictable. Take the drugs, rest, watch and wait.'

He writes a report for my boss and one to take to my doctor when I reach home, detailing the tests, diagnosis and treatment. He has been my saving grace. Mrs. Q. arrives to take me home. I tell her the results and she responds,

'You must stay and take complete rest'.

Now I can lie peacefully in the garden and wave as the family leaves to attend another wedding. Writing to my boss in a spidery hand I try to disguise with humour the desolation that is in me. Hope is temporarily buried under the realisation that all that I love is in jeopardy.

Sunday 27th November

Telling Mrs. Q that I will stay in bed all day, I read and think, pain dulled by the large doses of drugs. My clothes are washed and a bath is run at mid-day. The effort is worthwhile it is so refreshing. Lying in the garden passing time with the servants would have been idyllic if I was lying there by choice.

In the evening Mr. and Mrs. Q. are out and their eldest daughter joins me for supper to talk of life in England where her brother has been studying for the last two years. She sounds a little envious, wanting to see something of the world before marriage. Her social position calls for her to learn to be a gracious hostess and her college course in Home Economics does not interest her greatly. She would have preferred a career in medicine but that is not a suitable choice for her. Her younger sister studies relentlessly every night as examinations approach. She too has ambitions of a career. I have the career. All I want is not to lose it.

Monday 28th November

It is exciting. The ball of my foot reaches the floor. A friend of Mrs.Q's arrives and I inveigle a lift with her to post my letters. Conversation flows and, as rapport builds between us on this short journey, I am delighted to hear her inviting me to stay in her home in Rawlpindi, the very location I had so wanted to visit. She has visited England many times and assures me she has all the amenities I need for my recovery. Warmed by her kindness and invigorated by my own improvement, I feel moved to accept, however caution prompts me to discover whether I can stay upright without any relapse and we put the invitation on hold. At last I find my way into a bank, cash some traveller's cheques and as I make slow progress to the post office a cultured old gentleman stops and asks if he may walk with me. He introduces himself as the curator of the local museum and invites me to take tea with him in the museum gardens. This is not a tea-party day so I decline, which is just as well. As I exit from the post office the tiredness sweeps over me. The nearest place for sanctuary is a hairdressing shop, where I take a manicure before a swift ride home and back to bed.

Mrs. Q is delighted by my progress today and suggests an evening ride around Lahore. I appreciate this gesture and enjoy a drive through the bazaar but do not attempt to shop. As I close my bedroom door without the slightest warning, the signs of a relapse knock me sideways, the fatigue, leg drawing backwards, the stiffening and feverish heat...

Tuesday 29th November

Back to square one. Waves of pain hitting me. I have tied protective scarves around my wrists as every fractional move grates. I can hardly speak to Mrs.Q. as she leads me to the breakfast table with a shawl over my night-dress. Suddenly I find I cannot control my movements and clumsily knock over the tea pot. Cutlery slips from my right hand which has the lead weight feeling. I am causing chaos. A cup of hot sweet tea is placed in my left hand and my fingers curl around the handle but it spills as I lift it, bending my head to meet the cup and hide the tears so near the surface. Mrs.Q. moves me back to my bed.

The edge of the bed is the edge of my world. I have no energy to move to the middle, the covers bear down on my leg. Floating in and out of consciousness... where am I, where is home? I cannot remember. The nightmare is reality. I am lost inside myself. When I wake my mind is still unsteady and I cannot immediately recall a myriad of little things. Are the steroids slowing down my brain process? Does this thing attack the brain and have they kindly omitted to tell me? Reading my journal pulls me back into reality but brings scant consolation as I remember how far away home is and I have yet to reach there.

Mrs. Q. had a surprise ready for me that she felt unable to present at breakfast. She had thought yesterday that as I appeared mobile again, I would enjoy a holiday in Rawalpindi with her friend. They had talked together that evening and she had booked a plane ticket and a warm welcome was assured.

My mind is a whirlpool. To see Rawalpindi after all! New horizons again, people to meet, anxieties and excitement flooding in together. I am on a roller coaster, upright and mobile one moment and prostrate the next. All I have to do is step aboard a plane, it must be possible! So what is the plan? To go to Rawalpindi and then to go home. All my hopes are pinned on tomorrow. I would cross my fingers if they would cross.

19. Rawalpindi Retreat

Wednesday 30th November

The physician had mentioned 'jaw and neck'. He was right. Jaw *was* next. My jaw will only allow my mouth to open wide enough to slip in my tablets and a soft banana. It is utter madness to be going further afield now. Logic has deserted me; I simply receive my ticket with gratitude and am driven away.

Freedom! I have reached the heights and spirits are soaring. Peering through the window I drink in the panoramic views of the terrain I had hoped to travel through by land. To the east lies the Mangla Dam. I cannot see it but I know it is there, covering the soil that was once Mirapur, flooding an area the size of Yorkshire. A new town of Mirapur has been built on the Kashmir border but many of the old population have dispersed, some migrating to Britain's industrial cities in the 1960's. Gradually wives and children had joined them. I can see why they will not be returning. The piece of land they knew as home is under water.

A colleague had asked me to visit a Pakistani woman living in the Mirapur area who had grave problems. I know it will not be possible now and am sorry that is so, it would have been a new experience for me and could have been rewarding for someone down there. As the plane flew lower I feasted my eyes on the lakes, muddy inlets twisting and turning, straggling their way along, petering out in the middle of nowhere. Clusters of square shaped mud huts blend in with the soft yellowish brown landscape, a contrast to the sandy orange soil of the Punjab.

We land. There are crowds of people but no-one approaching me. I sit awhile in a corner then look outside as Mrs. F. arrives. She is taking me to see the new house she is having built in Islamabad, the capital of Pakistan. Islamabad is a new town, its boundary blurring as it merges with old Rawalpindi. Nestling at the foot of the Murree Hills elegant residences are being built for ambassadors, diplomats and ministers. Mrs. F. is overseeing the building of her new house personally. She deals with plans, materials and workmen while I wait comfortably in the car. She then takes me to confectioners and buys boxes of assorted cakes and small bread rolls. Then we go home.

This home is an old ranch style building, sprawling, long and low, set in well fenced grounds. This is gracious living indeed. Mr. F. is a government minister and owns his own business. The dining area, with its huge oval table and exquisite displays of silverware, is on a raised level overlooking the spacious lounge. A meal is waiting. The bread rolls join the salad, beetroot and hot paté. My mouth is watering so much that I am able eat more at one meal than I have taken in days. Servants stand well back behind our chairs darting forwards to pass dishes and pour water, knowing the exact moment when anything is required. Best of all I do not drop a thing!

After an hour's rest Mrs. F. suggests we make a tour of Rawalpindi by car. It is an old town similar to Jullunder and yet there is more orderliness about the traffic and the way people behave generally. Animals do not wander about; there are more cars and pavements; less noise and confusion; and no beggars to be seen. It is so much easier for me to cope here.

We return for tea and cakes by the gas fire. The weather is cooler here and breezy but the cooler climate seems to suit my body better. I am relaxing more every minute, and the leg has held up well. It is very heartening. Perhaps it is due to the overdose of tablets I took in desperation in the morning but I feel certain this is a good place to be right now and that I have been led to be here, the same as everywhere else.

Thursday 1st December

No dramatic relapse and I am holding steady. After a communal breakfast there is activity all around the house as the family prepare to go to a wedding. It has been agreed that I can remain at home in the care of seven servants. That is probably enough! The chauffeur will remain on hand to drive me anywhere I want to go. The cook will prepare a menu similar to yesterday. This is a perfect recovery zone. It is also the first day of December, which brings thoughts of Christmas drawing near. Where to go? The Murree Hills are capped with snow and look bleak and lonely. I dare not head out towards villages so my choice is to take the car into the back streets and alleyways of Rawalpindi that look so intriguing.

My driver does not speak English but we manage well enough, even stopping occasionally to make a few Christmas purchases, the driver insisting on walking behind me and carrying all packages. My last purchase is a black leather jacket, which my son had hopefully ordered for Christmas. It is good not to feel an oddity. No one takes any notice of me here, and the women, some heavily veiled, pass me by without a second glance.

The morning is a great success, so is lunch and a relaxing afternoon writing and sitting in the garden. I have not even fallen asleep! The family return in time for us to spend an hour by the fireside before I leave for the 9.30pm plane. I am totally content. I have been to Rawalpindi and that, in the circumstances, must be enough.

Too dark to see outside the plane window I welcome conversation with the lady sitting next to me. She is the wife of a wealthy landowner with property in a village two hundred miles from Lahore, where they now live. If time had permitted she tells me she would have been delighted to be my hostess and chaperon for village visits. This is a real disappointment, but definitely not possible, however I take her telephone number and promise, if possible, to visit her at home for lunch the next day.

We land. I am the last to leave the plane and find myself in a pool of blackness. There are neither direction signs nor people. A circular tour brings me to an empty waiting room. My heart sinks. At last I find Mr.Q. patiently sitting in his car waiting outside for me to discover him. It is a rosy welcome from the family. We talk of my impressions of Rawalpindi and of my trip until midnight. It was a success despite everything and the family are truly delighted.

There has been a telephone call from the I.G. requesting my return to Chandigargh on December 3rd. He is right. It is time to return.

20.Deported

Friday 2nd December

Sunday is a day at home for all the family. Mr. Q is watching cricket on television and I decide it would not be bad manners to go out to lunch. They are surprised but also pleased to see me more buoyant and making my own arrangements. Mrs. Mahmood answers the phone and she says has already arranged to send her son to collect me by car and was waiting for my call.

Mrs. Mahmood has an attractive house in Gulberg and I have a mobile jaw. Over lunch of rice and vegetables we exchange family information. She has four children, the eldest is studying law but it is the youngest that joins us. He is going to USA to study and may be visiting England on the way. He has many questions.

Remembering that I said I have not seen much of Lahore, she asks if there is anywhere where I would like to visit. My answer is unexpected to say the least. It so happens that I have with me an address in Lahore of a young man who had been deported about a year previously. His parents and a large family of brothers, sisters and extended relatives all remain in England, his home since the age of ten. He had committed a sexual offence and had been sentenced to seven years imprisonment which he had served with remission for good behaviour... and then had been deported. I had never met this young man personally as he was not my client, but had been visiting his cell mate during the time of his sentence and had heard a good deal about his situation. I had with me a tape recording from his ex-cell mate, now released, as surprisingly they had kept up a correspondence. The address, which I gave to Mrs. Mahmood was, from her expression, in a disreputable area of the town, but her son and his friend are more than willing to go on a detective hunt.

They find the very spot in the middle of a maze of dingy side streets. A neighbour tells us our quarry has gone to the cinema which seems to present no difficulty as there are plenty of curious spectators willing to dash off to locate him. My escorts decide to wait in the car leaving me to venture inside a large dilapidated house. It is bare, unclean and uninviting. I am shown upstairs, given a seat and left alone. It is not long before Harbans arrives, registering tremendous surprise and pleasure to see someone from England. His spoken English has a Black Country accent, his clothes are completely western and he looks out of place in this setting.

At first he finds it unbelievable that I have taken the trouble to find him. I explain that my interest in him is to discover the effects on someone 'replanted' into a culture after all this length of time. A dam breaks. He has bottled up so much feeling and there has been nothing he could do with it! So he gave it to me.

'Can you understand that it is NOT POSSIBLE to do this thing! I do not belong here. I have no work. It is disgusting to be dependent on this uncle who owns this house. This uncle has worked in England as a bus driver making money to buy this house and set up a business making leather wallets. Sometimes I help in the business but his family have first chances at everything. I'm charity. Just charity! To live the rest of my life here is impossible. I can never be a person again, never see all my family again. I did my punishment. It was a bad thing and bad punishment.'

Vehement about the judicial system that had punished him with imprisonment and then taken away all hope for the rest of his life with banishment and separation from his parental family, he feels trapped in an alien world from which he has no hope of escape. He implores me to tell him if there is any way in which he can return. I know none. He knows I am right. He has explored every avenue of return both legally and illegally and assures me that the only way is to create a new identity, which needs money, and he has none.

I have my answer. I can both see and hear the effects of deportation in this kind of situation. Because he had an early childhood in Pakistan does not mean it is possible to pick up the threads of a distant past that he had been happy to forget. I give him news of his friend, play the tape and record a message back from him. He reminisces about their days in prison; there had obviously been some good moments to remember. The escorts are waiting and I leave, understanding just a little more of what it means to put into action the oft spoken phrase 'send them back to where they came from'. There are many forms of life sentence.

Now I can be a tourist. I am given a running commentary about the buildings we pass and am particularly interested in the Courts where the trial of Mr. Bhutto is taking place and where I might well have visited as I have an introduction to a judge in my pocket. Seeing people gathered at the tomb of Allama Iquabal we stop and join in a simple prayer ceremony. I had recently been reading some of his mystically beautiful poetry and had copied the words: 'If thou art living, aspire and create', into my journal, making this experience even more pertinent. It has been a lovely day in which Lahore has shown me a different face.

The Q. family is at home and at last they see me in my natural state, enthused, and busily creating my life again. Together we enjoy an evening full of warmth and laughter. My train leaves at 2.15pm next day. I must be on it.

Saturday 3rd December

These are my last hours in Pakistan. Mrs. Q. has arranged a morning visit for us both to Jasmail, the neighbouring benefactor, a perfect finale, ending where I began. In the familiar colourful lounge, the courtesies of refreshments and enquiries about health are completed and I can sit and listen to Mrs. Q. and her neighbour becoming acquainted.

The car has been ordered for the drive to the train. Mrs. Q. is to escort me personally and I am grateful for this kindness, the last of many. I still feel I have been an anxiety to these good people; if only I could have been more myself, what exciting outings I could have enjoyed with Mrs. Q.

Apprehensive of the long journey ahead I am grateful for my first class ticket. A porter places me in a lone compartment. It is a dirty train with hard wooden seats but my compartment has a toilet and wash basin. Pakistan slips away from me as I peer through the grime on the windows but as soon as the door is closed the heat begins to build. There is no possibility of opening a window, I cannot move the catch. Though the pain has dulled to a pulsing ache the power has not returned to my fingers and what is more I am worried that I will not be able to turn the handle of this heavy door.

Akari, and a renewed acquaintance with the Railway Police. Thankfully they open the door, deal with everything efficiently and escort me back to my compartment. It is being 'cleaned'. Buckets of water are being sloshed in every conceivable corner and straight in through the door of the toilet. Everything drips. The water is cold with no added detergent and is poured out of a filthy bucket in a seemingly pointless exercise. Now everywhere is slippery and steaming. If only he had thrown some on the windows! I am hot and bored and want to be on the move. For something to do I decide to lighten my load again. Outside is a porter in threadbare clothes, beard scarcely disguising his gaunt features. I beckon to him and invite him inside to help empty contents onto the steaming seat. He does so with interest and watches as I make two piles, one for me and one for him, except he does not know his luck is in. His treasure-trove includes food, clothes, books and pencils, towels and sandals. He is at first beyond speech then, in halting Punjabi which I can understand, he tells me he has a wife and children who God will make happy this day. For good measure I empty out all my change and just wish that I could be present at his homecoming that night. It has been an enjoyable diversion but the next one proves to be the opposite.

A railway policeman, who had been in the photo line-up on my outward trip, arrives to visit. He talks, but I understand very little, then it suddenly clicks that he is intending to move into this compartment, complete with food, gun and bedroll. When he goes to fetch his bicycle I become distinctly edgy. My senses tell me this is not right. He could not afford first class and it is not part of his duties. There has to be a confrontation. I stand on the steps and refuse entry, knowing there will be onlookers and if he is in the wrong he will have to back down. His face is thunderous. His voice rises higher and higher. People begin laughing and I feel the situation is becoming dangerous. I have no doubt now he was trying to take advantage of me and had probably told someone I had asked for his 'guarding' services. So I close the door, exchanging the sun and laughing people for damp darkness and kick the bolt across the door shrieking as my toes take the impact. The door is under siege. I hide in the toilet cupboard which is a windowless steaming oven. My imagination runs riot. I imagine them opening the windows, climbing in, the gun pointing at me, being dragged out, wondering which side of the border they would take me. I am not showing a very smart English style today. Painfully slowly the train begins to move. I am all in one piece but my legs have turned to jelly and toes are throbbing. All I have to do now is move the bolt back again. At least it is something to do during the five and a half hours it takes to complete a two hour journey on which I had wished that I could be deported straight back home.

Amritsar. I have thought out my strategy carefully. A bandy legged red-shirted porter opens the door and swoops on my luggage without question. I tell him 'Office, Station Master'. He understands. I stutter out my rehearsed question asking times of trains to Chandigargh. Answer barks back 'Two hours. Through train'. The next bit is trickier. I ask him to make a telephone call to the I.G. as previously instructed. He refuses. Telephone calls are allowed to Amritsar area only. Desperation makes my brain work harder. I ask him to telephone the Superintendent of Amritsar Jail to pass on the message. He throws me the telephone directory. I counter with getting out my notebook and passing him the number. He tosses me the receiver. I make the connection and to my huge relief 'Madame' is welcomed back and all arrangements will be made at Chandigargh. I cannot have failed this time! But the Station Master wins the last round. I know it is possible to hire bedrolls for the night trains and that they are necessary to combat the cold and wooden slats. 'No bedrolls!' And I just know that is not true.

How to fill in two hours? That is easy. I can see a cafeteria with a group of white faces inside. I join them, we swap travel stories and time flies. They have very little money and travel by a variety of methods, sleeping often in Gudwaras and eating from their free kitchens. Well practised in the art of dodging ticket collectors they buy a couple of tickets and pass them round.

I think they find it fun to tell their indiscretions to a Probation Officer. It is not such fun when their food arrives and they find the rice is crawling with bugs. Some pick them out, others eat them. I cannot face food, with or without bugs.

My porter returns on the dot and tosses my bags into an unlit empty carriage. Just as I am shaping my bag into a pillow the door opens and an unpleasantly scowling man makes a rude gesture and in perfect English shouts 'SHIFT' reinforcing his message by thumbing motions towards the door. I shift. Am I in the male portion of the train? This sex segregation can be so complex. An Indian business man rescues me. He takes my bags in hand, places them in a compartment further down the train and shows me how to bolt the door, which he insists is necessary. He then tells me he will be positioned in the next compartment and will be at my service if needed, suggesting I knock the wall to attract his attention. He has a bedroll. Everyone has a bedroll except me.

Seven hours pass on a tattered Rexene covered bench, seven hours of knowing that I would pay the price for this mad jolting motion, jerking me in and out of consciousness. At least I am safe. I did not knock the wall.

21. Slipping Away

Sunday 4th December

Chandigarh Station; at 4am. Stepping down cautiously between bundles of bedding encasing sleeping bodies I see the boys. Loving hands hold the promise of no more worries now. Few words... gentle Kalmi waiting to tuck me into bed. Brain and body rest and sleep eats into the day.

The household is quiet, sober. A last letter home is posted in a box outside the Nan Kari Mission. Mohinder is with me. 'Shall we go in, Auntie?' People smile a welcome. This is a fitting place to pray and prayer comes easily for the frail ones and for the strong who have lost their strength. A feeling that I am slipping away from the outside world is taking hold, living inside myself where no one can see me.

A College Fete is on the afternoon programme. Jostling crowds, noise, and uneven ground, all those things and yet I am hardly aware of them. Christmas gifts find their way into my bag, embroidered tablecloths and hand made dolls. A tasty mouth-full of fish for supper, and a revival long enough to talk of the crossing to Pakistan, the place that they had left so long ago. I hear my words as if they are coming from far away, telling tales of golden tassels; of the people who have upheld me and for Sheshi the grim details of the body's demise.

But I discover that Sheshi is visiting home especially to take me back to Patiala to meet her friends at the Medical College.

'No, please! No more travelling. My body will not take it'.

Have I become a beggar now? No one will allow Sheshi to disappoint her friends. They have been told they will meet me and are waiting for that pleasure. I will be given Sheshi's own bed. There will be many people to care for me. I have only to speak for a short while and they will be satisfied. I tell myself to let go, just let go. I am simply being treated as a member of the I.G.'s family which carries with it responsibilities that over-ride the wishes of individual members. It is impossible to withstand the pressure. I have had to experience this to understand it. My identity is lost in that of the family. I am to leave for Patiala at 4am.

Monday 5th December

A biting wind chills me to the marrow. It is dark at the bus station and there is no shelter. Wind billows my thin cotton skirt exposing dry, flaking skin. Pushed into a corner seat, I am one of the lucky ones. Around us India comes to life to greet another morning as I slip further from it.

It is a long, bone-shaking ride. I know because I can feel bones. It seems to be where feeling lies, waiting to crack. In Patiala there is a different morning, crisp and clear, people emerging from their chrysalis of sleep, some clothed, some draped in scrappy rages. Oh the cold! I feel it for myself and I feel it for them.

The long, familiar College block appears. We thaw in the canteen with hot sweet tea and Sheshi escorts me to her own bed just as she had promised. Her room is small, full of the personal possessions of living.

'What can I get for you, Auntie?'

'Books please... Medical text books.'

It is time to face the pages, to read in solid words what is taking place in my body, fouling the machine that has given me such good service. She brings them and goes to her studies. Sleep claims me and it is later when I awake a little more refreshed that my own studies begin. Reason has not completely deserted me. I am thinking that it is the unknown and unpredictable that brings the worst anxiety. Am I facing the inevitable? Hope and faith are hard to crush and miracles do happen. Never the less I turn the pages, searching for signs and symptoms that will tell me whether the type of arthritis ascribed to me is progressive or reversible. For what it is worth I learn the exact biological process that carries a rider explaining that, even with a reversible form of the disease, irreparable damage may be caused if the activity is not arrested swiftly. To arrest such activity massive doses of aspirin are prescribed and absolute immobility of the patient. Large doses of steroids, such I am taking, are not recommended due to the production of unattractive side effects.

I seem to have two problems to ponder. I am immobilising myself with sleep and rest for only short bursts, any advantage gained being lost when I move or am moved, as the case may be. It is the outside world in which I am caught up in constant motion, so I am retreating into an inner world of stillness. But that will not solve the problem. Sooner or later the motion of the outer world must also cease. I am merely putting off the inevitable until maybe it will be too late. The second problem is the medication. Do I want to become the bearded lady or whatever other delightful oddity steroids produce? I do not. But in the short term they are holding the worst of the pain at bay and I am apprehensive at changing medication with a long journey ahead. My thought processes continue bringing a little more clarity if not a resolution. Constantly at the back of my mind is the notion 'it will be alright when I get home' the place where the Health Service will triumph with some great recipe. Rubbish, probably, false hope likely, but my job is to survive and at least test the system. It is time to close the books and play the awaited guest.

It is a good play. A gentle ride, clip clopping in a colourful cart around the bazaar with Sheshi leaping out to purchase black braids used for thickening long hair that I think Charlotte will have fun with, plaiting them into her pony's tail. We enjoy an hour of English music in a shadowy corner of a comfortable café with delicious snacks and conversation. Sheshi gives pen pictures of the friends who have been invited for an evening session in her room. All are English speaking.

The room is too small by far for all the guests. More and more young women squeeze into every available corner. Then suddenly music plays and they are on their feet, dancing! I should have remembered nothing happens around Sheshi without music. These are all medical students. Their minds are polished and honed, not only to their own subjects, but to questioning the social structure of society in which western society takes a battering. I am hard pressed to keep up! It is necessary to concede that I recognise western society is perceived as materialistic, immoral, ego-centric, ungodly, and what seems to be their most serious accusation of all, totally lacking in respect and care of the elderly. I tell them that I neither wish to justify nor defend my culture or the systems, which operate within it. I do, however, ask them to recognise that one must find a way to experience a culture from the inside, to begin to understand its traditions and its process of evolution, as I had been doing, before making challenges for change. They take my point. The day ends in warmth of friendship. I am glad I came to Patiala.

Tuesday 6th December

Sheshi has a busy day ahead. It is Davinder Singh, the Superintendent of Nabha Jail who visits to ensure my welfare. I ask only that he escorts me to a bank and after supervising the swift transaction he has a treat up his sleeve. We are to take a turn around the Historical Archives. The history of the Punjab is recorded visually in different art forms; old manuscripts display rare ancient texts. Here I come face to face with the plunder of the Punjab by invading forces, not least the British. This is a place in which to study, history is such a living part of any culture. The battle scenes are striking. The Sikh is a formidable enemy and a fiercely proud warrior. It is as if my companion is an illustration of a warrior who has stepped straight out of a history book. What a way to learn history!

Sheshi has arranged for a gentle afternoon's chat with two male medical students. Always the young people of India seem eager to converse and explore beyond their own horizons through the world of words.

I am to attend a working dinner at Davinder Singh's home. The I.G. has arrived to meet with the Superintendents of Prisons. For this occasion I dress carefully and feel I look as reasonable as possible in the circumstance. It is a joyous reunion yet the men are obviously disconcerted by my appearance and talk amongst themselves. I ask what bothers them and it is Davinder who answers:

'Madam, you are greatly reduced!'

Scales are fetched and I am weighed as if I am fragile china. My 9 stones on arrival have indeed been reduced to just 6stone 13lbs with my clothes on. There have been few mirrors and I had not noticed this all over weight loss to this extent.

They want to hear of my experiences in the villages and to listen to some of the recordings I have made. Then they invite me to enjoy their business meeting as it may be useful information for me. Accounts of the sale of goods made by prisoners at Amritsar Jail are examined and discussed; what has sold well; best trade outlets; profit margins; and orders in hand. My impression is of dedicated, intelligent and astute businessmen, with a sincere interest in social progress. Dinner over, farewells have to be taken. All our goodbyes convey the same joy that our paths have crossed for a span and the sadness that we now move in different directions. I will surely remember these men who bring light into dark places.

Gurbax is waiting to drive me back to Chandigargh, the I.G. beside me. Today has been good. And I thank him for it. It is not yet over for him, he talks on the telephone to ministers until late into the night with reports of the day's meeting.

Wednesday 7th December

This is my last day in Chandigarh. It is right that I should accompany the I.G. to his office and I need no persuasion. Greetings, questions, thanks and farewells leave me feeling the need to be alone for a while. I tell the I.G. I would like to wander unescorted through the shopping centre. He smiles his understanding, yet I believe Gurbax will be notified to keep an open eye. Slowly I make my way across the square knowing exactly what I want to do. First choice is to browse in a bookshop. A chair is brought and lists of stock available in English are handed to me. They search their shelves at my request to find an alphabet chart in Punjabi for my office, books written by prisoners, facts and history of India. It feels like Christmas already. Then there are presents to be purchased for all the I.G.'s family plus a soft woollen shawl to cover old Kalmi's bony shoulders. It is done and I must return. Gurbax is waiting with a message that Miss Keith has arrived and is eager to hear of my tour.

Words are inadequate today. Miss Keith and the I.G have made all things possible and I have no regrets. They have held me to the task. Nothing has been left undone that could have been done. I could have asked nothing more of anyone or them of me. They tell me it will be to their eternal regret that I return physically depleted. I reply 'It is karma'. This they understand though I cannot resist adding that I shall redress that karma with the help of our Health Services when I get home. There is much laughter and Miss K. leaves us with her soft smile as gently as she had walked into my life.

I know the I.G. has made arrangements with a friend who is travelling to Delhi the following day. He will take me by car to where it all began, to Uncle Pritam Singh's. Tonight this gentleman is the I.G's guest. Who is he? I don't know, yet I would entrust myself to any one of these good people who come for me when I need them. We eat a strangely silent meal. Mrs. I.G. moans softly and holds her head and old Kalmi tends her gently. I have become so much a part of it that to be leaving is unreal. There are parts of me distributed everywhere, Katani Kalan, Jullunder, Hariapur, Katarpur, Haus Khas, Ambala, Patiala, Ludhiana, Lahore, Rawalpindi in homes and in jails, wherever I have met with people who have been as loving family to me. The last ounces of my energy are to be spent on the journey to Delhi. Kalmi folds my clothes and places them reverently in their allotted bags.

Thursday 8th December

A set of glassware handmade at Amritsar, so heavy to carry but so precious, a bead handbag, wall scrolls, photo albums – presents are exchanged, material tokens of our esteem each for the other. Coupled with the value of the gift, is the joy of being thought a worthy recipient. Bags are heavy, hearts are heavier. Kalmi weeps for us all. A white pavement, not a wisp of wind and the road to Delhi takes me from them.

My companion is obviously a business man. The Grand Trunk Road to Delhi slips past the window as I slip in and out of a restless sleep. I hear the man talking, he's asking a question. Will I accompany him to a dancing display to celebrate Haryana Day at an Exhibition Centre in Delhi? How little time I have had to enjoy the arts! Why not end with a celebration? I hear my ridiculous reply, 'I would be delighted'.

We break our journey at the home of a friend of my escort. She is a lawyer. How coincidental that she should live near the courts of this small town! It is inevitable. We go to meet her colleagues. If I had found this lady earlier she would have become a friend and I would have learnt so much from her, but an hour is all we have together.At least I met a Master Advocate, an expensive man to engage as he has a reputation for winning his cases.

The journey continues through the orange heat of the afternoon and there is Delhi, Haus Khas and Sheshi in a long brown velvet dress, warm and welcoming. She cannot believe her eyes.

'What has happened to your body? It is bent!'

Shaloo comes to sit at my feet. Her eyes are huge. Jam sandwiches are pressed into my hands. Nibbling slowly I try to pull words together but my tongue seems unravelled and my adventures like a disjointed dream.

The clothing I had left behind is freshly laundered; water from the tap is warm. I tell them I am going out and must dress for a celebration. It is Shaloo who brushes my hair, fastens my buttons. Sheshi drapes me in a shawl, large enough to hide my clumsy swollen hands and I am handed over to my escort for my last night in India, still on my feet.

Pure amazement! The Exhibition Centre is a vast collection of Pavilions, one for each Indian State, in exotic architectural styles typifying the State it represents. Each building houses its own exhibition of regional crafts, art, machinery, models and projects such as irrigation schemes, educational and medical advances, programmes of research on fertilization of crops, housing developments, social welfare schemes… and more. Each state by individually depicting progress showed a face of India on the move in a technological age. My escort was knowledgeable. I was impressed.

The sight of crowds milling around a raised platform concerns me. I cannot afford to be jostled. We walk towards the platform. Officials come towards us, the crowds part and we are bowed towards two empty seats awaiting us in the front row. It is only then that I learn that my companion is Director of Industry for Harayana State and this is Harayana State Celebration Day. India is full of surprises and I am in the limelight once again and hardly fit to be seen.

It is easy to loose my self consciousness in the beauty of the exotic Bangra dances performed with vigour by lithe young bodies; the heights to which the young men jump, their energy, their sheer delight in performing makes an electrifying atmosphere. I had been told of Bangra dance competitions held in Smethwick at the local cinema, but I had come thousands of miles to learn to appreciate it. The programme was being recorded for television, the antics of the camera crew making for an additional entertainment as they dart amongst the dancers with coils of wire.

Too soon it is ended, and my Director is naturally in great demand. He is to lead a tour of the Harayana Pavilion. I walk behind, worried by the vast expanse of exhibits, appalled by the steps which wind upwards ahead of me. A young man is detailed to assist me. Oh for a day here and a good pair of legs! We visit three pavilions but my concentration is on negotiating steps, slopes and wires, all the more difficult because I cannot use my hands to clutch the handrails and it is not appropriate to be physically supported by my assistant. I feel off balance all the time as my right side no longer functions in the same way as the left.

My crowning glory is to be drawn towards an exhibit of weavings where a large floppy rainbow hat is dropped on my head and they all stand back to clap and admire their own handiwork! Then they show me this pretty sight in a mirror and I am aghast at the drawn white face accentuated by the brilliant colours. It looks ghoulish to me.

More walking and talking and the hour grows late. I am resistant to any idea of food, embarrassed at the thought of trying to manage both the mechanics and protocol of eating and exposing my hands to public view. There is a conference and the decision is made. The party will return to the Director's hotel. The assistant is despatched to a restaurant to order specialities to be cooked especially to my liking which I can then eat in private. There is no retreat from such kindness.

In a large modern hotel the Director's bedroom is comfortably furnished and the party settle down to talk on into the night. An age later the shopper returns with boxes of food. Oh - such food! Fish which crumbles to the touch, diced vegetables plus other numberless and nameless dishes. I do not care that my spoon wavers. It is worth every creaking mouthful and, what is even better, no-one remarks on my 'condition'. I am returned to Haus Khas, my first home…eventually.

Friday 9th December 1977

My plane leaves this evening. One last task awaits me, to report back to Dr. Hira Singh at the Institute for Social Defence. Ramoo fetches a scooter. There is no anxiety about this journey. I have learnt the ropes. Dr. Hira Singh's greetings are warm and yet I am distressed by his distress at my appearance. Despite all his efforts my body has been wilful and evaded his care. He is even more determined that in future western guests will be equipped with a car, cook, driver and servant and everything else that he considers necessary. Well they must all fight their own battles or follow their own star. I had found what I was seeking and had been exposed to the heart of India. There is so much he wants to hear; impressions of the prisons and conditions of prisoners, the Amritsar celebrations and meetings with the ministers, so much… too much.   I promise to set it all down in writing one day. He had hoped I would speak at a meeting today but can see it is not possible. Soberly I am returned to Haus Khas.

A canvas bag had arrived for me just after I had left. I ask Shaloo to unpick the twine stitching and wrappings. Golden slippers, the gift from Davinder Singh, my Maharaja of Patiala are tumbled into my hands. They are the last item I pack. Stumbling into the taxi I hear Shaloo's last words:

'Have you enjoyed your holiday, Auntie?' I nod.

It is easy for the touts to see my baggage will be overweight. I am pressed for money to have my bags passed through customs without excess charge. I refuse all offers. The baggage is 80lb overweight. No-one cares. I cannot lift it. No-one cares. I drag it up the gangway over the crook of my arm.

The journey is finished...and so am I.

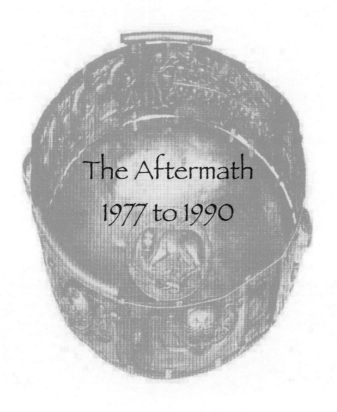

The Aftermath
1977 to 1990

22. A No Body

Passport photo   *Out of hospital*
October '77   *December '77*

Derek: I was struck first by the wheelchair then by the woman in it, so shrunken and aged it was inconceivable she was the same person. Seriously ill, seriously changed she was hidden behind dark glasses. Not nice, not nice at all. We, Marc and myself, loaded her into the car and Marc carried her into the house. At first there were tales to be told, tragic and comic and the insights, such insights into unimaginable lives but nothing could assuage her pain. She was trapped in it, locked in the body obviously but in something else bigger, something was wrapped around her that she was fighting with an aggressive volley of words. Fear was a part of it, of the illness progressing, self doubt perhaps, self rejection at her changed appearance, frustration certainly but she struggled to overcome her weakness and me. She definitely saw me in there with her demons for which she no doubt had her own reasons which were far beyond me to understand. I felt helpless, thinking mainly that rebuilding the body would begin recovery, maybe even lead to the return of the attractive, stimulating wife who had left. There was grief for me, but more so for her for the state she was in. Three days after arrival home she gave up the struggle, gave up the ghost you might well say. I came home from college to find her being loaded into an ambulance. They closed the doors. She wouldn't let me in.

My leg, toes and hands seemed to have solidified. Unable to deal with opening food containers I had by-passed all food trays and had no option but to ask for a wheelchair exit. The coldness of December bit into my bones as, draped in Marc's Christmas present of the black leather jacket, they had their first dark glimpse of the returning body. I saw them seeing me, reflecting what I already knew. India had wrought an unspeakable change in the person that had left.

Marc was a seventeen year old life line. He carried me over the threshold of home. Home was no more than an empty word. I had invested my sanity in the false belief that home would be an antidote to pain. It was worse than pain to see, to feel, the shock, the recoil of people who I knew had been the closest in my life and now seemed strangely distant. Charlotte, self contained, independent and responsible was a watchful presence, an anchor in the maelstrom of the disconnected world in which I found myself. One minute I ached to re-enter it, to take my place, to move on from where I had left off but it felt as if the grass had grown over where I once stood. At the same time I wanted to turn and run and not look back. Possessions were material trappings without significance or meaning. Worse was the notion that Derek saw me as a gargoyle. I could see it in his eyes. I needed reassurance of my own existence and drew the opposite when a wedding invitation arrived from close friends. My name was not on it. It was addressed only to Derek, trivial on the face of it but it acted as the catalyst for an outburst of emotion.

'Where is my name? How could they not ask me?'

'You're not well enough to go'.

'An invitation would have let me know they would have *liked* me there. I've brought presents. Ask them just to put my name on. I need to see my name'.

'No.'

'Then don't go'.

'No.'

Stalemate. I am battling raging torrents of perceived rejection. Emotionally exhausted on the third day I crawl to the telephone calling Derek at college to come home but he cannot be found. I call the doctor admitting to her and to myself that I am collapsing. Derek arrives as the ambulance revs up. I tell them to close the doors on him but it is more than that. I am trying to shut out the remnants of a life that has turned sour. Trollyed and tagged for isolation, I am glad not to have to respond any more.

'India has done this to you?' An Indian doctor, compassionate, understanding, touching me gently, probing what has become 'the body' as I distance myself from its embarrassing ownership.

'Now there will be no movement. Not a flicker of the eye, no books, no talking'.

I am being cast in polystyrene, being warmly re-moulded, remodelled in pliable white sheaths, strong and light that hug both legs and arms as the bones are teased into their accustomed places and held there, trapped, and glad to be so. Figures move around me gently accepting my state without recoil, advising me to let go. Drops are poured into ulcerated eyes. Closure against all light is necessary. Doses of aspirin are fed between spoons of mash. As soon as the body is in safe hands I leave it to its own devices.

There is a space, a place somewhere beyond the physical world. I went there. A deathly stillness settled. Unable to see, sometimes I could hear snatches of muted voices and feel the vibration of the tea trolley.

'Don't bother, she's past it' whispered one trolley-lady to another. My mother, given to exaggeration it is true, I later learnt, was intimating the same dire outcome although she did not venture near. So I was left to hover in that formless place unimpeded, unreachable by the 'real' world but reachable by something or an invisible someone that knew I was there and in a predicament. A question found its silent way into my mind.

'Do you agree to stay on the earth plane in this body or not?'
A silent response formed without hesitation: *'Only if I can become whole'.* I neither gave nor received further explanation knowing that it meant something far beyond the recovery of the physical body. Then I was left to get on with the vagaries of a twilight life. There seemed to be no power source in the room on which I could draw. People held no vitality that they could transfer to me and I remained untouched, by anyone other than the nursing staff, until my boss visited with a gift of a pot of violets and I was aware of a soothing beam of violet light bathing my eyes. When daughter Sandra came I could see her.

Sandra: 'I was living at The Red Lion in Watford training in Pub Management with my boyfriend Clive and full of plans for our wedding three months ahead when my father phoned and suggested I had better get to the hospital. There was a body in a bed. It was not my mother, nothing like her. It was something else, something unearthly. There was no life in it. Its skin was flaky, dry, and scaly. I will never forget nor understand what I did … or what is worse what I failed to do. I gave it its orders. I told those legs that they were to be walking down the aisle at my wedding but I gave it no gifts or kind words, not even the touch of a finger or a listening ear.'

Sandra's message reached me placing a date as a marker point on a distant horizon. All tests to identify whatever had caused the condition were negative; no virus identified; nothing to account for the demise, no antidote was therefore possible.

The cause I am told will have to remain undetected and, if it relates to an unspecified virus it could be lodged in my system and reactivate at any time.

'Do not go back to India. Do not expose yourself to infection'.

Though taking notice of the warning, the suddenness of the shock pain in the night of Diwali seemed to me to be at the root of all that had followed after. The remote possibility of a repeat, of waking to some new state of deformity was unthinkable and yet I thought it, constantly.

The splints are taken off. I am pleased. The pain has lessened substantially but my fingers are glued together. I now have mittens, two kitten-like hands. They test my grip on a machine to measure pressure readings. It hardly registers. Stick insect legs are a limp flaky white. No power, no life force flows through to create the strength needed to function. They can do no more for me and despite my fierce protests send me home for Christmas unable to get a grip on life. On the way Derek stops outside the village butcher's shop. There's a scream inside me. It seems I cannot bear the sight of butchery yet it is something more than that. I cannot relate to the world around me at all.

Downstairs I lie in a makeshift bed, semi-conscious during the daytime when alone, trying to be present in the evenings when Charlotte sweeps in from school bringing waves of the great outdoors that I still cannot reach nor do I want to. Derek's cooking starts to make its mark and my aggression towards him begins to abate. India has brought about a shattering and I am in pieces, unable to connect thoughts together in any logical sequence; unable to 'pull myself together' because I have so little pulling power either physically or mentally. This inability to think leaves me unable to comprehend emotions when they surface without warning.

Who sent the healers? I do not know. Eric Hatton, President of the local Spiritualist Church and his wife Heather arrive. With no experience as a giver or receiver in the laying on of hands I had no preconceived expectations. Through their hands, touching lightly above my head, it felt as if a current was moving through my body, kick-starting the life force in me that had fallen so low. I did not leap up nor fall back in hysteria but I felt a warmth and aliveness. Did their hands pass a message to my body reminding it of how to use the power it once had, or was it an energy that just poured through from somewhere beyond my comprehension? At least I now know there is life in there, somewhere.

In the days that follow, movement begins to reach both limbs and mind. The hospital had not arranged nor recommended any physiotherapy so, still unable to hold a tea-pot, I set about designing my own, rediscovering pressure levels and trying to tease the glued fingers apart by striking disjointed clumps of notes on the piano. Derek is still working hard on the same Probation Training course that I had completed five years previously and at times we find ourselves dialoguing as colleagues ... or nearly so.

Mohinder's wedding to Kamla took place in Southall. The date was immaterial; there was no way I could travel and play the part I would so much have enjoyed in my livelier days. After all that they had shared with me I was a pathetic hostess when the Inspector General arrived on my doorstep with his ailing wife, driven from London by faithful relatives. We had no rose gardens in mid-winter, no dancing parties or servants to bring down mattresses at his request into the warmth of downstairs rooms, as Mrs. Shenmar, frailty hidden under a voluminous fur coat, struggled with the grey chills of winter which quickly turned to snow.

The telephone is my first saving grace as I organise a meeting with Chiefs at Head Office who in their turn arrange a tour of Birmingham Prison, one of the I.G's prime objectives. Derek was my second string, enjoying the I.G.'s company and tale-telling. But the snow settled, only four-wheel drives and the milkman could make it up the steep gradient of Adams Hill, so it was prudent to curtail the visit, and have Mrs. Shenmar carried out to a Land-rover rather than a milk cart. The laughing adventure held an edge of concern. It was far too much to have asked of Mrs. Shenmar who, I later learnt, died shortly after return home. The call of her son's wedding had drawn her here no doubt but I deeply regretted that I could offer little else celebratory. Those sun-drenched dancing days seemed so far away in both time and distance. It felt as if I had lost a life, and struggling to create another identity that could function effectively was proving to be difficult.

It's the last day of January. My mother is the Edwards family matriarch and her birthday marks the annual family gathering in Handsworth, Birmingham our old home territory. Long red woollen socks hold the still spindly legs together under the scarlet cotton of my 'Exhibition Skirt'. Now I am the exhibition. There is dancing. At my ridiculous request Derek shuffles round with me propped up on his feet. Sisters, brothers and all manner of relations are recognisable but I have no voice for family affairs and they have no comprehension of my journey because I do not talk of India, not real talk, remaining devoid of anecdotes. I leave feeling an isolate in a world that is little more than a sea of faces.

Spring approaches passing milestones on the recovery road. Shopping, unable to unzip my purse or pinch out the coins; slithering down a doorpost in the street overcome by the weight of the body which still feels as if it lives in a diving suit; believing I was grasping the wheel of our motor home and learning otherwise when it shoots backwards into a neighbour's wall; trapped in muddy furrows unable to lift my feet to traverse a row of cabbages when kindly taken for a strengthening walk. So much I did not know how to rectify.

On the first of April Sandra's wedding takes place perfectly to her master plan. She had escorted me to buy an outfit. It must have been a particularly bad day. I ended up top heavy, dressed in a wide brimmed hat, topping a short fake fur coat, tottering on the high heels I was determined to wear. With little exercise and food galore in the urgency to be rid of the shrunken appearance, a new shape had formed. From under seven stone on return the body had ballooned to over ten stone producing a shape that appealed to me no more than the shape of the sedentary unproductive life I was leading. I did not know this person, nor did I particularly want to. The wedding never-the-less was delightful.

Work is a challenge waiting to be tested. Colleagues had been covering my caseload for months and continued when in June, to test my staying power and legs, I return to the more sedentary role of Court duties. The taped messages from India burn a hole in my cupboard. Probation work is all consuming. In my office personal matters remained personal. Apart from the polite and obvious questions there is no debriefing, storytelling or sharing of the massive body of information I had collected but not yet collated. The sense of detachment did not abate; it grew as I performed my duties mechanically. My former zest surfaced only when at last I was in a position to visit my prisoners, clients or the relatives of those I had met in India; then my tongue loosened and a stream of anecdotes and taped messages kept families enthralled. I seemed unable to step back into the western mode of being. It felt as if I had switched cultures.

Now in a position to begin the treasure hunt of seeking for Selima's errant husband, I eventually found him in the south of England and enlisted the help of his local Probation Officer to mediate on my behalf. Eventually we met. He had not prospered and was at low ebb but after learning more of his family's circumstances agreed they should have a chance at reunion in Britain. The paper work alone would have been beyond his capability, but we worked our way through, officials were intrigued by my authentic evidence and day came when the family was re-united. The story of their subsequent adventures is not mine to tell. This family, for whom I felt a loving respect, stood for all of those for whom I could do nothing.

After five years service an Officer is in line to be assessed as potential material for middle management if they choose to go before a panel of inquisitors. There were many willing and able to climb the promotional ladder though promotional vacancies were infrequent. Managing a team of colleagues and carrying the can for all and sundry had never appealed to me; even less so on my return. I wanted only to work at the interface. But my five years were up and I had an option. I had not been in a position to undertake any preliminary study and my Senior Officer, realistically supposing I was not up to it, checked out my intention. Just about to agree with her I hear myself reply:

'Thank you, but I will be applying'.

Derek laughed. 'I would expect you to. Go for it!'

I thought he was being kind rather than realistic. With neither time nor inclination to study I thought my best move was to wear the faithful white woolly dress of the fateful bursary day and trust it would not all turn out to be an embarrassing charade.

Interviewers consist of the Chief Probation Officer, various other senior ranks and members of the Probation Committee. Mostly they are strangers, members of a hierarchy outside my Smethwick boundary line. Delightfully courteous and deeply probing, their questions zip across the table. Each one elicits an answer from me that has never seen the inside of a manual. My answers are eminently sensible and strictly truthful if a trifle unusual. But what was more, they had done their homework. They knew the contents of my files which now contained the latest entries of my visits to the families in India, so they could ask about specific cases and listened with some amazement at my deeply felt replies. The past months when I had felt gagged were wiped away. They were touching something in me of substance that was intent upon an honest revelation of itself. I had a voice; a voice that was, at critical moments, somewhat ahead of my thinking mind; a voice that appeared to be working to an agenda of its own design.

A week later their spokesperson came to tell me that promotion was assured. It was probably around then that I began to realise there would be a life after India. It is just that it would be different.

23. The Wise Advisors

So far I had experienced a healing force and a voice ahead of my thinking mind with an interest in my future. But there was something else that I was keeping firmly under wraps. On my road to recovery I had visited the healers at the local spiritualist church to thank them by showing my increasing progress and had enjoyed a friendly reception. A woman was pointed out to me as someone I might be interested to meet. Her name was Marael Robertson, a medical photographer working in the local hospital. She told me that she had been experiencing the phenomenon of automatic writing and asked a surprising question.

'Would you be interested in seeing if anything happened if you were present?'

Marael was single and lived alone. Intrigued by her invitation, I accepted and found myself visiting her at home one evening. There was no attempt to get to know anything about me so we met virtually as strangers.

'Ask a question' she said picking up pen and paper. I complied.

'Is there any information that we need to receive?' was my first question.

Writing with abnormal speed, the words running into each other, the pen wrote that it was a source of intelligence that could be of service. It wrote of life being like a diamond and of the necessity to polish all the facets and in particular mine and there was no doubt that it knew what facets needed polishing. Encouraged to continue I carried on dialoguing with the pen until, after a while, it was laid aside and Marael began to speak. As the pen had written in a flourishing style quite different to her usual scripted hand, so her voice took on quite a different inflection, the flowing words holding a vibrant quality. And that was how I met the first of the unseen Communicators who became my wise advisors and an integral part of my life.

By the end of 1978 I am back in my old working routine and content to be so, when a vacancy is announced for a new Senior grade full time post. The first of its kind in a Probation Service nationally it would carry the title of 'Ethnic Advisor'. The post was going to be well contested and a hornet's nest, of that I was certain. Candidates and their supporters were jockeying for position. Whoever was appointed was at risk of becoming an Aunt Sally for racial issues, and grievances which were many and various. I kept a safe distance. In the climate of the day a white, middle class, middle aged female would be likely to receive zero votes. Through the management grapevine I was advised to apply. In front of a panel of astute questioners I am on the spot again being asked how I would approach such a job. There is a sense of letting go of any prescribed thought and allowing a more noetic intelligence the space to engage. It is from this space that I hear myself lay out a carefully designed and thoughtful plan beginning with a sweeping piece of county-wide research to provide the evidence from which to reshape policy, followed by training programmes to convey the policy into practice plus other detailed initiatives. It sounds good to me, and to them. They appoint me, trusting I can do the job that I did not of my own volition seek and do not relish. I have received no formal training in statistical research and this will be a high profile job for which there is no blueprint, with other Services watching to see which way the West Midlands will jump in this contentious zone of race relations.

On the home front I'm running on an even keel, body functioning effectively and emotions coming gradually under control. Derek was scheduled to finish training around the time that I would leave my post in Smethwick to move to Head Office in Birmingham. When Derek applied to West Midlands Probation Service for a position he was immediately appointed to Smethwick Office to take over both my soon to be vacant desk and my clients who were delighted to remain in the family as they had met Derek during our darts nights in the pub. What a family concern! It's all unusual to say the least.

I move to Birmingham City Centre into a role without prior existence and a sketchy job description of what needs to be done but without indication of how to do it, hence it will have to be crafted whilst I too will need to craft a working identity as an Ethnic Advisor. Life is becoming increasingly perplexing and intriguing. Having been filled to the brim my mind, after India, felt as if it had undergone a shattering, and having requested to become 'whole' was now having to reassemble and assimilate a much greater spectrum of thought including the metaphysical.

The inner voice that slipped to the forefront of its own volition seemed to me intent on keeping me on a prescribed track whilst Marael's wise communicator was setting about teaching me what it was considered I needed to know. Either way it was all a private matter and that was definitely how it needed to remain. Then my inner voice took to the pen. This was not automatic writing as I had seen but was more like some-one occasionally making an advisory comment on events as they occurred from a more enlightened perspective. It added a much needed dimension to my life that kept me afloat when I might well have become overwhelmed by the vitriolic behaviour of those colleagues who had supported another applicant and who consistently sought to unseat or at least unsettle me. Advisory notes were quick to drop out of my pen if I became edgy or disheartened: **Do not take up the sword. Hold integrity; respond without rancour; hold silence with an outstretched palm; and move with the noetic current. There are many who covet the task of another; if it is not their task then it is their ego that desires it.**

A noetic current was a good description of the inner advisor but when it was in full flow I discovered it could cause difficult situations. Daily I walked a mine field. In their political wisdom my managers had convened a 'support group' substantially made up of the opposition which made my life and the task infinitely more challenging. I was busily compiling a substantial research document when I received an advisory note: **You need a symbol for the cover; an image that holds the goal.** I tried to produce one diplomatically by suggesting a competition to devise a logo. The strength of their ribald humour barbed with distain, caught me off guard. Silently I deleted the item from the day's agenda, went home and engaged Carmella, my number two daughter who, with her artistic flair was well able to create a logo that 'held the goal', which was really all that mattered. It was later that I was taught more of the power and purpose of a holding symbol that displays not only true intention but holds the energy of that which lies behind it. It is the face of the word. Since that day I have never worked without a holding symbol.

Snippets of fore-knowledge that I was being offered, was another matter and extremely dangerous ground. I had never been to Brixton nor had conversation with anyone regarding the racial situation there, so it was a surprise to me when at a conference where I was speaking I found myself advising action to forestall impending riots in Brixton. The opposition had a field day accusing me of inflammatory comments, even insinuating I could be involved in subversive activities. The ears of the media began to flap with delight but to no avail. I survived unscathed having learnt the valuable lesson of taking full responsibility for words spoken or written whatever their origin. There was no-one to hide behind. I was the spokesperson and that was that. I learnt from experience ...fast.

The research went ahead; statistics were meticulously gathered and issues aired. Areas of deficiency on my part were rectified immediately by intensive training at the Home Office in London. The final document caused a furore. It could remain an internal policy document in which it would be likely to fizzle amongst a welter of opposition tactics, or enter the public arena, exposed to the mass media. **Publish and have no investment in the outcome** inner intelligence firmly advises. The Service hierarchy finally agree.

The Commission for Racial Equality saw it as a gift and offered to pay all publishing and distribution costs on a first run of 5,000 copies. Probation and After-Care in a Multi-Racial Society, published in 1981 with wide media coverage, was to be the first Probation statement on racial issues on the market. Blocking tactics proved no match for the current that swept it, logo and all, into the limelight and when the predicted Brixton riots followed  shortly afterwards, the carefully worded recommendations were examined by Lord Scarman and his tribunal proving their validity. They went national. The West Midlands Probation Service was on the race relations map and I was there, television, radio, advisor and all. Working with the media is hair-raising. Seeing behind the scenes was another learning curve. The bargain had been that The Commission could call on me for promotional tours across England and Wales. At last it was possible to draw on experiences in India to illustrate the many issues on our agenda and at last to share the cultural essence that holds the intrinsic patternings of life.

There were surprises on these jaunts away. People who had never met me before would sometimes wait for a personal word on various topics. Some tentatively shared that they had seen a haze around my head; others spoke of seeing light in the room that had enveloped them. The usual question that followed was: 'What is it'? Do you see it?' I did not; had no readily expressible explanation and was as cautious as a hawk as one word can often lead to another that is one too many. It was imperative to protect the Service from ridicule which would surely have followed with headlines that would have sunk the ship. However, it was of great interest to me that a fair sprinkling of people appeared to have a degree of clairvoyant ability.

Outside the parameters of the Service, my now weekly meetings with Marael and my Informers had expanded to include Grace, a nursery school teacher and her husband, Albert, who worked for the Midlands Electricity Board. Our meetings were nothing like the old hat séance. At no time did we ever attempt to contact 'spirits' or anyone who had died. No physical manifestation ever occurred, nor were any objects involved. We sat in a well lit, comfortable lounge in Kingswinford near Dudley. After our social exchanges, initially Marael, later Grace, became the spokesperson for streams of Wisdom, freely given.

Initially there were three main areas of focus which interwove: personal insights; informative discourses; and energy work. Insights offered reflections of our own personal natures and characteristics which needed polishing. The

Communicators explained it was a simple matter for them to see what was in need of attention and alteration. Invariably they were right. There was nowhere to hide.

To aid us in our development we were given discourses on all manner of themes such as truth; integrity and service all meticulously taped, transcribed and studied. We were encouraged to question, examine and absorb the essence of the content but more so we were always reminded to put any information to the test by application and experience of the outcome. We were advised that we would draw towards ourselves challenging opportunities. My work provided a perfect testing arena.

The energy work was fascinating. Our unseen tutors were able to change the energy frequencies in the room and we were taught to identify changes of temperature, frequency and density. We were taught of healing, not only at the physical level but of mind fields of crystallised thoughts (the very prejudices I was dealing with every day); instructed how to sense power points and negative energy clusters. It was all invaluable to me.

There was a fourth area that was present from the very first word of the very first day, which had no explanation and needed none. These communicating streams of Intelligence were what I can only describe as 'ineffable', a word from childhood hymn books, never relevant until now; a word conveying the essence of something too great to comprehend or describe. 'Love' is an ambiguous word often used to identify a multitude of emotions or preferences that is inadequate to convey the gentle yet penetrative radiance of my Communicators in both their words and presence. 'Ineffable Love' is a phrase that I ascribed to it. My wise advisors knew me and loved me despite my weaknesses; appearance or ignorance. This was not the Eros of human attraction, possessive and emotive, demanding to be loved back. Ineffable Love does not need to be loved back. It already IS. It sees reflection of itself in all things animate and inanimate, great and small, even in whatever opposes its expression. It does not need to explain itself, market or prove itself. Sometimes it felt as if the room was full of something tangible, other times as if it concentrated more around one person or another. It felt on these evenings as if it was outside and around me and yet when my inner advisor spoke or wrote and the words held that noetic quality, it was inside me. Even recognising that such a thing exists, it has to be experienced and expressed to witness it at work.

Though we were not informed that our responses were in some unfathomable way being monitored, I had no doubt that a system of observation operated on some higher register. Analogies were often used that evoked images such as of polishing the diamonds of our lives. Informed that we were receiving tuition in the Principles of the Quality of Life, where there was a shortfall it had to be rectified. Then, when we were considered ready, a short statement heralded a move of focus from the individual to the collective. Far from being a privileged few, we discovered ourselves to be in a programme taking place on a wide scale. These are original words as spoken on 24th September 1979 when the term and concept of a 'New Age' was not widely in vogue.

There is a way within your time, the starting of a New Creation, a new way. There must come to Earth's humanity a new realisation of thought; a new concept of 'God'; a new way within the world. There are small groups of people of many countries, many nationalities, many ways, many minds, not just those of deep intellect, but those who are simple people and each now receives this impetus of thought; this depth of knowledge of Spirit; this way of truth; this concept of a New Reality; this acceptance of what has been soul-matter, what IS soul-matter.

This is the New Creation; the New Beginning – a new power that must spread from a nucleus of homes of ordinary people and must spread to the city, to the town, to the village, to the countryside, by words and by deeds that will interlock. They will cross and they will weave and they will reach out beyond the world that you know into the very firmament of the worlds that are beyond this one ...

We have the bigger picture. People everywhere are being moved into place and made ready for the challenges to come as they discover the nature of their contribution to what is being described as Universal Harmony, hence all the polishing. Work is in hand, a far greater hand than we could envisage. Consciousness is shifting, rising, which, as it expands, will have immense repercussions for the development of societies, cultures and human evolution. It is already happening; happening behind closed doors that we were advised were about to open more widely.

Those who have been activated to make their contribution to Universal Harmony will work wherever they are impulsed to move in a way appropriate to their potential and their capabilities. They will create new paradigms; raise vibrational frequencies; present the Teachings for the Age; and bring about the merging of polarised living and polarised thought. All these things they will do and more. They work to ease the transition from one Age to the next; one Race to the next. To do so it is vital to grasp that ALL IS ENERGY and to bring the subtle senses into play.

Our metaphysical experiences had in effect been our training for whatever lay ahead.

The phrase 'they will work wherever they are impulsed to move' was in itself enough for me to recognise and accept that a force greater than I could comprehend was doing the impulsing; generating the opportunities necessary to perform an ascribed task; and aiding in the background. The vista of what this merging of polarities could mean was incalculable; mystic and scientist; male and female; east and west; rich and poor, black and white and so much more. The transition would bring massive disruption, stirring the cauldron to create a very different cultural brew.

Reviewing the work to which I had been assigned in the Probation Service in this wider context brought more realisations. Immigration is about transiting, from a familiar culture into another and dealing with the pressures and effects at physical, emotional, mental and spiritual levels as communication and coping skills are re-learnt, needs reassessed, beliefs are challenged whilst dealing with the constant sense of loss, maybe even rejection. It is not only immigrants that are in transit. The whole of humanity is on the move. It is a massive concept. Will they too feel themselves to be as strangers at their own gate? Or are there other ways to claim entrance to a New Reality?

24. The Melting Pot

In 1866 Lord Lyttleton sold a plot of land for £30 on the borders of his estate that fringed the village of Clent in Worcestershire. A dwelling house was built which from the outset appeared to have a task of serving the community ... and beyond, in diverse ways. It had provided residents and visitors with water from its well; tea from its tea-shop and beds for needy travellers. Eventually it had lain empty for a year until in 1966 when, almost derelict, we had claimed it, pouring into it our growing family and the proceeds of our working lives as a labour of love. Adam House, with its seven bedrooms, seemed to have a capacity for adapting to whatever was asked of it, and we had, over the years, asked a great deal. But time had moved on since the early years before the Probation Service had claimed my life and the youth of Clent had laid claim to the cellar with its bales of straw and a table tennis table. The Advisors had a few ideas for further development.

Individually all the family members had from time to time received personal advice and a variety of experiences during evenings with the Communicators, Derek being pointed more towards applying the energy through healing. After four years of tutorials the request was made that a room on the topmost floor of Adam House should be set aside for healing and used only for this purpose. There was no reluctance on our part. Both Derek and Carmella joined with me to make a trio enabling us to put into practice the training we had received with some fascinating results. Though we had also attended a course given by the National Federation of Spiritual Healers we found we did not quite fit into their structure and so we continued to develop on our own. There was never any advertising, merely being available for friends and those who found their way to us by various unusual connections and one of our three attic rooms became referred to as a Healing Sanctuary; later simply The Sanctuary.

Interested to stay abreast of what was happening elsewhere, we offered free bed and board at weekends for mediums serving the Stourbridge Spiritualist Church enjoying communication with a wide variety of people who shared with us at many levels, including their personal paths and metaphysical experiences, providing useful research. This phase lasted for only a year when I was given the news of a pending change. It is a bombshell. I am required to leave the Probation Service and take aboard a very different kind of task with a metaphysical component. It is to be experimental and experiential Energy Work and the location is Adam House; not just the Sanctuary but the whole of Adam House is now needed for 'the Work'.

Information given was detailed and specific. Adam House was to be developed as a high frequency energy zone and my full attention was necessary as I had to discover how to do it. As with the Ethnic Advisor's job there is no existing blueprint. The family home as we have known it, will now have to go in the melting pot along with my carefully constructed identity as an Officer of the Law complete with career prospects, substantial salary, and a great deal more that I had yet to discover. Scepticism as to the wisdom of following this new development simply cannot be counteracted by reason in such circumstances. That does not mean that reason does not clamour to be taken into account, so it is helpful when confirmation comes from an unexpected source.

Carmella had also been undergoing training for a shift in direction with a metaphysical component. As a student in Fine Arts she had opted to specialise in photography then had added editing skills by working for a magazine, later moving to Psychic News interviewing mediums and assessing their talents and integrity. Journeys to a Kibbutz in Israel had followed and after our year of healing work she had left to study with Paul Solomon at the 'Centre for Inner Light Consciousness' working as a volunteer at the "The Edgar Casey Foundation' at Virginia Beach in America. Already with experience of working Light Centres, and with a developing metaphysical awareness, she had independently become aware that it was time to return home to 'work' in Adam House. If we had needed confirmation this was it. Carmella returned home; I reluctantly tendered my resignation, explaining vaguely that there was something else that I had to do, and so they published my epitaph which, under the circumstances had some points of interest.

' Wendy Taylor pioneered the West Midlands Probation Service in the field of race and racism. She took the Service into territory which was unknown and unmarked; territory which was hazardous in giving rise to extreme, opposed opinions and feelings.

She bore the brunt of much of the frustration and discomfort of anyone who tries to move in this arena. There are always those who will say that one is moving too fast or touching things that would be better left alone. There are others who will accuse one of not moving fast enough, Wendy weathered those storms of protest as much by her own buoyancy of spirit and belief in what she was doing as by whatever support others were able to offer her. She brought the West Midlands Probation Service to the point of a definite avowal to address itself to issues in quite practical ways.'

Barrie Bridgeman ACPO

The choice of words was pertinent. I was about to engage in an area of metaphysical research, which many might say would be better left alone and was certainly unmarked territory.

Practical Wendy Taylor's identity was also about to go into the melting pot. My name had become synonymous with racial issues about which I had been writing prolifically. Mhaletta is the name by which my Communicators had told me I was known 'elsewhere'. Clearly familiar to me, I had answered to it from the outset using it as a pen name for the few esoteric articles I had published. Wendy therefore went where old names go, leaving Mhaletta to emerge and forge an identity in keeping with the next task which was progressing well. But then there is always the unexpected lurking.

A Conference on Humanistic Psychology made what I thought was a light weekend break as a gift to myself for my 50th birthday. I was on the train to London when the pre-warning came that I should stay alert as this would be a significant event. In one of the first small groups the phrase 'Divine Love' was being explored. Without divulging any personal experiences I commented that I regarded it as an un-earthly experience. Moving on into another room I heard a man speaking. What followed was explosive, dangerous, and totally unexpected. Here was someone with an experience similar to my own who had left the army, become a Consultant Psychologist, was having metaphysical experiences of both vision and voice and was also aware of Divine Love at a metaphysical level. The connection was instantaneous; the dynamic electrifying. I had not realised until then the intensity of feelings that my experiences had generated and the measure of control I had needed to employ. Now I did. And Derek knew the moment I walked in the door.

'You've met someone haven't you?'

'Yes'. There was no useless subterfuge. Neither was there any display of anger, or recriminations.

'I was afraid one day you might'.

I cannot explain other than that this is something different, more than.... The danger is obvious to us both. Was a thirty year roller-coaster marriage also heading for the melting pot? And what about the commitment to the Light Centre assignment? Way beyond reason by this point and unable to fathom what was happening I found myself in an agony of indecision. Everything seemed to be spinning beyond my control. All known advisers were silent. Derek offered me the breathing space that I needed.

'Do what you must **but do not leave**. You would not be able to sustain life four hundred feet up.'

It took three months in which I brought the two men in my life together to walk and talk, trying to understand this unsolicited event that was having such an impact on us all. Then I learnt of a man who could read the map of the hand. In an extra-ordinary act of trust I knew it was essential to listen to him and make a decision on his reading of the situation. A long train journey to meet him brought the answer, carefully, confidently reflected that there was work 'in hand' from which I could not deviate but the experience of human resonance had been a vital part of it. It was indeed Derek who, on this occasion, had played my wise advisor. What we had all three learnt from this encounter was inestimable. So, I faced the inevitable and let go. Then I needed all Wendy Taylor's 'buoyancy of spirit' to focus on the project ahead and became the one who welcomes strangers at the gate.

There was something else my map reader told me; that India was imprinted on the template of my palm.

25. The Foundation

Our original healing triangle is back together for a new venture. Carmella had invested her heart in people and places in America as I had in India and Adam House was ready and willing to reflect the best of both. It was essential that Derek remained in the Service to keep us afloat financially, joining us out of working hours.

MetaCentre: Foundation for Human Potential was launched unofficially at Christmas 1983 when we hosted fourteen complete 'strangers' for what became the beginning of a wider sense of family. The official opening was at Easter 1984. Thirty-four people gathered in the sanctuary for an Opening Ceremony as we made personal commitments to the work ahead. All were invited to speak, to share thoughts, visions, wisdoms, ideas or blessings as they chose. This would be how it would remain.

Easter Opening 1984
Carmella, Marael, Grace and Albert, Derek and Mhaletta.

The sense of freedom of release from the 'outside' world was revitalising. We now found ourselves in a position to design our own Centre life. There simply **was** no structure unless we created it. No rule book unless we wrote it. At first we did neither, instead we discovered the most profitable way forwards was simply to attune to the currents of each day. In that way we discovered that each day **had** a different current which could sweep us into creativity; physical activity; contemplation of the long view; planning events; pushing us out for unanticipated adventures. Every Day brought laughter and learning which was to continue in everything we did. We invented a paper clock without fingers, so that we could jump between time zones as we chose and sometimes confiscated watches to discover more of how it was in India when days gave the impression of elongating of their own accord.

Though I'm enjoying this huge change in lifestyle I soon realise that having delved into the field of research the urge is still there for gathering information and sculpting it into new paradigms from which changes in perception will emerge. Our prefix 'Meta' which had dropped from Carmella's pen accompanied by a symbol, is from the Greek, meaning 'beyond'. To go beyond anything it is wise to know what is there in the first place and so the research began in earnest.

It was obvious why we had not been given the green light to publish the transcripts of our Teachings. Bookshops had begun to open New Age/Spiritual sections and much of the same information we had received was appearing, written in a variety of different styles tucked into all manner of enlightening works. Other people had obviously been assigned the task of sharing this major informative wave in published forms. Books were already showing diagrams of the rising consciousness curve as those who had been in training to be a part of this major shift stepped forwards into a more active form of service. Our activity covered four areas. Firstly we collected books for our own research library; secondly we provided those people at the cutting edge with facilities, and a safe space in which to test their developing therapies and ideas; thirdly we attended talks and lectures on a wide variety of related subjects; and fourthly we visited any other Light Centres that we could find. There were no prototypes; and language base had to be built by collective use. We were all experimenting with our individual pieces of an ever growing jig-saw.

A holistic view was a key concept to relate to every subject we addressed, together with the challenge of finding ways to bring minds to bear on the unification of opposites. Triangular models kept appearing as we sought to use imagery to shift perceptions of a polarised world. Put together, we stretched our creative talents to new limits. Colour, music, drama, use of symbols, poetry and dance; all found their way into an increasingly active repertoire. All our research was funnelled into the prime task of discovering ways of building a sustainable high frequency energy field; the Alpha Field. People needed to be able to feel it, to step into it when they walked through the door; to absorb it and to leave replenished. In the first two years we counted one thousand eight hundred visitors participating in a wide range of gatherings and groups, and reflections began to tell us we were getting closer. The Plan which encapsulated the areas in which we had been working reflected our interpretation of a working Light Centre.

The Plan

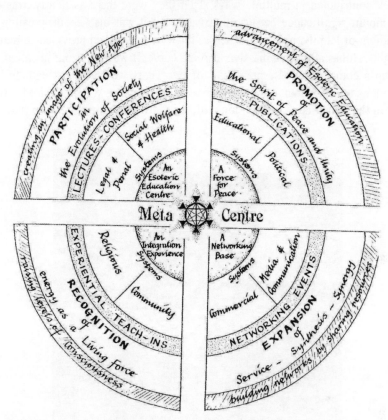

In 1986 the pen went to work and we published Evolution of the MetaCentre; a Centre handbook, in which we shared some of what we had learnt on our journey so far. Others too took threads of our work and ideas to weave them into their own. The Plan was published in Diarmuid O Murchu's book 'Coping with Change in the Modern World', under the caption: 'The Plan encapsulates the dream and vision of a new reality unfolding; eagerly awaiting realisation in our hearts and in our world', echoing our sentiments exactly.

Sir George Trevelyan had, along the way, become a father figure and yet another wise advisor, staying with us overnight when in the area. There had been evenings when we had sat beside the fire talking of the way ahead, sharing dreams and visions and he had spoken with a passionate certainty of Future Earth as a crystal sphere. **Always hold that image and its replica will form within the mind** was his wise advice.

Though Carmella worked with me full-time Sandra, Marc, Charlotte and Derek contributed in multiple ways. That they were there as family, was of paramount significance because that was what it was also about; creating a paradigm of Family, in its wider sense, for which India had provided so many insights. It has all been a massive learning curve. It was never our intention to set up a commercial enterprise and for two years we made just enough by donations to stay afloat. Then we sense change brewing. We are advised: **Stay within the parameters of the Plan within a state of readiness to respond.**

*With Carmella; Sir George Trevelyan; and our
Star symbol.*

26. Birthing an Archetype

In January 1986 Carmella went to a workshop in Devon and came home with a boyfriend, Abel, who became her partner and remained living with us at Adam House. My pen soon revealed the prediction that Carmella would become pregnant and that the coming child would be called **'wondrous one'** and would work from the moment of birth. Having no idea of how such an extraordinary notion could work out I left it at that. A pregnancy was soon announced with a birth date at the end of October. We all felt this event would offer significant learning as Abel and Carmella's inner guidance was that the birth was to be in water. It would take place in the sanctuary; needed to be recorded and publicised (whatever the outcome); and the holistic principles we had been testing were to be applied. Challenging, fascinating and many would say a little crazy! Birth in water was a method already in use in both America and France but not yet in favour in the UK. There had been no recorded water-births in the Midlands. Unbeknown to us we had been preparing a high frequency energy field in which to welcome a brand new life form and were ready to add the element of water and discover it effects.

New levels of trust were reached amongst us all as Carmella contacted *The Daily News*, a Birmingham based paper. The editor was on our wavelength, having had personal experience of our healing sanctuary, so he passed it to the News Desk. Two delightful reporters were sent and remained at the ready to find a 'quirky' story. First headlines announced 'birth in a fishpond', bringing a television crew to the doorstep resulting in Adam House making its television debut as the six pointed star symbol on the front wall played herald to the coming event.

The Health Service let its ego reign for a while as all manner of attempts were made to stop the plan. It was unstoppable. The birth of Benjamin Jaya took place in a beautifully converted garden pool in the Sanctuary. In what was literally a 'pregnant silence' twelve astounded people played their part as the silent watchers ensured there was a chalice of loving stillness to welcome a new life form as it broke the surface of the water. It was a photograph taken in the soft dawn light that was to convey the archetypal image of birth. Encapsulating a trinity of Father, Mother and Son we had caught an image of that energy of Ineffable Love in the moment of arriving life. Long ago we had been advised of our responsibilities: **It is the responsibility of those who experience Love Incarnate to share their**

expressions of those experiences that others may respond to the consciousness of Love within themselves.

The Joy and Miracle of Birth,

The Birmingham Offices of *The Daily News* came to a standstill as the photo taken seconds after the birth emerged from a hastily developed film. Filling the top half of the front page on the morning of 31st October 1986 our responsibilities were well met. Beside the photo stood the bold caption proclaiming the joy and miracle of a new birth; perfect for the breakfast table news, heralding a new life, a New Reality and water as a birthing medium.

Below the column referring us to the full story inside was reflection of the words that I had caught from somewhere in the ether months previously **WONDER BABY** (see page 3). So words, well tucked away, found themselves making news along with my own Page Three Girl! How we loved the synchronicity of it all. The only regret the reporters had was that the timing had not brought it out closer to Christmas when it would certainly have inspired a plethora of 'Nativity' captions. No doubt 'the timing' had its own reasoning!

Phone calls poured in; the media, from tabloids to The Times, wanting reproduction rights. The photo went international; we started to write; and Abel began to design and make Birthing Tubs in the cellar, experimenting with the prototypes in workshops which, for the next two years, drew midwives and pregnant parents responding to titles such as Water Birth and Culture; Spiritual Midwifery; and First Breath. By the time Abel's pools were operational he found a market ready in the hospitals. No-one else would need a converted fishpond! A new birthing paradigm had arrived via an archetypal imprint. What then is an archetype? The question formed the focus of a lengthy discourse from our Communicators beginning:

Of this word 'archetype' we would say that it is the Essence. It could be called the Presence. Again, it could be termed as energy, for the archetype is that which is formed upon which the future patterning can be matched; that an energy held in its original purity can be reproduced in matter, to hold as nearly as possible, its original patterning; the prototype. The physical bodies of Man have changed through a process of evolution because the shape of the body was not the prototype. What was the prototype was the energy that would be contained within that physical body, energy that is known by its effect...

Did this image hold energy more closely aligned to the original prototype of human life? It had certainly resulted in a wide ranging and positive effect. Benjamin Jaya B'Hahn, known as Benjaya, the 'water baby' became the face of water birth and that was how he began to 'work from the moment of birth'. Water-birth quickly became an accepted birthing method inviting enquiring minds to delve below the surface exploring the ancient practices and symbology of water, its healing and revitalising powers whilst making their own discoveries through their experiences.

Throughout the night of the birth, chants had echoed the voices of the monks of Taize. Their hill-top home in Cluny, France is a powerful high frequency energy point, which I have visited several times and witnessed a Brother-monk making a life commitment to the community. He is told of the way he treads:

This is a way contrary to all human reason; you can only advance upon it by faith, not by sight...whether you wake or sleep, night or day, the seed springs up and grows, you do not know how...

The words feel relevant, never more so than now when the wheel is turning yet again.

27.One Armed Signpost

Four great leaps set the direction for the end of the Eighties... the peaceful death of my mother; Carmella and family leave to set up home at Hill House Community in Bristol; the house is reduced to a building site for much needed extensions and I leap headlong into a Psychiatric Hospital. Derek had instigated my leap when he heard of a temporary vacancy for a Psychiatric Social Worker. It was his area of speciality at work, not mine, and I thought the suggestion ludicrous. He thought I would fit the bill very nicely and it was high time I produced regular funds. I applied, reluctantly, certain that I would be smartly rejected if this was not a useful move.

Interviews had previously been telling occasions. This time I have nothing to say. It consists of a walkabout around wards where people are in such extraordinary states of mind that conversation is not on the agenda. Energies produced by this conflagration of minds are haywire, swirling in dream-like nightmares, past memories hold minds trapped, scrambling to escape, inciting the physical body to hunt for exits; others search vacantly for someone or something non-visible. The hospital with its reinforced windows and locked doors holds innocents who have become their own jailers, unable to release themselves from time warps, memory traps, addictions, ephemeral worlds; a miasma of unrelated thoughts and loss of the ability to speak cohesively, or sometimes at all. Those well sedated convey a vacancy behind the eyes and shuffle or weave their way on limbs that don't always work out their pathway correctly. It is devastating and my heart aches.

I'm being told the nature and scope of the work. It is all irrelevant. I simply do not want to **be** here. I do not **belong** here. This is the most massive polarised leap that I could have imagined, other than being a patient! It is not a popular job and I am the only applicant, over qualified, under prepared. I sign a dotted line appalled to find myself becoming an instant Psychiatric Social Worker. I don't even know what I'm supposed to wear let alone do and I certainly have no affinity with hospitals.

It's an anti-climax to be allocated to the psycho-geriatric ward where the majority of patients are in advanced stages of dementia with which I am painfully familiar as my mother had been living in a twilight reality for some years. Allocated a private office tucked in the corner of the ward I make that tiny space into an oasis, a stress free corner, where people want to come to escape the madly swirling thought-forms of minds that are out of synch with the everyday world. Every patient has a file. I start one for daily jottings, hoping for enlightenment on this extraordinary turn of events, eventually recalling a recent prophetic phrase: **You approach a signpost that has but one arm to point the way.** Succinctly telling! I consider that I've passed the post. After my cushioned years in a high energy zone how will this chaotic energy affect me? Can I affect it in any positive way? What am I here to learn?

The post is temporary I'm pleased to say, but when offered three months at Birmingham University to take an added qualification giving the unenviable power of 'Sectioning' those considered a danger to self and/or others, I can see more of where the path is leading. There is no contest. I'm committed for two years of invaluable insight into the established world of Mental Health.

The learning has well and truly begun as I discover how to put people into boxes and categories, diagnose, discern between a range of reality states and write definitions of consciousness. With little opportunity to contribute from a personal perspective I jump thoughtfully through all the hoops, and receive my piece of paper. I am qualified to work alongside the Consultant Psychiatrist and watch him at work as he tries to re-anchor wayward minds. He uses a careful regime of questions that determine a person's reality state, a critical field for study when exploring meta-physical levels. It is essential that the grip on our physical, everyday reality is sustained whatever other-worldly experiences are taking place. It is necessary to know who we are, where we are, our age, where we live, the date, the Prime Ministers name and so on to put us squarely and securely into a common reality. I have innumerable questions of my own which cannot be asked of a psychiatrist or I might find myself in a box of trouble. A commonly used definition of consciousness that produces the common reality is: *'a person's usual state of alert awareness of himself, others and environment during waking hours, fed by a reservoir of past experiences, thoughts, feelings and environmental stimuli'.*

But what happens when the reservoir fills with uncommon experiences and uncommon thoughts bringing about an **unusual** state of awareness? For some it is a trip into oblivion or a psychiatric hospital...for others it is learning how to BE; how to function in the mainstream. I am back once again in a system, hiding my thoughts, unable to share the most enlightening and rewarding experiences of my life or add a definition of consciousness from where I stand. Never-the-less interesting opportunities are on the way.

It is discovered I have been a trainer. Would I be prepared to train staff from a social welfare perspective in what is referred to as 'the dementias.'? Yes, and thank you. I am given equipment, freedom to develop ideas, test materials, and explore methods of presentation as long as I deliver a balanced and useful contribution on the subject. Course evaluations from participants will be the proof of the pudding. At last. I am able to apply whole brain theories of learning by balancing analytical information and overhead graphs with colourfully creative depictions of energy at work; introduce a holistic approach to both work and life; and slip in my own reflections on consciousness! My favourite evaluation comment says it all: 'It was as if I saw the information you had given us in Technicolor'. A very metaphysical comment!

Next moves are to write a training manual and run an Alzheimer's support group. I have learnt to adapt, to contribute and to travel safely through these illusory worlds. And I have met death, the Great Teacher, many times. How differently relatives react. Some are distraught at not being called in the middle of the night to be present at 'the last breath' yet many deaths occur peacefully in the dark hours. What an anomaly after our intensive work with birth as 'The First Breath' that had been so inspiring. Why can the last breath not be the same?

A lucid elderly patient who had been brought in because of her refusal to eat explains to me that she is 'ready to leave'. I am required to 'talk to her' in other words to persuade her to comply with regulations. She is being drip-fed. I find her wanting to talk about the here-after she is not allowed to reach in this way. My tactic is to encourage her to speak of her New World that she is eager to reach, strengthening her mind with the awareness that she can travel there at will while waiting peacefully for the body to let go in its own time. These shared moments change her intention to leave. She chooses to eat and return home to a waiting husband. No one ever asks me for reassurance that there is a beyond. They hold their own knowing and maybe their visions are not all illusory. Every person I meet is a mystery, a storehouse of the unimaginable; each a teacher, and each touchable in ways that reach beyond words.

At home Adam House has survived the onslaught of the builders. The ground floor has expanded, having now a toilet and cloakroom, a large veranda and archways in the kitchen. It is ready for something else, and so am I.

28. The Recall

Eileen has been my friend through childhood and marriage to Ray, a man of many parts and places. A solider in his youth, Ray had tramped a trail in India. Years later, after his death, Eileen and her daughter celebrated his memory by reconstructing parts of his India journey. One of his duties had been as a guard at the Nazim's Palace in Hyderabad, India's fifth biggest city and capital of the state of Andhra Pradesh. On arrival at the airport she was approached by a man who earned a meagre living by assisting travellers. His name was George. Hyderabad flows into Secunderabad, creating a sprawling metropolis, so she engaged George as a local guide who led her with respectful courtesy that fitted the occasion. Persuaded by him to take a photo of his family, she visited his shoe box room and snapped them into her camera where they remained well hidden for two years until I arrived at her house for a visit. Looking through her albums I saw the photo. There he sat, a boy not yet of school age, perched on the edge of a bed, the first of a new generation, eyes straight forwards like a soldier on parade, looking *into* me! In that first glance I knew there was a connection. I felt it and said so.

'Over to you then', said my friend who had not felt any continuing connection, handing me the photo and address. Of all those thousands of children in Northern India years ago, none had spoken silently in this strange way. So I wrote to the unknown George, told him what had happened and offered to sponsor his eldest son's education. He replied:

As usual on the night of 31st December we thank God for the protection of the old year and welcome the new. On this night we asked for only one thing - a sponsor for Steven's education. We had strong faith that God would hear our prayer. It is true that God moves in mysterious ways.

We live in a small single room. The size is 15ft by 12ft. One portion we use as kitchen and the other for all purpose. We pay 300 rupees monthly rent £9. We have agreed to live on one meal a day if necessary and list childrens school fees first in monthly budget...

I began to make small monthly payments to cover Steven's school fees, gradually through letters, learning more of their environment, the rigours of their lives and the continuous struggle to balance the physical and educational nourishment of their growing family. Though life in Hyderabad was certainly impoverished it compared favourably to life in George's home village:

> *I come from a simple family in a tiny village in Orissa State. Its name is Rakeshponka and it is 900kms from Hyderabad. When you come to the village you will see that hills and forests are all around. It exists without electricity. People are laborious. The main crops are rice, dhal, oilseeds and banana fruit but during famine people depend on wild fruits, leaves and herbs. In summer men go hunting birds and wild animals. Men and women cover their bodies partly while children remain unclothed. You may name them as Stone Age generation. Up to this day the entire village is between the walls of illiteracy. The total population is around four hundred. In the entire village only I had the opportunity to learn English.*

George's ancestors originated from somewhere in Malaysia. His father had been the eldest of five brothers who had founded the village of Rakeshponka in the depths of a wildly forested area in the interior of Orissa State. George as the head man's son had been taken under the wing of a Belgian Priest, his introduction to English language being through the Bible stories. On the death of his father he had to return to help care for his big family of siblings carrying his thirst for education. In his early twenties he had left his village like a Dick Whittington to look for good fortune. Travelling around India he deliberately sought out places where English was spoken, first becoming fluent in an idiomatic way, rather than through text books, though his grasp of the pen soon followed and his thirst for knowledge was insatiable. He had found his good fortune in a marriage with Jenny, the sister of a man he had met on his travels. An Anglo-Indian from Calcutta, Jenny was slim and fair skinned in contrast to George's dark warm-brown complexion. Jenny was one of fifteen children, five of whom had died before the age of five. As a child, rescued from life on a railway station she had profited from the opportunity of schooling. Her mother tongue was English and both George and Jenny had long since determined that English should be the family's first language. So that is how the thread of a common language linked the East with the West.

Steven progressed and George arranged a transfer to a bigger school where more funds were needed to keep pace with uniform, books, and travel costs. He thrived. It was not surprising that George would suggest a sponsor for his next son, Stanley, assuring the family of two future wage earners. But the next child in age was a girl, Sandra, the same name as my eldest daughter. How could I in all western conscience pass her by? The situation had an immediate solution. I shared it at a reunion with two friends I was visiting in New York, Linda Loffredo and Nicoletta Cherubini. Linda who worked in the Women's Division at the World Trade Centre volunteered sponsorship of Sandra and Nicoletta, a professor from Sienna University (Italy) took on Stanley. Angela, the next in line, later found a sponsor in Karen Stratton from Wakefield UK and a prototype of a small global family unit began to emerge.

Elias (George's brother); George & Jenny
Sandra; Stanley; Angela; and Steven
(Genevieve, the fifth child has not yet been born)

By 1989 the tenor of George's letter had changed. In June he wrote:

There has been much improvement in my living and I can see that education and friendship have promoted me and my children to this wonderful world. As you know the world accepts today that primary education is one of the essential parts for every human being. But in our country it is different. A good education in India is equal to good shopping in a super market with a pocket full of money. That is how prosperous and influential families grasp the best school territory from early centuries and decades. I am inspired by my children's schooling. Do you know how many small children are deprived from schools because of family deficiency?

Yes, I did know. But did I want to think about this big question any further? An even bigger question was on the way.

Would you be interested to encourage us to extend opportunity to more children through a small kindergarten school in English medium? English is the key to the world's knowledge and a tongue for the future generation.

Despite the school sponsorships the family were still living hand to mouth. Was there a project settling on my doorstep? Could they handle such an initiative? How would I know unless I met them? And was there a problem gnawing away behind my mind, blocking my inner knowing? Obviously! The warning had been given and heard. Do not return to India, it may activate that sleeping giant that can screw your life up overnight! Yet India was reaching out for me, calling, daring me to return, and testing my ability to balance courage with prudence perhaps. I agonised, and then I let the agony go, because suddenly I knew. Sandra, my eldest daughter simply said, 'I'm coming with you'.

The knowing brought with it another. My hospital work was coming to an end. My mind had been well filled but my heart had never really left the Probation Service. Pension rights determined that I must work on for a few more years so I applied to re-join the Service on my return. Even after my six years of defection I was welcome and was offered various options of a post. My choice was to join a peripatetic team of old hands assigned to travel to wherever there were knotty problems to be solved. In the meantime I needed to solve my own. Our leaving date fell into place. October 24th 1990, an October departure again and we had only three months left in which to raise some funds or there would be nothing to discuss. We set ourselves a target of £1,000 and met it by the usual money raising ploys of car boot sales, talks, and workshops, crowned by India Day at the hospital. The ward was electrified with colour, saris and images, staff and relatives brought gifts, made donations and asked questions. India was tangibly and visibly present. The closing entries in my day's journal encapsulate the sense of closure and a new door opening. It reads:

'My work here is over and a sense of finality overcomes me. It looks and feels as if the gods have amalgamated on Windsor Ward. What difference between gods and people? All play their parts in making journeys possible for those who must carry the ticket to travel. What a bouquet! All the colours of India translated into perfume. Exhilaration, exhaustion and feelings beyond expression as I recognise I am leaving more than a hospital. It has been a plane of existence and certainly a Hall of Learning. Now I have truly begun to feel the magnetism of India again. If this is another assignment then so be it.'

Wisdom words are a part of our display. One verse from the writings of The Mother of Pondicherry whose words have become an intrinsic part of my life reads:

We are at a decisive hour in the history of the earth.
It is preparing for the coming of the superman
And because of this the old way of life is loosing its value.
We must strike out boldly
on the path of the future despite its new demands.
The pettinessess once tolerable, are tolerable no longer.
We must widen ourselves to receive what is going to come.
THE MOTHER 29th December 1971

We had been given the name of Mr. Mohan, a businessman in Hyderabad, by a friend of long standing. He had been alerted to assist us with accommodation and advise us in any way necessary. Unbeknown to us, the day before our arrival there had been an insurrection and violence in the city and Mr. Mohan had been sending calls in an attempt to stop us travelling. What is known as a *bundh* was in progress - when activity ceases and a strict police curfew confines everyone indoors. We did not receive the message. We would have gone anyway. It was a recall on another turn of the spiral both to India and to the Probation Service, those twin teachers who had entwined themselves around my life had come for me again and now Sandra is a vital part of it.

The Second Part

The Hand Over

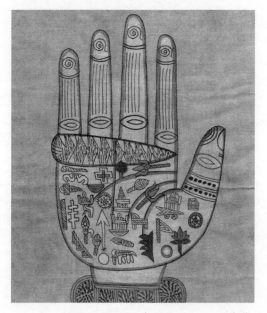

Every culture is a power that rises and fall prey
to the stirring of the cauldron by the Hand of Destiny

29. The Gates of Hyderabad
Journaling in Tandem
Two people writing independently of the same experience are as two mirrors.
No one sees the whole, yet each can see into the whole, one perhaps
to catch the sunlight while the other reflects the Hand of Destiny

23rd October 1990

Sandra: Who would have thought of it? Not me. Definitely not me! What do I
have to do with India? Nothing at all so far except in these last months of trying
to help in raising the pot of gold. Am I a seasoned traveller? Nothing much
beyond teenage adventures with a rucksack to the Riviera carrying a large alarm
clock and high heeled boots! Then, after a Cyprus honeymoon life had turned
inwards instead of outwards. Home, family and my inner life has been my world.
So how did it happen? What an amazement that Clive simply agreed to look after
our three children for twenty-five days. I'm not in the work-a-day world so have
no personal finance available. We have raised just enough by family donations.
It's incredulous to me from any angle. My mind can't get a grip of it. I'm on
tip-toe with a travelling bag packed full of toys and gifts and iron rations. The
only trouble is I've arrived at Adam House for a 2am launch and have forgotten
to pack my carefully chosen travelling outfit. My saffron coloured persona is left
hanging firmly to my wardrobe door. If I'm leaving something behind, let's hope
this is all. After what happened to mother I'm a bit wary and intended to be fully
prepared. So what to do?

    Clothes breathe identity and I do not have one just at the moment.
My mother is smaller than me in some ways, not in others! Rather strangely **she**
is wearing a saffron travelling suit borrowed from my sister, Carmella! My legs
are long, so my father handed me his trousers that have seen many a journey and
returned safely. Mother provided a matching top of hers, so here I am in parental
disguise and rather beside myself!

24th October 1990

Mhaletta: Dawn take off. No tears, no tearing sense of loss, loneliness or
trepidation, all superseded by an immense joy at the return. Charlotte has been
kissed a 2am goodbye in the safety of her bed and a warmly smiling Derek has
waved us away, yet the notion lingers that he has not gone. His presence is firmly

anchored beside me in those blue trousers.

An electrical storm slices the clouds below us as we ride high, writing lists of questions for George, ways to raise funds, places of interest to visit. The writing triggers the realisation that we are not only immersed in a massive mushroom of thought but we feel that we have merged into one rather over-active mind, albeit with two oddly assorted bodies!

Lunch mats carry imprints of lotus feet, triggering thoughts of the golden threads woven into slippers on the last journey. I know that there is no right or wrong path, decision or act – only the unwinding of a thread already spun for the purpose of this journey. We will discover what we make it... or it of us!

25th October 1990

Bathed in the vibrant orange of a risen sun one minute we land to find Bombay in darkness and the night air is a heavy blanket. Switching planes we fly into the dawn as the sun follows us to Hyderabad.

We spot George immediately, then Jenny and some of the children amongst a swarm of imploring brown faces, hungry for our luggage and a rupee for breakfast. Our bags are wrestled away from us. George is serenely watching it all take place. He had organised our 'handlers' as he had organised everything else possible to draw us into the heart of his family.

Sandra: The shock of it had to come sooner or later. It was sooner. Bundles of wet humanity prone, as if dead to this world already; shanty towns; street dwellers cleaning teeth in gutter water and relieving themselves freely. Squalor is in the air. I'm breathing it in, together with plaster from crumbling walls and animals in various states and stages of life. Three wheeled scooters swerve around craterous rain filled holes. We're in two of them... the scooters, not the holes, yet! We cannot talk. I cannot speak at all. I'm overwhelmed by India.

Mhaletta: The twin cities of Hyderabad and Secunderabad (our destination) merge in a central lake. The city cloaks me like a net, a filigree of human life. George's room opening from a communal courtyard is windowless brick and blackened plaster. One single webbed bed serves a family of seven. Baby Genevieve lies sleeping on a mat on the stone floor in near darkness. One flickering candle reflects on the paraffin blackened patches and a few worn posters. Children give shy smiles. How is it one can reel with love and shock at the same moment?

Coffee, delicious, in tiny cups is served by Jenny and their eldest daughter Sandra, as our whispered words begin bridging miles and cultures, adding living illustrations to the vivid pictures of their letters. Dawn light reveals the beauty and vivacity of the children as they warm towards us. Now we are a group of nine, four adults and five children. Their neighbours and landlord, who are one and the same, invite us into their home in the courtyard. The introduction which works so well in India is to show photos to place oneself in the context of family, home and country. We are well prepared and the faces of our family arrive to make their presence known. We already feel an immediate sense of inclusion in the awakening lives around us.

When the city opens its doors we set out on foot for the bank. There had been a problem in that George had been unable to withdraw the funds I had sent out weeks previously. The reason was evident. Piles of dusty slips of paper were stacked in all manner of boxes and trays awaiting entry into Dickensian ledgers. Amazingly they found my remittance, deep down but retrievable. We are solvent.

It's time to find Mr. Mohan and sort out accommodation. George accompanies us to Banjara Hills, an upper class area of Hyderabad. Mr.Mohan is at home working in his office on the ground floor of a pleasant corner house. He is a business man engaged in making training films. There is consternation at our arrival, having expected we had received his advice to cancel and his house was now a safe house for relatives plus an American exchange student. What to do? Assuring us the problem was his, we were plied with refreshments whilst he made a booking for us at a city hotel insisting that he would pay all expenses and oversee our welfare during our visit ending in an invitation to speak with his Rotary Club friends the following evening.

Our room in the hotel is large, darkened by wooden panelling but with its own bathroom. We are gratefully pleased to have this private space to regroup our senses. There is no question of jet-lag as we plunge into sharing our first impressions and agree that we move on further to explore this family's dreams.

26th October 1990

Sandra: 7am. Hammering on the door to deliver a newspaper. Mhaletta reads it selecting bits to read aloud to me. She reaches the engagements column interested to learn what entertainment is on offer and what dignitaries are visiting.

'It's Mrs. Mhaletta from U.K.!'

She isn't joking. Her face is a picture. We've only been in the country a matter of hours and she is listed as speaking at The Gateway Hotel on 'Britain's concern for Third World Countries'. How on earth did she get into that?

'Did you give him that topic and agree to speak?'

'I don't think so. I thought he meant just speaking to his friends informally.'

'Are you going to do it? What will you say?'

'I don't know yet'.

'Do you know anything about the subject?'

'No. It's political. I've no mandate to speak for Britain … or anybody or anything. I'll just have to stand up and see what happens.'

We laugh and forget about it.

Mhaletta: We're not keen to test hotel food yet so we breakfast on oat bars and apple juice then take a cycle rickshaw to see George who said he would have a plan. He does. We are taken to a small private school in the suburb of Mehendiputnam. The proprietor wants to sell the goodwill and hand over the rented premises which are licensed for education. The school premises consist of the ground floor of a large white house, smart on the outside but unfurnished and unpainted inside. The children are a captivating motley of all ages and sizes between three and eleven years old. Two women called 'teachers' are untrained and little more than minders. A few tattered books are shared. A few scattered benches try to look as if they are filling the space of a large central area with dusty rooms leading off. Oh what a challenge to provide resources that would transform this into anything like a western style classroom with visual aids…and the rest. Schools have to conform to the Indian School Curriculum. Much is learnt from books and our school would be in English Medium meant to assist the young ones in applying for places in more prodigious schools, opening the gates to higher education. Our minds run riot with the size and responsibility of it all.

It was Jenny who told us in her own quiet and gentle way that she had been coming here as a volunteer for over a year getting to know the children and the curriculum. She was holding a dream whilst working to make it a reality. She would be the strength in the care of the little ones as she had cared for her own without question. George would be the organiser and the Principal and her children would grow up in an environment where they could share their learning. How many nights and days have they spent talking, planning and preparing to hand over the dream? They had also found a flat nearby as the school was not habitable to double as a home.

We try to discuss pros and cons rationally but this is well beyond logic. George has all the answers anyway. We only have to transfer the ownership, re-register the school and re-open as *MetaCentre Public School in English Medium.* The four of us will need to be registered as *MetaCentre Educational Society.* It was our second day in the city, still morning and we were in the throes of becoming a Society and the owners of a school.

Lunch is taken at Sandra's school a fair ride away. We are welcomed by the Headmistress who takes us for a tour but there is little of note except for the absence of facilities. A large concrete area is surrounded by rows of box shaped classrooms. 1,700 girls are divided into groups of seventy per room.

The local bazaar looks tempting but it is time to return to the hotel to unleash the shower of books, toys, clothes, maps, and gifts we have collected over the last months. Little Genevieve aged three, the baby of the family, laughs on and on, rolling balls, tossing dolls. It is a deluge of loving sharing when the material world gives the pleasure for which it was surely created.

Mr. Mohan phones to remind me he will be collecting us within the hour. My brain has been otherwise engaged. A shower and change and we are off to meet a challenge of a different nature at the other end of the spectrum. The Gateway Hotel sits in pride of place on the edge of a lake. The Conference Suite is filled with men who are clearly at home in that setting. A talk on European Economy is the opening session. I do not enjoy it as I have been given pen and paper to write a synopsis for introduction to my contribution which will follow. It is short and to the point although as yet I do not have one. But the adrenaline begins to run, nerves are taut and I know words will present themselves if I make a beginning. And so when I have to, I do.

'Gentlemen of Hyderabad Rotary Club, I am honoured to be with you tonight to speak on 'Britain's Concern for Third World Countries'...and a theme evolved. This is the gist of it.

The commercial response of Britain to calls from the East is not my concern, though indeed the West is coming with its technology and skills honed by years of focus on providing the infrastructure of an ever evolving society. And you, as businessmen will be the vital links that make change happen. There will be great benefits and risks also of the dilution of cultures that are the very fabric of India. Yet all cultures in the world evolve, that we must accept and be ready to join the guiding hands that influence direction.

Beyond the Halls of Commerce is a body of people, the nature of a nation with a history to assuage and a future to ensure for our children, mine and yours. They may play no noticeable part in corporations yet they hold a corporate energy that, when harnessed, has the potential to bring change where change is due. Thousands of individuals contribute towards the education of disadvantaged people in many parts of the world each being drawn to their own marker point in Eastern Europe, Africa or Asia

*by many and extra-ordinary means, each having their own story. I am here
tonight to tell you of mine, a mystery, and a tale that has brought us here
together tonight to ask you to wonder at it with me and share with me in
a night of thanksgiving....*

So I told of the prophets from the East, the claim that India has made upon my
life and how I have answered...thus far. Then instead of eliciting questions from
the audience I become the questioner.

*Tell me. Is this a mission of goodwill to open further the hearts of
the West? Is it a personal debt I have to pay, a working out of karma, or
is this affinity for a country of many cultures the memory of some once
lived life? Is it any of these things or something else, indefinable? How I
would enjoy talking more with you all about unknowable things. All I have
discovered yet is that I have to come when India calls and hand over to a
Guiding Intelligence greater than I can comprehend that knows me better
than I know myself. So now I have taken that first step and am here for
your guidance and advice. But before our work begins, George, the father
of our education project tells me that a journey must be made to meet
with his elders in the village of Rakeshponka in the interior of Orissa. This
I know you will understand and I ask for your blessings on that journey
into the unknown that each of us travels every day of our lives, and
thereafter.*

*I salute you gentlemen for the work that you do for your
organization is well known in England...*

I'd enjoyed the telling of it and so it seems had they. We accept
invitations to a Muslim wedding; meeting with a man who had set up a village
school; an invitation to speak on Holism at a Radionics Conference and a dinner
party. Then we are whisked away through a downpour to the Nazim Club for a
lavish dinner and talk of radio and television programmes and even an offer to
take us by car to Sai Baba's Ashram if time allows. All doors are left open until
our project is under way. It has been a substantial day.

27th October 1990

Sandra: The world seems to be in quite a hurry to get us off the mark but here
comes a gap when we seem to have a morning to explore on our own and I want
to buy some postcards. We learn they can be bought at the Ritz Hotel. So where
is it? We follow a map navigating on foot amongst craters and chaos and find

ourselves climbing a winding side street of stalls leading to the glittering white Venkatashwara Temple. Barefoot now we move with the flow of Hindus up flights of steps to circle a great golden rod pointing skywards, drink holy water and gaze at the twin cities spread out below us. Well, some of us drink holy water. Mhaletta copies the man in front of her and throws it over her head only to find he had drunk the water first and was just wiping his hair! She is given a second go, thank goodness. In front of us the sun reflects on the lake acting as a giant mirror and behind on the horizon looms the Golconda Fort, our destination for the afternoon. Cards and all manner of souvenirs are here and we never do find the Ritz. We emerge from another labyrinth of pathways opposite Thomas Cooks, reminding us to fill up with rupees. Our feet have a life of their own this morning! We arrive back at Dwaraka Hotel at the same time as George and Steven who have come to take us to collect Jenny and the children for an afternoon OUT!

Mhaletta: Golconda. Is it the biggest fort in the world? It looks like it with its seventeen mile circumference. Gigantic gates are studied with iron spikes to stop elephants battering them down. Formidable, but it's a weird energy. More steps, three hundred and sixty five, I'm told, one for each of the king's wives. My mind is a mixture of silly images and an inexplicable pressure. History hangs all over me and I can feel the weight of it. The walls still stand and though there's no visible roof it feels as if there is a heavy stone ceiling above me. Images of gods are carved all over the walls of stone holes where prisoners spent torturous half buried lives. The atmosphere is oppressive to me yet the children are in high spirits. Dancing and leaping they clap to hear the echoes whilst I am contending with the echoes of the past and its clinging imprints. Caught in a wave of sadness I am glad to leave.

Sandra: I've been getting to know the children this afternoon, five of them between the ages of three and nine. Angela is the quiet one who likes to hold my hand; little Genevieve skips tirelessly around us; Sandra is Jenny's right hand, the motherly one; Steven the family runner of errands bursts with energy and confidence whilst Stanley seems to absorb everything. They are a mixture of characters yet the family have an intensely close bond. Mhaletta reckons they have incarnated as a group and that is one reason we have been linked  to them. We travel back in two auto rickshaws the children goading the drivers to race, screaming with laughter … or is it fear? It's a dead heat and we fall on the bed in a laughing heap.

Enough! Darkness just drops out of the sky here and we feel like dropping with it but we are in an auto rickshaw trying to return and are being driven in an unfamiliar direction. My adrenalin is rising ready for a fight, verbal or otherwise and Mhaletta is rehearsing frightening Punjabi phrases. We've taken a back route to avoid the traffic that's all. How quickly imagination can kick in. We rush upstairs feeling silly and tired. Mhaletta is engrossed in her journal drawing diagrams of connecting lines between the Temple and the Fort. We know there are underground tunnels between the two built as an escape route for the king if the fort is attacked. She is drawing light lines above showing nodal points at each end. The Golden Rod and the Lake are conductors she tells me. I think she senses more than can be explained by words.

28th October 1990

Mhaletta: Its Sunday. George has matters to attend to and so have we. He is following up the negotiations for the transfer of the goodwill of the school and also needs to procure tickets for the train journey to Orissa. We have agreed to leave on Thursday. Today we plan to visit the Shri Aurobindo School and meet Dr. Reddy for advice on our school project. It proves to be a huge building with a side entrance to the Centre for Human Studies. A courtyard full of plants holds a photo of Shri Aurobindo in pride of place. Gentle voiced people smile and invite us to sit in an oasis while an unknown man gives an introduction to the history of the Centre and the School. Dr. Reddy had been instructed to set up a school in the 1960's. He gave his house which is now the Centre and the school now houses a thousand pupils who follow the Government curriculum but use Montessori methods. We are invited to take breakfast with Dr. Reddy, a tall imposing presence. A diabetic, he is served with respectful concern for his health by his wife who oversees our unexpected breakfast of eggs and juices.

Next we are taken upstairs into the Meditation Hall. On the dais where the remains of Shri Aurobindo lie, orange and gold flowers form the shape of a six pointed star. The sun streams across the marbled floor. The energy in the room is electric, empowering and familiar. It is the opposite of the previous day at Golconda when darkness seemed to be pressing upon me. Today it is light that pours into us both. We are drenched in it. Moving slowly, we step next door into the Sanctuary of The Mother. Her chair stands empty, yet it is not. Her energy presides. Here she has remained a living Presence, still manifesting Ineffable Love. Her chair is surrounded by symbols of significance in her life … and ours. We sit, Lotus style, facing 'her'. In silence I acknowledge her as True Mother and all that implies. She has been an invisible influence on my life for many years, now it feels as if that invisibility has entranced me, that energy of pure love impregnated with wisdom is a living force- field here. It is contagious and once realised is indestructible. There is an aspect of her Being that will go with me. But in these moments we are far beyond words. Dr. Reddy is waiting with information for which we had asked of salary structures for teachers and the like but we already had what we had come to find and our concentration seems to have been dissolved by our experience.

Sandra: Sublime is my word for this morning. I cannot find a word for what came after. The Charminar Gate is Hyderabad's central archway in the middle of a Muslim bazaar. We can't walk about here. I'm pulled physically, dragged from side to side by ragged women. It feels as if they are trying to pull the flowers off my dress. We escape down a side street. Bad choice! All around we hear chanting voices full of aggression. I feel vulnerable, exposed and very white. There is something wrong here and we dare not go further from the main square so it's back to the Gate. Police are lounging by vehicles, watching, waiting. We reach a police car and stand with our backs to it but the crowds are thickening. They are like no crowds I have ever seen or felt before. Then on the fringe we spy an old, thin-as-a-stick man, peddling a bicycle rickshaw and make a dash for it. We are IN and he is peddling away. We give no instructions other than 'go... GO!' Anywhere will do away from this place, anyway we don't know our way back and dare not take a map out. He peddles on and on. Suddenly we see the familiar lake and recognise the road to our hotel by the position of the Temple. How could he possibly have known where to take us? Mhaletta is busy overpaying him as I jump thankfully out into a pool of bullock dung. It splatters up my calf and over the hem of my flowery dress. We look for water and find a slimy puddle. I take a tissue from my bag and try to make do. It's not the slime that bothers me as much as the energy that we have just come through. My nerves are shot to pieces. A group of boys are bearing down on us. I cringe. What next? They only want to shake hands and hurry on. My hands are shaking already! The sun is blisteringly strong and I need a drink. We try a roadside café . No-one moves to serve us. We move off on jelly legs and I purchase something from a stall. It tastes rough and slithers of undetermined things lie in sediment at the bottom.

Our room is our sanctuary until a cleaner enters sweeping the carpet backwards and forwards raising clouds of dust mites. What a morning of contrasts! Two worlds, one in which I feel I fit and the other never ... NEVER! I can hardly breathe in it and will not have it creep in here. Mhaletta is recovering by writing poetry. She reads a sample to me. It's about our rickshaw man:

> *Take us in your rickshaw thin man,*
> *Carry our fat western purses through the dust.*
> *Take us to the river next thin man,*
> *Show us washing covered rocks and buffalo.*
> *Take us; take us further on and on*
> *What matter if your bones are cracked with pain?*
> *Take us, take us; do not let us stop*
> *Lest we should wipe your sweat with silken scarves*
> *And bid you sit while we take up the shafts.*

How to reconcile these two worlds? I simply do not know.

Mhaletta: A messenger is at the door. We had agreed to meet with Mr. Bala Krishna at his home at 3pm but he had called in our absence to say there was a change of plan and he would be coming to the Hotel instead at 4pm. This is good news. Neither of us wants to venture out again this afternoon as we have an evening dinner party. Mr. Krishna proves to be a most welcome diversion. He is a learned man, a great raconteur and we are able to ask a wide range of educational questions and listen to his informed answers and innovative ideas.

By evening we are back on track, find an auto rickshaw driver who locates the address of Mr. Ahsan and family at the end of a very dark road. They are amazed to see us arrive unescorted at night and promise an escort home. Three generations of this delightful family are our entertaining hosts. Mrs. Ahsan is a teacher at the prestigious Hyderabad Public School. Mr. Mohan is also a guest and we are able to share with him our travel plans to Orissa which raise a few eyebrows as if they are glad they are not in our shoes. Swapping anecdotes there is much to laugh at as they tell us of their houseboy who refuses to use their brand new vacuum, hence they too suffer from the abundant dust mites. Dinner, a mouth watering spread of choices arrives at 10pm and we are well ready to be escorted back by Mr. Mohan and the American student, Steve.

It is late for journaling but images of the day are crowding in pressing to find imprints on the page; but it is the energy of The Mother that I hold to and have no doubt that she also holds me.

30. The Bundh

29th October 1990

Mhaletta: The seventh day, the ending of our first week starts well. It is George's choice of programme that takes us to St. Francis's Girls College and the bank. We arrive to find he is already out on a mission and it will be Jenny taking us out. It is good to be out with Jenny taking the lead. What we had thought of as a lack in confidence was only shyness and because George, as the male is the acknowledged spokesperson in this family.

The College is large, cool, spacious and well equipped. Posters carry maxims such as 'do not mind mistakes, that is why pencils have erasers'. The energy feels warm and friendly as is Mother Christine, the Principal. She speaks of George and Jenny who she obviously knows well, as courageous, very determined and tenacious; characteristics we are discovering fast. One of the nuns has already visited the proposed school premises and stresses how it will be an impossible undertaking without regular financial support if the intention is to reach disadvantaged children whose parents have nothing spare to contribute. George and Jenny already have the nuns blessing.

In the bazaar we stock up with fruit and return home just before George arrives clearly concerned that the School negotiations have become complex. It is now too late to go to the bank today which we will need to do before our journey so we return to The Dwaraka.

This is the day of the Muslim wedding so we spend time arranging each other in our finery. It is time for my silver and burgundy sari to have an outing and Sandra is in soft folds of a lilac and blue sari with a silver shawl. Feeling elegant enough and appropriately dressed we float downstairs and are immediately called to the telephone. It is Mr. Mohan.

'Please go to your room and close the door soundly. A bundh has been called. There is curfew. No-one must be on the streets'.

Sandra: I feel ridiculous now sitting in a sari. It comes off quicker than it went on. Our window overlooks a police station and busy thoroughfare. We watch as gradually traffic flow ceases. Only the police are a visible presence. Sounds of gunfire, rifle fire I think; the hotel gates are slammed and padlocked and guards are posted. Instead of being at a wedding we are in a fortress. The speed of events in India is just mind blowing. When things get out of hand my favourite phrase is 'how interesting' which covers a range of unspeakable emotions. Tonight it does not stop at being interesting, it is downright scary! We are alert to every noise. Sounds of furniture being moved about make me wonder whether people are blocking bedroom doors. I switch on the television for the first time and am amazed to tune in to a programme in English. It is like having someone arrive to tell us what we need to know. Hyderabad is indeed under curfew for thirty-six hours following insurrections, demonstrations, stabbings, looting and killing. Guess where? The murder was at Charminar Gate! Can you sense murder in the air, on the way, closing in? That is the nearest I ever want to get to finding out. Thousands of police are being drafted in. I suggest that we both draft in a few of our own security forces so we spend a safe night guarded by everyone from my father to The Mother; my special guardsman Guru Gobind Singh, a formidable warrior whose maxim is 'when all else has failed it is just to take up the sword'. We have a peaceful night.

30th October 1990

Mhaletta: My first thought on waking is that it is Benjaya's birthday. He is three years old. We wonder how he will be celebrating and doubt if anyone at home could imagine where we are spending it. There are neither papers nor water other than a small bowl delivered to the door. We open the balcony doors, well secured last night, and have a view of police activity. The police who yesterday were wearing flip flops, today have shoes and jaunty red crash helmets. A few people are trying to run the early morning curfew but have no chance at all. They are caught. Even a scooter is beaten with canes and a motor bike is confiscated. The energy is electrifying and dangerously unpredictable. Gently strolling buffaloes are bellowed at and flicked on their rumps for good measure. Nothing and no-one is exempt. We cannot sit out as we feel exposed to stray bullets. I want to take photos of incidents but prudence wins. I would never make a reporter in a war zone.

George phones. He is ready to run the curfew to bring food and spend the day with us. We give a graphic account of police activity and refuse to let him come near. A rare day in India of compulsory free time stretches before us in which to rest and use our day in constructive reflections. So we do.

We have been moving swiftly through extreme polarities such as:

❖ **Poverty** (everywhere) to pockets of **affluence**
❖ **Upliftment** (at the Temple) to the **weight of history** (at the Fort)
❖ The most **holy** (at the Ashram) into the most **unholy** physical violence
❖ The freedom of the **open city** to **entrapment** of the bundh.

India is a pendulum. She forces you to extremes, to discover where your trip wires lie. At any moment we must be ready to move whilst keeping our balance, good humour and our focus on the purpose for which we are here without any personal investment in the outcome. Sandra is working on the trip wires so she isn't caught napping!

Sandra: I am at the ready to be an expert on trip-wires and fill a page or two. Pressure is the big one, so I list what comes to mind of the lessons that India is offering on a daily basis that are most likely to become even more stressful on our jungle journey.

- Bulging conscience. What can I do about this?
- Pressure to be drawn into events which can then escalate beyond control.
- The very physical world to be dealt with constantly in order to function
- Violence of any kind
- Communication: Reading non-verbal signs (what does *this* head shake mean?)
- Accents, cannot always hear or interpret.
- Difficulties in walking about safely due to holes, traffic, pressure from beggars.
- Hygiene. (Flies on food etc.)
- Maps (or lack of). Finding the way amongst unmapped paths.
- Fear!

And that is only for a start!
We are here to DO SOMETHING ABOUT SOMETHING so at least I am dealing with No.1. on the list. I intend to be intrepid, non-judgemental, positive and safe!

Mhaletta: That gave us plenty to talk about then inevitably we followed with lists of the difficulties we already foresee in starting a school (too numerous to even mention at this stage) followed by the benefits of the bundh. It is good to end our swathe of mind-work on a positive note. After a game of dominoes we sleep the afternoon away and wake for the early evening news. The bundh is to continue until 6am on Thursday. It is only Tuesday so this is not good news. We have not opened our door all day and are eating whatever bits and pieces we have in our diminishing food store.
The benefits of the bundh do not seem so plentiful now.

31st October 1990

Mhaletta: Another internal day at the ready, and why not? Why should the external bustle of life always take precedence? Why should inner contemplative days be enforced as if they were the best one can do when imprisoned. So much is taking place in here, in us, as a part of the preparation for the next spool of the thread to unwind. I have a sense that we will look back on these Dwaraka days as a haven.

So the day begins by gently reading a newspaper which has slipped silently under the door. A moving article informs that fourteen million children die every year; nine million of them being in India, Pakistan and Bangladesh. That is thirty eight thousand children dying every day! The day has turned sombre as we try to comprehend the magnitude of the statistics. Then George phones. He is not pleased at us being here. He and Jenny would like us to be **there.** I explain we are unable to leave. George insists he will run the gauntlet. He arrives having been to the airport where he is well known and has a pass valid until tomorrow. We are suitably amazed. There is still no transport. He had hitched a lift from a police inspector! The pass does not include us so we settle down to enjoy the hot sweet tea he has organised while giving birth to the School on paper. We are all agreed on the name of MetaCentre Public School, Hyderabad and the school motto emerges at Sandra's suggestion as JOY IN UNITY, words which are to be set around the circumference of a circle holding our six pointed star within a lotus. At some level the school is becoming a reality although the delicate negotiations are now at a standstill because of the bundh.

We had sent George a copy of our MetaCentre Handbook and he was well prepared to talk holistic philosophy, adding ideas of how we could also care for the health and welfare of the children by daily drinks and regular health checks. He is so keen for our school to be different, full of colour, creativity, sports activities and fun!

Tomorrow is Thursday which should see the end of the bundh and our departure to Orissa. George has managed to procure four tickets for the 1.30pm train. The fourth is for his eldest son, nine year old Steven, who George feels should be a part of this historic journey to meet his ancestors. We ask for an outline of route and how long we will be gone. It is somewhat sketchy as much depends on transport connections and accommodation, both of which seem to be unpredictable. The train will only take us as far as Berhampur on the Orissa coastline. We will then have to organise transport to Mohana a small town closer to Rakeshponka and then somehow cross a substantial river which isolates Rakeshponka in a loop.

He estimates we will stay a couple of nights in the village plus travelling time both ends. We are at a loss to know what to pack as our outfits are more for city wear. In any event George is proposing to take bags and bundles of his children's clothing plus some of the toys we had brought for the village children so we are advised to travel light and leave the rest of our luggage with Jenny.

Our last task of the day is for me to give Sandra healing as a bout of diarrhoea had caught hold in the last couple of days and travelling was causing some disquieting thoughts on this and various other fronts, not the least the prospect of sleeping in mud huts.

31. The Great Escape

1st November 1990

Mhaletta: We are instantly alert on waking. The plan is to stock up on rupees from Thomas Cooks and go to George's for breakfast. We are packed and urgent now to escape. It is strangely quiet outside. We sign the bill as agreed with Mr. Mohan who will settle up later. At 8.30am we are on the doorstep discovering that the bundh is still on and they have not been able to contact Mr. Mohan. We wait. The bill is settled and we are released into the empty street where there is no transport of any kind. I am told by the guard that I need a pass to move out. Its time to step into the police station.

There are thirty or so policemen milling around who wave me away to wait at control (which is closed) with a jostling crowd who tell me 'ten to one'. Thinking this means the office does not open until ten minutes to one o'clock I say forcefully 'TOO LATE!' Amongst this mayhem I hear voices calling me. The hotel has obtained a scooter with driver willing to take us (without passes) for double the price. We pay and roll away safely through the empty streets. George is at the Airport trying to get us passes as we learn the bundh is not over. The curfew is to be lifted only between 10 and 1 o'clock to enable people to shop. He's exceptionally pleased to see us.

Sandra: We've escaped from the bundh, and out of the Gates of Hyderabad and into what looks like a travelling prison, bars at the windows and long thin bed/seats swinging from chains. All are full. We have numbered tickets. George removes people who are reluctant to give up our numbered seats. Our twenty three travelling hours feel like a sentence but then I find life around me is a fascinating entertainment if at times astonishing such as when a little girl is swiped with a knitting needle for spilling her drink. George orders his supper supplies which appear hours later, piping hot rice surrounded by a mixture of small bowls of dhal and dips all delicately presented. Thankfully Jenny has packed us a box of salad, so we are safe! And I need to be after my bouts of the last two days but thankfully do not have a twinge and put it down to mother's healing as the antidote. As it is I have to borrow her shoes to get in the toilet as the floor is in an unmentionable state. It falls to me to entertain Steven with a pocket calculator which passes the time until everyone changes into their sleeping wrap around dhotis and seem to sleep soundly, even those on the floor. I am chilly and the noise is incessant. Trains pass each other sending out body-shattering whistles; tea boys bang the barred windows at every stop. My blow up pillow is my best luxury and I am thankful I am not amongst the floor sleepers. I'm discovering a great deal to be thankful for by the minute.

2nd November 1990

Mhaletta: We wake to a whole new outer vision. We are in Orissa State. Clusters of grass roofed huts amongst groves of palm trees. Snaking paths cut through the head-high sugar cane. People in skimpy scarves and or sacking as covering for the morning chills heading for the field latrines with toilet cans; people bathing in muddy waters; old women balancing giant pots on their heads; lazy dogs and buffaloes meandering; scene after scene to draw the eyes into a cultural explosion. Despite the poverty this terrain has a beauty and tranquillity that moves me deeply. Maybe it is the pools of Lotus flowers that are catching the heart. Orissa is about to draw us into her net.

Elias, George's brother, and Benny his cousin, meet us. Elias who speaks no English is family, instantly. His smile is enough. We embrace. All bags are swept up onto the men's shoulders and we move out towards the painted cycle rickshaws … and past. Elias has booked us into Hotel Geetanjali near enough to the station to walk. We will not be moving on further today.

Our room is green, flaky and grimy with grey stained sheets and a reasonable enough bathroom. Anyway it is Hobson's choice. Outside a Puja is underway in honour of the full moon. Hindus are singing and playing an assortment of instruments at a shrine next to the hotel. Loudspeakers relay it across the town. It is rather loud inside our green room. We take a rest unpacking necessities, including our duvet covers which act as sleeping bags and are our nightly protection from all ills. The Hotel provides some buttered bread and a blend between tea and coffee. Our immediate priority is for an outing to the bank as the bundh had prevented us from reaching our rupee supplies and we have only been able to buy one way tickets. A 'CLOSED' notice tells us the bank will be reopening tomorrow 10.30am until noon. Today is a holiday. It is a holiday every full moon.

Sandra: We walk in a block, the three men in front, Steven between us following behind. They lead us into a central market area of stalls, carts and a bus-stand. The ground is a slimy mixture of buffalo dung mixed with the rain that has begun to fall. Obviously this is not a tourist resort. We are stared at from every angle. Stopping to speak draws bunches of people who listen enthralled by our conversation or at least to the flow of English which they may well not often hear.

When George asks for pen and paper a crowd gathers to watch him write the bus timetable. There is no bad feeling from the people. It is just curiosity. We make good entertainment I think.

We have to reach Mohana about 64 kilometres away. Elias will take a bus today and return to Rakeshponka to prepare for our arrival. Benny will remain with us and we will follow on tomorrow. We buy some fruit and opt to take a short ride to a beach at Gopalpur before dark. As we set off the rain slithers off the roof down our jutting-out legs. Nipping over black sand and dodging wild pigs we suddenly emerge at a fabulous beach and frothy sea. Being so wet already I just wade into the curly bathwater waves giving George a fright. He thought I was going for a swim! I wouldn't have taken my clothes off though; it would have brought out the whole town! What are coming out are big black umbrellas. We stride about in pattering rain but the air has become clammy and chilly and I for one am glad to be back in Gitanjalli even though the Puja is still pounding.

George hunts down the chef who produces boiling water and our main meal of the day is our own packet soup, cream crackers and bananas; quite a feast in the circumstances. Entertainment before bedtime is to learn a few words of Oria so that we can greet the village people. It is similar to Punjabi so Mhaletta has a head start on me. I'm astonished to learn that George doesn't know the names of his brothers' wives. They are not allowed to speak to him face to face, only sometimes, if they stand well away and do not make eye contact. He also confesses that he has to pass us off as English relatives on Jenny's side as it is not appropriate for him to be alone in bedrooms with two strange women. We also have cousin Benny along to ensure all is above board. The Puja, which to my ears is grossly tuneless, is inescapable so when the men have left us we decide to have our own full moon meeting. We have a tiny book of wisdoms with us called Jewels of Knowledge. Opening it at random Page 59 reads: *I carry myself softly beyond my physical awareness, beyond the scenes that are before my eyes. I let the purest music of silence; the soft sounds of peace carry me to my home.* What perfect advice; only a hand's turn away.

32. The Rains of Rakeshponka

3rd November 1990

Mhaletta: The rain has pounded away all night, nature's drumbeat to the sound of the Puja. I learn that we are now in the path of a cyclonic deluge. Everywhere has turned grey-brown. The sky is pressing down like a wet army blanket. I stand on the balcony watching the street scene where cycle men huddle in doorways in coolie hats. The road is awash.   I nibble half an apple while Sandra attempts bread and jam. George arrives. He is determined the rain will not prevent us reaching the bank so he sets off to get both a rickshaw and a soaking. We are

both on tip-toe itching to leave. It takes half an hour to secure a cycle rickshaw.

We ride, dodging floating mud cakes. The bank is OPEN. Rain is pouring in through the roof over the stairs. No clerks have yet arrived. We sit. People push in front. The clerk arrives and promptly loses a man's traveller's cheques so there is a full scale search of the premises. They are found sticking damply together. Time is passing as everything is slowly and meticulously posted by hand in ledgers while Sandra's sparkling shawl is staining brown. We take our numbered chips and enter the money cage. 8,750 rupees? The bank is broken! It has no notes larger than 100Rs. We take them in a cumbersome bundle tied with string. Mission complete. Or is it?

Now we cannot get OUT! The well by the bank steps is flooded . We take off our shoes and prepare to wade. George insists the rickshaw is dragged to the door. So we are shoved out into a watery world in which sight of solid ground is fast disappearing.

In the green room, feeling now both rich and marooned, discussions begin. I am having inner signals not to take the bus. George does not want us to spend a wedge of money on a taxi even if we could find one willing to drive us inland in this weather. He feels we should postpone the journey. I will not. The green light is showing and I know we simply have to trust and go on but definitely NOT by bus. The lines have gone down and telephones are not working. George knows of a Government Tourist House on the way to Mohana where we might be able to stay if we can reach that far. If we cannot we are taking a huge risk. Understandably George feels a heavy sense of responsibility. Finally he capitulates and agrees to go out and hunt for a taxi.

A taxi and driver is found and then the taxi's owner decides he wants to come too. It takes an interminable time to even get into the car. Even when we are off a stop is called to buy flip flops, torches and umbrellas. Roads are flooded and rivers overflowing. It is hard to tell one from the other. People are fetching their cattle inside any shelter they can find and roads are teeming with buffaloes, goats, and pigs. The ditches are fast flowing streams being used to propel logs along. Even the rains are used to capacity for transport. The rain now is falling in sharp sheets, beating the big palm leaves flat to their trunks.

The taxi door is opened frequently by the driver to spit out red betel juice. In these gusts it could easily fly backwards. Scrunched up behind the driver I am trying to see through the water falling over the wiper-less windscreen to catch every vista of these unimaginable scenes.

Sandra: I've been asleep for the first part of the journey and would have liked to have stayed that way but ear splitting music is bursting out of the speaker near my ear competing with the drumming rain. When eventually George gets out, investigating a possibility of overnight beds, the taxi owner begins to take liberties, putting his hand on my knee, trying to persuade us to ditch this expedition and go to Madras. We deal with him. Saviour George is here again. We have reached the Government Guest House and they will find us beds for the night.

The room is spacious; two beds with white sheets. We accept gratefully. George and Benny disappear leaving us with Steven. We want to write so we give Steven a colouring book but after one picture he plays for attention, so I teach him how to use our tape recorder by asking him questions and recording the answers.

'How will we recognise your grandmother?'

'Her skin is very black and her hair is curly, pressed flat on her head in a plait and she is **so** small you won't even **see** her! If she is a long way away she is **this** big' (holding his fingers two inches apart).

Steven is good fun with a quirky sense of humour but tonight he is restless and hungry. Mhaletta has only had a bit of an apple and our stomachs are rumbling. George brings a menu. We choose vegetable fried rice and finger chips. We would like it soon. It is 5.30pm. George goes to the kitchen and returns.

'It will be ready by 8pm. I will stay in the kitchen and supervise'.

The plan is to eat in the dining room. It does not happen. At 8pm George supervises the entry of the dinner. We quickly improvise by laying a small table, the others all joining in to give it a party air until the waiter ruins our stage set. Using the overlong ragged curtain that the previous man had wiped his hair on, he polishes our plates and spoons. My stomach turns over and Mhaletta's face is a picture. I leap for a towel, re-wipe the plates and cutlery and we are ready for a banquet. It is delicious and we don't notice any stray hairs! Best of all it has warmed us up. We are cold and clammy most of the time now and worst of all my bag has been put down in the wet, my sleeping bag is sopping at the edges and nightclothes too wet to contemplate, so I slip into my shroud-bag fully dressed...but not for long.

First it's the slow creaking of the door handle being turned which George had warned us to lock. We have our suspicions of who that might be. Then comes forked lightening followed by ear crunching thunder. We're in the haunted house and I've got the shakes. Mhaletta's not much better and says she dare not close her eyes. We decide to put the light on to deter intruders. Mhaletta's getting out of her bag while I shine the torch. The beam highlights an army of cockroaches. They are all over the floor scuttling between our beds and the door. Mhaletta won't be deterred. She makes stepping stones out of the chairs, having A+ from me for reaching the light switch which doesn't work. No electricity! By now I've discovered the columns of ants marching up the walls, and things that look like winged spiders. It is now 1.30am. We try to raise our courage by reading a piece about the 'Eight Powers' from our Jewels of Wisdom, deciding we need a few more than eight tonight. Mhaletta opts to sit up journal writing while I choose to suffocate as I will NOT put one hair outside my bag. I expect we both slept sooner or later.

4th November 1990

Mhaletta: I'd be the first to admit that last night I was pining for my pink frilly life. By 6am George has us installed in the taxi again listening to negotiations about payment. George is a stickler. We have a deal regardless of the weather and the taxi owner must complete the ride to receive his money. What I do not think the driver knew was that we were about to make a round of George's relatives who live in this area! The rains are still with us but are softly warm today. Everywhere is still awash.

Our first unscheduled stop is at the home of George's father's sister. We stand in the road and an elderly couple emerge from a grass thatched hut. They have a group of children with them. Polite greetings are given and received. It is obvious that George commands great respect, People are pouring out of neighbouring hut-houses, silently running. It gives pleasure when we take their photos but we have little time to spare and move quickly on to stop again at Elizabeth's home. This is different. Elizabeth, George's greatly loved baby sister is close family. She lives with her husband and his family whose five sons live in a row of five huts with their families. Ramesh, her husband is the youngest of the sons. It is necessary to digest this information fast as it is important to know who is who.

Their hut-homes are in the middle of flooded rice fields a distance from the main road, Benny is sent to alert them. We see him waving his black umbrella as he paddles through a small stream. Some of the family are already running out towards us but George has not seen them for four years and wants us all to go inside. Jennie and the children have never visited. We recognise the significance of all of this and that whilst George is taking the opportunity to see his relatives he is giving us a first hand insight into rural poverty.

Elizabeth and Ramesh reach us with their children a boy of three and a girl of six. They are hesitant about us crossing the fields but we convince them we are willing and able. Elizabeth touches George's toes followed by mine and then Sandra's. She wears a plain soft brown sari with golden ear rings and nose rings and has a lovely slightly wistful face. George had said 'She will cry'. She does.

We take the journey barefoot through mud, grassy bogs and ford the stream. George is animated telling us how lengths of cut grass are dried to make the roofs which have to be replaced every two years. Then we are there, inside in the darkness with the people, many of them, who have crowded into the tiny rooms. It is Grandfather who sits in state at the entrance. They pass us a bundle. In it is a tiny baby girl. It feels like a message that we are shown we are welcome from the oldest to the youngest. We are moved beyond words. We wash our feet, a clean woven mat is placed for us to sit and we take breakfast of sweet black tea with lime juice. It is delicious.

There are photographs to be taken. Grandfather changes into his best clothes and turns into a statuesque patriarch. Each family group must be pho-tographed separately and buffaloes and chickens must be admired. I am drawn towards Ajit, a sixteen year old boy who wants to be a priest and speaks a little English. He asks me 'How is this possible?' I have no answers. How I would love to be a closer part of this huge family. I can see the ancestral heritage of Malaysia here in their more rounded features. No-one wants to part. We have to.

Sandra: I just don't know how to express the feelings these people have stirred in me. It's the heart, just bursting at the seams. The taxi men have redeemed themselves by their patience this morning. Now we are off again on a good road to Mohana and people have been waving to us for the last mile or so. No, they are not waving to us, they are trying to wave us down to give us news that a bridge ahead has collapsed. We don't understand the significance immediately. Kiosk shops outline where the road should be that is now an expanse of mud. It is Sunday. The black umbrella-people are out in force moving in the same direction. They are on their way to view the spectacle of the collapsed bridge. We arrive to be the day's spectacle number two.

George is fielding numerous invitations to visit which he declines. Benny goes ahead to inspect the bridge situation. George then decides we will alight after all and are welcomed to sit in deck chairs on a veranda amidst a variety of religious symbols. George talks while we exchange smiles and greetings with the usual gathering crowd. An elderly man who is the father of the Brother Priest we had hoped to visit in Berhampur appears and we move to his tiny house, pitch dark inside. He lights an oil lamp and we sit crossed legged on his bed, the one and only piece of furniture. I don't know the protocol for any of this and am just trying to follow suit with whatever is going on.

Back at the taxi we have a report from Benny. Half of the bridge on the main road through Mohana has been swept away. Surprisingly it is classed as a National Highway and officials must come immediately to inspect it and consider repairs. The river is in full flood. The way ahead is impassable. On the other side of the torrents people from Rakeshponka are waiting to escort us on the 3km walk to their village. We are all stunned by the news.

Mhaletta: No-one has any immediate solutions. We head for the Roman Catholic Church for sanctuary and paddle through the flooded churchyard. One wall has a crucifixion scene that covers the whole wall, painted Indian style with a brilliant blue sky. Clouds make a pattern that mirror the shape of the rocks below depicting the age old axiom 'as above so below'. Calvary is covered with flowers and trees sprouting new growth. It's a symbolic feast holding my attention while George disappears inside to negotiate for a room. I notice they are unloading the luggage. It does not reach the church. There will be no room. Someone has gone off with the keys and cannot be found. I silently query whether anyone has looked. About turn, reloading us and the luggage. We try the Government Rest House. It is empty and silent but they are holding it for the Bridge Inspectors and there will be **many** inspectors.

A rapid fire conversation is taking place with the taxi men, which is then graphically conveyed to us. It is estimated that the river will be impassable for at least a week. By then it may be possible to wade across but we cannot wait for a week. The taxi men want to turn back, returning to Berhampur. That is impossible. A bridge was demolished behind us yesterday. The overloaded bus that we might well have taken was washed away and all seventy passengers are reported as drowned. We can go neither onwards nor backwards. There is only one possibility of a sideways loop to Chandragiri. The taxi driver is adamant he will go no further and anyway has no more petrol. A settlement is made Indian style. He commits to take us to Chandragiri but not an inch further. I understand this is in the opposite direction to Rakeshponka. Someone is despatched to shout across the river to our waiting hosts that we are on the way to Chandragiri. We have plenty of time on our next ride to contemplate our narrow escape which is sobering.

Somehow we appear to have lost direction and find ourselves in a Tibetan Colony. This is a restricted government area. No foreigners are allowed in or there will be trouble with the police. Regardless they drive into the settlement as we can see three parked vehicles. We are on the hunt for another vehicle, another driver and petrol. A Tibetan lady appears. She is charming and takes us into a colourfully painted house where a Tibetan man, speaking perfect English, listens thoughtfully to our dilemma. He regrets there are no solutions. On Sundays there are no drivers; maybe tomorrow according to the state of the roads. We leave.

By some unknown means we pull up at a Revenue Inspectors bungalow where we discover a caretaker, a guest room with two single beds and a toilet. We have shelter and must share it. Sandra and I take one bed, George and Steven the other while Benny takes a mat on the floor. The inevitable calculations are underway. We are committed to pay our taxi man two rupees per mile! Altogether we have travelled only about 50 miles on a journey of two days. I'm on the taxi-man's side in this equation! George says time is immaterial and that they have to pay for their own overnight accommodation as they should have slept in their taxi which is usual. Somehow a settlement is reached but I cannot see where they can go from here or where we can for that matter. Their last assignment is to drive Benny and Steven to a shop for provisions. We hope it will not be far away.

Sandra: I'm keeping a low profile, glad to be alive and thinking about the people on that bus. It's dusk when they return with a supply of grapes, apples, bananas and biscuits. That is to be our main, and only, meal of the day so we add half a glass of watery Horlicks each. George and Benny take off to investigate our options for tomorrow. Suddenly its pitch dark and we have only torches. We take to our webbed beds because there is nowhere else to be and after last night's fiasco we are tired. Steven can't settle so Mhaletta tells him the story of Charlie and the chocolate factory which he thinks is silly.

George and Benny return with candles but no luck with transport. They bring news that three bus loads of passengers have arrived. Unable to find any passable road in any direction they, like us, are trapped. There is only one room and we have it. They have a few old mats and mattresses and will be sleeping on the veranda floor outside our barred window. Their voices rumble on talking the night away while we share the luxury of two in a rope bed doing a bit of talking ourselves. It is a pretty serious situation. We are committed to this journey and are determined to keep going until we find a way in to Rakeshponka. We both feel confident that tomorrow, come what may, we will reach there and focus positively on a safe arrival before sharing the night with whining mosquitoes.

33. Journey of the Peacock

5th November 1990

Mhaletta: Sunrise reveals forested hills appearing through a misty vapour rising from the trees. It's eerie. There is a way through to Rakeshponka on foot if help can be found to carry the luggage. George and Benny who left at first light to hunt for a bullock cart and guide return despondent. We drink tea, breakfast on fruit, and they leave to try again and are gone for a long time. Then at last success! Transport arrives. They have hired one bicycle porter. Three bags are roped onto a wooden frame made of branches. The other two are humped up to balance on the handlebars. It will be a dead weight in the mud. For fifty rupees our guide will push our luggage to the river but he will not cross it. We will then have to find porters. So we **still** have to cross the torrent! By 10.30am the inevitable photos have been taken; spirits restored we set off on what we understand is a three or four kilometre short cut to Rakeshponka by the forest route.

Sandra: There are good omens about. Mhaletta is dressed like a peacock in an old cotton sundress with this giant bird on the front and Steven has found a peacock feather which he's waving at everyone and everything including the bicycle. And of course we have our umbrellas up in what is now a fine sprinkling of rain.

We roll along a well constructed road with bridge intact although water is pouring over the edge; sandals off to paddle here and there; slinking past bathing buffaloes. Steven skips along picking flowers and talking interminably. Gradually the surface worsens, becoming cobbled and stony and we turn off onto the forest trail, plodding on and on through a world of lush vegetation; rice, mangos, banana, date and coconut palms; all surfacing through still lakes touched by a watery sun. In places the volume of water has made islands. We could be in Bali or some exotic South Sea Islands.

The problem we have is that what was once a path is a quagmire, stretching our soaked leather sandals and sucking them off our feet every few yards. I test the next choice of the cheap flip flops we had bought to paddle through puddles but they are hopeless. Mosquitoes had made themselves at home between my toes in the night and the toe thongs soon rub my bites raw. More ingenuity is needed. I cut the toe pieces off and tie the rubbery soles on with a strip of rag out of the clothes jumble bag. It is slow progress as the bicycle has to be maneuvered through the mud. Here and there we pass clusters of mud huts and people who look at us silently, showing no surprise. George always asks the

way ahead followed by Steven's big question 'How far NOW?' George's replies of 'not far, Bapu, few minutes more' are meant to be encouraging. I have become doubtful. After two and a half hours and one heavy downpour we stop for a snack of bananas and a couple of sugary sweets each and to dry off. A watery sun is shining on idyllic scenes of waterfalls gushing down the hills.

Mhaletta: We have entered the forest now and can pick up our stride along a trail that twists and turns between the trees. Another hour and a half and I realise my legs are tiring. It is about then that George slips in a stray comment: 'they **will** be surprised to see white people who can walk eighteen kilometres'. This is when we truly realise the size of the challenge. There is still the river ahead to be crossed (we have no idea how) and a sizable walk the other side of it.

Sandra rests on a rock. I step behind her putting my hands on the nape of her neck and feel a massive inflow of energy. I had asked for nothing, the move being an instinctive reaction to the obvious tiredness of her physical body. In that instant my inner eye saw the image of golden liquid tipping out of my cupped palm and coursing down her spine. To this point it had been the body's journey, the body's responsibility to carry us to our destined point. Now it was something else. This simple action alerted us to our need to draw consciously on resources beyond the physical. We say not a word but we both know it.

George has information. The river is still a racing torrent but there is a point on the bank where a tree has fallen across by natural means to lodge in trees on the opposite bank. Incredible!

Sandra: The porter has reappeared with bicycle, minus luggage and is paid. George has engaged a lady carrying a baby, a girl of twelve or so and a boy of six to carry the bags on their heads. They don't even steady them with their hands as we climb a steep muddy slope. Then I'm down, slithering head first on one knee among laughing children who are gathering to see the show. But that was only a minor excursion. I can see the river. It looks even worse than it had in Mohana. It's a raging torrent. The pace at which it is carrying logs and debris means a body would be swept away like a leaf. On a gigantic palm tree which disappears into the tree tops opposite, a man is slicing chunks out, I suspect to make footholds. It looks horrendous. There is no consultation because there is

no choice. This is the only route. Benny demonstrates. The tree is sloping upwards. The trunk is wet and no doubt slippery. The footholds show the tree's yellow insides at irregular intervals. And it is HIGH. I face the inevitable and am ready to get it over with. It's Mhaletta that I am worrying about. My mother suffers from vertigo. This is not the ideal place for the world to spin and the legs to freeze or turn to jelly. George is to cross with me holding one hand. I'm on, wobbling step by step watching my feet to find the notches.

'Don't look at the water whatever you do' comes George's warning voice.

It's in the middle when I become gripped with fear, aching legs turning to jelly. Three quarters of the way and I collapse to my knees, clutching the log; half crawl and half drag myself to the tree top's branches that feel like strong arms…oh yes, those are there as well. They help me to the ground. My camera is in my hand now ready to catch what I hope will not be my mother's last walk.

Now what is she doing? She's opened her luggage bag and in front of all the spectators she is taking off her peacock dress and is putting on a white shirt and black trousers. Then I get it. Black and white – yin and yang - perfect balance. Now she's at the log. It looks as if she is talking to it. She could be doing anything; drawing on its life force; blending her energy with it perhaps. Was I surprised when she stepped on the log and walked across like a ballet dancer, with George holding one hand and a village man the other? No. I'd been too busy wanting to get it over with that I'd done it the hard way.

Mhaletta: When I saw the tree and the churning river I could not conceive it would be possible for me to cross. There is a brief discussion with George who suggests various methods and then makes his pronouncement. 'We will walk'.

I face the river, first looking at the direction of the flow. If I fall I can see which way the current is running and the slim chance that I could hurtle toward a sand bank with overhanging bushes. Then it comes to me in a flash that I will not have to take the plunge. That tree has sacrificed its life for us. Why else did it fall in our pathway when we needed a bridge? I did not need to ask it to uphold me. That was what it was there for! It was that one realisation that sustained me and blocked the ever lurking fear of vertigo. All I had to do was create an image of balance in my mind which I did by changing my clothes and then I quickly made up a simple mantra, an affirmation. 'The tree is holding me steady and straight', was all I repeated on the silent passage over our bridge. I didn't even notice the river as I visualised the log being on the ground. George would have known intuitively it was best not to speak to me. As we step into the nest of branches I fall into George's arms and tell him 'Now I am a Rakeshponkan'.

4pm. We hear that the village is only a short way now. I know that darkness falls at 5.30. Benny, a village man and the young girl become our porters. They are pushing on ahead to the village then people can be despatched to come to meet us. I hear George's instructions to leave us the torch and to tell the villagers to bring kerosene lamps. This is the clue we need. There is still a long way to go yet.

Now the hazards really begin. There is no marked trail as the tree has fallen at random. It is difficult for George to get his bearings as he has not ventured in this area for many years, terrain changes so quickly and we have no guide. We walk barefoot through rice fields, scramble through rocky ravines, up and down muddy slopes, wading fast flowing streams. Every step is getting harder and harder. Sandra stops to gather some grains of rice and gives them to Steven. He asks if we know that Orissa means rice. We didn't. So now we all carry some grains of rice and talk of holding Orissa in our hands. 'What part of Orissa?' we ask each other. Rakeshponka of course! Any game that comes to mind we play and coin the phrase 'The Peacock Journey' as the feather becomes our flag and Steven the standard bearer. We have to keep each other going and talk to Steven about the energy in everything even the rice and the feather. He is intrigued and holds our focus until darkness creeps over us.

I have been keeping an eye out for mud huts – any kind of huts or shelter for emergencies. There is nothing but what now seems to be a tangled wilderness. George has been navigating by contours of the land and soon we are unable to see in front of us. He keeps moving from side to side trying to feel firm ground and finding nothing except the will to lead us on and on. And our legs continue to respond. Sandra seems to have superhuman strength. Steven clutches his feather as a lifeline. He never complains, which has earned our admiration. It's 5.30 when my left foot steps on a sharp pointed rock hidden in the grass. I shout. George grabs me tightly not knowing what has happened. The sudden shock of pain takes my breath away. It's too dark to see the damage. He helps me limp towards a pool of water, but we walk straight into an anthill. My right foot is bitten and Sandra is shouting she is bitten…where I don't know. I feel there is a flap of skin loose and cannot put my heel to the floor. The terrain now seems impassable with tufts of spiky grasses hiding black ants on the prowl and muddy inclines. We have only one torch between us. Ours had been spirited away in our luggage.

We make a chain, George leading me by the hand, Steven with the torch behind, shining it ahead and Sandra brings up the rear.

Pain is shooting up my leg. My only hope is that Sandra can anesthetise it with healing. I explain to George who waits calmly as Sandra works on my foot telling me that energy is pouring through and she is also dealing with the shock wave to my auric field. We move off again gingerly. After about ten minutes I feel my foot go numb and am able to walk unaided. It is the same as the effect of an injection. We are facing the worst patch of all so far. With slopes and rocks ahead there is neither path nor foothold. George leaves us to find a way round. We follow his voice and the faint torchlight and are guided to reach the top of the incline. Breathless and exhausted we take a respite break on a log listening to George's voice echoing through this invisible world of darkness. He is calling for his brother Elias, who should be leading the rescue party. We are lost sheep!

34.Beyond Darkness

5th November continued

Mhaletta: There are voices, then sounds of cracking branches and faint lights and people coming towards us. It is George's brother, Elias who takes me in his arms. Others touch our feet and garlands of sweet smelling golden flowers are gently placed around our necks. Between the trees more women are appearing singing in softly haunting tones *Ha Ma...Hail Mary – Mother of Grace.* The refrain rises and falls, an exquisite melody echoing through the darkness, lifting now, as the kerosene lights are held high revealing their faces, and ours, tears blinding eyes that no longer need to see the way.

Sandra: Are these real people? It's all surreal to me, the absurdities of our day and now this overwhelming sense of absolute joy as this choir surrounds us with what is not just music, it's a loving protective circle, overwhelming, just out of this world. There's still further to go. It doesn't matter now. I've gone beyond feeling my legs.

We are a procession. Mhaletta has a man either side of her holding her arms. Young women cluster closely around me holding my hands, taking my shoulder bag from me, vaporising the aches and pains away just by being there. Words don't seem necessary. It's their touching presence that is everything. It is still a long haul, and I am hauled over boulders, and across expanses of boggy pools. I can see Mhaletta in front, arms around the men's necks being swept up and over obstacles. I've lost sight of Steven.

Rakeshponka exists. We arrive from the back of a line of huts and into the 'street' awash with mud that now feels cool and soothing in the chill of the night air. A rope bed is waiting for us on the porch and as we sit in state people pour out of their dark doorways to crowd around us and it is up to Mhaletta now to do the greetings in Oria. She has at least learnt to say 'I am fine'. I've forgotten every word.

Mhaletta: The elders must be greeted first. The first elder, the matriarch of the village is Ma, George's mother. We embrace. I too am addressed as Ma .It is the greatest honour they could give. It is an acknowledgement of more than the matriarch of a tribe, needing no explanation. George interprets as I tell them I feel as if I have walked from England! Yet there is no exhaustion now, the feeling is one of awe and a sense of invincibility.

Drinking hot sweet tea we are told the position. Half the street is flooded where a hut-house had been prepared for us. A family have offered us sleeping space. We are thankful and willing to accept whatever is offered. Our luggage has already been placed in there. We are to take a supper of rice that is waiting in George's house. We are able to add a slice of cucumber and tomato. It is enough and we are ready for bed but firstly George tends personally to cleaning the gash on my heel. We add antiseptic cream and plasters so I am put together again and we are led away to our sleeping spaces.

Taking off our garlands we hang them over a nail in the wall and when our eyes become accustomed to the shadows from the lamp we discover we have hung them over a picture of the nativity, a perfect gesture. This is not our time of 'no room at the inn'; this is truly a most welcome shelter in our Bethlehem. Motioning for us to sit on the bed the women then begin to massage our legs with saffron…we are turning golden from toes to knees. We are told this will alleviate the after effects of the journey and will reduce the swelling in Sandra's ankles.

Sandra: It's all sublime and other worldly until we are brought back to the physicality of life by being tutored in the toilet routine. The earth offers an ever ready toilet area and our spot is pointed out close to the back door. How I keep my face straight I do not know when Mhaletta, due to age and rank is shown first how to stoop down! Do they think westerners legs don't bend? Flashlights are trained on her ... or on the spot, I don't know which, as she performs before eagerly watching spectators. She's done this before and it doesn't phase her. I haven't and it does! In my haste to get the job done I manage to soak the hem of my grimy dress. Next error is to use a wet-wipe and then find I have nowhere to put it. Naturally there are no rubbish bins and the ground is too hard to dig with my nails. It could be I have a lot to learn.

Next thing to be learnt is that we are to sleep in the one roomed hut with two of the young women and their parents. We are allocated the one and only rope bed (single) and a corner of the floor. Guess who has the bed? There is a strict status code. Who cares? I urgently just want to stretch out my golden legs. I have my treasured blow up pillow in place, the last sounds of the day are of babies crying, a mournful sound. I wish the women would sing to them.

6th November 1990

Sandra: Sunshine is streaming in through the open door and so are the chickens, wandering about and pecking away. We dress, suitably watched, and sit outside on the porch to survey our surroundings sipping sweet tea. Mhaletta tells me she has had a twisting night with cramp in her legs but she looks as if she's survived well.

The views are magnificent. Without even taking a step we see a panoramic view of mountains, palm trees, rice fields, pumpkin, tamarind and banyan trees and we can hear rivers rushing about somewhere beyond the backdrop of foliage behind the huts. It is idyllic, peaceful, innocent and lovely, a perfect setting to bathe behind a screen of banana leaves. I work up a golden soapy lather as the saffron colours everything it touches, working its magic all over me, including my hair. This seems a good time to wash out our food bag of dwindling provisions discovering that our bags, clothes and all are a new found world for invading ants while the women watch and smile at our shaking antics, not understanding our distaste.

Mhaletta: A veil has simply dropped away. All the pressure to focus on finding the path and walking the path has been released. We are in a totally different energy field here beyond anything I have ever experienced as if I have stepped out of the known world into something far more subtle; more enveloping. I recall a line in some old scripture that describes it: *'He uncovered the two, Earth and Heaven, eternal and in one nest.'* We are in the nest and now I understand why. George tells me that before we could work together we needed to prove we could journey together. He considers it proven. So do we!

George's father and uncles had been the founders of this village, fifty-four of his relatives now making up the main population of Budapara Street, the oldest of the three village streets. Making a round of the village is an important ritual. Grass roofed mud huts define the edges of each street. There are no shops or facilities other than the village school which is no more than a shed with a blackboard. We are told a teacher seldom arrives. It's a gently ambient morning yet at the same time deeply reflective.

Sandra: We settle for rice and a chopped onion for lunch then negotiate for an hour's free time for writing as our pens are burning to capture our impressions of our Peacock Trail and a few other things besides. The rope bed appears on Elias's shoulder and we follow as it is placed under a shady tamarind tree. In front of us stretch fields of golden flowers harvested for their oily seeds. Our writing is great entertainment for the children as they close silently around us watching as our pens propel us back onto the trail in our minds eye, recalling and recording as we try to express the elusive sense of having crossed a boundary into another reality.

We are urgent to compare notes but have promised Steven that we will go with him to see how fast the river level is dropping as we will have to wade or swim it at some point to reach Mohana on our return journey. The children dog our every footstep and its fun to watch city boy Steven's antics as they all dig connecting tunnels in the sandy banks.

Mhaletta: Ma is here. So far we had only exchanged greetings. Now she has found a way to connect to me. She kneels and with strong leathery fingers

 massages my feet and legs. I had not realised how much they ached but the heartache is greater. **We are the same age, fifty-seven,** but it is evident which life has taken the heavier toll. Ma is not only the matriarch; she is the wise woman, the power centre of this village and a healer. She too calls me Ma, and though we are unable to speak our thoughts aloud I am aware that this woman is in some way familiar and means more to me than could be expressed in words. Maybe we have known each other in some other life, time, or existence or maybe it is one of those soul to soul connections which need neither acknowledgement nor explanation. Whatever it is I have certainly not arrived as a stranger at **her** gate. Her touch has been given and received. Just maybe it was for the touch of Ma that I had come these thousands of miles! Who knows? Next it is Sandra's turn for a massage and then we have both received Ma's blessing.

Sandra: It is dusk when supper arrives of what was planned to be some of our delicious packet soup. Unfortunately, the water is tepid and the powder is turned into unpalatable lumps, but not as unpalatable as the chicken who we had met earlier being strangled right beside us as we relaxed nicely on the porch.

Now here comes another night. I do have my own rope cot which is yet another blessing. Mhaletta's flash light is trained on a cockroach army advancing along the shelf beside our beds. We make a quick decision to reverse and swivel our heads to the foot of the bed, further from the shelf. There is something going on with the other people in the room, shouting, lanterns, moaning, snores and dog fights. In the morning we learn someone had been bitten by a rat. Twice Mhaletta wakes up thrashing about and beating the bed. She says cockroaches are crawling over her face. I believe her because one's gone inside my sleeping bag. Definitely we're in the underworld at night. Mhaletta is a picture getting dressed. I accidentally sprinkle a pocketful of sweet corn over her and her nerves jerk her into wild thrashings thinking it's another invasion of creatures. We're not very good at this!

7th November 1990

Mhaletta: We reassemble our nerves in the sunshine. This is a day for an outing to the nearby village where George attended school. I've been limping about until this morning when I find I can put my heel to the floor again just in time. Villagers pour out of their homes to join us and we have a troop by the time we arrive at George's old school, a straw shelter with teaching space outdoors. Then we visit the Roman Catholic Church. Eight years old and blackened by the weather, it's a large shed housing dusty remnants of altar regalia. Two more visits to neighbouring villages are lively. Firstly we pay our respects to one of George's disabled friends while drummer's drum and people gather to sing. It's delightful. At the next stop, as confidence builds, people begin to ask us questions with George as interpreter. We soon realise that the answers are not too important as their enjoyment is to hear us all speaking English for which accomplishment

George is so highly regarded. Always there is protocol to follow of the village elder being presented first, some such as Moses, have the look as well as the names of Biblical characters. Children swarm out of every nook and cranny, all wearing the minimum of tattered clothes, many with obvious health problems such as ear infections and pox-like facial scars. None have any kind of footwear. George had his first pair of chappals (flip-flips) when he was seventeen.

Sandra: A splendid morning out and about and a splendid dinner of potatoes and onions. I'm back under the tamarind tree and have just learned that George is not ready to return tomorrow as we had expected and wants to spend another day with his family. Now this doesn't seem a good plan to me. I'm resistant to another two nights and need to be clear with myself about why. A list seems a good idea!

1) We don't know the score as to how we'll get back.
2) The tortuously uncomfortable nights have now become fear-filled with the added possibility of biting rats.
3) Food is scarce, not too nourishing, and we are running out of supplements.
4) We will have no time left the other end to move on with the school project.
5) We cannot talk directly to anyone except George.
6) We are always concerned about hygiene; toilet facilities; have insect bites and dirty clothes.

That will do for a start. I'm at the ready to do some serious talking. We track George down and give him our side of the picture. He is perfectly understanding of our sleeping problems and is already working on it by arranging for us to have a hut to ourselves across the road. Elias has been detailed to sleep on the porch outside the door which we can leave open. Oh bliss! I'll have to cope with the rest.

It's our task to choose a name for a baby girl, the daughter of George's brother Gervaise who will be baptised when a priest comes around in two months time. We agree on Carolyne, my second name. She is a dear little thing. At two months old she only looks like a newly born. At last we are seeing that the toys we brought have been handed out by Ma. So far we have seen the children batting tin cans with sticks when they are not rolling down sand hills, standing around or holding babies. Now they are experimenting with balloons, balls, gliders and dolls. It's hilarious. Even better when I join in and learn their names which I write down for them. I don't think they have ever seen their names written before. I give some of them paper and pencils and try to show them how to draw balloons and little stick people but they have no idea at all of how to control a pencil. They have pulled me out of the doldrums though and I can even look forward to bedtime.

Mhaletta: We're sipping our soup supper on the porch when we can see there is a problem with the removal of our beds to the house on the opposite side of the street. It slowly dawns on us that there is not room for both beds and they have to remove some sacks out of the way. The beds are then wedged in one behind the other. Sandra opts for the back corner leaving me by the open door. We clamber into position and have time to scribble and talk a little before dark.

We know that dealing with this massive cultural shift is taking a great deal of our attention and there is a momentous project hovering over our heads needing constructive thought, yet we are both aware that we are experiencing something beyond either of these considerations that we have not yet grasped. We decide that for now we will settle for the notion that here, we are more conscious of the 'one reality'; to the merging of the material physical world with a more subtle energy that penetrates and impregnates everything, revealing an inner beauty. The word 'Ma' seems to hold everything in that single syllable reflected in the face of the elderly woman. Musing to catch my drifting thoughts a few words tumble from the pen.

What is Divine Sight? Divine Sight lies in the eye of the beholder where beauty lies awaiting that mere flicker of the 'I' to see beyond mind's coating.

What is Divine Sight but sight of the Divine? And when you see the Divine within all things, all people and all Self, then is your sight Divine for you will have become the Eye within the Darkness.

At some level maybe I understand.

Sandra: Sublime to absolutely ridiculous! There are loud voices outside. We peer out and see people peering back towards our hut. There seems to be some problem related to us. We don't understand. We know Elias has been designated to sleep on the porch. Elias's wife suddenly appears in the doorway gesturing that the door must be closed. We refuse. Air of some sort is part of the luxury. She leaves and we sleep … for a very short time. George is visiting and I am too cross to speak. He has been sent by Ma to tell us to put passports and money in our bed bags. It seems neighbouring villagers are not all trustworthy. We comply. Night is not working out well so far. It gets worse. Elias, our watchman is now grunting on his sleeping mat. I've drifted off with my feet dangling over a shelf that has now come to life with munching rats. I take a flying leap on top of Mhaletta. Flashlight on and they scamper but they'll be back as there are sacks stored which they are investigating. A quivering jelly yet again, I refuse to return to the rat corner. After hysterical disbelieving laughter I put on thick socks and creep in beside Mhaletta to lie stiff and straight pinned up the furthest wall. When all is quiet she decides to brave the rat corner bed. We're settled, safe and drifting off when my bed starts to shake and rise in the air. How Mhaletta moved so fast I'll never know. In a leap she was on top on me holding us down and we can hear her bed now clanking up and down. We can't see why and dare not look under the bed. This is terrifying! In the moonlight we see the spooks leave through our open door. They are mangy wild dogs roaming about looking for their supper no doubt. Our webbed beds are so low they had to push their way under. In a state of after-shock we stay in the same bed not caring whether we sleep. We have definitely not yet become the 'Eye of the Darkness' although we are certainly getting some practice!

8th November 1990

Mhaletta: Daylight at 6am brings activity outside as the street it swept with twig brooms, bed mats are rolled and life begins afresh. This is George's day. It has all been a momentous experience for him and a family council has been called for this morning. Who knows how long it will be before he can return? With the eventual death of his mother, George, as the eldest son, will be the head of the family with all the responsibilities that ensue. How difficult to take on such a task from such a distance! It is a certainty that he will never return here to live. The world that he went out to seek is expanding now, taking on an International flavour. Today we can become the watchers and the planners.

Our priority is to have a meeting of our own council of two and address some of the big questions that seem to be growing bigger by the day. Acknowledging that we are both becoming increasingly aware of the vast areas of need here, we recognise that we must not deflect our energy from the main Hyderabad project. This is our chance for a spell of creative thinking. A magic mushroom of ideas grows fast. The starting point for raising interest and funds we decide could be a free booklet written as an illustrated story suggesting readers might like to be a part of MetaCentre International's 'Global Family' in a social welfare and educational project. Then we give ideas how it might work, such as sponsoring a child for £5 per month, to donations, not necessarily of money, but of the things needed to create a colourfully attractive school. Sketches and layouts take up our morning as we have a creative bonanza basing our thinking on the premises we have seen so far. We even choose the colours for the school uniforms which we call 'raspberry and sweet corn' to remind us of the piles of sweet corn being laid out to dry in the street as we talk. The focus of our task may well lie in Hyderabad but the seeds are already growing in our minds here. We want the work ahead to carry the energy of Rakeshponka into the city.

Sandra: George is with us again bringing information. There is a story circulating that we set out back to Berhampur last Sunday by taxi and that there was an accident in which driver and passengers all died. We guess no-one has found our bodies yet! How strange those images of our deaths have been floating around for the last four days; we have certainly felt ourselves to be in a different world!

We've abandoned an earlier idea of scaling the heights and go for a gentle climb instead to where a stream trickles down the stony hill. Rakeshponka lies in a bowl at the bottom, protected by the hills. A sacred spot is pointed out to us where a rosary had moved from Ma's house by means unknown, to be found by Lucy, George's sister. George tells us that he saw it as one of several signs in those long ago days that led him to hold to his knowing that one day something special would happen to him. That we are seen as the special happening brings a quake of responsibility.

Mhaletta: Our main meal today is a feast of potatoes and sweet corn. We are full, happy and relaxed. I want to take a photograph of Ma on her own. She runs away and I chase her with the camera. Everyone is laughing as we are drawn further into the inner family circle. George tells us more of what took place at the family council meeting. As we had expected hopes were high that help would come in some form for the village. While we had been brainstorming, so had they. For instance with two teams of buffaloes they could plough additional land that is uncultivated and sow more crops. Half of the produce would go to the owner and half to the village. All we can do is to listen and learn.

   The family have decided to send a girl back with us to Hyderabad to help Jenny. The small amount she will be paid will go back to her family. Her name is Sasoona. She is only twelve years old and has never been more than a stone's throw from the village. What a massive challenge! Does she want to go? That does not matter. The family have decided.

   Our contribution to what becomes an evening's celebration is to play our tape of Junior Hits. Steven has a musical ear and had been learning what had become his favourites during the journey, so we give an impromptu concert of 'Puff the Magic Dragon' and 'I Can Sing a Rainbow'. Ma is entranced and will not leave to have her supper. We cross the compound to our hut when we both look up and gasp. It's like a mirage. The sky appears as a perfect dome, clear of cloud, and the stars are hugely bright, hanging like lanterns, so low, almost touchable. It is Sandra that catches it in words: 'It's Bethlehem; it's all about birth … of a school, of everything …'

9th November 1990

Sandra: We made a rat blockade last night and it worked. We stood one of the beds up against the shelf wedged it with bags and covers and slept head to toe on the single rope trampoline. Ingenious! The night provides no horrors. Scuffles and squeaks can be taken in our stride. I feel so good after a full night's sleep or maybe it is the prospect of hitting the road again. The river is crossable. We are packed and ready but is George ready? Not quite.

Mhaletta: Today is Speech Day. George is preparing to gather all people of Budapara Street to make a public announcement. It seems that so far he has only told his close family about the School project which can now be shared more widely.

All the men and boys gather with the closest male relatives in the middle. On their left sit the women, girls and babies. On the far right are all distant relatives, the rest of the village people and passers by. We are both in position at the front with George. It is beautifully orchestrated. George speaks to an audience who are intent upon hearing every word Even the babies are quiet today. He is speaking as if something exists that isn't yet anchored in bricks and mortar. Is it his faith in us, himself or something greater than all of us? His sense of destiny is certainly unshakeable, but just look at the effort he is putting in to bring a result!

People ask questions. George answers thoughtfully and patiently. Someone questions our motives and George asks me to answer directly. Words come from somewhere which I sense George is interpreting exactly as spoken. The gist of it is that I tell them that we know ourselves to be 'family' in a wider sense and want to find a way to express that connection through George. Ma is crying; people nod tearfully. Then whoever wants to speak stands and delivers words that we know to be heartfelt. There is no doubt we have been accepted as English family and exact relationships are unimportant. Then it is time for the baby to be publicly acknowledged. She is to be called 'Carolyne', Sandra's second name. Asked for an interpretation Sandra tells them she knows of it as Beloved of the Ancestors, one who has been blessed with Divine Love throughout the Ages; 'caro' meaning beloved, and 'lyne' the line of ancestry.

The Next Generation of
The Nayaks of Budapara Street.

A discussion begins about the Government and we have to make it clear that we have no connections and are not intending to be involved at any political level. Some of the men are then moved to stand, each giving words of thanksgiving and the blessing in Oria: 'May God's Hand be upon your work'.

A task is then allocated to us of completing a photographic record of our visit. All the large groups must be taken first, followed by all George's relatives in separate family units standing in front of their own homes. The camera is passed between us as we are urged to join the group photos. This all takes some time. And then there are the goodbyes which cannot begin until George has had his lunch. We decide to wait to eat until we reach Mohana. It is in the tiny home of Gervaise that close family gather for more loving exchanges as each kiss and embrace us. Ma is bent with weeping, begging our forgiveness if there has been any inconvenience to us during our stay. We are told that our story will be recorded in the history of the village and we are presented with a carefully notated list of George's Budpara Street relatives; thirteen families totalling fifty-seven members, all named Nayak.

It is a group of young women who come holding a folded sari waiting to escort us on the first leg of the journey. As we step outside the sun is blazing, the sari is unfolded in a sweeping movement that lifts it to form a vibrant orange canopy over our heads. Benny opens a black umbrella and is our guardsman walking beside us. They are all there. George and Steven; Elias and young Sasoona who are to return with us to Hyderabad to help with the physical work ahead, the family, the village people, young men balancing our luggage on their heads, all processing through the pumpkin grove and the oil seed fields to the Big Tree.

That is where many turn back and Ma must return home. Can you go somewhere beyond emotion? If so then we are there. The Sari Canopy is folded and in it is folded a precious fragment of my life, maybe even of myself.

Sandra: Rumi is Sasoona's older sister. We have discovered an unspoken way of communicating during these last days. She steps beside me and drapes the corner of her sari over my shoulders; two in one sari. We are closer than sisters. I have known her before; we have both known this family before in some form of existence. They have appeared from our soul memory. They are both real and at the same time unreal. In stepping into their world we have stepped back in time. It's all been a dream of lives beyond lives; lives within lives. Now we have to step back into a different rhythm. Slowly we walk the next four kilometres in silence. It is a meditation.

Mhaletta: I walk alone separated by an inability to express that inner world; that inner knowing that sometimes offers vistas of realities beyond the traps of physical existence. I am moved beyond words by the experiences of these last days. The whys and wherefores do not matter.

There is a good firm trail. Shallow streams to cross; sandals off and on and always hands there, waiting to steady us. At 3.15pm we reach the river boundary. Beyond it is Mohana. A narrow forest trail leads to a crossing point. Though it is still flowing with a strong current and is chest deep, we are to wade across. After we've changed into trousers and shirts our luggage makes the crossing first on the young men's heads.

It seems to be Sandra's task to lead in perilous places. Immediately she slides down a slope falling in the river backwards. There's a look of rapture on her face at this baptismal plunge. She's up, laughing. I follow cautiously. The bottom is sandy. Its luke warm, refreshing. How I want to strike out and swim, floating with the current. My escort holds on to me, tightly. As we near the bank his hold loosens and I cannot resist it and swim. George stands aghast on the bank. This river has meant something more than providing us with a challenge to be faced, it has come to symbolise for me the crossing of The Rubicon, a boundary line which, when crossed, means there can be no turning back.

Sandra: Mohana is still there, the mud is not but the crowds are, surrounding us immediately. George questions people, anyone, everyone, because he doesn't want to believe their answers. There IS no bus. There IS no transport of any kind. We haven't eaten today other than an apple breakfast. Is there any food? We walk up and down the main street impeded by the crowds, peering into the shacks and netting a haul of luke warm Sprites; biscuits and a pineapple; ten bread buns and a bag of toffees. A feast in store!

People urge us to walk on to view the broken bridge, a devastating sight. A giant tree has crashed into the supports demolishing them. There is certainly no way out in this direction and we cannot return via Berhampur as there is still no way through where the bridge was demolished behind us. We appear once more to be marooned in Mohana. However, it is not long before the owner of a jeep offers us a ride to Palasa (wherever that is) for a fortune of 750 rupees. We keep the offer open but it is too late to leave tonight anyway. This means a night in Mohana, but where?

The 'unavailable' Government Rest House is now available and able to offer us one room between us. We accept, gratefully. It has electricity, a toilet and two single beds with wafer thin coir mattresses. There will again be four in here sharing, George and Steven in one single bed and us in the other. I'm almost getting used to sleeping soldier straight by now. We are installed and then George goes out to see that the rest of the party of luggage carriers, Benny, Elias and Sasoona are sheltered somewhere else. What responsibility!

Our first move is to have a monster picnic washed down with sweet tea which arrives in a flask. The luxury of electricity is not lost on us as we settle to our journaling while Steven draws colourful peacocks. The crowning glory of the day is that George returns to tell us that he has discovered a bus leaving for Palasa at 6am. We all agree that come what may, we will be on it!

35. Back from the Dead

10th November 1990

Mhaletta: There are seven days left with still a massive challenge ahead. I have had to accept that we will be missing the Homeopathic Conference and the visit to Sai Baba's Ashram is a non starter. It has been a fragmented night hanging on to a sloping bed, my mind filling the hours mulling over events and priorities. How much can we achieve? Have we achieved what we came for already? Was this 'initiatory' journey the point of it all, the real reason behind the impulse to let India back into my life and open its gates for Sandra? How will she pick up every day life again after this? Will it change her, if so how? My mind is running riot with thought filled questions.

I am clock watching. We are up at 4.30am and out at 5 o'clock to be in position for the 6 o'clock bus. Carrying our own bags today we meet Elias at the bus stop. What a magical time of day! The mist is rising over the black contours of the forested hills and I feel I am standing in a greeting card. Nothing seems physically real and yet it is the physical world that is creating the beauty and wonder of our surroundings. The main street is waking. We by-pass the breakfast stalls as we see the bus is already waiting. It looks a wreck. Buckets of water are being thrown over the thick dust on the windscreen, its only window. They push it to get going. Luckily we are early and are in place with seats but the scrambling surge to board continues well after the bus is rolling as it begins an entrancing visual journey through mountain valley roads.

The word is that it is a journey of 110kms to the railway station. After six hours, we stop in a town believing we have arrived, only to find we are to change buses for the last 40kms. The wait is unpleasant in the heat with the usual crowds gathering round us. We have already accumulated various extra pieces of baggage, mostly field produce to take home for family provisions, now we add a sack of rice and huge bunches of green bananas.

The second bus is another two hour drive. This is much worse. It is full of students staring, laughing and making jokes at our expense. There are no backs to the seats only iron rails and the road is sandy and potholed. At 2.45pm we reach Palasa, a small train station.

'No tickets today. Quota is sold'.

This station is allowed a quota of fourteen tickets per day. We are told to take the train to Berhampur which is 100kms in the opposite direction, to buy some tickets.

Even George has no sway here and can only suggest we go into town to have a think and a meal. Or perhaps we would like to take a room in the town?

'NO, no more rooms, please!'

We opt to remain in the station while Steven and the men go to eat hoping our presence will jog some compassion. Something works. When they return I tell George to try again and insist on having two tickets for the ladies compartment. They are purchased, plus a little extra I suspect. The others have no tickets yet. Then begins the long wait; 3.45pm until midnight. Waiting in a station is LONG! A chunk of a day just sitting, feeling out of chat and rather out of sorts. This very moving day lurches on into tomorrow.

11th November 1990

Sandra: The train's arrival is pure TV comedy. George races up the platform with our luggage to meet a fat policeman with plaits who is supposed to 'look after us'. Steven and Elias are searching for any crack of space for the others. We are standing at the wrong end of the platform. The Women's Compartments are in No.3. Carriage at the front. The train stays here only for three minutes. George is on a race track loaded up to the gills. Sasoona balances the bag of rice on her head. We are all running through jostling crowds, barging and pushing our way. It's a disgrace! It's also vital to get aboard and I could also add by any means!

We are on. Ugh! Wooden slatted two tier berths. George is there positioning our luggage, meticulous to the last. The train is moving. George is hustled off by policemen and is last seen by us running down the platform. We don't know where he is going. Last night Benny left us. That was sad. He has been a major connecting thread and a perfect server on our journey. Now our party is split and we are ladies only. Somehow Sasoona has been pushed in with us without a ticket no doubt. She has never even been on a train and I would think is terrified. How would we know? She does not speak in *any* language. Let's just hope this train is going in the right direction!

As it is the middle of the night and we have already caused an upheaval I force myself to swing up to the top bunk via the window frame and sleep on the slats for six hours while Mhaletta shares her bunk with Sasoona. As the sun rises I realise I am in the wrong place. This side of the train is red hot and there is no air, no ventilation at all nor an inch of room anywhere and I'm scrunched up a corner with a sloping ceiling and cannot get down because it's too crowded. Eventually I crack, slither off, discover Mhaletta is still alive and she moves six inches so I can sit ramrod still until 6pm when we reach Secunderabad Station after eighteen hours of purgatory. I have existed on a slice of pineapple and an ice cream bought through the train window, eaten with a squashed banana. We must be living on prana!

Mhaletta: An unspeakable journey though I fared a little better than Sandra as I had been able to buy coffee, could reach the luggage and found a book in which to bury my mind. After Sandra descended we planned our own moves on arrival. The priority is a hotel with swimming pool, a restaurant and a bath. We are now determined to have a measure of control over what we do during these last days. The journey has taken every ounce of our stamina but what we have received is immeasurable and we would not have missed an iota of it … now that it is over. We head straight to George's house with George and Steven who had also survived in some unknown corner. It didn't matter any more. We are in a taxi on the last leg HOME!

The household is in a state of mourning. It was thought that we had perished in the floods. They had learnt from the television of the deaths of the bus passengers knowing it to have been the most likely bus that we would have taken from Berhampur. Not hearing from us in all this time, because we had no access to telephones, they drew a conclusion that left Jenny, neighbours and the family in tearful disarray. Jenny was about to contact Mr. Mohan to ask for his aid in a search. News had reported no survivors. She had sent for her brother and sister from the neighbouring State to help her prepare a wake. The joy at our homecoming was multiplied a thousand fold. Strange indeed that whilst we were in our Rakeshponka Heaven we had on two different accounts been thought to have left the physical world. I think in some weird way we probably had.

Sandra: The Decca Continental is the best hotel in the world right now and we are IN it. Cleanliness, smiling service, white sheets and embroidered coverlets, springy mattresses, hot water, just everything, plus a live band and delicious choices of food. We are overcome by this latest massive shift in polarities. Out of the mud hut and into the palace!

Mhaletta, equally ecstatic, phones my father who knew nothing of the floods so had not been at all worried. She tells me how eerie it felt to hear his voice sounding out in India. It's interesting his voice has reached here before his body which keeps a safe distance.

People had stood politely close to the phone listening as Mhaletta related our death defying adventures and want to serve us and talk to us but words are elusive tonight. It is all too much to comprehend or express.

The meal is a fantastic Chicken-a-la-King, French fries and vegetables and a Decca Special ice cream eaten while the band plays their heart felt version of 'I just called to say I love you'. We are in a man-made heaven and thankful in every pore to be here. And just to top it all we realise it is 11th November, Armistice Day at home, the day when the country honours its dead. I'm in heaven here honouring the living!

36. The Hand Over

12th November 1990

Mhaletta: We linger over breakfast, revisiting events and memories of the journey; reluctant to release this energy of wonderment that is pouring through, unleashing renewed vitality to begin what we expect will be a day of decisions.

Our filthy clothes go to the hotel laundry. Smartened up with outfits from our spare bag we set off for the Nayaks. Letters are waiting for Sandra from her children, giving a tearfully happy start before we are catapulted into Jenny's urgent request. The vacant flat she had found is waiting to be viewed. Will we go? We think this is a little premature as we have not yet secured the school. We go. It consists of the first floor of a corner house, having a lounge, kitchen, two bedrooms and bathroom. Jenny's dream home for her family. The rent will be payable from the income George expects from taking some paying pupils at the school. We are hoping to manifest a plan that will enable financing on a continuous basis for the school rental and teachers salaries from the sponsorship of the disadvantaged non-paying pupils and fund raising events. In the meantime we have enough money at the ready to pay a deposit on the apartment. Jenny never makes outward show of her feelings but her incredulity when George receives a key which he hands over to me and I pass it on to her is unmissable.

We visit the School premises again, considering its potential. George has excelled in his organisational skills on our journey and we do not question his ability to master-mind the project. Jenny is designing her own part in it drawing our admiration for her quiet certainty of which way to move forwards.

Next visits on the agenda are to Steven's, Stanley's and Angela's schools so we can learn in situ the good use to which sponsorship funds have been put so far. We are impressed. These are some of the best schools in the city and University entrance will be accessible to them in the future. The sky's the limit as far as this family are concerned.

Though there are more details to sort out and papers to be signed in regard to the school , George and Jenny are acting as if we are already the tenants and insist that we have an Inauguration Day before we have to leave. It is scheduled for Thursday. I do not know what you do on an Inauguration Day so hand it over to them to make the programme. So much handing over is taking place it is mesmerising! This is trust at a level that I have not experienced before. Usually all loose ends are tied up in business transactions before taking over a business.

We have no lawyers involved. It is all ad hoc and yet feels completely right.

We return to our Decca haven with a load of homework, have another meal, listen to the band and then work until midnight. One of our tasks is to write a prototype letter to all the parents telling them that MetaCentre Educational Society is now taking over the management of the school and that they are invited to a Parents' Day in three day's time.

13th November 1990

Sandra: We are at George's by 8 o'clock as pre-arranged to present our homework. The letter passes scrutiny. It will be photocopied and given to all pupils today. It will be up to the parents whether they choose to keep their children at 'our' school or move them. I don't doubt for one moment that when they see there is some new financial backing they will be as intrigued as we are to wait and see what happens. This will be good as it will give the school a starter income while we discover what funding we can find in sponsorships.

I'm on stage today taking photos of their Airport Road house, residence of the last ten years. They are moving out this afternoon! Today I learn that the children have never been inside what they call a 'real' house before and neither has Jenny! Jenny is off to organise the cleaning of the new house in the district of Mehendiputnam. There is very little to pack. George has a multiple choice day - from dealing with the invitations, completing purchase negotiations, to hiring a lorry.

By 8.30 we are on the road to visit Hyderabad Public School at the invitation of Mrs. Ahsan. It's palatial from the outside, set in rolling green playing fields and well tended gardens. We know the work standard is high but inside we are surprised to find pupils crammed in rows of chairs, not nearly enough desks, books on knees. We visit various classes and Mhaletta is asked to speak to a class of seven year olds. She asks a few simple questions.

'Can you guess which country we live in?'

'England!' Beams all round when they hit the right answer.

'Can you name a town in England?'

'Portsmouth.' Right, if a surprising choice.

'What is the capital of England?'

'Japan!' The teacher is embarrassed. Mhaletta moves on.

It's more useful to talk with a group of teachers who explore ideas with us for cultural exchange visits for the teachers who felt they could be inspired by experiencing a western style curriculum and more creative ways of working. It all comes down to money as usual and we are unable to make any commitments in this direction. The Art Room displays an array of creative talent but we learn it suffers from a grievous shortage of paper, paints and resource materials. There are no typewriters, computers or signs of any technology at all. We guess this will be one of the first schools that technology will reach eventually.

A housekeeping matron shows us the dormitory accommodation. Sixteen beds are crammed into each room, each with a bedcover and tin locker, shoe space and communal shelf for toiletries. Should we ever decide to become residential she would be pleased to act as our advisor. I spot Steve, the American exchange student, looking super-smart in a khaki uniform. He has been staying at a farm in the mountains and tells us anecdotes of his encounter with a panther. We've met so many interesting people today, thanks to Mrs. Ahsan.

Our next adventure is to visit Noble House School in Jubilee Hills. It is a wonderland. We are beginning to envisage how our school could be. Here there is a Western style environment and style of teaching with masses of resources and visual aids. We meet the Principal, briefly tell him our story and learn more about teachers' salaries, though he admits that even with Teacher Training credentials their status is low and is reflected in their salaries. This school caters for 250 children with 200 on the waiting list and he needs a bigger building. His children are all fee paying, a cost of 300 rupees per month. We tell him we are investigating sponsorships for those well under the poverty line and he suggests we provide them with some basic food for lunch as a priority. What an inspiring visit!

Here comes an interlude when we can investigate the shops. I've been waiting for this as I've presents to find for my children. We find an accommodating auto rickshaw driver, and ask for 'bazaar'. We don't know where we are but he must have read my mind for a start! Our first spree is in a Rajasthan shop ablaze with multi-coloured mirror-ware soft furnishings, from cushion covers and table cloths to bed covers and wall hangings. It is a treasure trove. It is their lucky day and ours as we fill bags, load them in our rickshaw and speed on to the Sultan Bazaar. Half an hour left to grab a dress for Amy, skirt for Summer and shirt for Josh. It's really hard to remember their sizes. I'm thinking they will have grown in all this time I've been away as if it has been months rather than weeks. Time is just elastic in India.

We are expected at George's new home ready for the grand arrival of a lorry load of belongings. We arrive. Jenny is standing there in a shining, clean, empty space. George has gone to organise the lorry. How well they work together sharing out the tasks. We discover that it is Steven's birthday today but no-one appears to have taken any notice so while we are waiting we escort him to a local shop. He has a bonanza buying cold drinks, ice creams and chocolates, rushing back to share them with the children who are running riot and shouting with excitement as they chase each other from room to room. Birthdays in India I'm told, are more about giving than receiving. Children take sweets to school to share but presents are not much in evidence.

The lorry has arrived. The one single bed is placed in state in the bedroom. We all sit on it drinking and nibbling. Jenny is exhausted and still has so much to think of that we feel its best to leave the family together to get the measure of living in their new space. So it's back to our oasis. How I love this hotel! Mhaletta takes her tape recorder to the restaurant to record our song and the waiter is mortified as he drops a bottle of vinegar over the microphone. Could anything spoil a day like today?

14th November 1990

Mhaletta: Something has happened to Sandra. One minute we are chatting about yesterday and the next she is dancing and jumping around, doubled up with laughter and talking on and on. In jumbles of words and sentences she is trying to convey the utterly amazing energy she is experiencing.

'I've gone up... UP, UP! I'm detached, separate.....letting go of the world. I'm in a massive thought-form... a magic mushroom. I'm brain-storming how we can create this; generate this; share this energy. It's magnificent!'

She is bubbling incoherently with ideas for the project which I am trying to catch and write down but then I too am swept up and into it and it is just exactly as she describes. At some level it seems to me that we are experiencing metaphysically that essential sense of joy in the coming work; devoid of apprehension; fears or stresses of responsibility, but the JOY IN UNITY symbolised in our school motto is real and alive. We are physically being infused with the energy of it, enthused by it and enwrapped in it. In the work to come in the days ahead we will remember this as we work to find ways of bringing this energy into being.

George is late arriving this morning and we are glad to have time to internalise our experiences. Is the plan moving forwards? Not entirely. The inauguration is tomorrow and the invitation has still not been typed up. I refuse to allow him to send out my scrappy handwritten page telling him that our paperwork has to be first class. It is our publicity, the outreach face of the school that carries our collective energy, symbol and word-power. George concedes we are right and it will be done somehow. Now George's priority appears to be the making of an embroidered school symbol. We go with him and buy some white satin. The embroiderer is an old man inside a dark shack with children lying inert on the floor. He shows us a range of delicate silken threads and jointly we make decisions of the colours for the symbol. One by one they are added to make up a delicate rainbow. We are by then delighted and he promises two pieces will be completed by 2pm tomorrow.

Shopping is next on his list for an Inaugural Day sari for Jenny. George knows exactly what she would like. We don't doubt he is right. It is a sari swathe in softly flowing sky blue. We then buy bed sheets, two wicker chairs and a table and he leaves us to tend to more vital details. Its shoe shopping time for sandals for Derek, then the rains fall in their usual drenching sheets, sending us scuttling home.

Tonight we are due at Mr. Mohan's to dinner and I have the jitters to such a degree that I want to cancel. It is in fact more than the jitters. It is fear that I can feel, physically. Sandra persuades me as far as reception where we learn there are disturbances outside and reports of stabbings. We try to find a taxi but no driver wants our business, which is unusual. We agree to give up the attempt to travel, return to the hotel and phone Mr. Mohan to apologise. His immediate response is that he will have friends with us in half an hour.

I'm standing in the bedroom still feeling disturbed and uncertain about going out when I realise it is something more that what may be in the air outside. Today I have been phoning the Airport to check our flight and have begun to reconnect to home, but memory-association is playing fear-filled tricks. My last journey back from India, albeit thirteen years ago, was a journey into darkness and rejection. There is still a memory imprint somewhere within me that has surfaced and is affecting my judgement, impeding my movements and giving my body the jitters. How fortunate that Sandra is with me as together we can deal with it. She has practiced a variety of ways of moving entrenched patterns that have impressed themselves deeply into the cellular systems of memory. Tonight as we have little time, we create a simple ritual using the colourfully embroidered squares of mirror-ware. It is the mirrors that seem significant for me as we use our will power to dissolve this old reflection that has no place in today's world. We are ready to travel when the friends arrive to take us to a bountiful dinner of spaghetti pie and sweetbread and a delightfully sociable evening.

15th November 1990

Sandra: The family circle is growing. We arrive at George's at our usual 8am to be introduced to Jenny's brother Philip and sister Jean who had not been needed at a wake but instead find themselves needed at an Inauguration. They have arrived by train from Guntur, a small town hundreds of miles away. Jean is a school teacher with two children, Cynthia a shy four year old and Royston who she introduces as being 'very naughty boy'.The house is shining and we realise what a joy it must be for Jenny to share their good fortune with her family. Elias is still with us and of course Sasoona from the village. For each of these families life is a constant struggle and we wish our funds could stretch further into the extended family.

This is all delightful but we still haven't any signed papers regarding the school premises and goodwill. Leaving them all behind, the four of us set off for a chaotic, tense and tiresome morning.

Mhaletta: We have no information as to how this transaction is to be accomplished. The vendor is found in his canteen shop of a big school and is reluctant to do **any** transactions. He stonewalls. 'Come back tomorrow'. Tomorrow will not come as we will be on the plane. The School Principal is asked to assist. He refuses to become involved. The vendor then agrees to transact. He is willing to receive our 10,000 rupees in exchange for a tatty receipt merely stating he has received it without notation of what we are purchasing. His brother will witness. I refuse to hand over the money, feeling suspicious of the vendor's tactics. We then all traipse to another school to transact at the back of a book stall with a man introduced as another 'brother' willing to act as witness. George now writes out the receipt which I insist is still not suitable. It states that the 10,000 rupees are **towards** the purchase of furniture and goodwill leaving it wide open to pressure for further payments later. So now I have a go, re-writing the receipt as **10,000 rupees in full payment of** …etc. We are now on a repeat round returning to the first brother who again resists witnessing a signing. It is turned 1pm. The Inauguration begins at two and as yet we do not have a school. At 1.15pm the vendor's signature is witnessed. Relief sweeps through us all with revitalising momentum.

At home nobody is ready. It is 1.45. We inject urgency and everyone rushes about dressing for the occasion. Out come our saris again but we cannot compete with Jenny, poised and elegant in her sky blue as we process, with the dignity of very new dignitaries towards the school. Then we see our names, up there, painted on a monster banner swinging from poles. A second  banner of equal size welcomes the parents. Amazement grows as we are faced with an orange tent awning in the middle of the road; three red thrones on a stage and row after row of chairs; music playing through micro-phones; children looking like performers, made up and in extraordinary costumes; parents arriving by the score and ragged street children, sitting in wide eyed wonder waiting for the show to begin. We all mingle talking with parents, and children. The nuns are there with a friendly priest and even the bank manager! George goes missing for a while returning with a giant board that is immediately erected.

George and Jenny have their school. I am so moved by what has been

accomplished in such a short time that I quake to think that I had dared to lecture George about good publicity. The whole neighbourhood is being treated to an afternoon of MetaCentre energy like it has never before been presented. India does not always work best on paper; she has her own methods.

Garlands encircle us as we take to our thrones to be introduced. George and I both make brief speeches then move into the body of the audience to enjoy the children's entertainment of poems, songs, dances and plays which they must have been preparing for many a month. It is Jenny that has been their teacher of the performing arts and it is mostly in English. It is Sandra and Stanley who lead in the performance of a dancing drama of 'The Golden Bird'.

Coffee and biscuits are given out. This is the first time in the three year history of this school that there has been a parents day. It is a huge success. We expect that every parent there will be re-registering their children. George and Jenny now have a business with a small income on which we can build. They must have been planning it all in absolute trust that it could happen and it has.

It is all over now. We wander back to the New House mesmerised, take refreshing drinks and say our goodbyes to Elias and Sasoona, Philip, Jean, Cynthia and Royston, Steven, Sandra, Stanley, Angela and Genevieve and a bunch of their friends and neighbours. Where **does** family begin and end?

George and Jenny are returning with us to our hotel for a quiet celebratory dinner together. George asks our permission to take a drink of alcohol. We reckon he has truly earned his choice of two whiskies and it is a delight to watch him unwind and laugh as he pours out a stream of the most outrageous compliments that either of us have ever received. We return them with interest, including Jenny in our mutual admiration Society. These are not four egos sitting round a table tonight, they are four very human people that just for a while are allowed to feel super-human!

George is the one, whose tongue being loosened, gives recognition on behalf of us all to the Great Guiding Intelligence that has brought us together, leading and protecting us on our journey. We ask for nothing, knowing that it is all in hand and we will all work to the limits of our abilities ... and beyond if necessary.

The Gates of Hyderabad are open. We leave at 1am for Bombay.

16th November 1990

Mhaletta: Sandra has organised a one day stop over in Bombay. In her efforts to earn her fare she had discovered Gita, a social worker living nearby who needed help in keeping her house in order which had led to them becoming friendly. Knowing we were passing through Bombay she had suggested we contact her brother Anil who, she assured us, would be delighted to host us for a day out. It had been a frenetic, exhilarating three weeks when we had held such a strong focus on the journey and its purpose and we both felt we needed this respite care and time to unwind.

After booking into a small hotel we have a couple of hour's sleep and phone Anil. We are just in time as he is about to go to work. He takes the day off, collects us and takes us to his home for breakfast of pastries and tea where we meet his wife, a psychology lecturer. They take us to the roof of their high rise building to see the vista of Bombay laid out below. Acting as our protector and guide Anil is the perfect host. He drives us around the city, stopping for us to see a treasure trove of jewellery in Bombay Tiffanys and introduces us to the renowned Jehu Beach with its miles of sandy shoreline edging the city. There are horses in garlands and tinsel dressed for wild galloping on the sands (not for us though); decorated carts and superior looking camels; round-a-bouts, and every kind of stall. We had no idea Bombay could offer such a holiday atmosphere.

The sun is the hottest we have experienced yet and we both paddle up to our knees to cool down, then, seeing we need some shade Anil shepherds us into the Sun and Sand Hotel. It is five stars and luxurious, tempting us to take snacks and drinks in an idyllic setting. It is there that Anil gives us a message from his heart.

He speaks of acceptance and of always seeking out the best life has to offer in people, in cultures and environment. He has travelled the world, loves beautiful places and has met beautiful people. So have we. Brothers of the Way are to be found everywhere. Anil is yet another. There has been no pressure on us today to be anything other than the tourists which, for this one whole day, we are.

17th November 1990

Sandra: All the information screens at the Airport have gone haywire. They're showing all the wrong information and can't work out who is supposed to sit where on the plane. We end up in seats two rows apart. It doesn't matter. All I have left to say is 'I've been on an Indiana Jones Extravaganza!'

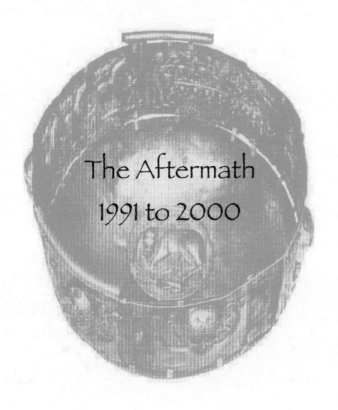

The Aftermath
1991 to 2000

37. The Beggars Bowl

We returned as beggars for the next twelve years. In this way India sat on my outstretched palm. Again we placed ourselves on breakfast tables with news articles and a three monthly magazine was quickly in production, MetaCentre turning into MetaCentre International as we launched a drive to find sponsors at £5 per child. India made her presence felt in primary schools in Dudley Borough as children began 'Letters to India' projects, penny lines were measured in rupees; anecdotes of our escapades were told and models of straw roofed huts were designed amongst yards of foot tripping saris. India afternoons in the classrooms caught on.

All donations for our workshops and groups at Adam House were channelled into the 'Hyderabad Project', collages of photos lining the hallway. India had stepped inside. She was visible, purposefully so. On many an evening I was out and about talking to the theme of *Journeys in India ... and beyond* offering a wealth of material to explore, the 'beyond' being an integral part of it. India, ever synonymous with the mystical East, was a catalyst for dialogue ranging from material needs to metaphysical possibilities. Always the question arose as to why I had taken on such a time consuming challenge of this nature and I had no answer. Then, one unsuspecting day while journal writing my pen gave me something different to contemplate. Thinking at the time that I had begun to pick up the thread of a short story which sometimes appears in this sudden way, I simply wrote on. It felt as if I was writing from a different place, a place where memory was vibrant, alive. This is what appeared on the page under the title:

The Eye within the Darkness

Admi was the name they called in the ear laid upon my mother's cradle back. A tiny child, wizened even then, ill nourished by the breast flattened by poverty, given into the hands of a wandering monk.

'Place this in your bowl' said my woman-mother as she held out the folded scraps of cotton cloth, wrinkled as the skin that scarcely covered the frame of bone. 'A gift for the temple... this is my rice, last grains of my womanhood'. And she faded from my ears yet not out of my heart for the rhythm of the blood coursing through her veins still ran, though thinly, in my own.

Monk's hands gathered in my drooping limbs that had not strength enough to hold to the only strand of life-giving warmth that I had ever known. Then, as now, I felt the current leap to set the body on its soul-filled course. A circuit, solar fired, connected and I knew myself as humanness laced with fire. He took then my burnished body and placed it within the folds of his robe, colourless to me, as my eyes knew only the darkness of delight as memory flooded my cells with the awareness of life. I knew this current. This was not the awareness of earthly existence but the pure knowledge of the Divine spark as it bursts into beingness, though cloaked by the roughest of cloth. As my mother gave me into nameless hands, that spark of the Divine called out and in its calling broke the seal.

How clear that moment returns to me. What of the after life you ask? What of that spark? Did it fan into a flame? They did not even know my name, for my tongue could not shape the word, so only my puny heart held it in safe keeping and, as I grew but slowly, they knew me as Jeva-luendi, the one who hides beneath the folds. So the cloth became both my mother and father that shielded me from the rigours of the world, from the dust bowls of the months of heat, from the torrents of the months of water, and from the eyes of the Masters whose season began with birth and ended never.

Yet I felt their presence, the Knowing Ones. The more tightly did I pull the cloth about me the more their eyes pierced the threads. I could not escape them either by night or by day. Neither did I wish to escape for the sounds of their thoughts were like music, the music of a thousand nesting birds. Every moment they fed their young by the purity of their beingness, by the potency of their minds; and by the emissions from their hearts. To be a Master myself was never a possibility. I had not been bred for mastery within that scheme, but I had been bred with purpose. And the purpose was to feel, to sense, to identify the presence of the Masters in human form and to do so without the energy of sight. Ah, have I not yet told you? Yes, I was blind, from birth.

My mother, knowing I would never serve my filial duty as her son, never protect and succour her in her infirmities did give me up into the begging bowl, begging even as she gave, that I should live in my enshrouded life. For the folds of the cloak were the folds of mine own eyelids also, those cowls of flesh that would not lift to allow the eyes to breathe in the glories of the world of sight. Yet I felt no sorrow. For what is sorrow when the spark is kindled? It is nought but a longing for that which is not and I would not have given up the spark of my soul for the eyes of a princeling.

And so I worked out the purpose of that life knowing how many grains of rice fell into my bowl by its weight; learning my prayers by the imprints of the hands of the Masters upon the Wheel; knowing the path to the snowline by the smell of the wind and the sweet sharpness of the rock-strewn paths. Was I handsome or disfigured? How should I know? I could not tell and no-one told me so. For it was not the way of the Master to give heed to the features save that they should be tranquil as a lake upon which the perfect image of the Buddha may rest without ripple.

'Be still in the name of holiness' they called to some, but not to me, for to me they seldom spoke. It was as if my sightlessness had deprived them of sight of me! I could not feel my hair. Though I knew not the meaning of dark or fair I could feel its power, its strength ... until the day they took it from me. They spoke then saying:

'Power is an inner attribute that needs no symbol to proclaim itself unto the world. Let the power within grow even as the hairs of thy head will never cease to reach out for the light'.

I could work. Have no doubt of it. I knew the weeds of the fields by their odours and the sweet herbs by their rich perfume. And I garnered well those plants which the mendicant monks culled for their remedies. But because of my sightless state I was of greatest use to carry forth the begging bowl, and into that void was placed the holy gifts, as I myself had once been placed. And in return I gave them joy, for in my coming was released in them a thank-fullness for the sight of their children, for their vision of a world made manifest before them. And I knew as I walked amongst them that I would come again and would create visions of beauty; that I would become a see-er. Yet in my ignorance I knew not when that day would come, nor how I could unfold the sacred visions beyond the imaginings of my formless mind.

The wheel turned. Age was no criteria for death. The alertness of my living did not forsake me when the day of my completion came. I had trodden my path with fortitude. It was enough. There were no farewells for they, the Masters of my days, knew each and every thread of my existence. It was a joy to climb the mountain, to feel the snow, soft yet crisp beneath my shoeless feet. If only I could see what whiteness was this once! A wisp of longing touched me then and in that moment the mountains seemed to breathe from their cavernous depths as the snow began to move, to gambol and to roar as it cascaded down her craggy sides. Oh yes, I saw with inner eye, and heard with inner ear as it enfolded me – another cloak, pure, soft, with the warmth of the heart of winter, enfolding me, embracing me ... whispering my name, Admi, for he who hides within the folds shall be no more. And the cowls fell as the eyes saw that which they had always known as Light Supernal.

A past life some might say. Perhaps. There may be other explanations. All I can say is that this is not a story culled from imagination or desire for as I wrote I could see not only images of the scenes described; it felt as if all emotion was gathered in the heart. Even if I had not lived this tale before I had lived it now. I knew this blind monk who saw within his darkness. He is familiar, real. I feel his feelings of being 'in hiding' though I live in a world vibrant with life; the urge to work with colour and all manner of creative arts; to create beauty is always with me; the loving wisdom of unseen Masters surrounds me; Buddhas are my watchers, sitting in their appointed places always ready to receive the jewels or the dross of my life. And then there is the well of compassion that never leaves for the prisoners of darkness; of ignorance; of poverty; or of minds buried under mountains of unleavened thoughts. Maybe the snippets of wisdom that I catch are his silent voice: *'Those whose lives have depended upon it truly know the meaning of compassion'*. His love is of the unseen world, his unseen Brothers and the way ahead…and he found joy in darkness. Maybe he is that wise advisor, or aspect of that higher mind needing no human eyes to know my way. Imprints of the experience remain indelible, unblemished by interpretation.

India visibly and invisibly had in thought and deed en-cloaked my life.

38. Finger of Death

Someone in the close inner circle of my family will die soon. There are no words advising me, I simply sense it and with it comes that noetic certainty of an event that will happen, inevitably. Yet no finger points to this one or that. I write registering words I do not want to pen.

Carmella is in Devon and we have met in odd times and places as we join our creative ideas for a book based on our water birth experience and research. We like the finished article. Publishers show no interest. It is shelved, Benjaya has started school and life moves on.

It is two years since the creation of the Hyderabad School, two years of re-investing my energy in the Probation Service, earning enough to fund a return to India to see the progress of our project that has remained ever present in our daily lives. And it is time for the next generation to find its footing in India. My companion on the road is to be Sandra's eldest daughter Sommer, now twelve. She has collected eighty books to start a school library, so we plan a weighty journey together in the month of February 1992; but by now I am carrying the awareness of the nearness of death. It is necessary that I tell Sandra. We hold to the plan telling no-one else. Sommer gives me a drawing of some Arabic wisdom words: 'God grant me a goodly entrance and a goodly exit and sustain me with your power'. What does **she** know?

George and Jenny are at the airport, sombre faced. Ma has died. George could not reach the village in time to be at her funeral. He is in a state of mourning that is palpable. And so we are met by images of death, talk of death and yet this is not the one. Sommer describes seeing Ma's face superimposed over mine as I lie in the bed. She has not seen her photo yet describes her features much as Steven had done. It is weird, unsettling. Sommer greatly enjoys spending time with the Nayak children but after three days we decide to move on as we have a programme of visits to make further afield. Jenny's teenage nephew is in a bad condition and in need of a kidney transplant. We have collected funds for an operation which we are to deliver personally to his home in Guntur, a long distance train ride away at the same time meeting Jenny's mother and more family members. Warmly welcoming we enjoy their hospitality and, mission accomplished, we move on. We are heading for Pondicherry and the Ashram of Shri Aurobindo and The Mother, stopping overnight in Chennai where a work colleague has arranged accommodation. After a somewhat adventurous overnight train journey we find our next hosts and a nearby hotel with a swimming pool where we plunge in. Sommer repeatedly lies face down in the water floating after giving me the chilling instruction 'don't let anyone save me'. I watch her, hawk-eyed.

Our host lends us his car and driver for the journey to Pondicherry. At last I am on the ground, hallowed to many, where that great soul known as The Mother lived, worked and produced volumes of wisdom. Her life was focused upon reaching supramental consciousness asserting always that 'supramental change is a thing decreed'. The energy that I had experienced with Sandra at the Hyderabad Ashram was overwhelming here, held in the perfume of banks of flowers covering her resting place visited by hundreds every day. We flow amongst them, leaving only to take a taxi out to Auroville, the Soul City which she had planned in her later years that was taking shape, its focus being the Matrimandir which houses a magnificent crystal in its sanctuary. We arrive. It is closed and still under construction. I obtain permission for us to go in and then I am unable to make the climb up the steeply winding concrete ramp, unfinished and as yet without a balustrade. Vertigo is for me a hazard of some proportions. Sommer, dressed in my clothes that day, will make the climb for both of us. I watch her disappear beyond the ramp. The crystal was to be the highlight of a visit to Auroville. Thwarted by my own fear I sink to the floor amongst dusty shoes and concrete rubble, fraught with disappointment and disbelief at my persisting weakness. Suddenly I am aware of a phrase imprinting on my mind **the light body now takes precedence**. I interpret this to mean I can let go of my desire to see the physical 'body' of the crystal and sense the light it emits. Sommer returns intact. I feel disorientated. It is enough. We return to Chennai and determine to fly back to Hyderabad.

The plane flies out. We are both in the same quiet thoughtful mood. The plane circles in thick fog and is not allowed to land. We return, re-circle Chennai and repeat the flight to Hyderabad. At the second attempt we land feeling as if we have been lost in space. George and Jenny have been busy in our absence orchestrating another colourful celebration, the parents are once again present and it is now Sommer's turn in the spotlight as, garlanded and with full honours, she is presented with a carved eagle for her work in initiating the school library.

We are relaxed; delighted by the event and are ready to discuss the business of finance and future plans, but first it is time for a swim at a local hotel.

It is there that George and Jenny find us to give us the news. The police had just arrived to inform them of the death by drowning of Benjaya in the River Avon two days previously. The finger had pointed to the little one, the youngest in our family. *The light body now takes precedence* again has meaning; I must let go of desire for the sight of that much loved physical body and remain focussed on the Light Body … his and mine! What do you say when you hear such awesome news. My only expletive was 'Oh My Love!' Sommer spoke only through her eyes.

Sometimes I had played with Benjaya on the beach, a game of chasing the Golden Bird as he flapped wildly with a yellow towel. We all return to light the school lamp. It is a two foot high golden bird. This is no time for a grim reaper. We have our own symbol that holds us as we create a Ceremony of Light for Benjaya's continuing journey. And the memory returns. I had foreseen his life would be short when he was six months old and had locked away the images I had seen. It is obvious why our book on birth had not found its way out. It was only half finished. Birth and death will combine to complete that work. We flew home immediately

Carmella was not fending off the media publicity; she had stepped in to share the truth of her perceptions of the immensity and continuity of life. The media were taken by surprise but clearly interested and took the synchronicity of the water birth and water death as their headlines which were valid, not quirky. She knew already that we must start to write immediately unfolding the holistic principles that had brought about the birthing archetype while we lived them day by day. And so we did. I interviewed everyone involved from police to water-bailiffs, family and friends, discovering Benjaya to have been aware of his forthcoming departure in water as Sommer, and others, clearly had. The Great Finger truly does point. We have not yet learnt to read its writing on the skein of our lives.

It was inevitable that we would plunge straight into the same learning pattern as we had for birth. Workshops, talks, and gatherings brought together all manner of people engaged with the business end of death, the professionals and those who death had touched personally and closely. The continuity of consciousness held as the core concept. Darkness and secrecy gave way to a changing paradigm of language and perception of reality bridging the polarities of physical and metaphysical states of existence. It was to take us four years to complete *Benjaya's Gifts*. Published in 1996 it too circled the world.

My journey had ended abruptly and we still needed to gather histories of all our pupils and details of finances. Charlotte offers to go for three months taking two young men with her. They leave with funds to purchase equipment with an assignment to introduce sports, crafts and teach English. Task done, Charlotte takes to the road alone travelling to the Taj Mahal and on to Dharamsala, home of the Dalai Llama, receiving his blessing before returning safely home to find changes in store.

Charlotte is our youngest child. Born in 1967 she is the only one to have been born in Adam House and she fully intended to give birth here when that day came. It came. Yasmin was born on 10th December 1993. In the September of that year Charlotte was committed to begin four years of teacher training at Worcester College. What to do? I was not available to become a full time grandmother so we engaged an au pair, Charlotte's partner moved in and a new family unit formed as Adam House became predominantly a family home again where life comes and goes wherever and whenever it is called to go.

39. Caged Birds

Prison is looming on the horizon once again. Wherever there are shortfalls of staff our peripatetic Probation team allocate someone to fill in temporary gaps. I'm sent to prison, a Young Offenders Institution for 500 males between seventeen and twenty one for a brief spell of duty. It's strange how the prison is sectioned into so many 'wings', with everyone 'doing bird', talking of being 'caged'. I'm intrigued. I don't need a finger to point out that this is exactly where I need to be. There is no resistance on this turn of the wheel. It is where I **want** to be, experiencing a very different kind of training.

No.1 instruction is about the keys. A key bunch swings on a chain that must be tucked securely into a leather pouch worn on the right hip. They never leave the prison. No.2. is about emergencies and hostage taking. No. 3 ... and so on. I'm on the inside, not a visitor this time, allocated to the Vulnerable Wing. Being identified as vulnerable in prison can increase a person's vulnerability, drawing unwelcome attention and more derogatory labels. What makes a prisoner vulnerable? The nature of his crime which here can well be amongst the most serious on the statute books; his size and physical appearance; his tendency towards self harm or suicide for a start. Every morning I am at my desk at 8am ready to assess and assist those brought in from the courts the previous night, sorting out muddles they'd left behind them; helping them to deal with their emotions; giving essential information on how to cope, especially to first time offenders; assessing for suicide risk and self harm. I'd arrived at a perfect point. The Vulnerable Wing was in the process of changing its name to the Personal Development Unit. I will certainly be amongst those developing. It is a new world to explore, an internalised world. Opportunities to develop experimental programmes were already on the agenda. Willingly I apply to convert my short term cover into a long term post and am seconded to the Prison Service for the foreseeable future. Many initiatives were taking place. I was asked to work on tactics for encouraging prisoners out of their cells with the aim of integration into the main body of the prison. I choose to form an innovative group of very mixed characters. It proved to be hilarious, profitable and a voyage of discovery for us all. Prisoners collect labels. They are frequently described as mindless, thoughtless, brainless individuals. The title I chose was simply *'Open Your Mind'*. They did. What came out and what went into those minds they asked me to record and send it to 'everybody'. I did and it became my training material. A Prison

Officer was allocated to join me on the group. He thought he would be playing guard but even he was drawn in to be a part of it all as we used the analogy of the mind as a cage, and thoughts our birds. It is usual at work to keep one's personal life under wraps. Mine wouldn't stay under and neither would India who swept in through every available crevice, and what a teaching resource she made!

They came out of curiosity and to stir life up a bit, bravado hiding their nerves as they jockeyed for status. Young as they were they had many children between them, often from different short-lived relationships.

'What do you think about babies? **Do** you think about babies?' a question they had probably never been asked. Someone starts a sick monologue:

'Babies should be put in the microwave' continuing with a lurid description of the result. It's too obvious. They are testing; wondering if they can wind me up. Some snigger nervously. I say nothing. Three of the group are on murder charges. I lay the front page of *The Daily News* on the table. It's Benjaya's picture. Someone tentatively breaks the silence.

'What's the baby's name Miss?'

'It was Benjaya'. They pick up on the 'was'.

'Is he dead Miss?'

'Yes. He was, is, my grandson.'

There's a focus of eyes on the table and I sense a shift as if their veneer has been disturbed. We're past the joke stage and I have their attention as they wonder why he made headlines. I wait for the next question or comment. One scrapes his chair back and jumps to his feet.

'It's not fair Miss. You've got PERSONAL!'

We'd hit the jackpot. Prison depersonalises. They'd opened the door for me and I went through, fast.

'Life is personal. Life is personal and it is precious; all life, including yours. We have all been affected by other people haven't we? Some lift us up and others knock us down. We have to decide where we stand in the game and whether we can be knocked down like skittles. When you come to my office you are personal and I am personal. You want me to care about your situations and your feelings and the last thing you want from me is a knock down. Its snakes and ladders and you need ladders to lift you up to look over the wall of this place and the walls you have built in your minds. My life is about ladders. That is what I can offer. You can choose to see where they lead or clang the iron door on yourself.'

They chose ladders and no 'put downs'. They came out and we had some perfect symbols to play with, snakes, ladders and birds just for a start. My challenger who had tried to lay a snake, asked for an interview next day and we discovered he had been speaking of himself when he said of babies 'destroy them'. Abandoned as a baby, he felt he been emotionally destroyed. Words have roots. They can be rooted in the past and who knows what can gnaw away at the roots for a lifetime.

The group became the highlight of my week Bit by bit they let me see into their inner worlds and I enticed them into mine. Deprivation of the senses is a massive part of the punishment of prison life. We did experiments on loss of the five senses; sight, hearing, touch, smell or sound. Their illustrations were personal and poignant. They learnt fast, building mind pictures of a world they were being brought to see in a different light, to value what they had and to realise the cost of their actions. In effect I was teaching the Law of Cause and Effect … and a few others!

India was an ever present part of it. Coloured cloths, artefacts and pictures sparked minds and imagination of a wider world. The Education Department took up our project helping them to create adverts and slogans and write for the magazine. Releasing laughter is easy. They need no persuasion to try on saris responding with:

'Women are just floaty aren't they Miss?' As they step in willingly to discover more of a woman's world they begin to write poetry, and their love letters take

on a very different note! Their most exciting discovery is that we live in a world of constantly changing energies and I find many ways to prove it. Reaching, always reaching, touching minds, igniting sparks; loving my work and those whose lives are thrown together in this ever churning cauldron called a prison.

At home there is another prisoner, one that I can find no way to reach. Derek has been sliding deeper and deeper into the darkness of depression. The situation has become critical. It is affecting his work and our lives at home. He is given sick leave and chooses to go to the Gambia for recuperation time. To the depression is added a mystery illness on his return. He takes to bed, sweating, hallucinating, and seeing the bed covered in water and a flashing light in the corner of the room. Pills and potions have no effect. He worsens. I am given compassionate leave and call the family together. We prop him up, Marc shaves him. I have no presentiment of death approaching and yet **he** is no longer present. Sitting at his beside I give thanks for his life, then call yet another doctor, our third. An ambulance is sent for and I go with him to the Hospital for Tropical Diseases. He is diagnosed immediately with Falsiparum's malaria, the most virulent strain. We learn that half an hour longer and he would not have survived. It is a long, winding road back that does not lead to the Probation Service. In 1995 he retires on the grounds of ill health. I am left uncertain whether he is truly home. He does not seem the same person. Has he too become a stranger at his own gate? Depression too is a prison and I could find neither key nor antidote.

On the India front a situation was developing causing us concern. Both George and Jenny's extended families were undoubtedly in need of help and in India those who prosper are expected to share their prosperity. They were feeling pressure from all sides. Though we realised the need was genuine we were not in a position to keep increasing the fundraising. To finance an intensive training course in hypnotherapy Sandra was working and with three growing children to consider had little time to spare. We did find a school sponsor for Elias's eldest son in Rakeshponka but the prime focus had to be the everyday maintenance of the school, its fifty pupils and the spiralling expenses for the five Nayak children as each one made the grades towards their goal of College/University.

To cut expenses George had given up his flat and converted some rooms in the school as living space.   Looking long term he had found a small piece of ground on which he hoped one day to build a small school with living accommodation and become self sufficient. We raised funds to buy it. From the outset it was a disaster. It was as if the finger of death pointed squarely at our plot and we had not seen it coming. Squatters tried to establish themselves on it. Unable to afford a wall we bought barbed wire trying to cage it in and George employed a guard, a man from his village. The man died and the villagers demanded compensation for his death on our land. Shortly after a girl was kidnapped in Rakeshponka and there was a question of ransom money, a question we did not answer. We had already purchased four buffaloes for Rakeshponka and George had the idea of using our plot for keeping milking buffaloes, providing free school milk and selling the surplus, an idea he put into practice. There was a fierce drought, the animals skins dried up, their milk dried up, and when the roof blew off the buffalo sheds in a gale our finances dried up! The gale was devastating as George had planted coconut palm saplings around the perimeter. They were all destroyed. With all these weather extremes his efforts at planting vegetables came to nought. Unbeknown to us George had taken out an ill advised loan, was unable to keep up payments and the bank foreclosed. Clearly the development of this land was not in the wider scheme of things. These were hard lessons on all sides and George suffered greatly. He too saw the inside of the cage of depression and found his faith to be the saving grace that aided him on a lengthy journey to recovery.

So far the nineties had clearly been about applying the lessons we had been taught, number one being judgement and the subsequent laying of blame. Blame is a mind monster, easy to create, difficult to dispel. My pen slipped in a timely reminder:

Blame is a foolishness that wastes life's summers. Blame sets the trap, exposing pride in many a self-righteous act of feigned forgiveness. Where there is no blame there is no need for forgiveness. Where there is blame the need for forgiveness is of one's self alone. Think well upon it.

I had much to think well about, knowing I was certainly amongst those who both apportioned and received blame when circumstances cried out for understanding. Blame too is a cage where one can become a prisoner of guilt and regrets.

40.Beyond Friendship

All those amazing people I had met on life's journey who stepped out of the daily pattern of their lives to journey with me; uphold me; draw the best from me; nourish me at every level from food to information to spiritual upliftment, were more than friends. Friendship is defined as a relationship of mutual affection and goodwill. Beyond friendship is something else. What is it?

Beyond friendship lie the dissoluble bonds of Brotherhood, a bonding without ties, a merging of minds; and lives within lives emerging from the webs of solar kinship...

Brothers are not known in the same way as one 'makes' friends. Such connections are not made; they already are. Beyond friendship I am aware that there is recognition of a connection that has purpose; a powerful sense of service; a noetic awareness of need and a readiness to respond; the ability to aid in the next onward step or stage of a life's journey even if that means delivering a test or challenge; and an ever loving Presence, even in silence. There are Brothers everywhere; solar/soul kinship can be found in the most unlikely places; and family **can** be both.

During the fifteen years of discarnate teachings my notion of Brotherhood had stretched far beyond the physical. Our Informers had consistently spoken of us being under the canopy of The White Brotherhood explaining that the Order was composed of many smaller groupings each with their own specific part to play within a collective evolutionary Plan whilst extending the Spirit of Brotherhood and the essential qualities of Love, Wisdom and Service. During the Nineties our Teaching Group gradually came to an end. Marael had moved to the South of England and both Grace and Albert died after succumbing to illness, a poignant end to an era that had played an immense part in pulling me back from the brink and catapulting me at full tilt into a fast moving current. By this time Elizabeth Child had stepped into my life arena.

Dr. Elizabeth Child is an extraordinary person. We met in the Eighties when MetaCentre was in full swing and she too was enjoying running a variety of groups at her home which she had developed as a Healing and Meditation Centre. As a practising Doctor of Psychology, Liz had expanded her work by the study of hypnotherapy and alternative healing methods. We had joined a networking group to keep up to speed with developments in our fields of interest, hoping to make links with like minded people. An instant affinity sparked between us.

Life events that might well have appeared as bizarre, even catastrophic to many, drew us together, not to sympathise or bemoan, but to reveal and release with laughter the tensions of our 'cloaked' lives. We unravelled puzzling events, squeezing out the last drops of learning, placing them within the bigger picture of changes taking place at so many levels. We have a similar approach to life; speak the same language; have both come from professional backgrounds; and have both been involved in inter-cultural studies, even having shared the same University tutors. Certainly when we come together we never fail to lift each others spirits. We knew from the outset that our meeting held more than friendship, though friendship was clearly held firmly within it, it was a meeting with purpose.

Ancient Mystery School traditions tell of two main methods of instruction; the oral tradition, known as *Mystes*, and the second way, the more interactive method using vision, analogies, and symbols known as the *Epoptic School*. Liz was essentially of the first way. I had been developing the second. So we put them together. Though I had said plenty in the past, Liz became the prime spokesperson on a series of joint workshops, introducing streams of information; metaphysical insights and correspondences. My task was to encapsulate and visually depict the energy of the themes using a range of creative resources, in other terms to make energy tangible; the invisible visible. We were given to understand that our work was part of ever developing programmes of experimental energy work taking place, orchestrated and monitored by Advanced Minds who held the long view.

As ever at home the wheel keeps turning. It's 1996. Charlotte has one more year left of Teacher Training and is pregnant with daughter number two, due in September. There is no dispensation. She can have only an extra month off college or she will have to take a gap year and complete later. Another 'what to do?' situation. The answer slips out before thought. I had heard there were a few packages available for early retirement but had not been interested. Now I am suddenly interested. A package is agreed. That is how retirement came about and I became resident grandmother. We dispense with au pairs and I'm housekeeper as well. Sandra is living in Birmingham now working with her hypnotherapy practice at home and offers to share all the tasks in my lap. Charlotte's daughters, Yasmin and Daisy become our companions. In a group of four we re-enter a child's world, playing and studying each other and the energy we produce. These are delightful days after the intensity of the prison and a rosy future beckons except for one thing.

Derek has neither recovered his spirits nor his old demeanour. Affection and goodwill are in short supply. Both have 'gone with the wind', at least the wind is not blowing in my direction. Mindful of how rejecting I had been after my illness and that I had substantially recovered in a month or so, I bided my time hoping for him to see me in a different light, he however is adamant that he has 'lost the spark' and the light stays out. The only advice of note is: **Do not try to change the direction of the wind**. A bond which I well knew transcended friendship still held but by the merest sliver of a thread.

41. The Claim

In the afternoon of 31st December 1999 Derek and Marc landed in the tiny State of Goa on the south west coast of India for a two week package holiday on their first ever holiday abroad together. In the twenty two years since India had invested herself in me, Derek had touched only the hem of her cloak through his work. Any passing thoughts of a visit had remained vague and unrealised. Now India had beckoned to both father and son but not to me. I remained at home, alone. At 6.30pm that same day I switched on the television and there, the flat darkness of the screen erupted into myriad star bursts as the presenter announced 'A New Millennium has arrived…in Goa!' They were five and a half hours ahead of GMT. So that was how Goa made her entry into my life and Derek his exit. That moment of the turning of the century heralded the turn around of the established pattern of our lives.

Marc returned as planned. Derek remained. India had lost no time in laying her claim. Marc had sensed the rightness, the inevitability of it and I was left wondering what India had in store. These were uncertain days as Derek tried to find his anchorage. It came in the form of a three roomed house in the fishing village of Maddo Waddo where patchwork pigs meandered amongst the palm trees.

It was three months before I was free of commitments and able to join him for two weeks but it was with an increasing sense of apprehension that I left. On the plane I began to shiver, an inner coldness taking hold. There were no blankets. I covered myself with newspapers until, before touchdown, changing into an alluring dress, I tried to arrive. I do not think I ever really did. I wasn't much more than a talking body that wanted to be so much else and yet in three days I was too ill to engage with food, Goa, Derek or anyone. A sickness erupted. Whatever I had contracted had me in its grip and I couldn't bear the sadness of it all. Derek became infected and worsening fast, we agreed he must leave for home immediately. That was the first week. I had seen little more than the pigs and a seascape or two. The second week alone was spent trying to recover in a hotel room. Goa was of no interest to me. I saw her with dull eyes and a withering heart. She expelled me next and I went home.

Derek had rented the house for another full year and returned for the winter. His plans did not include me. It hurt. He had begun to see his Goan house as his home and family life in Adam House was receding.

'I'm not on holiday in India. There's a difference. I'm not a tourist; I live there.' I felt what he was really telling me was that he was alive there in a way he no longer felt alive with us. *WAIT* was all my Advisor had to offer. *Do not interfere,* was definitely implied.

Derek's second Goan winter passed but I didn't stand still while I waited. Returning home with Liz and Sandra from a talk at our local library by a traveller of Wisdom Trails, we experienced what I had come to call a 'noetic flash'. Liz and I were to travel to the Yucatan to study the pyramids. So began our Mayan adventures and a whole new sequence of learning as the pyramids and the Mayan culture became our Wisdom Teachers in a wider understanding of Universal Law, a subject which we then developed into workshops on our return.

An English summer was under way. My life was full and stimulating. I had no quarrel with Derek wintering in India, it was my exclusion that was so difficult to bear, yet I was forever hoping that he would bring back that aliveness with him so that we could find our way together again. It didn't happen. *It will,* said my confident Advisor. *Have patience.*

At the end of August 2002, a few days before our 47th wedding anniversary Derek announced that he was leaving permanently and would never return. He had already moved his belongings whilst I was away for a few days and within the hour he had gone out of my life. A marriage guillotined with quiet certainty.

'There is something else I have to do', was all he told me as he left to be with someone else.

What did I feel? The question is how to allow feelings their accustomed place when a deathly stillness is pervading the senses and numbness is forcing itself into every cell and cavity. No tears. That is not my way. Make it real. Tell the children and listen to words saying the unthinkable. I know only too well all the prescribed steps and stages of bereavement. Number one: Registration. Allow the imprint to form without denial and, if possible, without anger, blame or guilt. Tough! Just get it registered. This is a real happening, not a nightmare, a mistake or a rotten joke. So I made it real as events demand in the 'real' world and yet even then the Advisor was trying to register as well, insisting as always that nothing is as it seems. Well it seemed real enough to me and to the family, so each in their own way dealt with the surging diversity of feelings as they surfaced.

My journal at this time was unintelligible and then within a few days, to my immense surprise, I found I had a clear head and could sort out all the practicalities of separating lives. In the last moments allotted to me I had asked if he wanted a divorce but his expression had looked puzzled as he answered *'No!'*

Somewhere on the back shelf of my mind I was aware that *his* voice had sounded soft, distant, and slightly hypnotic as if it was coming from a long way away. Was his guiding principle orchestrating this cataclysmic event? That was something I had to take into account, when I was ready.

Then two things occurred. The first was that Marc returned home while sorting out the ending of a long partnership and stayed. With both our lives in a state of flux there were so many common denominators. We have always been talkers, both using images as we wrap our minds around concepts and ideas and the vagaries of life. And this was the ideal time for unwrapping some of the parcels and particles of events that had gone beyond our mind's grasp for the present. So together with the loss came an experience of the joy of sharing that had been missing for a long time.

Then the Twin Towers collapsed. Massive thought forms were instantly created by the devastating imagery impacting on the brain. Suddenly we were all carrying visions of a world rocking to its foundations. Death, grief, and loss was no longer an individual's private suffering; it was collective, it was shared, it was acknowledged with compassion and courage beyond measure. The death of a marriage found its place within a bigger picture. People came with open hearts to be in the peace and healing energy of the Sanctuary, and to hold or to express their visions of the regeneration that must surely come after such devastation. The sense of loving union they generated was exactly what was needed. This was a time of critical mass movement, of separations on many different levels, leaving relationships, jobs, homes, old beliefs and life structures falling, separating from the known, entering the unknown. I was certain then that Derek had been impulsed by the timing. Whatever he felt he had to do, this was the time to go and do it.

Dressed in our best we met for lunch in October for the signing of bank papers as we acknowledged the bizarre nature of events that seemed to have overtaken us. In November he paid me a visit in such low spirits that we went to the Sanctuary where I gave him healing and a blessing for his untrodden road and then he left for India, alone. The position with his Someone Else who had been a shadowy presence in my life for many years was left hanging in the balance yet it seemed that a line had been drawn under our lives together. An accounting was taking place and as I saw it, though there was no road back … or it seemed forwards, I remained aware that our journey together was as yet incomplete.

In the safety of his Goan house Derek settled into his thoughts and I into mine and the new life I intended to build. Then the Advisor's *Wait* messages changed to *Move!* The green light was on and there was clearly a plan under way. I felt like a pawn that was a vital piece in the game. A *Move* message often calls for immediate action without allowing thought to slip in. The rational mind can usually think of dozens of reasons for prevarication. I only had to move a hand to lift the phone, call the Someone Else and make a visit to her home.

Meetings between women in such situations might be expected to be delicate, with both parties trying to get the measure of the other and to have the upper hand in the situation, not to mention the unpredictability of emotions running riot. This was not the case. I felt neither vulnerable nor was I trying to do or get anything. No animosity surfaced. She suggested that in other circumstances we might well have become friends. I agreed. We held the high ground calmly and courteously enabling us to discuss and discover whatever was necessary to begin unravelling the tangled web of our lives.

What is the point of all these years of developing awareness of energy at the subtle levels if I could not identify whether Derek's presence was anchored in this house or not? Had he made an indelible imprint upon it that would draw him back? Was it on his Life Path to take this turn in the road? Is this the place where he truly belongs? I sensed that it was not. This was merely a place where he had been and lived a slice of his life inaccessible to me. Whatever imprints he may have made were no longer active. The knowing was clear enough that he would not be returning to this house and person; but it was not for me to say as that was clearly not the outcome for which she was hoping and planning. It was enough to explain that we had not yet completed the journey on which we had embarked together. Derek had to find his own knowing … if he could.

42.Hearts in Aspic

Christmas loomed on our horizon. The Spirit of Celebration would not rise in me. In New York there are those who have been my guardians and guides in that city, with whom I have worked and played and evolved beyond measure in their company. I call. New York is in mourning and there is room for two more. Marc is coming with me.

We are welcomed into an apartment overlooking the Hudson River and into the hearts and homes of those who know themselves to be bonded by invisible threads. Teddy, my host, an ex-Jesuit priest who had initiated Spirit Theatre, is the answer to the unanswerable questions. His home is filled with all manner of artefacts, a riot of colours and cultures. Reading the situation with few words he tells me that Derek has 'shaken the web'. I nod. It is our way to use symbols, laying out the situation on a cloth in the formation of a web. Teddy is the shaman/priest; I am called on to surrender the thought of any outcome to the situation and then together we shake the cloth and the pieces fall into a different patterning. We do not attempt to read it. It is enough to know that change will ensue.

New York envelops us both in the pageantry of Christmas. This is not tinsel town; this is a people who need life that has been stopped in its tracks to re-assemble. Christmas Eve is to be our last night in New York as on Christmas morning we will be travelling with Linda and Alex to their home in the country. I ask Marc to leave me alone as there is something I know I have to do. He leaves to go out revelling and I head out alone for Ground Zero-The World Trade Centre.

At first it seems unreachable; most roads blocked off; cranes; rubble rolling out on lorries; coldness warmed only by the heartrending letters, flowers and pictures. Looming over the desolation the only tower block still standing is completely draped in black topped by a USA flag; surly this is the biggest grave stone in the world. Slowly the energy it symbolises begins to infuse me, seeping into my cells, finding connections to a depth of sorrow in me that I never even knew existed. I could sense sorrow, aware of it like never before. Sorrow is beyond sadness. It feels to me like one huge penetrating vortex of sorrow; a hole of sorrow. Yet from the Zero point it was sweeping out on all sides attracting towards itself wave after wave of compassion. People who were walking in sorrow were being touched by something else as I am, that offers transformative power for the task of re-constructing lives; buildings or the heart of a city. The Black Tower is the symbol of potential for transformation standing majestically over the scene of devastation. The energy of sorrow infused with compassion that had subsumed me was a transformative power and this was a massive transformational point within my life.

A tiny church on the edge of the Zone is open and it gathers me in. A sermon is in progress. We are being asked:
'Will **you** hold the Christ Child even if he cries and screams and does not smile upon you? Will you take him in your arms, soothe him and hold him with all the love within you? Will you hold your brother, your husband, wife; a friend, a stranger? Will you hold him as the Christ Child and give to him your bed, your succour and your heart? And will you make condition that he must behave according to **your** screed? Or will you allow him to BE that which he truly is?'
    I understand the Christmas message. It is of relevance in my life. I give a silent answer there and then and walk out into the darkness. There are few people or traffic, no subway or buses. A garbage lorry has overturned tipping its load of putrid smells. Always I can find my way home by some means and so I walk.
    Carmella is also in New York for Christmas with her son, Asher. Our groups of friends overlap as we come together to give recognition to the immensity of the events and their aftermath. Carmella whose pen had been flourishing for the last five years researching and writing on the wisdom to be found in the aftermath of trauma, was ready to play a part in the years of support work to follow.

Derek has fallen under India's spell and the winter becomes his burning ground as his travels begin. India leads him to the North along some of the pathways I had travelled so long ago, Delhi, Chandigargh, Agra, Simla, as well as tracks of his own choosing. As the New Year begins I feel a newness; an honesty and freshness in his increasingly frequent Emails as he writes of missing 'the hand of the family'. Cautiously we correspond and then he sends me a book *Set my Heart in Aspic* a gift to him from its author, Nisha da Cunha, a lady he has met in Goa. I'm intrigued. They are short stories, mostly sad, about people who had realised their true path … or loves, too late to reclaim them. Its essential message is to **act** even if you think it is too late, at least then you will know one way or the other and will not be forever wondering 'what if'. Often a speaker through symbolic gifts he had tucked inside a golden key. So, he had acted. He is ready to come home to be where he belongs. He, or the gods, had decided and I am immeasurably glad of it.

We put each other to the test by taking time away from the watching world, travelling in Europe in our old motor home. Strangely, in this restrictive space when on the road, we find ourselves to be at our most compatible. Derek had made it clear to me and to himself, 'You are the one I journey with'. Correct. He knows. The indissoluble bond between us is acknowledged; the journey is not yet over and we have to move on.

Too soon, it is September and I'm rocking at the thought of India looming. Derek is certain it is a part of our newly emerging life together. I am shaking with apprehension laced with anger that India is inching her way back into the life we have so recently redesigned. Derek has no interest in Projects. He wants a peace-filled co-existence in the world of the Lotus Eaters. His dream could be my nightmare. I certainly had not felt at home in Goa. I do not lie on sun-beds toasting, sip concoctions and talk of this and that and am certain that I will not fit as a tourist, but what else is there? India has been my work place. What if my body has another  battering? What if I am expelled again? Is it possible to step into his dream and make it my own? Is it a marked path? Confusion and commitment are uncomfortable bed-fellows. I'm definitely wobbling. Now we're both in the aspic! Unable to grasp the nettle and buy a ticket it is Marc who, having been in at the beginning of the Goa saga suggests I stop prevaricating and 'give it a go'. Family are of the opinion I will soon be back. With a sigh and no signs to the contrary I buy the tickets. 'Take care of her' I tell Marc who is left alone in charge of the house and then let go of everything that is solid, the foundations, the family, the familiar buzzing world and set off to take on India once again.

The Third Part

The Blue Print

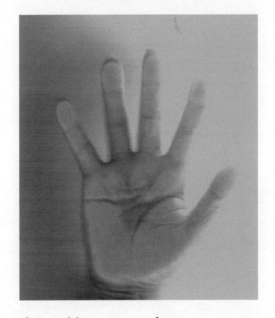

The cauldron waits in fiery expectation
For those who handle the life to examine the brew

43.Shadows of a Muse
2002/2003

The Cycle

A travelling companion is a magician whose presence or preference can change
a plot or plan in an instant. For the next seven winters Derek held me in Goa.
Was he the magician or the instrument of the cyclic force of India that was
beyond either of us to withstand?

The Missing Presence

I sense the house that Derek has been renting is a can of worms waiting.
Festooned with lingering memories of my unhappy previous visit and shadowy
images of events that had taken place there both before and since, ghostly webs
of the past lay waiting to be faced. A note of caution is sounding: **It is possible
to view the past from the vantage point of the present but if pulled into its
slipstream then there is a risk of recoil.**

    I know I am not ready. These astral imprints, mixed with imagination,
are powerful and I am undoubtedly feeling vulnerable. Stepping warily we book
into a hotel for a few days but despite every attempt to absorb the sun soaked
beauty and bustle of our new world something essential is missing. Derek hires
a scooter which widens our horizon of the immediate physical terrain. He also
has a proposition up his sleeve.

    'Let's go to Poona!'

    On his travels of the previous year he had met a couple on a train on
their way to Goa with whom he struck up a friendship culminating in an open
invitation for him to visit them in Poona, plus wife if he had one. I am willing,
more than willing, the feeling of adventure brewing; a road to be travelled, the
known meeting unknown. Ramesh, a property developer owns a motor museum
with some rare vehicles of interest to Derek, another incentive. He makes a phone
call. It is arranged. All will be provided, just come! All trains are fully booked
but we cannot wait so buy bus tickets for the 570 mile journey north across the
Western Ghats, vacate the hotel and step over the threshold of the House of
Shadows to sort our luggage and spend a night at ' home'.

    On the outside the house is pretty with a small veranda overlooking a
sandy compound. Inside it feels empty; its three rooms are three shells in a row
waiting for the missing presence of people. The strip of kitchen, a perfect lizard

run, is at the rear with dilapidated fridge, toilet and shower tacked on at the end. The middle shell is the bedroom with two single wooden based beds; a metal cabinet; and a trestle table under the barred window. The square front room houses eleven assorted chairs and dining table. Clothes, bedding, cupboards … everything reeks of mothballs. The dust of ages has settled. It looks and smells as if nothing has been touched since Derek left. It's formidable but I can see something that I had missed on that first visit. It is a small, dilapidated wooden shrine hanging lopsidedly opposite the front door with nothing in it. By no stretch of the imagination can I envisage this place as 'home' yet I feel an immediate compassion for this untended shell.

We go out to dinner. It's idyllic. Kingfish on a balcony as we watch the moon's reflection riding the waves; bursts of fireworks lighting the night and Derek thoughtfully telling me: 'You can change anything you want in the house, you know'.

I think that I just might.

Krishna's Brothers

It's a twelve hour ride, 7pm to 7am. It's surreal. We can see the moon riding with us through a missing hatch in the roof. Frozen and deafened by the obligatory four hour manic movie we arrive at dawn shell shocked. Poona is a vast sprawling conglomeration of shacks, thrown together buildings; huge new structures and temples galore. We give the name of a hotel, South Court, as instructed. It's a colonial mansion in an oasis of tranquil gardens. On the steps waiting are our hosts, Anjana and Ramesh, serene, warmly welcoming. If there exists a polarity to the House of Shadows this is it. We are in a suite with ballroom size bedroom, lounge and balcony, a table ready laid with breakfast foods. The day is to be ours until we are collected at 6.30pm for dinner. They leave, presenting us with a bouquet of red roses and a card picturing two children carrying suitcases. Emblazoned in gold are the significant words, *'Welcome Back'*. It is extra-ordinary, beautiful and moving. Is India welcoming us back through these two 'strangers'? Who **are** these people? Brothers, undoubtedly.

I've noticed the Rajnish Commune is in the same road so set out to explore while Derek sleeps. It looks interesting so buy two tickets for an afternoon tour which begins with a film of Osho, its founder (long since deceased) speaking on Human Transformation. He speaks not of birth and death but of 'visiting this planet' and matching the richness of the inner life with the outer, then we are introduced to the philosophy of the ashramic way of life followed by a silent tour of the grounds. This is predominantly a Meditation Centre with over a hundred therapists working with Reiki, Tai Chi, massage and dance, in what is described as 'preparation for the inner journey that must be taken alone'. A young man asks if we will be joining the commune. Derek tells him that we have just finished an alone bit and are trying to find out what comes after that!

Ramesh's Metro-Museum housing fifty plus vintage cars is the evening treat. A car-keeper runs ahead lifting bonnets and starting engines and Derek is well impressed. After a tour of Ramesh's building projects we meet their friends over a sumptuous dinner at home. Falling naturally afterwards into male and female groups the women succumb to the fascination of exploring each other's lives. Our hosts follow the Krishna Path. Morning begins with a prayer ritual of awakening the baby Krishna, feeding him with milk, returning for evening prayers and to put Krishna to bed. We are told that in this way the Krishna within is always awake and well nourished.

Next morning Anjana is our guide around an ancient Museum with 17,000 exhibits where I am entranced by the energy of the past. Some objects draw me as if they have a magnetic pull and are waiting for a reaction or response giving recognition to their presence. Drawn towards an imposing carved wooden figure I ask Anjana who it is. 'Jaya, Lord Krishna's Assistant' she tells me with a smile, knowing the name of Jaya holds significance for me. The notion comes to me of seeing life as a museum filled with memorabilia, many of which have stood the test of time and greatly increased in value, whilst others which have lost their potency and purpose have no energy. This is a concept to be mused over later as I may well be holding onto various skeletons hence have been dropped neatly into The Shadows to take stock. Later, at an Art Exhibition we meet Krishna again in exquisite poses. In a laughing exchange with a yoga teacher she tells me that on a bad day she will say 'Krishna is being a rascal today'. What a fun way to approach life!

One more day to go and tickets are presented for an extensive tour with seventeen stopping points at temples, museums and all manner of cultural delights. Overwhelmed by the pace of Poona and fortified at every level we climb at last onto a sleeping slot in the roof of our next rickety bus for another moonlight ride ... home.

A Living Museum

We're back and now there **is** a Presence in The Shadows. It's us; enlivened, uplifted and with a sparkle. Whether it comes from Krishna, Poona or the sheer joy of life is of little consequence. What we now have to do is to reflect it in our environment. I've found a book by Parker J. Palmer a man who, having given up his career to live in a Quaker community felt that he had stepped off the edge of his known world and was in danger of disappearing. I have no intention of disappearing into the shadows so take good notice of what he says next. He determines: 'I am here to become myself and to write'. Thank you Mr. Palmer. Perhaps I can do the same whilst cleaning up The Shadows, physical and otherwise.

The shrine is polished and candle lit, encircled by a large silvered ceremonial pendant, a leaving present from Anjana. I shall keep my journal in it too as a reminder to pen enlightened thoughts. Straw mats, rainbow striped, cover the now shining red tiled floor; sequined cushions are the smiling faces of the chair brigade; floating lilac dupatas drape the bars and harlequin duvet covers are the touch from home that make for inviting bedtime thoughts. The wall-hanging is the crowning glory, over-lighting the room. It's a batik of The Great Chariot arriving on the battlefield. Anjuna stands, arrows poised, behind Krishna who holds the reins of four lively horses representing control of the senses and the three bodies; physical, emotional and mental; a goodly reminder! We are now a far better match for the sparkling sea shores of Goa dressed exquisitely with palm trees, fishing boats, intricately made bamboo beach shacks and a plethora of sights to delight the eye.

People are not at the forefront of my life at the moment. Derek has a group of friends with apartments at the hotel where he first stayed so I leave him to socialise and carry on with my next task of setting up a writing corner on the veranda ready to muse a bit with the pen, clear out my Museum of the Past and discover any lurking skeletons. Old half remembered lines of poetry are touching on my mind. I jot them down: *The moving finger writes and having writ moves on ... not all thy piety and wit can alter but a word, nor all thy tears wash out a word of it* ... and then the pen continues:

Can that be so? What if that finger was your own that writ the scripting of the life; and having writ the script enacted it; then having played the parts of your devising do you discover you had played that scene in darkness and the audience, long gone, left not one clapping hand nor unwiped tear. There were no witnesses to genius neither to mistakes, to a prancing ego or a soulful stare. None saw, nor cared; none laughed aloud or wept with you at your behest. What then? Could you look again, illumining the darkness and see that what you thought was emptiness was merely that you had not fanned the fire. Perception is the taper that can set the life aflame. Revision the past from the light of experience! Illumine the stage and you may see the trap doors into which you fell; you may hear the prompters; see the scene shifters ... and see a different play.

It is as if The Book of Life has opened. This is not something I am doing, it is simply occurring. Many and various aspects of my life appear as characters in a play each having their own stories, insights and energy. In a trice I find that perceptions of events clouded by time, by ego, grievances, ill conceived beliefs, notions of failure and so much more, are changing. It's a revue, though who is doing the reviewing is hard to say. Nothing is exactly as it once seemed. Each character, from No-body in a bed to the striding Officer the Law, plus the many before and since, is a creative expression of energy enabling a range of opportunities for experience and for learning. I can see there must be an effortless flow between them if they are to fit together to make a cohesive whole.

Derek has returned. 'Fancy a game of scrabble on the beach?'
Scrabble at sunset is very fitting whoever I think I am … or might have been.

Spirit of Tagore

Rabindranath Tagore, a man of many parts, was described by Ghandi as 'The Great Sentinel'. I've picked up a book of his Poems and Plays and copy out a stanza at the top of each day's journaling so it can sit as a sentinel in my mind keeping extraneous nonsense at bay. Through touching daily on words conveyed by this Wisdom Mind I begin to sense the man behind the words and the Source of his inspiration. **To touch the Mind of a Master is to touch his Spirit**, says the pen. Tagore's words urge me to stop thinking. He writes: *'A mind all logic is like a knife all blade. It makes the hand bleed that uses it.'* It is time for my musing to take a back seat and accept Tagore's invitation to the beach. His words beckon: *'Come to the edge of the shore and stand with your eyes tight shut and you will be carried out upon the waves… And no-one in the world will know where we both are.'* I go to the beach, alone, and am there, still in the physical world and at the same time beyond it.

Boys at Large!

What have we done? Some while ago we had written to invite Steven Nayak for a week's holiday to help his recovery after a motor bike accident. Steven now wants to bring his brother Stanley; however we seem to have created a cocoon of two and my mind has wanderlust! Now we are in dire need of a plan that will give them the unforgettable experience we feel ill equipped to orchestrate. Then we discover a plan is already under construction in the form of Marc who will be arriving on holiday the day after the boys. We book two scooters, a room in our compound and create our Christmas for two with a Chinese dinner on a far-flung beach.

It is seven years since I was in Hyderabad. The 'boys' are now young men; tall, confident, energetic and overjoyed at having their first beach holiday.

Stanley has the more serious, responsible nature whilst Steven is still effervescent and boldly adventurous. Seeing Goa through their eyes is enlightening and enlivening! Marc then enters the equation master-minding a whirl of activities. There are swimming lessons, hazardous lilo rides down the river, pool matches, wild scooter adventures and musical evenings in the beach shacks as Steven plays and sings to a borrowed guitar; a music-master in the making. Combining with a family with teenagers from Marc's hotel adds another dimension to events and we flow in and out as we choose.

New Year's Eve is a highlight for us all. It seems so long ago that I first saw Goa light up the screen whilst playing Cinderella at home. Now I am IN it on the shore of Baga Estuary. The whole expanse of Calangute beach stretches for miles, shacks silhouetted by the blaze of bonfires and barbeques topped by effigies of *The Old Man* representing the fast receding past; sands stock-piled with fireworks ready for the biggest annual firework spectacle in India. Thousands have gathered, travelling from all over India and beyond. I'm watching the river. We are sitting high on the bank at the point where the incoming sea meets the swirling out-flowing tide as if the ocean has come to collect its new waters to become part of a greater whole. Fireworks cascade, each spark having its place in this panoply of light. The three boys head down to mingle with the crowds. Derek drives the scooter homewards finding all main roads closed leaving us to brave a maze of unmarked, unlit, pot holed paths. We arrive out of the darkness laughing and shaking with relief.

Uma's Music

The German Bakery is a gathering place for late Sunday morning breakfasts. There we are introduced to Uma, sister of Nisha, Derek's author friend. She has lived in the far north of India in an isolated ashram for some years and has an air of quiet wisdom about her. She invites me to visit the old family mansion where she is staying. What a joy it is to explore each other's way in the world. She offers me old treasured manuscripts to read and return but the music tape is a gift. It is the Bhagavad Gita set to music; a rendering in exquisite sound of our wall hanging as Krishna and Arjuna dialogue in verse. We are absorbed into it, listening firstly without understanding the Sanskrit and then follow an English translation. Firstly it was the words of Tagore that led beyond the shore; now it is the music ... and it takes us both.

Another wall-hanging is in my hand looking for its place. It is of Ganesh, the elephant god, holding a pen, symbol of his appointed task as a Scribe of the Eternal Truths recorded by sages in whose hearts and minds they were said to be 'heard'. Ganesh with his great elephant ears is an ideal image to represent 'hearing' the Wisdoms. Another of his attributes is as the remover of blockages. Frequently positioned at the entrance to Temples his Presence is invoked at the beginning of significant events to clear any impeding energies. It is significant to me that Sandra and Clive are attempting to reach us for a much needed holiday, their first ever in Goa, but Sandra has been going through a debilitating menopause and it is touch and go whether they will make it. As we hang Ganesh under the shrine adding Sandra's photo over the top of it, jumping firecrackers are being set off below. I'm wondering out loud if it's some kind of holy day celebration when Derek tells me, 'It's Ganesha's Birthday today; I thought you knew'.

There's a notion that's been teasing me overlong, of India and her impact upon my life. As it's a birthday kind of day I make a beginning with a first flurry of ideas under the title of 'Under an Orange Sun'.

The Lotus Master

Sandra and Clive have been here twelve hours. From her arrival, debilitated and exhausted she has already made an astonishing recovery. What is more she is ecstatic and sets about blissfully absorbing the whole ambience of Goa. They are staying in a nearby hotel. Slipping into the rhythm of sun soaked lotus living, we intermingle in the frothy breakers, over pineapple pancakes, or lazy strolls to the massage parlour. I continue to write of the Orange Sun while they are well content to lie under it.

After the Nayak boys left Marc had arranged a boat trip. He had learnt of an old man who gave massages using local mud so while Derek went bird-watching we had trekked inland and found him sitting cross legged by a clear pool surrounded by yellow rocks. There we submitted to deeply penetrating massages then, spread eagled in the sun, caked over every available surface with a yellow substance, we had dried into golden stone people! The last act was a dip in the pool. Sandra is determined to have this experience. We hire a boat; the men take off elsewhere and we trek inland. The Old Man is not there so we wait. At last he appears out of the trees. There is time left for only one massage before the boat leaves. It must be Sandra, leaving me to witness him working his magic. In Rakeshponka, only our legs were coloured saffron gold. I watch as Sandra's whole body takes on the golden glow, aware that energy from the yellow substance is being absorbed through the pores. Our yogi then demonstrates yoga postures, floating in the pool smiling as he tells us 'I am a Lotus'. Then Sandra is invited into the pool to be washed by our Lotus Master. I see it all as an ancient ritual.

Ring of Hampi

We are going to Hampi. An inauspicious start with a puncture on the way to the train begins an interminable ten hour journey, uncomfortable in more ways than one. Bitten on toes, feet and ankles, appalling scenes of poverty also make their mark gripping my thoughts that have found no rising agent yet today. This is inland India with less amenities and frenzied struggles for custom as Derek valiantly negotiates to find a habitable room in nearby Hospet. Hampi, an ancient city, once capital of the region, is a scooter-rickshaw journey away. We book in and wait for a new day to make our entry. Next morning we are about to leave when a man jumps in our auto. I ask who he is and he replies 'Your guide'. We have not engaged one. Derek does not need dates and details and I choose to be alert to whatever touches my eye and senses in the moment. We ride on unaccompanied by physical guides. Soon we are standing in the past; great crumbling temple walls looming above us; walls still alive with cavorting images of gods and goddesses in all manner of poses. Every posture tells a story passed from Age to Age reminding the people of the day of the qualities and attributes of Brahman, the God Head and of the codes of conduct which they would be well advised to employ in their daily lives. Interpreting the symbology of it all is way beyond me. We take a scooter to tour the many acres of rocky outcrops and smaller temples.

We're about to return to the hotel when on a sudden whim to have a memento of a memorable day, a ring catches my eye. Derek says he will buy it as a gift. It's not of any monetary value, only a couple of pounds, but Derek becomes embroiled in haggling over a few rupees. Suddenly I find myself tottering on the edge of a dangerous ravine of thoughts. How can he be feeling, conveying the joy and graciousness of giving, reflecting the light of the day, when his mind is wrapped in rupees? I leave the shop in disarray, angry and giftless knowing that anger for me can be a mask for tears, betrayers of some hidden hurt. A nudge to the mind tells me: **The Ring of Hampi is its silent sound, not a bauble.** Knowing we've already absorbed it I no longer need a gift but it has disturbed me as it always does when we run into a pocket of dissent. The pen has the last word:

Living in equanimity takes precedence over the vagaries of life. The sculptor sculpts. Only the end product has relevance. Does he care whether the milk in his cup is curdled; where the day begins or ends, as long as the tools are ready and leap to the hand as he creates that which Beingness dictates?

We have sculpted a winter in India without many curdled days and lived as Beingness has dictated. Is there to be a return? Derek's 'Yes' is emphatic. I tell him that though I too want to return, next year will have a very different flavour. He accepts the risk and we are committed, with or without a ring.

44.A Yogi's Cloak
2003/2004

Corsica: 7th June 2003

We were robbed two days ago on Marseille docks. Derek sat at the wheel of the caravette route mapping, while I was out and about chasing up boat tickets to Corsica. A red crash helmet and a black-leathered hand and arm were all he registered as the door burst open. The hand swept the well and the seat claiming my work bag as its Prize Draw of the day. Passports, tickets, cheque books, even my pen! How little they matter to the loss of my notes and scripted pages, fruit of my winter's work. Orange Sun is most likely consigned to the bin by now as unintelligible, valueless! There is no copy. Derek took the brunt of the shock wave and is reeling from it. I've dredged up some French to make a police report; held down the emotions and we are feeling weird, travelling without any provable identity. Is that the point of this? Have I unwittingly been writing to prove (or even improve) my identity? Are other people now preparing to masquerade as 'us'? It's all surreal. Or is it just another opportunity to practice the art of letting go? Plenty of questions; all unanswered. The pen digresses with a question of its own:

What does the word 'yogi' mean to you?

My answer is briefly insufficient and so a lesson begins:

A word is, in itself, little more than sound and structure until activated by the power of living thought. So often meaning is culled from notions of other minds devoid of the depths of experience. Examine the word; experience the word and sense its nature, only then will it enter your vocabulary as a Living Word.

This, to a degree, I understand and so the examination of a Yogi's way within the world begins as the pen fills page after page.

Yogis are energy fields that vibrate on the organic, natural frequencies. Their home is neither in East nor West; to them the Earth has no states other than States of Being. They inhabit form, yet cannot possess it. Yogis will speak of the body; the mind, not my body, for beyond possession is dispossession and beyond that formlessness.

A yogi has recourse to a greater compassion; greater awareness; greater resilience; greater strength of character, fortitude, love for human life for are these not the qualities he has practiced and built into the scheme of his unified life? And if those same challenges beset him over and over, day beyond day, year beyond year, does he not have the will to pursue a purposeful path losing neither his equanimity nor integrity but holding to the course of the river of life?

A yogi quests for nothing for All That Is is perpetually omnipresent. That which he perceives with the outer eye is immediately recognisable as reflection of his inner landscape. The yogi is perpetually open for the shields have fallen and he has passed the mechanistic state of closure. In contemplative stillness he resonates, receives, transposes and transmits. In the motion of the day or the slumbers of a seamless night yogi continuously emit a life force.

To entertain the mind of yogi it is necessary to give credence to the possibility of dimensions of existence beyond bodily life for a yogi enjoys multi-dimensional experiences as he traverses the inter-dimensional boundary-less states.

Does a yogi know all things? No, indeed; to be conscious of the state of All Being, is not to be conscious of All Knowing. He rests within the knowledge that all is known that needs to be known within each given moment.

To the yogi, Mind is his cloak. It envelops the totality of his Being. It is his abode, his raiment of life and his purpose for existence. The Mind Cloak is permeable. It is a resonant web; tissue of etheric light anchored upon the Earth plane yet free to raise antennae far beyond.

The Yogi holds the blue print of the Kadmon; before the Great Corruption... and so the teaching continued filling both pages and mind; and offering much for depth of contemplation. But why, I wondered had this teaching appeared following my disappearing manuscript? A fair exchange! There were many more passages; one noting that a Yogi does not lead a personalised life therefore has no need to 'rest upon identity or upon the exigencies of others'. Teaching comes in many ways and we have just had that message demonstrated loud and clear! In my experience to date whatever is received is usefully followed by opportunities for application. Maybe the winter will prove to be a testing ground.

Out Runner

It's November again. Letting go of Adam House is easy this time. What is waiting, The Shadows or something else?

Lank streamers straddle the chairs; empty beer crates tell a story reflecting the aftermath of a celebration that is over. Ours does not begin. The house has not retained its sparkle in our absence, Derek is unwell and on our second day back takes to bed coughing. Shivering yet feverish he slips into a cocoon of one whilst I slip in and out on the run dodging pigs, people and my unhallowed thoughts as I hunt down antibiotics or his favourite bacon sandwiches. He struggles with lethargy and a mixture of unpleasant symptoms whilst I become increasingly disenchanted and restless. My advice of the day is simply *let go; change is coming.*

I choose to help change along. We agree it's a good idea for me to make a visit to Hyderabad and the Nayak family to return with fresh energy. We either have to revitalise this house or move on. Derek is not in a moving mood so I leave him with the Powers-that-Be, to influence him as they choose, pack a bag and catch the inevitable long distance overnight bus. It's already the first of December. I arrive five hundred miles later on the misty morning of the second.

They've no idea I am coming and I've no idea of the direction of Safilguda, their latest address. My brainwave is to book into a hotel; find St. Francis's College for Girls and take it from there. It works. It seems in no time I am standing before the Principal asking for Angela and she is brought to stand wide-eyed in front of me. Slim, tall and elegant in soft blue sari she has the same calm gracefulness of her mother. We then surprise the 'baby' beauty Genevieve in the school next door; skip school and pile laughing into an auto rickshaw for a long trundling journey to the outskirts of the city. George answers to our ring, his face a picture of incredulity. I'm already having such a good time and it's getting better by the moment as Jenny appears and I discover that I still have a place in the heart of this family. Words race through the years covering the gaps and one by one the others arrive, Stanley, Steven and Sandra.

The week ahead assuages every need in me as I feel India surrounding me; listening to each one's hopes, fears, plans and successes. Sandra wants to pursue her studies in England but that is a step too far for us to finance so she, it seems is likely to become the first wage-earner. There are family conferences; meals; outings; as well as private talks with George and Jenny ironing out issues from the past though on some things we also have to acknowledge widely divergent viewpoints. One such is my feelings of support for Steven's musical talent. George is adamant that only academic success will put food on the table which I understand, never-the-less, I am impulsed to buy Steven a guitar, an act heart warming to us both. George is still hard pressed financially to maintain five teenagers and hold to his determination to realise his dream for their future through education but he has not been able to find work and our monthly remittances are his only financial life-line. We acknowledge that though the pressures are different from where we each stand we have both faced challenges, 'day beyond day, year beyond year', and have found the will to pursue the purposeful path for which we know we have been brought together. Glad that I came, whatever the reason, it is time to let go and return to await developments.

Bodies and Souls

Its the 19th December when I hear the words that are my best possible Christmas gift: 'I think I'm ready to let go of this place'. The compound looks like a building site with new extensions going up fast and Derek has learnt a new floor is to be added on top of us. I am out on the hunt immediately and come across a small house on the beach under renovation. We think that this will do until we discover another option, a brand new apartment with view of that orange sun setting over the sea and a regal flight of steps leading to the entrance through imposing French windows. We name it The Steps, symbolic of moving forwards and upwards. The downside is that it will not be ready for a month. We wait, in the meantime accepting invitations to a confirmation service for local children; a carol concert and visits to two charitable projects run by nuns; an orphanage and home for elderly women.

At St. Alex's orphanage one of Derek's friends plays Father Christmas handing each child a school satchel of presents, all donated by tourists. I find it heart wrenching as the girls hug, kiss and stroke us, hungry for our touch. Dressed in their best, an assortment of bits and pieces and in some cases outfits made out of newspaper, they sing and dance holding out their hands for us to partner them.

Next door is a Home for Elderly Women. It costs each one three thousand rupees (£35) a month for a dormitory bed and food. Each has a small cupboard with little in it. We've brought soap and toiletries which are treasure trove though old well thumbed photos are their prized possessions. Many speak good English and tell me their fees are paid by relatives living abroad. Mostly they have no income and no-one left to care for them in India. All are hungry to talk, to share stories of their lives and ask questions. I am finding it difficult to let go of all these faces young and old who are so greatly in need of care of body and soul, for whom change in their circumstances is only a dream. We eat our Christmas dinner in a beach shack, thoughtful and appreciative.

Paradise Regained

Liz Child has arrived for a Goa Experience. We spend the days out and about together, joining with Derek for mealtimes, beaching and at our favourite swimming pool at a nearby hotel complex named Paradise Village. The evenings we spend in her bedroom contemplating all manner of things and planning an event to mark the opening of a large new room in her home. On a temple tour we find ourselves drawn towards images of Lord Shiva that abound in all manner of creative forms and agree that this is the energy we will draw on to create a celebratory workshop where I will be able to use some of my yogi wisdoms. Rich in mythology within the sacred texts, Lord Shiva is the third person of the Hindu Trinity. Shiva is the Maha-Yogi (the great ascetic) patron of all yogis. Though known by multiple names he epitomises the Destroyer, destroying only to regenerate on a higher plane. When he dances the *Tandavas* he is known as Lord of the Dance. In the vast markets of Anjuna Liz purchases a wall-hanging of Lord Shiva as the mendicant sitting in lotus posture whilst I choose him dancing tip-toed in the ring of fire. I hang mine to represent letting go of the shadows in every respect and we hunt out books to study later.

The Steps is nearly ready and we are able to visit and lie on the beds facing the French windows and bask in the solar rays. Goa has offered the best of herself to us both and we are ready for our last day which Liz wants to spend at Paradise Village.

On Friday 23rd January I am with Liz at the poolside. Derek has gone to pick up his e-mails and we hear him calling to us over the gate waving a message from Carmella with news we had not heard heralding the death of Derek's mother.

> ' I know by now you must have heard about the passing of your mother on my birthday (20th). It is the passing of an era in our family– an important moment. I heard the news from Sandra just as I was sitting down at my birthday party. I told my friends who began to sing and play music on all their amazing instruments. We had a happy birthday to me and a happy re-birthday to her. It was very magical with her picture in the middle.'

She writes on to say how the family will all convene at home and asks if Derek will be returning. He goes immediately to book a flight. I am to stay and organise the move; two more circumstances in which we must let go, each different yet both physical and metaphysical. Once again it is in India that I learn of a family death three days after it has taken place; days during which I have been thoughtfully contemplating the cycles of life. Liz leaves the next day, followed by Derek on Sunday and on Monday I will leave The Shadows; each letting go, each on their separate cyclic journeys, all inter-woven.

By Sunday night I'm alone. Tonight the shadows are real, boxes and bags silhouetted as eerie shapes on the walls; trappings of life stacked up and waiting to re-appear somewhere else. I would rather have returned with Derek but know I have to do this bit alone. The Shadows has been our Tardis, transformed as we choose into our Saturday night football stadium; a minuscule Temple, Concert Hall, and Art Gallery; a restaurant for Derek's gourmet cooking; a Museum and much more; yet it has still at times felt like a prison. I am grateful to have been brought here for all that has transpired but immensely grateful to be leaving.

Virgil's Vigil

Monday: feeling like an itinerant I climb into the cab of a rattling truck, furniture precariously balanced and make an entry up the steps. The house is washed in soft pink inside and out; shining with newness. Unpacking can be gentle and this place needs no ornamentation. Derek will be away for at least a week and this is my time.

I fancy a quiet vigil and have a book waiting; a novel 'I. Virgil' by David Wishart. On the cover Virgil holding a scroll, is seated before a fully fanned peacock's tail. Maybe it is the image that drew me to pick it out of the jumbled pile in a beach shack. Virgil is known as a visionary, a poet and social commentator of his times. The author writes in the first person. He **is** Virgil. Vigil has become for him a Living Word as he touches on his Spirit; the Core Substance. I neither know nor care if I have been alone for a moment, a day or a week. Virgil's world is my reality; a passport to that boundary-less state of the yogi. This is a vigil though I am not vigilant. There is no effort; no need for prayer or praising; no sensation of letting go; no intruding thoughts; no distractions of physical needs or responsibilities; no intention or desires, simply a state of All Being; an awareness of existence without physical form.

I know that I did not go out anywhere during the week other than the few paces to Ocean Blue, a beach shack where Nicholas, my landlady's cousin unobtrusively prepared whatever simple food I requested. Neither did I write a journal. I had even let go of the pen together with everyday notions of reality. I know that I slept and that when I awoke the state was still there, enfolding me like a cloak.

Inside everything is in order at every level by the time Derek returns. I hear the details of **his** significant journey and he reflects that he can see what I've been doing, an acknowledgement of the visible work which had all but done itself! How to offer a glimpse beyond the boundary is a perennial puzzle.

'It's been a vigil. Virgil took me off somewhere'.

'It was a good book then?'

'Brilliant!'

Though I cannot explain I hope that he will feel the effects. Perhaps he does as at long last we begin to feel a cocoon of two reforming and life up the steps begins.

Family Steps

The Steps is open plan, one large multi-purpose room, twin beds doubling as couches in the day. It does not take long to identify a few challenges needing a good dose of fortitude. We are at the end of a track which is a thoroughfare to the beach for motorbikes; tourists; fishermen and beach vendors. The vendors come from Karnataka, a poorer state to the south, leaving tiny children with minders. An old lady minder lives opposite us in a sort of tent. She also has a stall so leaves tiny tots to run wild which includes up and down our steps, even into the house at times. Derek calls it 'the circus' and neither of us want to perform.

Electricity supply is so temperamental we are often in the dark especially at overload times such as Saturdays when our weekly football treat is as often as not swiped off the screen, ensuring yet another game of candlelight scrabble. Do we keep the windows closed to keep out noise, mosquitoes and uninvited callers and live in a concrete oven or leave them open and live in a goldfish bowl? What's more we've had our washing stolen off the line. None of any of this had been evident during my vigil when I had not even noticed the temperature.

On the other hand the vista is amazing. The well, also a few yards in front of our windows is the community water supply for the tap-less. We are fascinated by processes that take place there especially in the early morning. Still protective of the remnants of our privacy I make heavier curtains and we stop fidgeting because we have more to think about. Family are coming.

Carmella and ten year old Asher, are due to arrive on 15th February to be followed a few days later by Sandra and Clive plus their family of three, Sommer, Joshua and Amy, bringing together three generations. Carmella and Asher draw us out into the beach world of spades and surfboards and Derek zooms out on the scooter with Asher while I have some time with Carmella, a rare treat these days; then the Casey Family arrive exuberantly, at the ready to engage with Goa and not miss a trick day or night! Sandra and Clive are the nucleus of the group and Asher is in his element with his older cousins as they generate their own power centre. Our cocoon of two holds and we flow in and out as we choose.

There is news of significance. Sandra and Clive feel they have temporarily to let go of their home *Hafan*, a stone cottage near Harlech in North Wales and want to move back to live with us in Clent. Their cottage will be used as a summer retreat for friends and family. Marc is still at home which means we will become a unit of five. It is the same with Adam House as with India, as if a silent call goes out, is picked up by family and answered. This move is welcome to us both for a whole range of reasons, but this is not so much about reason as about knowing this is the next piece of an ever expanding jigsaw of interwoven family lives. We begin to look forward to a different kind of summer. It's been a different kind of winter.

Our landlady offers to store our furniture which seals a deal for the following year when something more than furniture will be in store for us no doubt.

45.Buddha's Gifts
2004/2005

Thailand: July 2004

Its summer and I am on holiday in Thailand with Liz. We have travelled a wisdom
trail of golden temples, met monks galore and are being taken by friends of
Marc's on a tour of a remote area in the north. The darkening sky is heavy with
rain as we pull up at yet another temple tucked well between trees and bushes.
This is not one we would even have noticed; it is not like the others we have seen,
ablaze with images of Buddha covered in gold leaf. These Temple doors are huge
and heavy. I push one open. It's dark yet I can see on the inside this door is made
up of small panels, each intricately carved. One panel is riveting. A man and a
woman, walking hand in hand, are highlighted in gold. The light is bad but I try
taking a photo. There is nothing else much here of note and we move on.

A week or so later we have our films developed. Nothing is significant
except for this one picture. It is a holding symbol for words as yet unwritten
speaking to me of alchemy, of human transformation. And strangely they look
Indian, not Thai.

The Temples of Thailand have made their mark both visually and
energetically. Back home, buzzing with enthusiasm I enlist Sandra to join me in
painting over the pastel shades of our Upper Room in rich temple colours.

Sanctuary of the Word

India has a surprise in store for our third winter. The track to the beach has been
firmly fenced off just before reaching The Steps preventing motorbikes and such
like roaring, tooting and parking. Our steps are now the centre-piece of a garden
of healthy foliage but the crowning glory is that the pale pink façade has been
painted in Tibetan Temple colours of rich green, terracotta and mustard gold. The
synchronicity of it could not possibly escape us. Buddha is ahead of us, colouring
the way! Well, that is how it feels to me, as if our sanctuary has been visibly
transferred!

We've been in place for two days and I am aware that Derek is
struggling. His voice is flat, a monotone. Everything is an effort. I ask 'what's
the matter'? He cannot articulate, just says he's not awake, that it must be the

humidity, a pain in his elbow, not enough water in-take, looking always for a physical answer. Is there any other? The atmosphere in the apartment that has been empty throughout the rainy summer season feels similar to that in the Sanctuary at home, also to that which I have experienced in the Thai Temples which I call 'intense tranquillity'. Certain high energy fields produce a hypnotic effect with symptoms equivalent to inertia as the brain rhythms edge into theta wavelengths. High frequency energies that appear completely motionless hold a powerfully active core. I explain to Derek that I sense he will need to acclimatise to the shift in atmospheric conditions indoors, as well as to the humidity. He does, gradually. I am well content to remain immersed in it and wait.

Master Minds

There is a beach shack where we sometimes eat named *The Ritz*. Lawrence, its owner, notices the books I read and tells me that he will look out booklets he brought back from an Ashram where he goes for silent meditation. We talk of energy and he reveals how he watches the tourists; returning to the same sun-bed; seat at the table and so on attracted by their own magnetic imprints. A few days later on an early morning walk Lawrence appears from across a field, hands me a booklet and disappears. There are three introductory papers entitled 'Vipassana Journal for the Benefit of the Many' by S-N Goenka. They contain a goldmine of wisdom emanating from Buddha's teachings opening with a discourse on how sensation can lead to aversions and cravings. I read: *'Between object and reaction lies sensation. To deal with reactions one must become aware of where they start: i.e. with sensation'*. There is rather a lot of opportunity for reacting in India but also some bigger issues in my life surfacing to have an airing. The Big Question is whether this perennial urge to pick up the pen is a craving or something else; something that I cannot not do because it is part of my life template. Is there purpose within my scribbling, scribing and journaling? Am I constantly registering the world as I see it for some Greater Eye? Anyway I find the action of writing to be sensational in that it quickens the senses; and stirs the mind.

Another thought comes to mind. It was essential during the Punjab assignment in 1977 that I recorded detail meticulously and comprehensively as a foundation for the next wave of work. By doing so I had learnt discipline, focus, awareness to detail and a great deal more. All this training and observation at a physical level now appears to be transferring to the metaphysical; to Worlds of the Mind for which the physical world around me is merely a catalyst. And what IS around me is India. She has provided opportunities to engage with people within the working world and to a degree to engage in some form of service; and has provided Brothers of the Way, so evident then in human form on past journeying to hold me to the task. Now I sense 'Brothers' in a different sense appearing wrapped in the ragged jackets of well thumbed books and ancient imagery pointing the way to Wisdom Worlds. The pen is my reflector ... and theirs.

Master Minds are having a field day; wisdoms arriving thick and fast. My next prize from a cupboard bookstore is a little book of Sutras by Osho of the Poona Ashram, accompanied by a card deck, each carrying a wisdom stanza. I learn that Sutra means 'a thread' and that Masters speak and write in small maxims, without elaboration, explanation, or decoration in order to sow seeds that contain the promise of realisation. **Now live the sutras, ...** is my next advice!

Yet another wisdom thread has worked its way through the beach shack jumbles of treasure pages in a book called 'External Echoes' by John O'Donahue. A line imprints immediately heading the day's journal page. *'Your 'self' is the total gift which every moment of your life endeavours to graciously receive with honour'*. Surely it is, at least in part, an answer to a question as to why I am in Goa where I am being given gift after gift yet feel unable to serve in any discernable out-giving way. I am here to learn; not only to learn how to receive the wisdoms graciously but to do so 'with honour'. I think that means not to flip over the page or the mind but that to receive with honour is to listen with the ears of Ganesh the Scribe; to contemplate as Shiva the yogi; and dance to the rhythms of Life. And when the gift is of Life itself, then honour must be given to The Source; the Godhead; Krishna; the Creator; whatever or whoever represents The Great Giver. A Mystery School for one operates daily and I'm trying to keep up!

Garlanding the Brain

Another gift is just around the corner. On our beach wanderings we meet a Dutch couple who had been our previous neighbours. They have moved to the first floor of a big house that is quiet and shady. There is a spacious apartment which they think would suit us perfectly. We visit and do not even have to discuss it, just a glance does it. A hall with curved archways opens onto a large kitchen; a bedroom and lounge, both with balconies, shining bathroom, everything! Paulo a fisherman lives on the ground floor with his delightful wife Carmen and their three children, a Christian family as are many in this area of Goa. The apartment is already taken for the rest of the season. We book immediately for next year, well aware that we are only just into December and things can change fast in India. The immediate focus is that Liz is about to arrive for her winter holiday and we have already planned a journey together.

Liz has been a major contributor to MetaCentre International and had asked to meet the Nayak family. This time I had made arrangements in advance so after a few play days we are off; by the inevitable bus. George is there to meet us, books us into a hotel and then whisks us off to Safilguda. It is a huge treat for me to introduce all the family in person. Our opening entertainment, a video of Steven playing his guitar and singing at a party sets the scene for a celebratory reunion. The plan next day is to visit Stanley at the Loyola Academy where he is in the second semester of his second year. He is hoping to move into the Halls of Residence if funds can be found to cover fees, saving him the long daily journey. Liz wants to see the sights of Hyderabad and there is a secret mission that we have in mind to accomplish. After the success of our Shiva Day we had decided to recycle the energy back into India by buying the family a computer as the facilities of the internet would undoubtedly be an invaluable study resource.

The Loyola visit proves to be a great success. We meet the Principal who has high regard for Stanley's diligent studies and future prospects and tour the residential quarters. Our Hyderabad sightseeing tour comes next in which we include the Nazim's Palace and museum which I had never seen, imagining our friend Ray who had long ago set this adventure in motion by standing guard. In his day the Nazim was reputed to be the richest man in the world and had put Hyderabad firmly on the map. Our journey takes us to the Charminar Gate which today is a lively Bazaar, the energy so different to my last murderous visit. Restaurants and temples, nothing escapes us; the maelstrom of Hyderabad is vibrant with life lived at an ultra fast pace and we plunge in.

We have asked Steven to accompany us on a shopping round. He is delighted, even more so when he learns that he is to buy a computer. Had we been aware of his intrepid bargaining skills we may never even have started! Underground tunnels house endless rows of cupboard shops, computers in store of every conceivable make jammed in boxes amongst a motley of technical equipment. Nothing is exactly looking like a showroom! Steven wants to buy everything separately and build something extra special. And it has to be black. We agree to let him go ahead. He haggles for every rupee as we spend the morning standing listening in doorways with the amazing result that he has everything he wants within our budget. He drives home ecstatic with the promise that all will be up and running for us to view next day.

Never before have we engaged in a ritual for the installation of a computer but it happens. George has garlands for us all plus one for the computer which is being referred to as 'The Big Brain'. He places us all in position for many angled photos as we make our physical connections, then we are requested to give the blessing. Liz aptly says *'May you always work!'*

A concert of pop songs on computer follows and Steven demonstrates that he now has access to on line guitar lessons. Unbeknown to us we had bought him a music tutor! We were all going out to celebrate with a night at the cinema for a touch of Bollywood, something they could never afford, but as there were no

seats left ended up at a restaurant, also a treat but nothing could top the installation of the Big Brain.

The perfect ending on our last morning is taking a boat out on the lake where the biggest Buddha in India presides on a central island. He weighs 350 tons! We learn that men had drowned trying to get him into position, an unimaginable scene and a supreme undertaking. Buddha is assuredly to be kept in our minds eye this winter.

Another surreal bus journey leads us to be sitting in a Muslim cemetery at 4am after innumerable breakdowns. The bus now has three wheels; having no spare the driver has taken off into the moonlight to find a way of mending a puncture! No doubt he will succeed … eventually. After twenty three hours on the road we arrive back, good for nothing other than joining Derek on the beach. He is smiling; he knows about bus journeys. What is more he offers to pay Stanley's fees in the Halls of Residence. Yet one more gift, to be accepted graciously with honour to the giver!

The Christmas Tide

Liz has returned home. It's Christmas Eve and it seems that all roads lead to Goa. We're in hiding, feeling a stillness in the air and not wanting to shatter it by mingling in the bustling crowds. Deciding on a Chinese take-away, we time it to eat at sunset in the window and light candles when the light fades. Derek rides off returning with an array of dishes and we have a succulent Chinese tasting. All is very calm, silent, and safely gathered in.

We had a plan of riding further afield on Christmas day but the sense of staying in this still, peace-filled state persists so we stroll to the beach to breakfast at Lawrence's beach shack The Ritz, under a huge silver star on a pole. It's idyllic. There are two sun-beds left so for once I laze amongst a group of English holiday makers who are creating a real tinsel-town Christmas and absorb the spirit of the day. It's late afternoon when we wander home to eat the remnants of our Chinese dinner. Derek rents his scooter from an Indian family who to our surprise arrive with a cake and bowl of beef curry. As we chat on the balcony they remark on how still the sea is. Always there are frothy crested breakers lunging up the beach. We cannot hear them.

In the morning of 26th December we learn of the Tsunami. It seemed to have centred on Thailand and our first thought is of family and relief that Marc had decided not to go out there this year. The swell had reached The Ritz in the early hours of the morning. The community have been working through the night to safeguard the beach-shacks and fishing boats and no-one has drowned. Further south there was devastation and some destruction in the north. We are in a pocket between them. We do not know whether the sea will rise again and are on flat land 400 metres from the beach yet we feel it is over. It is, for us. I do not know how to view it as a gift.

Can you sense a tsunami on the way? We had sensed an unusual stillness in the air twenty-four hours before it reached the beach. How many stories will there be to come from those who acted on some presentiment of where they needed to be ... and those who had not? We are sobered by it all as the death toll rises. It is not until 29th that I feel moved to go to the beach. Alone, at the sea edge pre-dawn, I can see in the soft moonlight that the sand has been re-sculpted; fast running rivulets cutting new channels. Standing between the rising sun and disappearing moon in this changed landscape is my moment of acknowledgement of the ascension of so many souls; of the tidal waves of sorrow stirring again the depths of compassion. We have known of drowning, the way through the waters is especially pertinent for us.

New Year celebrations this year are not so extravagant. There is poignancy about the fireworks, a thoughtfulness, and gratitude no doubt that though India has been shaken Goa has been spared the worst.

Overtaken by the Heart

On 6th January Steve and Glenys, two of Derek's friends on holiday, invite us to share a day out with them to celebrate their engagement. It's a delightful day's tour south by taxi in which we take a close look at the coastal locations in case for any reason we want a change of location in the future. Nothing compares to Calangute. Derek speaks of how Calangute has provided for its tourists without spoiling its natural beauty. It is enough to add that the 'energy' of the place suits us. Derek goes with them to the beach and I go home. When he returns he looks strange. His pulse is racing. He monitors his blood pressure. It's massively high. I ask if we should find help.

'No, I'll wait until tomorrow. If I don't make it through the night you can leave my bits here!'

It's a long thought-filled night. In the morning with readings rising Derek is moved to action, drives off and returns without having found anywhere that felt right to seek advice. After a few days of no improvement he finds a Wellness Clinic returning with advice on diet and reduction of salt; complete rest; to stop riding the scooter and take diuretics to reduce water retention. He complies while we lead a stately life close to home but after no discernable progress we experiment by taking readings after different activities discovering that when I give him healing his pulse rate drops. Healing for me consists of laying my hands wherever they choose to go and, in this case, speaking quietly to the heart. Probably Derek hears very little but it feels to me as if the word can carry revitalising messages just as well as the hands. Though this gives respite to the thumping heart it does not hold for long and the erratic rise and fall continues, moving us to speak of heart felt matters.

I have been keeping a graph that Derek decides to take to the Don Bosio, a small local hospital run by nuns where specialist doctors hold evening clinics. He must undergo tests before they will give a diagnosis. He complies and we are joined in the wait for results by Sandra and Clive, here again, on holiday. I for one am acutely relieved. We are three weeks into the New Year.

Perpetual Blessings

Amongst the physical flurry we had heard a whisper that the tenants of our next year's apartment are planning to leave on 9th February. Without thought I blurt out: 'It will be empty before the fourth'. They leave a week earlier than planned. We move in on the second; into a new vista and a new energy field that is sublime. Overhanging the balconies, tapping at the windows, palm fronds sway gently. It is a forest of hands waving, offering protection from the sun; sending perpetual blessings. We name it simply The Palms. Derek, who has been started on a course of beta-blockers, watches every flutter in bird-land as he sits on the balcony, binoculars ever at the ready, while I meander happily with Sandra in our sun-drenched outer world, letting our minds run free to explore thoughts as they flow in. These are truly 'palmy' days a word long gone once ascribed to the victorious gladiator who receives the palm branch as reward for his prowess. The Palm Tree is said to grow faster for being weighed down by its heavy fruit, well we have certainly had weighty lives in some respects.

There is an article in the newspaper by an artist writing of the quality of light in Goa that is emerging through her paintings. We also recognise it, sensing that it is also emerging through us. What a delightful thought, that we too are paintings in process. The pen adds another reflection to our lazy musings: **The worlds of sight and non-sight work in tandem. The seemingly sighted merely see the sunlight's inter-play upon a physical world; yet within that Light are Rays of intensity that are changing the cellular structure of the human form...** There is much for our contemplative minds to enjoy, seen and unseen.

I intend to learn more of the craft of creative writing this summer by making a collation of short mystical tales, amongst other things. Our Golden Wedding, on 3rd September calls for a family gathering followed by a journey to high places, starting with Mont Blanc. And so we journey home again ready to reply to the oft repeated question: 'What do you find to do in Goa?' What can I say except that India is different every year, and so are we.

46. The Way of the Fool
2005/2006

The Opening Robe

I've found a cheap route this year which takes us on a detour to southern Goa for a week's bonus hotel holiday but we are restless, rootless, wanting only our familiar base. Derek plunges in and out of the pool while I plunge into a book that whisks me straight to attention. It's called 'The Zelator: The Secret Journals of Mark Hessel' by David Ovason. The title is intriguing, the contents even more so as the secret life of The Fool unfolds as an archetypal character with his own particular perception of life:

'The Fool has committed to the search of wresting from matter its hidden secrets. He does not eschew emotion, he enters into that strange world where feelings run amok, spearing the unwary heart, calling out Down you Go into the caverns of tortuous pride or doubt and fears until you have strung a ballad that can raise you up and you can sing of battles won; chasms crossed; dreams reborn; death defied; life lived unhooked from its pretentious past... and he knows the cave. A Fool knows that only the light of his own being illuminates the cavernous place'.

The Way of the Fool is not in itself a path but a Way of Being in the world. The Fool's robe is designed to fall open at both front and back, symbolising that when he chooses, the Fool is prepared to show those things which others prefer to hide. Though dressed ready to reveal, he must dress those revelations in the cloak of a life. A Fool does not deal in theories and beliefs but in experiences and expressions. I feel such a strong affinity with the Fool's Way that I think there must be a good dose of the Fool in me. Then I remember. On the wall, over my desk at home lives a Jester with a secret smile. I think he is the equivalent to Hessel's Fool.

Now I am looking at what is in my bag with a naked eye. During the summer I have put together a small collation of stories *Telling Tales; The Art of Mystical Storytelling*, my practice ground for honing the craft of creative writing. The manuscript has come with me for last chance additions. Though the tales are born of snippets of personal experience, there has been a Jester in my pen who slips in to put a twist in the tale, make a point, sort out some imagined hurt, fill an over quiet moment, add a quick insight between the lines. I have been practicing more than I realised, offering reflective snapshots of a Fool's way of perceiving the world in which everything from a diamond to a pebble is significant.

Reading on in Zealator I find the line: '*the Monk and the Fool can travel together*'. What does **that** mean? Am I the Fool and Derek the Monk? I don't think he's a Fool. He'll probably be relieved to hear that. Maybe these are two compatible archetypes and I have a measure of each. Either way it's been a fruitful week's holiday for me at least. Now we can go to our Goan home and I can be relieved that whatever I may come to write of more substance my Jester will certainly have a hand in it!

Derek slips effortlessly into the slip-steam of his sun-stroked world while I set to work rustling both pages and mind, at the ready to edit the proofs that Liz will be bringing shortly. It isn't until the last page that I realise they are all essentially love stories. Why not? We had been overtaken by the heart last winter hadn't we? My mind has a focus. I could be anywhere in the world I am so happy to be in a creative thought stream. It just so happens that I am in India and Derek has a journey up his sleeve. Sandra and Clive are coming in January and want to go travelling with us. Derek will master-mind the route. Firstly I will be hosting Liz who is booked to arrive in December but there are complications. Liz is in Surrey staying with her mother, Ursula who, with a terminal illness is in need of constant care. The passing comes and Liz arrives as planned. We are able to share the essence of what has been an awesome event and create a thanksgiving for Ursula's life in our own way. Liz is staying at a hotel with a swimming pool this time, a short bus ride away, so often I travel to her and we spend our time relaxing and talking over lives lived, battles fought and the world at large; interspersed with some delightful days out with Derek.

Bonny's Presence

When Liz leaves I set about the final editing work which calls for journeys up and down the lane to an e-mail cupboard shop. It's hot and claustrophobic and I am sometimes glad of a refreshing drink on the way home. Neighbours, a family of five, had moved into their newly built bungalow to which they had added a rustic restaurant area in the garden, an ideal relaxing space for me to sit without interruptions and check my pages of script. Bonny, father of the family, sees the cover image of one of my created figures photographed in candlelight, wanting to know how it was produced. He works for Saatchi and Saatchi in Dubai, and when he shows me some of his work that has won awards he talks knowledgeably of the significance and power of visual imagery. Bonny has a mystical tale to tell of his own. He had been diagnosed with terminal kidney failure and went to spend meditative time in an ashram. There he sensed an invisible Presence that 'walked with him' making him aware that he would recover. He did. The family have heard this many times yet tell me they never tire of listening to the story of the Healing Presence that had no image, only effects. That I tell them is how I also sense energy making its 'Presence' felt.

I've agreed with Derek that I will choose a Christmas Eve venue for dinner and he will decide for Christmas Day. My choice is Bonny's but the family are busy behind the scenes. I miss their inspirational conversation; the food is not to Derek's taste and I recognise my oft repeated lesson that food and drink alone do not lift my spirits; there are more magical ingredients that do not necessarily nestle in the food! It is the same on Christmas Day at The Ritz. Derek's King Size Prawns look balefully at me and the Spirit of the occasion keeps a safe distance. Maybe it's because I'm not entirely invested in the present; the family messages that had come with secretly packed gifts of music and candles have triggered a bout of home sickness. So Christmas slips by; Bonny slips back to his work in Dubai; and we both slip into the New Year looking forward to our mystery tour in the south at the end of the month.

Rock of Ages

Kanyakumari marks the southernmost tip of India; the lands end, meeting point of three great seas, the Indian Ocean, the Arabian Sea and the Bay of Bengal. Derek had spoken of a spectacular sunset that had imprinted on his memory from a brief visit there some years ago. We have tiptoed through January, and have train tickets at the ready for Clive and Sandra's arrival. They do not have to acclimatise. It is their pattern to step into a sublime space and stay there! 'We'll just go where ever you go' became their mantra for the journey making life easy for Derek as he led us onto an overnight train and onwards on a sunset trail.

We are not a band of jokers yet good humour is the bedrock of our travels. Travellers' chat seems an unnecessary intrusion into the theatre of the day as we step out of our everyday world into something else less tangible. People appear like actors on a stage, saying lines, disappearing into places beyond our vision or even imagination. Train attendants fling aside the straggling streamers of makeshift curtains, entering with a flourish of tin trays or buckets, steaming teas, damp sheets, bananas and items unnamed. Unfailingly polite and cheerful our favourite attendant returns empty handed at the end of the line, facing us bravely with the memorable words 'If you are happy I am happy and will have good tip'. Irresistible!

Time elongates. The train goes only as far as Trivandrum and the world is still dark, yet that indefinable magical 'something' remains with us. Derek hires a taxi for the last leg and we are driven away to what is beginning to feel more like the edge of the world. It is important to choose a hotel that has a perfect view of The Rock that will offer the best view of tomorrow's sunrise. We are in place and ready to step into the pilgrim world that is Kanyakumari.

I understand why Derek has brought us here, why this place is so memorable for him. It is the energy; energy sustained by the focus of the sun upon the Great Rock; an icon to Vivekananda, a monk of the people who in his day became the Spiritual Voice of India. I had known of him as words on a page but had not touched the essence of that life. A joyous dreamer and enlightened thinker, he journeyed from the Himalayas the length of India telling the people that he would wander on wherever the Spirit leads: *It matters not whether I wander in forest or desert, on a lonely mountain or a populous city, I go. Let everyone strive and realise their goal according to their light* … The Spirit had led him to Kanyakumari as it had led us and never-ending flocks of pilgrims.

The causeway between the mainland and the Rock is a frothing, churning cauldron drawing us towards a pilgrim-packed boat. Story has it that Vivekananda torn between wanting the ascetic life of a monk and the urgency to bring education to the poor, swam the causeway remaining on the rock for some days until he knew the direction his life must take. When certainty came he swam back and began his life's work in education in India, his enlightened oratory and his magnetising Presence reaching the Western world to make its indelible imprint.

We cross by boat. On the Rock is a temple/museum presided over by carved figures that draw the crowds. I wander around the perimeter drawn towards a glass fronted case holding a life-sized sculpted head of Vivekananda but because of the reflected sunlight streaming in I see only the reflection of my own face in the glass. As the light moves my face appears to merge into the head and disappear. Easily this would be set aside by most as a natural illusion. The Fool in me knows otherwise; that it is significant because there is a distinct effect; a sensation of wavering consciousness, a spell of light headedness; when there is that awareness of nothing physically extraneous, only the experience of being within a vast field of consciousness one does not need to comprehend. It is already comprehensive! This is the field I have come to know of as *The Mahat*. It's best to quietly make for the bookshop.

The return boat trip is manic and dangerous. There is no concept of overloading and people cluster on one side of the boat to shelter from the gusting wind. It is fine if I appear a little out of the ordinary. There are no words in me to explain or describe what I think of as an infusion of light. I'm wondering whether where a Master has walked, breathed, thought and proclaimed the truth of his knowing it is possible to be touched by the light of that life. Why else do pilgrims travel the world to holy places?

Morning breaks for us all, as we stand on the roof of the hotel watching for the fireball sun that appears as if rising from a watery grave, fingers of flame playing on The Rock. Never have I seen, or felt the sun so near. With the wind wildly fanning my hair Sandra takes a photo for the back cover of my *Mystical Tales*. I want to catch and share this energy; this moment. Every element is IN its element in full measure. Kanyakumari is for me, a point where earth, air, fire and the waters become the four in one in one massive explosion of power. Is this why Vivekananda was drawn here?

Four in One

The plan is to find our way back in stages crossing the inland backwaters by boat. An hour's ride north to Kovalam exactly fits our dreamlike state. Now we are the four in one, in tune with the elements and each other. At Kovalam a wide sweep of beach with tranquil sea is waiting for our floating bodies and minds. Sea View Guest House tucks us into her sea view bedrooms; a German bakery feeds us and Kovalam is our nesting place for two days in a perfect hide-away. My highlight is the Great Moonstone Walk. In my mind's eye I had been carrying an image of a moonstone pendant that would hold the energy of this journey but there had been no sign of one in any jewellers so far. On the second day we set out for an intrepid walk along the coast, dotted with clusters of huts, homes to the local fishermen and coir makers. When the others stop at a shack for a drink, I wander away until suddenly at the side of the track is a tiny jewellers shop. Through the sand blown glass I see my pendant. When the old jeweller fastens it around my neck it feels like an investiture! He tells me it is a special *Rainbow Moonstone,* all four colours merging; the symbol of the journey of the 'four in one'.

Derek's research has found a Government Guest House listed at Kollum our next stop. It is a star find. The lakeside colonial mansion where visiting magistrates were once housed is a step back into history. Empty of any drapery and soft furnishings we are bowed to four poster beds in bare cavernous rooms. Treasured faded pictures tell their tales of daring deeds; mystical stories of lives long gone. Here we are gathered into a web of the past becoming a living part of it; quietly, respectfully spooning soup at a baronial banqueting table wondering who had sat here before us. What world, what era are we in? Scenes seem to change around us as if all we have to do is put one foot in front of the other. And on the far side of the lake we can see the flat bottomed boats, waiting for us to venture into the backwaters.

We buy boat tickets to Adeppe, our landing site, to be reached after the eight hour journey across a wilderness of twisting waterways. There is a somewhat strange colonial breakfast which I pass in favour of an orange, my first and last taste of the day and we step aboard into yet another strange world. Soon we are gliding on a mirrored expanse of still waters that look as if they have never moved! There are other people aboard but they, like us sit silently unmoving, watching. There is no rustling of paper wrappings, music, children playing. All seem to be caught in this time warp, a hypnotic state of gentle motion pulling me further and further in until I am in a no-man's land, suspended. The shift in brain rhythm which began with the Vivekananda experience has reached its optimum point. I slip in and out of consciousness. There is a lunch break at an island restaurant. Derek and Clive sample the banana leaf platter. Sandra is also beyond food as we confirm that we feel as if we are in a mirage.

It is a rude awakening when there is an invasion of boys with placards trying to sell accommodation in Aleppe. We make a choice and when we arrive at 9pm it is too late to remedy our mistake. We find ourselves in the most unaesthetic, paint flaking, stains on everything stainable, apology for a Guest House. There is no food in situ but Chinese dishes can be ordered in. The others order. Fortunately I do not. Plastic bags of substances unnamed arrive eventually. Incredulous at this sudden change in circumstances we creep reluctantly under the grey mosquito nets and are glad to reach the morning unscathed. Breakfast is hilarious. Two old men try to serve us but having very little English between them we are served an old newspaper for pepper; our request for one pot of tea and one of coffee brings a jug with tea and coffee mixed together; and eggs are almost raw. Clive master minds our escape onwards to Cochin.

Cochin, a small sea side town with a mixture of alley ways, courtyards and colourful shops is full. I am volunteered to go hunting rooms as pillion rider to a young man who assures us he has answers to any problem or question. He has. We arrive at *The Ark*, a family run guest house with warm, delightful hosts. The significance of the name does not escape us as two by two we are ushered in. For the next two days it is home. Here there is a great deal to see and do. The central gathering place is a big square lined with stalls at the edge of the quay where the renowned Chinese fishing nets looking like huge ethereal sails, edge the shore. Our dream-like state has now been replaced by a burst of vitality as we savour the sights amongst which are well stocked book shops where I spend browsing time with Derek. It is there that I make a prize find, *Shambhala* by Victoria LePage and that is how I join her on a journey of fifty years research into that which she describes as '*a paradise of universal wisdom and ineffable peace*'. Shambhala is to her, as to me, not just a name but is the Seat of Governance, the World Axis from which that New Reality is being orchestrated, and activated. Her book brings it a fraction closer.

On the second day a morning out with Sandra leads us to Jews Town for a fascinating tour of shops and synagogue. My problem solver has persuaded me to buy tickets for an evening performance at the Kathakali Centre advising me to be there for 'make up' at 5pm though the show does not start until 6.30. Derek is willing to take pot luck so we are there at the front, promptly at five. The performers, all male, enter and sit on stage so the audience can watch the transformation into the characters they will play whilst we are told about the colours used, how some are extracted from stones, including the yellow ochre we had experienced in our woodland massage. We meet the lamplighters and the men who play 'rainbow walking curtains' that follow the actors shielding them as masks are changed. The story to be enacted is of a demon pretending to be a beautiful maiden who sets about charming King Idra's son. When she offers to make love he knows she is a demon and rejects her, at which point (behind the walking curtains) she turns back into the demon. A great battle takes place and the King's son wins which means that all the demons are kept out of heaven. When the story line has been explained the play begins. We are transfixed by the energy of it; the raw power unleashed on that stage. The demons are real screeching demons! This is a night when Shambhala is before my eyes. Why? Because I have been reading of Rigden Jypo, King of the World, who protects Shambhala from any invasive energies such as the impure in heart! It is the same story made visible; living legends bridging cultures, entrancing minds.

It is almost over, one more visit to the quay before we leave. Sandra finds the symbol we have been waiting for, a Tibetan bell. We will take a photo of her hand holding it that will be turned into an icon to ring in each of the twelve *Telling Tales* that she will take back when she leaves for home. Each day has told its tale, as each day always does.

47. Hanuman's Wheel
2006/2007

The pen is a traveller across the page so let us study journaling.
The feet are travellers of Earth's terrain so let us study journeying.
The mind is a solar traveller so let us study the Great Beyond.
But when the studying is done, then free the pen, the feet and mind
And ride on Hanuman's Wheel

Free Wheeling: Summer 2006

The pen has been freed for the moment. Twelve mystical tales troupe to the publishers returning bound together, and happy to be so, providing ready made material for Writers' Retreats at Adam House. This sparks the idea with Liz of combining twelve of our favourite themes into one bonanza workshop. *Mind Webs* is a creative feast and an exciting experiment as we demonstrate how everything merges at a Solar level. Then the mind sails free as the next task emerges. My office/bedroom is calling for a dramatic change of image which emerges through the paint brush. Sage green walls become the backdrop to vibrant electric colours of the peacock with feathers and insignia to match. I work to the axiom 'as without so within' so what is that all about I wonder? On the open road again in September we are free wheeling in the caravette along the Camino Way to San Diego de Compostello, a pilgrim route steeped in Templar history and on through Portugal sweeping inland over the majestic mountains of the Picos de Europe; vistas of beauty at every turn of the wheel.

A November Fall

Arrival at Heathrow Airport by bus is unnerving. My bag is wedged at the back of the hold and I can't reach it so I am waiting for help when a bus swings into the next bay. The mirror stanchion hits my elbow sending a juddering wave of pain through my bones leaving me floundering and disorientated. The bag is retrieved, but my balance is not as I stumble on the escalator, feeling unsteady and shaken. Derek who had moseyed on ahead has missed the drama. I'm not sure he takes me seriously when I tell him I've been hit by a bus. By the time we land in the breath catching heat of Mumbai my spirits have fallen to the point that I am telling myself its all too much, that I cannot do this again and do not choose this route to heaven.

On arrival I take stock; arm bruised, pain in lower back; and an increasing sense of vulnerability. Three days on I have been unable to sleep it off and haven't even made it to the beach. The shake is well lodged inside me. What to do? **Apply oil and water** is the notion tapping on my sluggish mind. Tending the body will, it seems, restore equilibrium at every level. The oil needs to be applied by Sumesh, my masseur who, I have no doubt, works on the subtle levels as well as the muscles, then I will need to swim rather than sleep. Not only does the recipe work but my mind is switched on! As I know full well any substantial shake up is so often a wake up.

Monkey Mind

Now that I am out and about again it is images of Hanuman, the Hindu monkey god, that constantly draw my attention. Hanuman symbolises the human mind which, like a monkey, can be fickle and mischievous, jumping from place to place and causing disruption. But Hanuman is a winged monkey, free to fly across mountains, continents or worlds in an instant, able to reach anyone or anything. Hanuman also represents the characteristics of loyalty and devotion because he has surrendered completely to Lord Rama (who depicts the inner or Higher Self), to whom he becomes a devoted, obedient and loyal servant. Mythological tales are full of Hanuman's exploits as, always mind-full of Lord Rama, he becomes able to assume miraculous powers. It is not long before I find a Hanuman image that speaks to me. Hand-painted on black velvet he becomes the centre piece on the lounge wall, looking perfectly at home in the leafy backdrop for us both to sense the Presence of Mind in residence each in our own way.

Hanuman makes an immediate impression. The title of *Mind Mysteries,* as a sequence of six evening groups next summer is already in place, but as yet has no substantial content. Six headings drop on the page followed by an explanation that we will be playing out a range of different aspects, or States of Mind.

The Spinning Wheel will demonstrate mind in constant motion; the *Peacock Garden* its ability for peace-filled contemplation; *The Living Ladder* is mind's carrier into higher realms of thought; *Ring of Fire* conveys mind's power to consume and recreate; *The Magic Cloak* is mind as revealer and concealer of wisdom; and lastly *The Lyra Creation* is mind resonating within the vast cosmic scheme; Lyra being the planet associated with Universal Harmony. Each theme has the potential for colourful and creative displays activating both right and left sides of the brain simultaneously allowing for a much stronger imprint of a theme. Hanuman adds a rider: **Ensure you dress the intellect in mystery and inlay mystery with intellect!**

The Living Ladder

What I had not bargained for was that Hanuman's arrival seems to be setting in motion a Mystery School for two. Derek noticed it first. When communication hits a torpedo we both sink. There was a morning when we sank abysmally. My response is a long hike down the beach to The Wreck, a tanker washed up on the shoreline. It seems an admirable symbol for the day but solves nothing. Day done, I return and we try to set about unravelling the situation. It's difficult and I'm shouting with frustration:

'I'm trying to create a living ladder to higher mind and we can't even get off the bottom rung!'

'You'd better show me the ladder'.

His reply is the beginning, not only of resolving that particular scenario but of forestalling other possible trip wires. Derek does crosswords. He is good at finding individual words, not always so good at stringing them together. I ask him if he can find a word to express the sense of when Nature seems to be speaking. He answers: 'Pan-sensory perception'. I think he's met our resident tutor! Pan-sensory perception enters our vocabulary as yet another rung on our communication ladder.

It's December and we set about some pleasure-seeking outings which will give us something good to talk about; a trip to the capital, Panjim; testing a new pool and of course the book shops. It's Shri Ravi Shankar who jumps into my hand intent on adding another dimension to our mystery school, and he does! Easy to read, filled with wisdom, humour and an all pervading sense of Love, his words touch us both as we dip in and out of a trilogy: Celebrating Silence; Wisdom of the New Millennium; and God Loves Fun. He writes: *'If you really love something you want to know more about it. If you love yourself you want to know more about yourself. You want to go deep into yourself'*. We're moving at all levels.

Often we find gems to feed the mind; go a little deeper into Lord Rama's territory and keep torpedoes at bay. We are well on the road to Christmas which arrives with an extra-ordinary illustration of our pan-sensory perception! I have given Derek a C.D of Maria Callas, telling him it is the highest note I know. Sitting on the balcony we play it Christmas morning and birds in their hundreds join in stirred into a cacophony of bird song heralding a Christmas day to be savoured.

Pilgrim Travellers

We've decided to plunge out further and take a journey south to Udipi, travelling there by train and then taking short hops back on local buses. Hanuman has a few words of advice: **Set the consciousness adrift on the seas of perception; travel**

with neither haste nor sloth; elation or despondency allowing the world to be that which it is, simply a wonder to behold.

The journey of five hours is interminable, sardine packed with loud, liquor-drinking back-packers. The wonder is that they remain on the train! Derek has booked a hotel in advance and we fall into crisp white sheets exhausted. Immediately the biting starts. I whip off the sheets hunting for any microscopic sign of bed bugs and can see nothing but already I am in big trouble as some types of bites cause a violent reaction and this is one of them. An anti-histamine tablet eventually knocks me out but by morning my face is a swollen mess with one eye completely closed. I look like a puff adder and have been chewed unmercifully. I hide. Derek goes out to see the wonders of Udipi and finds them in a magical old temple where he buys two gilt necklaces to charm the bugs away and purchases a potion, applying it he tells me, 'with a bleeding heart'. What a start! Tiptoeing out at dusk he leads me, still one-eyed, to the temple but the rubble strewn streets are hazardous and crowds are gathering ready for the evening arrival of a ceremonial elephant pulling a golden cart, so I return having been unable to behold anything much but sensing that Udipi is a holy jewel of old India.

Musing on why I've been advised to see the world as a wonder to behold when I am half blind I have a glimmer of understanding. When I was thumped by the bus I had been so shaken and out of sorts that I didn't even go out for three days, caring very little what the world was doing. Now I am being brought to see that whatever is happening at a personal level does not have to change the sense of wonder of the world at large so on the second day, still half sighted, I determine to go out to see what I **can** see. Derek suggests a trip to the beach where we sit in a garden restaurant. Enjoying a fruit salad breakfast I watch a servant creating a lotus mandala of floating petals in a bird-bath kind of dish on a pedestal. My eye is so sore that I visualise bathing it in that lotus water. Slowly but completely it opens. Indeed it is a wonder to be able to behold again! The phrase now has both meaning and a bit of Hanuman magic! It is not a blind monk day. I am fine and we are ready to find a bus to take us up the coast.

There are buses a-plenty but no hotels for 'long way distance'. So we go long distance to Kundapura only to discover the Rotarians have booked all available hotel spaces for a Conference. Another bus, to dusty Bhatkai whose best hotel is prison grey with barred windows and heavy doors with clanging padlocks but it transpires no bed bugs, so giving thanks for our night shelter we leap aboard the first available bus north. Crossing estuaries with palm fringed inlets we reach the fishing village of Honavar, with a market in full swing. This is more like it!

Friendly people direct us to Kamat Executive a modest hotel with a restaurant and an airy bedroom. Drumming and shouting draws us out again to discover a political rally is taking place. Hundreds, if not thousands, wearing an assortment of orange outfits and bandanas are on a flag waving march creating a massive surging wave of powerful energy.

Having found a comfortable corner we decide to stay and take a local bus for a round trip up the coast to Murudeshwar. The tiny sea-side town is alive with pilgrims, markets, and temples but dwarfing everything on the crown of a hill is the statue of a Lord Shiva, 132ft tall, destined I would say to become one of the wonders of India. The hill is a promontory jutting into the sea. On one side of the statue is RNS a newly built hotel with panoramic views and on the other a towering temple is being constructed which will be taller even than Shiva. We watch workmen chipping intricate temple figures and stroll in the markets. Pilgrims want to have their photos taken with us as we add to the colourful nature of this magical scene. I can see how we must stand out in a crowd with Derek at 6ft 2in being a head taller than most, and my blond hair looking its best in the ever present sun. Our journey too has begun to feel like a pilgrimage and the world here that has truly been embellished by human hands is a most wondrous place.

Still northbound we leave Honavar for Golkonda, where the standard of accommodation is questionable, unsavoury brown flowered curtains being indicated as bed covers but the scenery is magnificent. Hiring an auto rickshaw with English speaking driver we are introduced to every cranny and crevice of Golkonda from bazaar and market to tanks and temples passing stern looking old women sitting watchfully outside rickety houses. We are informed that we need to take a blessing from the temple priest, for a small donation. He asks for the names of our mothers and fathers and we discover they are to be the recipients of the blessings which I find an interesting scenario as they are all deceased and are probably in good spirits! The view of the famous Ohm Beach, formed in the shape of the Hindu Ohm symbol, is eye catching. We are told the hotel bungalows we can see fringing the shore are for 'rich Americans'.

Our last stop on the route home is Karwar, a naval base and large bustling town where we stroll the long beaches telling each other what we have most enjoyed which is encapsulated in the phrase 'free wheeling in a world full of wonders'. Derek's top pocket calculations tell us that the whole journey has cost about £60 (for two). It's 11th January. We have been away for eight days. Two weeks later we determine we enjoyed it so much we will set off again, so we do.

The Looped Road

We are ambitious. Derek wants to go south again but inland this time to Ooty to ride the small mountain train. That suits me as we can take the route that will pass through Madikiri, from which we can reach the Tibetan settlements in the hills and especially the Golden Temple housing a Golden Buddha. A Guest House, advertised as 'heart warmingly welcoming', is nearby and with five thousand monks in the Sera Village monasteries it has to be a very high energy area.

Taking the familiar train ride south we reach our stop, Mangalore, in the evening for an uneventful first night's stay. Up early and away on the long bus journey over the Western Ghats, we make it safely to Madikiri only to discover the whole Tibetan sector is out of bounds due to the forthcoming arrival of the Dalai Llama. Trying every avenue to secure a pass of entry ends in failure and we are left with no option other than to surrender to the long road ahead leading to the city of Mysore. It is on the way that I begin to feel distinctly unwell, worsening by the moment when we trudge the city full of tourists in search of a bed. Mysore looks a beautiful city of majestic architecture but by the time we find a room I can only slink into bed, shivering, feverish and with stomach cramps. Once again it is Derek who goes exploring to return and describe the sights. By night-time diarrhoea and sickness has begun in earnest. Apologetic and dismayed I dare not take another bus nor play tourist. Derek negotiates a taxi, scoops me up and I hold myself together just long enough to reach Ooti. The significance of meeting a troupe of monkeys blocking the road is not lost on me; there is certainly mischief in the air. Reaching the hill-town is an assault course of bumping and jolting and as we gain height the air turns crisply cold. By now I have double shivers and am desperate for a bathroom. Derek has booked a hotel which takes an age to find by which time, immensely grateful, I slide into yet another bed seeing no more of Ooti other than the ride through. The road has brought us here, the train station is in sight and Derek is on the job discovering there are no tickets available. We cannot escape down line; we are in icicle town without warm coats; the road behind us can only lead back on a looping trail of endless miles and I cannot move yet anyway. Surrender time again. We survive for two nights. Derek has an interesting day exploring and discovers a bus route over the Ghats; a seven hour ride if we can get aboard. It is usually full. No tickets are pre-sold. On the third day we lurk at the bus stand and physically join the fight to board the only exit bus of the day. The journey is magical. I'm living outside the window, absorbed in the amazing sights of life lived in these high places, high-lighted by a lantern-lit procession snaking along beside us; the creeping bus becoming a festive part of St.Joseph's Feast Day. Its nine o'clock and darkly mysterious as we end an utterly entrancing journey on a road we would never have thought to have travelled.

The terminus is Kozicode a large coastal town. Derek had taken pot luck and booked a hotel room at the Hyson Heritage. Only a step away from the bus stand it proves the perfect recovery zone and we are back on track; a track that will now lead northwards towards home. Our choice is between a long train journey and bus hopping. After a day of respite care we choose to hop. On our first day on the road again we make four connections sometimes with hours between hunting for shade in doorways or people watching at bus stations. After an overnight stay in a non-descript town we see Udipi inching over the edge of the map and there is no contest. Strange how certain places claim you; how you remember a name, an image or an incident that imprints itself in memory. Udipi had all those. We replaced the bed-bug hotel with a traditional Hindu hotel complete with an array of statues of welcoming gods delighted to find what are fast becoming familiar images, waiting after such a marathon journey. In the morning we discover the road is not yet ready to let us go. A moment's confirmation that we have the same destination in mind is all we need and the last leg of this great looping journey carries us back to Murudeshwar. And what is more we are agreed to stay at the RNS, the hotel on the hill with the panoramic views. Basking in the sight of the mountains merging into the sea we come to the end of the looping road that had claimed us, curving on patiently while we learnt of surrender to the inevitable with the best grace we could muster and a few other unmissable lessons besides. Hanuman's mystery school had taken to the road with us, depositing us unscathed at Lord Shiva's feet where even his shadow is a blessing shading us from the orange sun and words begin again to fill both mind and page: **Let the world delight the eye/I, for as you see the world, so will the world see you as a wonder to be held in her embrace...** We are content to be seen and held; content to be here or there.

A Silver Beach

Whatever has happened? We cannot stop travelling! No sooner are we home than the road is beckoning again. We have heard of Malvan a fishing village in the north, only a few hours bus ride away. There is time for a short foray of three days before home time looms; three unmissable days. Stepping from the bus the village greets us with namastes from people unknown, smiling, guiding us to the one and only hotel. The beach belongs to the fishermen. Spread the length of the sands are fish, silvered, shimmering scales sorted into their different sizes and families, the perfect symbol of absolute surrender to the Great Fisherman. Only poetry could catch the drama of such an army of lives laid down in perfect order and symmetry. We wander between the rows, my mind wandering into a profusion of thought. A visual analogy is taking shape. I see the beach as Pisces;

The World of the Fish. Sacred to Christians the fish symbolises the Great Piscean Age now surrendering to the very different energies of Aquarius, the Solar Age. It is a surreal vision of unimaginable vastness; moving in its immensity. The Blessing of the Fish will no doubt be performed at some time by the fishermen. Not knowing their words I make up my own.

Tahiti of India

Derek had found a picture of beachside bungalows in Tarkali. Six miles south of Malvan it is described as the 'Tahiti' of India, boasting of its virgin beaches and an array of culinary delights. We have a room booked there for one night. It's all quaintly different. Wooden bungalows with queer pointed roofs hide amongst fir trees, a step away from a magnificent swathe of empty sands. Empty is a useful word. There is no sign of any other guests except in a bus leaving, nor sign of food of any description. The bed however is not empty; it is sprinkled with biscuit crumbs and hairs. I request sheets are changed.

Request refused; *'bed-sheets changed'*. House-boy stares me in the eye. I'm staring back deciding on my next tactic when Derck arrives.

'Is anything the matter?'

I explain succinctly.

'Change sheets!' Two words barked as an order and the naughty one is running around the bed at the double rolling up the crumbs. Oh to be a barking male sometimes! Command is a well used rung on India's ladder of communication that isn't on mine; well not too often.

Night drops fast; birds sing a raucous chorus; houseboy disappears forever and we are in solitary confinement in 'Tahiti'. Morning only enhances the expanse of uninhabited beauty around us. The beach is ours alone; breakfast is ours alone and we take photos of each other to prove we are here!

The wheel, that has turned us in three different directions, returns us to our Goan home then onwards to our house on the hill where Derek will enjoy another season on the golf course and my 'Mind Mystery' evenings will begin.

48.Road to Bethlehem
2007/2008

A Shaman's Shoes

The notion of a mystery journey began in the summer. I had in my head the idea of setting out a couple of weeks before Christmas to 'follow the star' to wherever it might deliver us on Christmas Day. All that is needed is a starter direction. It becomes a summer talking point and remains our focus after arrival as we test ways of packing essentials into light rucksacks. No advice has been offered until we are ready to leave when it's suggested that I 'wear the Shaman's shoes'. There is much that can be said of a Shaman's way of being in the world, but my immediate thought is that they are subjected to many challenges in dark places before graduating to stand on the bridge between the physical and metaphysical worlds. If I have registered my message correctly this seems likely to be a formidable journey. That which follows is the essence of 21 unforgettable days, 12th December to 2nd January, when I had need of those shoes.

Making Tracks: 12th December 2007
Derek's finger has pointed to Adam's Bridge, a rope of rocky outcrops protruding from Rameshwara, a point on the East coast opposite Shri Lanka, reachable via our pilgrims' point of Kanyakumari. Nineteen hours on the Raj Express is a gift in contemplation time. The motion is hypnotic. Food comes; bedding comes; snapshot views are grainy with the growing filigree of window grime. Fields, rivers, shanty towns and temples; the sacred and secular merge effortlessly holding lives lived in ways unknown and unrelished by us. I love these first footings, stepping aboard, knowing the train is on its track laid out ahead; and so I suspect is ours.

Butterfly Garden: 13th December 2007
It's 5.15am on Trivandrum Station – the end of the line. We sit on a luggage trolley watching the cleaners swoop on unmentionable objects, as we tune into the motion of the day. Shall we stay or move on? There's a museum here of Nicholas Roerich's original paintings of journeys in the Himalayas on his quest to find Shamballa. I would like to see them but feel no holding energy here, neither does Derek. He asks if I want to move on. All it takes is a nod and we are away on the local bus for the 84k journey to the 'end of the world'. Dawn breaks,

everything is waking; people, goats, birds, flowers, temples, music. Colours intermingle, saris flow, school children smile and wave. This is India's enchanted world that shakes me alive, stuns me with her beauty. Too late for today's sunrise; we book into a modern sea view hotel. Breakfasting in the shadowy basement restaurant Derek comments on the darkness, wishing we could eat in the open courtyard above. Rambling the day away amongst the crowds as we reconnect to the Presence that pervades this town, we brave the basement again for an evening meal. The restaurant has gone, removed to the upper courtyard where a slide projector is creating a butterfly garden. The floor is alive with dancing winged images fluttering across the floor, our plates, our hands and hair and up the walls. Pure magic!

Roerich's Sunrise: 14th December 2007
At 6.15am I'm on the roof alone waiting for sunrise. As the sun's fingers begin to paint the rock I am aware my eyesight has shifted and I am seeing the sky as an artist's canvas of purple stroked clouds, soft grey edged mountains and ethereal shapes. This is why we did not stop at Trivandrum. For one enchanted moment I am seeing how Roerich could see, expressing through his brush the greater picture which no words could ever convey, no more can I.

A day's excursion out to Takkilal brings a connection to an Indian couple we meet on the bus, with whom we share the day's adventure into history. Our destination is the wooden palace of a long gone ruler of the area. Every day we are told 2,000 people were fed from the immense vats. Intricate carvings tell the tales of history with our friends adding their reflections. Drinks together bring an invitation to their home in Lucknow but regretfully we are following a different star route.

'Fawlty' Towers: 15th December 2007
Tourists buses run inland to Madurai but the shorter route to Adam's Bridge is along the coast where there doesn't appear to be much of a road, nevertheless we find a local bus, jump aboard and wonder why people are smiling. First we are driven into a sandy field to have urgent repairs before we lurch onto a potholed track. Prickly branches invade the windowless holes through which we can clearly see goats have taken over the world. For mile after mile they entertain us, lounging on doorsteps, draped over the tops of wells, wedged into scrubby trees and attacking anything that hangs from bicycle handlebars. Unexpectedly we are on the only visible road to a Nuclear Power Station. Buses, trucks, bicycles, any means of transport converge stacked with bodies arriving for work. Entranced by the suddenness with which scenes in India change we now have another. The rains begin with a splatter through holes in the roof; flapping shutters drop over the window-holes and the world outside disappears. Four hours later we leap out

into an umbrella world. This is Tutucorin and this is a deluge. Roads are a morass of mud, and any hotel will do.

The restaurant is a slosh away across an open courtyard. Derek's soup water is drinkable, my fish is a thin scallop of sharp protruding bones and the chips are smeared with coloured granules whose colour has run. The electricity fails and a pall of darkness settles inside as the rain lashes down. Bed is my sanctuary for warmth. Unable to explore outside Derek explores inside trying to order a pot of coffee. No-one speaks any English here. A genie pops his head around the door with a questioning face setting a pantomime in motion as Derek mimes his order by pouring out an invisible pot and blowing his finger to intimate 'hot' toast. Little genie disappears returning with a pot and two miniscule cups, pours thimbles full of brown substance but disappears with the pot. The toast mime was completely unsuccessful. Now I know for certain I'm in 'Fawlty' Towers, dip gratefully into my iron rations, find an oatmeal bar, pick up my pen and we lay escape plans for the morning.

Queen Mary's Voyage: 16th December 2007
The sun is out and so are we, heading for the bus stand at 8am which is good intuitive timing as we are on our sandy ribbon of road by 8.30 on the way to Rameshwaram, a temple town and nearest point to Adams Bridge. Bejewelled now with water-filled pot holes glinting in the sun the road once again turns on its magic. Every bus, every kind of vehicle has its own distinctive sound from squeaky to ear-splitting. Ours is deep and melodious like a ship's funnel. We're laughing as at the same moment we both say 'Queen Mary' as we steam our way through fast evaporating waters, through fields rich with crops, acres of low bush lands, saline pans and straggly villages. A Shaman calls his travels between worlds 'voyages' which feels just right for today. Feeling this sense of rapport with the road is euphoric and we are in high spirits as we cross the gigantic I.G. Bridge and arrive at Rameshwaram.

The Temple is the centre piece of this compact town of stalls, shacks and basic hotels. Enquiries reveal the best hotel which is cheap and super clean, the furniture all still wrapped in cellophane. Well tucked in we make our way to the area of the beach from which we can see the fifteen mile promontory jutting out towards Siri Lanka. To see the Bridge of Rocks we will need to take a vehicle of some sort and have had enough travel for today so we move on to see what is happening on the shore.

This is a pilgrim's town and they have their rituals to perform both in the temple and on the beach. We watch ceremonial bathing in a filthy sea. The sand is strewn with every type of litter. Saris, scarves, lungis and strips of cloth lie draped over every rocky outcrop, now all faded, slimed by sea and weathered into all states of disintegration. Something significant is being expressed here in ways unfamiliar to us. Each item will undoubtedly have been laid with a reverent hand. We are the only white faces evident and it feels intrusive to remain as watchers. No-one approaches us and so we leave in thoughtful mood to stroll the side streets in the town.

Cafes offer buckets and pails of dahl, rice and curds. As usual I choose fruit from the stalls and the inevitable biscuits. There are no women eating in public anyway and we try to be respectful to cultural traditions if we know what they are. Tonight I am introspective wondering what that phrase of wearing the Shaman's shoes was all about. The testing ordeals that a Shaman is challenged to face, often alone in darkly deserted places, is the first thought that comes to mind. The pen, not in a mode or mood to give a full scale lesson is content with just a couple of pertinent lines: **The Shaman is not fearless for it is that very fear-fullness that swivels him, spinning the thread that holds him in a state of transcendent composure.**

I have the point. Fear is fine if it doesn't pull you into its lair. Composure is the antidote. With what I am beginning to think could well be a forewarning I slip into a Shaman's dream world.

Lucid Dreaming: 17th December 2007
It is difficult to say where a day ends and a night begins when the windows of one do not close, neither do mine as mosquitoes slip in out of the rain to nestle on my warm cheeks. Waking I feel bites already swelling but slide back into sleep where lucid dreaming begins. I am watching myself being completely covered in the intricate designs of Hindu artistry. Every detail, every touch holds meaning which I am unable to interpret. When the work of art is finished I am carried into the Temple, the very one that stands in the middle of this small town, by a group of monks dressed in black robes and become the focus of a ritualistic ceremony. Vividly real I wake in the certainty that an event of significance has taken place at some level. There is neither swelling nor sign of bites on my face.

Derek is up early and out investigating. He reports on spitting rain and a thick haze over the sea. We agree it is pointless making the trip along the peninsular because the rocks would be unlikely to be visible. He asks if I want to go to the temple. I answer that I've already been there in the night, thank you. That being an acceptable answer he is ready to move on. There's a bus to Madurai already waiting that has both leg room, windows and a driver, all good signs for a trouble free four hour drive on a straight tarmac road to Madurai.

Madurai is built around a vast Temple complex. I had visited many years ago and had never expected to find myself there again with Derek. We find a road of hotels and book in at Golden Park where all is bright and beautiful, comfortable and clean. From our room we can see the four Great Towers (Golons) that make up the Temple square looking strangely mysterious in the misty rain. Our priority is for food. There is a continental section on the menu that looks hopeful. Dressed in our best we follow the signs to the indoor restaurant. It is closed. There is also one on the roof. It is blowing a gale and raining enough to float a dinner. They try to anchor a rocking table under an awning. Not suitable. They open the downstairs restaurant where we are served to a delicious dinner by hovering waiters as we sit in state, alone.

Baptism in Madurai: 18th December 2007

This is not drizzle and mist, this is a deluge of cyclonic proportions from a leaden sky that completely obscures any view of the temples, so we indulge in a lazy breakfast and read the newspapers confirming officially that a cyclone at sea is forcing the rain inland. It is unexpected and unseasonable but not unwanted by everyone. To the farmers it is a priceless gift.

Our expectation is that we can hire an auto rickshaw to drop us at the temple gate. A good humoured driver welcomes us to his 'boat' for yet another kind of voyage and we find he is not joking. We sail through swirling lakes of water stirred by tangles of traffic. He cannot reach the gates. Alighting into ankle deep water we are soaked through by the time we have negotiated the square. Waterfalls plummet from shop tarpaulins; nothing can hold the weight of this volume of water. Our hair is stuck to our scalps and I'm having a blissful time! Why; because I am realizing something BIG. We have not had to dunk in the sacred waters of the sea or temple tanks with pilgrims, ladling water over ourselves. The waters have risen, evaporating from who knows which sacred spot, and are pouring over us for a baptismal blessing. Is **this** the sense of ecstasy that pilgrims seek and maybe find? We had not sought it consciously, yet like the farmers the rains have come as a 'gift from heaven'.

Drenched, bedraggled and for me somewhat euphoric we enter through the South Gate. No other temple has ever moved me like this one. It holds an ancient power that still pervades every crevice. Derek is drawn towards a massive golden lotus floating in the Great Tank, a tank that the papers had reported would have to be refilled with thousands of gallons of water as it was running close to dry. Today water is pouring in from the heavens through every available pipe and overhanging roof.

Intricate Hindu patterns cover every available surface, etched, carved, painted or gilded and rows of fluttering papers carry designs for body decoration catapulting me back into my temple dream. Again I am aware of my decorated body and the analogy is clearly set. I am nothing more, nor less, than a microscopic pattern that is part of the Grand Design. Which part? Does it matter?

What matters is that the sense of delighted participation in something so immense enables me for just a moment to see perfection of the whole regardless of the imperfection of the parts. It's a tour of some proportions in both mind and body.

Plunging again into the downpour we cross the square to visit the Sewing Halls where hundreds of machinists work in rows creating the ordinary and extra-ordinary, enjoying banter with customers who are tempted into buying things they will never wear. I am being nudged to buy a warm garment but there is nothing woolly warm in sight. At *Golden Park* the room becomes a steaming laundry. Derek has a room service lunch but I am restless. A woolly garment would soak up the rain and it is not cold so why am I on the hunt for something I don't want? Nevertheless the notion is insistent so I go out again when the rain has abated. The few articles I find look garish and in desperation I settle for a salmon pink cardigan embroidered with green flowers. A hotel guide is busy booking tours, one of which is to Kodikanal, a high peak in the Ghats. We book to leave next day, have our last supper and all in the world is well.

Cold Poison: 19th December 2007

It's a good decision not to take breakfast as our 8 o'clock bus arrives at 7.30am. The bus circles Madurai twice hunting down its passengers and we enjoy the tour though the rain is still formidable. It worsens becoming a journey of survival. The road curls, and climbs interminably. The higher we go the faster the visible world recedes into dense grey-white vaporous clouds. This is not mist; it is water vapour hanging in the air, swirling over the towering Ghats. On my side is a sheer drop into space and on the far side of the mountain slope shale and branches have already fallen, boulders looking ready to follow. There are flooded patches of road where roaring walls of water cascade, searching for outlets under bridges still holding, but for how long? It seems impassable, impossible to go on but we do.

Bus boy asks if we want a hotel and before we know it have been deposited by a long drive-way. As he is running ahead with our bags we have little choice but to follow, the towels over our heads soaked in seconds. I think this place is run by young men who are the bus-boys friends. Reluctantly we book into a dismal room, heavy curtains draping a dark heavy atmosphere but worst of all is the cold, a biting penetrating, and wet coldness. Bed sheets are clammy as is the one thin blanket. We ask for more blankets. They do not come. Coffee does not come. There is no restaurant, no food can be fetched in and we cannot go back out. In any case there is no sign of habitation. We look at each other and consider survival skills. Our plan is to find dry clothes which are scarce, get into bed and huddle together. We are both trembling and it's not with laughter now. It's only just after mid-day but luckily we both fall asleep for a few precious hours then the drama begins.

Waking suddenly I lurch out of bed. An excruciating pain jack-knifes my body as if I have been stabbed in the pit of my stomach. All I can think of is that I've been poisoned but I haven't had a bite since the previous evening. It feels as if my intestines are in spasm, followed by a shock wave as if something inside me has burst, is exploding, violently forcing out the contents of my stomach. Lurching again, I make it just inside the bathroom as diarrhoea and a tidal wave of sickness hits with full force. Luckily the floors are marble, unluckily it is like a fridge and the shivering takes hold. From some distant place I hear my voice moaning 'Oh... Ooh... Ooooh' over and over. By the time Derek reaches me I've turned the taps on trying to swill the floor. 'Leave it, leave everything; come back to the bed'. But I'm still bent at a right angle, unable to straighten up. The next couple of hours are an unspeakable horror of shaking icy coldness, cork-screw pain, and a right angled body. Derek deals with all things possible. Managing to hire a small fan heater, he puts a chair in front but I cannot sit the body down. The suddenness of my demise has shocked us both. What has erupted inside me? How serious is it? In a poignant moment I find myself telling Derek that on no account must he leave my body on this mountain. He deals with that one easily assuring me he will find a way for us to escape. Something in me hears and knows that is what will happen, though somewhere within me lurks the fear of sudden inexplicable pain from the distant past. Derek goes downstairs to beg another blanket and meets an English guest who passes the news that all roads ahead are closed by falling boulders and debris. The only way out is back to Madurai if that road and its bridges survive the night. Shades of Rakeshponka again! Still there is no food available. We dress like scarecrows in our least damp clothes. The salmon pink cardigan is now my prize possession, and as soon as body allows me to straighten it I lay it down in the bed, thankful that I had acted on the timely advice from whoever knew this scenario was on the way. Now there are two of us, body and me. No wonder the Shaman chooses the Spirit Body! If I can find it I'll stay in it!

Ticket to Board: 20th December 2007

We have slept the sleep of exhaustion. Waking well before dawn we remain huddled in bed until 7.30. The rain has not abated one jot. In two shirts and with a borrowed rainbow striped umbrella Derek is soon out scavenging for his breakfast and an escape route. He finds neither. We have to leave and I have to control this body at all costs for this next leg knowing that I must not touch any food, even if there was any. Three times Derek ventures out following false clues. There's a possibility of a man with a car, we pack and wait; he doesn't come. A travel agent opens where he buys a bus ticket. No bus arrives. Suddenly we are called: 'Go, Go, GO!' Plunging into the rain minus umbrella, drenched again, we are loaded into the front seat of a car piled high with luggage on the roof; seven equally well soaked people inside. I am anchored on Derek's knee, bag wedged on mine as I refuse to let it ride on the roof. Our responsibility is to keep the windscreen clear, a formidable task. .

A huge tree that has fallen across the road has had a portion hacked out allowing just enough room for a car to inch through. The mists swirl treacherously and we are amazed when the car pulls up on a bridge for our occupants to take photos of the roaring torrents! Madurai Railway Station is our goal. We reach it. I have no appetite at all but body is holding together so Derek buys bananas and we plead at every kiosk window for tickets for the night train to Erakleum, the station nearest to familiar Cochin on the opposite coast which is well out of the rain band. There are no berths to be bought. We are at last sold a 'ticket to board' which means a pushing match for any inch of space that can be found. However we are advised the ticket collector, known as T.C. may, if we are lucky, sell us a berth. Train comes and we are aboard, but T.C. has no berths to sell. We stumble through the carriages, invited by a Belgian couple to share a few inches of their seat for a while; later a kindly Indian couple squeeze us into a corner of their berth and after four hours T.C. appears. Officiously he tells us he has kept full track of our movement and if we pay lashings of rupees we can be placed in berths A 15 & 16. We pay. The luxury of lying out flat now that I can is enough to send me straight into a fitful rocking sleep.

Finding the Stable: 21st December 2007
Erakleum is wrapped in darkness and we work on radar finding a bus for yet another dawn journey to Cochin only half an hour away. Both spent we sit on the quayside watching the fishermen hoisting their nets. On the bus my attention had been drawn to a particular house in a cluster of 'Home Stays', small houses with rooms to let. Knowing in this Christmas season accommodation would be scarce, we decide to follow my hunch and back track down the road. A young man answers the door, smiling. He has one room only. It's cosy, clean, light and airy, with en suite bathroom. It is ours. We shower, empty bags and our landlord gathers up the soggy mess of clothing. The sun is shining and we are hungry. I have sucked only a few segments of an orange since the demise. Remembering a continental restaurant from our last trip Derek orders a full English breakfast while I try a boiled egg and cup of tea, savouring every mouthful, but not for long. With aching guts and equally aching heart I make it home. Nothing stays down, not a crumb. The body must be tended and allowed time to recover. I cannot travel any further and am well content for Cochin to be our Bethlehem.

City of Stars: 22nd & 23rd December 2007

A totally different rhythm has begun. Days are seamless, merging into each other. Our room is our cocoon, our refuge, our hermitage. Days have a dream-like quality and a drifting motion as, whenever I feel able, we take short gentle strolls around curio shops, the nets and bookstalls. People stream quietly out of churches, an array of colourful floating saris; stars swing from balconies, lamp-posts, over shops and spires. Father Christmas sails by on a float leading a nativity scene. The next-door house fills with carol singers rehearsing and the Presence of Christmas that envelops us has never been closer. Everything we could wish for is here; what is more that driving energy that holds us to the road has been replaced by a serene tranquillity, an inner stillness that cannot, must not, be disturbed. It seems incongruous that my body is disintegrating. Apart from the constant nausea and inability to retain food I am becoming dehydrated and am loosing blood from internal bleeding at an alarming rate. Dizziness creeps in at sudden movements and there is a tight pain in my chest.

Derek is on a spree of buying second hand books from a cart. We could be anywhere as we enter into these massive mind fields of Paul Coelho; Vicram Seth; Khalid Hussein, journeys that we travel willingly, following their mind maps, completely absorbed by these enchanting storytellers. By putting our body-selves to rest we have set our minds dancing. Days, dates have little relevance. We are somewhere beyond time. A children's carol concert at St. Francis's Church sets my spirits soaring even higher.

Perfect Imperfection: December 24th 2007

It has been a bad night of serious bathroom episodes nevertheless we have a plan for a celebration that seems to be taking momentum. Boats run to Willenden Island across the river where a hotel, the Taj Malabar, sits waiting for us to pay her a visit. We both have a sense that if we can do it we must. Is it possible or ridiculous? I make a decision to focus for ten minutes on my body to discover whether it will co-operate. My hands are immediately taken over and make strong movements of their own volition. I am aware of my friend Liz saying 'Let go, I'll take care of body today' just as normally as if she was baby-sitting. Telling Derek I can do it, I dress and we move but find the body is not yet under control, hers or mine! It feels as if it is slipping away from me and she hasn't caught it yet. We take a rickshaw to the dock and by the time the water-bus appears I feel the familiar sense of light headedness that often occurs when consciousness is on the rise.

After our days in hiding it is a joy to receive a Taj welcome. The surroundings reflect a vista of order and beauty and those who tend their guests make Service an elegant art. Here begins our Christmas celebration. I order a croissant and coffee which arrive with a flourish and six different jams, accompanied by Derek's giant vegetable dhosa and multiple pots of unknowns. As we acknowledge the extraordinary way we have landed at this point of perfection, I find myself musing aloud on the question of perfection. Is it perfection when the world around us fits our design, when we are in perfect accord with everything and each other? Is it simply the wanting of something to be better or different that spoils a day, a moment or a life? Animated dialogue bounces across the table as we catch and toss seeds of thought, my favourite game! Our philosophical breakfast lasts until they come to lay tables for lunch. We have ranged far and wide on the notion of 'Perfection', settling for the stanza: **Divine Love is the Love of Imperfection.** Recognising the voyage to that exalted state will take some time, we wisely admit that an everyday kind of loving calls for something similar!

Our next course is a bottle of water sitting in the verdant gardens overlooking the river. Dialogue goes with us, continuing as we watch the flow of the river. It has a swift current that carries all manner of effluence, plastic bags, patches of tangled weeds and things various. A sudden realisation adds to the day's insights as I confess that at times I am intent on fishing out rubbish, trying to make the river into a swimming pool. The river of life is the river of life, not a chlorinated swimming pool, an image that opened another bag of tricks, as the afternoon carried us on a tide of wandering thoughts. How greatly I enjoy this Hanuman Mind kind of day.

The Empty Vessel: 25th December 2007

Lips and tongue are cracked and dry. The bathroom has been my night refuge. There is no way I dare hazard breakfast and our greetings are wrapped in a soft sadness as Derek goes out to breakfast alone. So here I am, with imperfect body de-solidifying daily. I'm losing weight rapidly now and ache to immerse in water, a Jacuzzi, the sea, a pool; instead I hold watery images in my mind and let the body be about its work of becoming the empty vessel.

We reach mid-day and I can neither leave the room nor drink a sip. Everything returns with interest. We have to talk of our next moves. Though the thought of a lengthy journey appals me Derek knows he must go to Erakleum next day to search for a berth on the overnight train home. By mid-afternoon I'm encouraged to venture out for a short stroll to the sea. The people are beautiful Christmas people parading in smiles. The vista is idyllic, the sea is tranquil but body feels insecure as if it is trespassing; and has no substance. I'm thankful to creep back where we are met by our landlord Sunil who invites us to Christmas dinner. He has invited two friends. Derek accepts. I am glad for him.

At 6.30 we sit to a small table aware of the special effort that has been made. Knives and forks are laid for us and four dishes appear. I take a spoonful of rice and eat it grain by grain. They lay a cutlet of fish on my plate but as I make pretence of tasting it the phone rings. It is Sandra and Sommer. The link to family is my best present. We return to bed speaking of this astounding journey; of our yesterday at the Taj being a for-ever memory; and of the kindness and generosity of the strangers who took us in.

Return to Sender: 26th December 2007
I accept now that I am in big trouble. Thoughts of hospital are looming. Only sips of water are possible. Boxing Day has no relevance. It is vital we reach Goa soon. Derek leaves for Erakleum waking me on his return with good and bad news. He has two tickets for the Navrathi Express tomorrow at 2.15pm but they are not together one is B3 and the other B60. We will manage. Body has become unworkable and must be returned to sender.

The Underworld: 27th December 2007
A gentle water taxi to Erakleum in the morning is followed by the worst of hours in a women's waiting room, lolling sideways, holding consciousness by a thread as bugs attack. The train stretches the length of the platform. Not only is there no B coach markings, it is a miracle Derek is able to force a slot for me to climb aboard and that is the end of me. I tell Derek to go on without me and look for coach B if he can. He tells me to wait and not to move and is gone into the heaving mass of bodies. I slide down the filthy wall. It supports me. The outer door stays open, swinging. There's a breeze on my face. I'm wedged underneath a public wash basin. People just step over me as if I'm baggage. Half an hour or so passes; Derek does not return. How could he, every inch is blocked by bodies. A man who smells of drink picks up my bag. Is he going to steal it? People are alerted as I call out and a barrage of questioning begins and demands to 'show ticket'. I cannot. Derek has it. The train is slowing to a halt, my bag is snatched again so I grab the basin, standing up to wrestle it back when I see Derek on the platform gesturing at me to get off the train. I plunge out and in a trice he has my bag and is shouting to me to run. I do my best but the train is getting up steam again. We have to catch the rail of the restaurant car and are hauled into the heaving masses of bodies again. The heat is unbearable. Derek forges a way through and then suddenly, as a partition opens, the chaos subsides. We are in B. carriage which is air conditioned and Derek's luggage is enthroned on a berth B60 in the midst of a smiling Indian family. He leads on to B9 in a compartment where a large Indian family is in residence. They re-arrange so that I can have a lower berth, seeing

that I would not make the climb, and ask if I would prefer to sit or lie. I choose to lie. It is my last choice of the night. Bedding arrives. Body can do no more than surrender to the rhythm of the train. Later Derek tells me that he had been to check on my longevity during the night but I do not remember that or anything more until Goa greets me in the morning.

No Respite: 28th December 2007

A miracle would be good. I'm back in The Palms gently testing a sip of this, a spoonful of that, as we savour the day in the safe cocoon that has become an intrinsic part of our lives; the lull before another physical storm as the body reacts violently to the unwelcome food; pains worsening under the heart now. Spasmodically napping upright in a chair I wake with the knowing it is time to go.

The Special Room: 29th December2007

I speak the words Derek was waiting to hear. He calls a taxi. My choice is the Don Boscoe Hospital run by nuns. Its close, familiar and they speak English. Serenely smiling Sisters in crisp white habits welcome us on the doorstep. Over the doorway a notice reads 'The House of God'. There are no doctors on site. It is necessary to order one and so we do. Dr. Bhobee, who is also a surgeon, examines and diagnoses. Dehydration; gastro enteritis; low haemoglobin levels due to burst blood vessels and excessive bleeding. Immediate surgery is essential. He asks 'Shall we operate'? The only possible answer is 'yes'. There is one decision to be made between open surgery and purchase of a staple gun. Derek is brought into the discussion and we all three are agreed. We will buy a gun! Admission is immediate and a round of tests begin to see if I am fit enough to withstand the operation. Failed! My blood pressure is 190/50. By the time I'm harnessed to drips times three, I decide it's time to call home and ask Sandra to set a healing wave in motion. Charlotte calls in; Sandra reaches Liz and friend Jill, who runs Reiki Courses at Adam House and has a wide healing circle. I am well secured. Dr. B. returns in the evening, slaps me affectionately on the back exclaiming 'We did it!' though who the 'we' is I am not so sure. B.P. is now 110/70 and I can now be moved into the private 'Special Room'. It even has a sign above the door saying just that. I ask why it is 'special' and discover this is primarily a hospital for the delivery of babies. I am going into the 'birthing' room. At present I'm hoping it's to birth a new body.

Derek has gone home to fetch my nightwear and returns with two Christmas cards which had arrived that morning. The first is from my old friend Eileen enclosing a photo of me standing on the doorstep of Adam House looking as if I'm about to enter. I see that as an excellent portent. The second is a card from Beverly, another friend, carrying the words 'you are a very special person'. It is all hilariously synchronistic. The Overseers have the most delicious sense of humour especially in dire times! How long ago were those apt messages sent? Already I have plenty to wonder about.

A True Surgeon: 30th December 2007

Dr. B. a most delightful communicator welcomes me into the morning with details of an operation to take place at 3pm next day. I am to have a spinal anaesthetic so he can talk to me all the way through and a man will be here shortly to demonstrate the staple gun. After information giving, Dr. B. asks me to share with him my approach to life. Somehow words are there and honesty is there, building a rapport that will allow for the best outcome in this most intimate adventure. I've never met a surgeon like it!

Derek arrives with his mobile phone so I can keep family contact. Sandra says she is going to put a placard outside the house with bulletins on it. I think she's getting a few calls. The afternoon brings a surprise visit from Paulo and Carmen (our landlord and lady), hugely welcome as they are able to advise me on aspects of hospital life. The second truckle bed in my room is for my servant ... Derek, who is supposed to sleep there, be attentive to all personal needs, make the bed and do all the odd jobs. We have ignored the bed and the odd jobs! Injections, drips and pills keep coming. Oh body – I'm so sorry.

Don Boscoe's Angels: 31st December 2007

At 8am distant singing grows louder until it reaches my bedside. It is the Sisters heralding the coming of a New Year singing '*Follow the Star where-so-ever it leads*'. It's surreal. They are acting in a pre-scripted play! Servant Derek arrives and we talk of growing sweet-peas next year, nothing heavy; it is body who is feeling leaden. My energy has evaporated as if I am preparing to slide right out. Derek leaves me to hide in my journal reviewing 2007 with instruction to return at 4pm when I should be out of ... where? I have no idea where I am going. I've spoken to all three of my girls but cannot reach Marc who is in Thailand. This bothers me. Its still only 12 noon.

Action! A cleaner who had mopped the floor earlier arrives to give me a printed programme which she reads: 12pm shave; 1pm enema; 2pm bath; 3pm operation, clapping her hands when she reaches 3pm. So it begins. At 12 o'clock a naked blade in a packet is put into my hand. I don't know what to do with it. She says 'new'. I nod and give it back. Gentle as a fairy she shaves my back! The 1pm enema is a non event as there's nothing of me left inside. 2pm 'bath' means that I am brought a bucket of water. Now I discover that Derek should have remained to wash me! I use a flannel and pass that hurdle. 3pm operation is now in hand. In wide prison stripes of green and grey top and wrap I am walked, supported either side, past a row of waiting patients with curious eyes. Double doors open and I'm inside a theatre, pristine in every degree with rows of shining silver instruments. Lying on a trolley I watch the gowning up pretending this is all a television episode. Floodlights come on and the spinal injection is endured without mishap. This is not an epidural as I had thought. It is something else, something that starts a process where icy cold creeps upwards through those now a little thin, brown legs; up and up through the body which is fast becoming nothing more than frozen flesh. The anxiety is whether it will go too far and reach my head. I do not think my brain would survive it.

There are five of them; anaesthetist; surgeon and assistant; nurse and observer/trainee. Every one is a delight, focussed, smiling eyes peeking over their masks; gentle, professional, friendly.

'How are you doing M'haletta?'

'I'm enjoying it, thank you'.

They laugh at my weak joke. Then I have gone beyond words. Not because of pain but because of memory. I am back on the mountain in Kodikanal on that freezing night and that same uncontrollable trembling begins in me that is shaking the trolley making the instruments clank; arms beating a tattoo in their metal splints. They drape more sheets but I sense they are struggling with whatever is in the depths of me. So this is where body must be left to its own devices and I find a place where my mind is safely held in total trust that all is well. I have seen that gun. It is heavy metal, about 18inches long shaped like a rocket firework. It has to fire metal staples into the right places to seal the burst blood vessels. It should take them half an hour. Is it going well? I'm uncertain, hearing hushed voices in a language I don't understand. After an hour and a half there is a mighty crack and it seems to be over. He has had to cut out a muscle and shows me a piece of myself I've never seen before.

Trundled back to the Special Room they lay body onto the bed, a dead weight. Derek has been looking everywhere for me, not knowing if I am a body or a person. Now here I am knotted inside a sheet, on yet another drip and frozen solid to my arm pits and thankful that Derek doesn't mention the striped outfit. De-frosting is slow and as darkness falls Derek leaves as he has to ride his bike home. Thinking the worst is over I smile him away. It is when the Sisters try to wedge me up to make me more comfortable that the jack knife pain slices across my stomach drawing a scream from me and the agonies begin. Engulfed in a wave of nausea, blood clots are pouring from me. I try to stagger to the toilet but am still tied up in the sheet. Sisters are running. No-one knows what to do. They bring a bowl of ruby red liquid and put it on the toilet to bathe me but the toilet seat breaks and I'm on the floor vomiting amongst who knows what. Nothing is real ... nothing is real, I keep telling myself. Sisters are praying around me. I suggest Sister gives me an injection to put me to sleep, the only escape route from this murky horror. Mercifully she does, stroking my arm, singing softly. I know nothing until I hear music and fireworks in some distant world. The Old Year is passing; another year or is it another life, beginning?

The Antidote: 1st January 2008.
It was expected I would return home today. Hope recedes during a day of pills, drips and injections. Each time I try to take anything orally the stomach spasms and violent vomiting begins. Derek is here. I tell him I am being poisoned. My mouth and tongue are crusted and furry; not even a sip of water will stay down. There are periods when Derek just holds me, then lies on the bed looking exhausted. At some point I tell him I don't know if body can survive this onslaught. Then Marc calls from Thailand. He is with a group of people in a hotel restaurant who have been helping him to find the telephone code for India. Picking up the urgency immediately his voice is a tonic as he says firmly 'I'll get the monks on the job. It will stop; NOW!' It is the last time I am sick. Derek stays the night on the creaking bed just in case and I sleep soundly.

The Measuring Stick: 2nd January 2008
I'm awake telling Derek I will go home today. I am not allowed out until I can eat. He cycles off returning with strawberries, bananas and bread rolls. I eat and it stays down. Sisters pour in congratulating me as I am thanking them. Marc calls: 'Its over isn't it?' He tells me people in the hotel had come together like a big international family to work on me and monks had performed a Water Ceremony. Maybe this is the kind of water I'd been calling for in Cochin! I'm laughing; telling him I'm eating strawberries and am going home. Something has certainly worked that is way beyond me to identify and the challenge is over. How much composure did I manage? That will have to be measured by some measuring stick other than mine.

By sunset I am on the beach, sitting in Oceanic Blue and ordering my favourite cauliflower lasagne. Derek can't believe his eyes. We never did see Adam's Bridge but what if that was only a red herring and the bridge we did find was the one the Shaman crosses on his metaphysical voyages. If we did, then assuredly we were both on it.

A Long Distance Exchange

Is it still only January? We both admit to feeling weird, reluctant to become involved with the daily doings of the world whilst I am feeling alienated from my body. It's like a piece of luggage which I drop down and it doesn't move until picked up. Derek too has been shaken by events and we agree that we just have to be okay with how we are and give our bodies' recovery time.

An earlier plan had been to meet George Nayak in Bangalore. Realising that's a step too far at present we ask if he would like to bring Jenny to Goa for a few days holiday and some gentle reminiscing. That does not prove to be the way of it. They would like to come but not without the family which leads us to realise we are neither ready nor able to do more than tick over quietly. So we remain in a world of two turning into a world of four when once again Sandra and Clive arrive, as they too want little more than recuperative time away from their daily round.

Two friends, Pam and Christina, who are also participants at Adam House events, are our last visitors with a tale to share. Christina has made a note of what she had experienced during the night I was in difficulties in hospital.

'I'm at home feeling a strange pain from the waist down that I felt did not belong to me. At our healing group I asked them to focus on it. When I woke in the night the pain was overwhelming but I didn't feel anxious about it. Next day travelling by car with friends, Lesley and Pam, I told them the pain was till there. As we were wondering what it could be, Lesley received a text informing her that Mhaletta was ill in hospital in India. We all then consciously connected to Mhaletta and the pain immediately dissipated'.

Intrigued, I thank them and add this experience to my list of all those who had linked with me, each in their own way. As we meet to share the ambient nature of life in Goa I feel them refuelling me with their familiar vitality. Such friendship truly holds a healing power.

49.Inside Story
2008/2009

Striking News

When you face the word cancer, as so many do, does it come immediately to mind to examine the word, and sense its nature? Maybe the mind would rather re-write the dictionary missing out the 'c' words. Peculiar symptoms in my right side, a pressure under the ribs had called for tests in the summer. Nothing untoward had been discovered, I was advised to see what happened next and report accordingly. Instead I went to India. Symptoms persist. Returning to Don Bosio to give my favourite surgeon a present I ask his advice which is … more tests; so begins November. It is the C.T. scan that reveals a small mass in the gall bladder which could be an innocent polyp; on the other hand … Doctor B. seeds the word. Derek raises an eyebrow. I ask several pertinent questions. I have the option of a biopsy in India; needless to say with more tests. We go home and settle in for an evening of conversation, pooling our scant knowledge of gall bladders and considering all the options. I really have to tune into this scenario because I certainly didn't sense it coming. It's obvious that neither of us want to return for a winter round of hospital jaunts, however common-sensible that might seem. We decide to sleep on it and wait for some clarity which is there on waking, in two parts.

The first decision is to return home a month earlier this year after our winter visitors have left in February. The second part is unexpected. I simply know I will not be returning next year; that my time here is over for the immediate future. Whether it has to do with my health I've no idea. All I can sense is that a door is closing for me though not for Derek who is clear that his Gateway to India is still wide open. Recognising that each will be in their appointed place, there is no dissent, yet when I set about enjoying the holiday everything becomes poignant; everything becomes 'maybe this is the last time' and I am left wondering whether India has finally struck me off her agenda.

There's no earth shattering news from other realms or this one until terrorists strike the Taj Hotel complex in Mumbai. I lock onto the news, watching the travail of the world; terror that comes from skies and sea; guns glued to hands steady or shaking with their determined intent to bring terror or deaden the perpetrators. Newscasters are lost in a torrent of words, sometimes babbling, incoherent with emotion as images of blood and bodies spring onto mind-screens around the globe. Amidst the chaos, India, that land of dreamy mysticism; stoic endurance; and formidable undercurrents of unleashed power puts out a forceful message for unification and a call for the sanctity of life. Can words covey the awesomeness of such carnage? Can words have impact enough to stem this tide? Words seem futile, a forlorn hope; purposeless in the face of such unbridled destruction. Suddenly the pen seems a puny instrument; but doubt, it appears, must be nipped in the bud immediately. Lessons begin with the familiar question and answer.

When the hand holds the pen what does the Word hold?
What the Word holds is its power as a binding agent as it laces together intricate patternings of thought transposing them into imagery that has value. Does it hold Truth; Wisdom; Beauty; Joy? Does it hold the present emblazoned with the crest of the past? Does it hold its receptors by the hand upon the journey; the heart in compassionate perception of lives in transit; and the mind electrified by the power of illumined thought? Those who are determined that reality rests upon human perception alone are those who have not yet recognised the vastness of consciousness that Wisdom seeks to reflect. Words are the transcription of Light frequencies into meaning; Words are the sound of Mind restoring itself.

And the Word is a vehicle for the holding and releasing of keys, codes, equations, imagery, symbols, sounds, and correspondences many of which are impervious to the human mind yet they have effect. They are impulses activating human minds subliminally. When Wisdom communicates whether it be from within or beyond the Treasury of Self it seeks to reach those whose minds are ready to journey into the vastness of beyond.

The pen continues with its self-imposed questions and answers. I learn of the **purpose** of the Word; what is **invested** in the Word; the **value** of the Word; and the **intention** behind the Word, being left in no doubt at all that the Word intends to be ever present in whatever form it chooses and has significance in my life. Yet it must be remembered that as minds are being activated to wider regions of thought pens will be at work everywhere on the endless search for the Unwritten Word.

A Different Being

Scientific discoveries in the nature of DNA have at last led to the realisation that the human form is not genetically fixed. The cellular structure of our bodies is evolving as a result of electromagnetic impulses which produce a spectrum of symptomatic effects at all levels such as those I experienced in 1977 and on other occasions since that time. In my archives of buried things are tapes, laced with emotion, recorded at a time when there was little understanding of such events. Feeling and sensing were my only yardsticks. Understanding that has gradually percolated through the ensuing years has not been set to paper. The pen, seeking to set this to rights is in the mood for hindsight and takes me back to the night of the Festival of Lights in 1977 for a commentary on events both personal and global. It begins:

On the night in question the demise of the Officer of the Law was neither tragic nor accidental. An infusion of high frequency light waves located a point of entry; a conductor. The unsuspecting body took an electromagnetic charge which, travelling through the skeletal structure exploded in the joints on the side of impact, firing thumb, knee and toe leaving a crystallised residue as it sought an exit point. The power of this initial strike flooded the systems as it tried to travel through existing neural pathways whilst operating in the unfamiliar dense and heavy substance of matter. The human system is not yet geared to sustain such sudden and forceful infusions; such intrusions; such high-lights.

Human body cells are light-encoded filaments, fine gossamer threads carrying coded information. Solar infused charges are opening neural pathways, setting in motion the next stage in human metamorphosis; aiding in the transmutation of the cellular structure, introducing the physical body to a metasystem that will gradually over-ride the archaic human form and formulae. A body, overwhelmed and losing power, fights to retain control, and when to no avail, withdraws, allowing the subtle senses to experience and interpret a changing cellular state. The common view of everyday life appears at times incomprehensible as the finer qualities of human nature seek precedence whilst the astral body, refusing to give way fuels emotions into a fiery state. Shifting brain rhythms are the cause of fluctuations in consciousness compounding the struggle in dealing with messages as yet impossible to interpret.

A temporary shift in the centre of gravity accounts for the sudden heaviness, sluggish mobility, and changes in weight and shape as toxic waste finds its apertures for release. Such activity can simulate physical conditions attributable to other causes. Treatment for that diagnosed as an acute arthritic condition was usefully employed by supportive re-alignment of the limbs allowing time for settling of the body into its new frequency to which it had to make adjustments at every level.

When Light invades with force its effects are both destructive and constructive. The sense of feeling like a different person, a stranger even to oneself is valid for in effect a different Being has formed because the Beingness is different. Identity has to be re-designed or modified to fit a revised, reconstructed, or replaced Blue Print for the ensuing life in which Advanced Minds may well have an investment. Think well upon it.

I have been thinking well upon it for over thirty years and am relieved to read words penned with authority that can be added to a growing body of evidence of escalating change at every level. Is it any wonder that I have been led to record what may appear as inconsequential details of my life when they could well have significance when set within a wider patterning? Though this commentary offers answers, it gives rise to many more questions; the very questions I was asking from my first footsteps in India when I questioned whether there was a Force influencing the direction of my life. I am at a point of answering that for myself. Assuredly there is. From that I deduce there is wisdom and purpose within it and a plan behind it of some substance.

Worlds within Worlds

Sandra and Clive are on their way and, at their request we have planned a journey to Murudeshwar, home of the magnificent Lord Shiva statue. Now we know the ropes the journey is smooth and simple. We book into a small hotel and are back strolling in that same easy flowing world discovering that underneath the Great Shiva, caves are open to the public. To our amazement inside we find ourselves on a circular tour of larger than life-sized figures set into scenes of Hindu mythology, magnificent in colour and intricacy, a power house of creative energy. It is a Wisdom World complete with giants, demons and dwarfs all playing their parts in a multi-dimensional pageant. Mystical tales in Technicolor! Mind is leapfrogging with thoughts, analogies, ideas, aware that we are both below and inside the Great Shiva, a world within a world; another inside story of great proportions. How often have I created life sized figures, archetypal images spinning minds into a spectrum of thoughts? Now I have another spectrum of my own. It is a National holiday. People are streaming in as we return to an ice-cream world below a green hill resplendent with Anjuna's golden chariot and statues of extraordinary dimensions.

A few days before Sandra leaves we find the pattern of the work waiting for our return home. It is surprising. There is a cellar in Adam House. In it is a living well where water flows through. For many years it has been the scene of flooding, waters rising to the light switch; firemen pumping snaking hoses through the library. We think the problem of a mains blockage is now cured. We hope so because the project sitting on our table is to convert the cellar into a Templar Cavern, our own underground cave. I have been scribbling red crosses and Templar symbols since last summer. What we have to do in there we have no notion other than opening it at Easter with a Templar Day, activating the well washed foundations.

And there is something else, a recurring image that made its mark before Christmas and is firmly lodged in my mind. It is of a group of three figures. I see them in Eastern robes and they are standing in the window of Adam House with the background of the far distant hills. They are three Kings of the Orient, each with their own powerful energy pervading the house. Next Christmas I will create them; make their Presence visible and their energy tangible. It will be as the pen has described, **patternings of thought transposed into imagery that has value.**

There's one more delightful interlude before India waves me away. Pam, who has returned alone for a holiday, is staying at a hotel close by with a swimming pool where we float and talk of history, ours and the wider world. The larger than life mermaid who lazes beside the pool sparkles at night with multi-coloured lights, her reflection floating in the water creating a touch of magic. Waiters sing and dance with guests; people warble to karaoke music and we are entranced.

There is no sadness on leaving day. India is sending me safely home without a vestige of thought of another physical demise to meet the seasons ahead awaiting re-creation.

50. The Greater Whole
2009/2010

Everywhere we look in nature we see nothing but wholes,
not just simple wholes but hierarchical ones.
Each whole is a part of a larger whole; fields within fields,
stretching through the cosmos
Inter-lacing each and every thing; with each and every other.

J.C. Smuts   (Holism and Evolution)

The Coming of the Kings

It's October and I'm enjoying a meeting at a local group begun as 'Open Minds'. We are foraging in a philosophical direction, defining words such as philosophy and theology. Musing on the word 'theosophy' we agree to do some research for our next meeting. That is how India burst through my defences. My research not only led to the Internet but to calling the Theosophical Society and asking for their literature. The International Headquarters of the Society is at Adyar in Chennai where a month long Wisdom School will be taking place in January 2010 and I am made aware that I am requested to attend and no doubt to be attentive. It is for members only. I am not a fellow of this Society, or of any other. I know of no member who can give me a reference so write my own introduction. By November I have the necessary paperwork and make a booking by post directly to India as instructed, however dizziness takes a hold accompanied by a feeling of pressure in my temples; the walls waver and at times there appears to be no space between myself and the floor. I check with the doctor. There is no discernable cause. This is becoming a repetitive picture of inexplicable symptoms. It had taken months to obtain the gall bladder scans which showed no sign of any polyp, cancer or anything untoward. Derek who had his ticket to return for a winter in The Palms left with the promise that he would fly to Chennai when I have finished School for us to holiday for a week in Pondicherry.

On the first of December I create the three life-size Kings in their Eastern robes as planned. As soon as they are in place, standing majestically in my front window, the pressure in my temples and dizziness dissipates. Each has a distinctly familiar energy I identify as reflections of three Spiritual Beings; El Morya, Kutumi and Dujwal Khul, long associated with the Wisdom Worlds of Madame

Blavatsky (Founder of the Theosophical Society) as the Mahatmas or Great Masters. But Masters are not personalised, they are vast energy fields of solar radiance. What I had not known, and discover when reading the theosophical literature, is that these Mahatmas had an earth incarnation as the three Magi; or Wise Men well known as Balthazar, Kaspar and Melchior, depicted in many creative forms at Christmas-time. The Wisdom of The Magi, an ancient priestly caste, is said to stem from the teachings of the Brahmin of India; wisdom that Madame Blavatsky, had sought to gather; translate; and disseminate in the Western world.

Sandra is well able to confirm that she too is aware of this Mahatma Field impregnating the atmosphere in the house. Calling together those who had shared group experiences during the year, included a fascinating Templar Day in the new cellar/cavern, we created a Christmas event 'Celebration of The Kings'. Each room had been dressed; each having its own visual themes to be explored from the Snow Queen's Palace in the veranda to the Golden Child in a sanctuary crib. The sense of Brotherhood is tangible both physically and metaphysically. It is a night to remember which stirs a long forgotten memory.

On my return from the Punjab in 1977 the bedroom that I shared with Derek was the one on the top floor of the house which later became The Sanctuary. It was in the daytime when I was alone, that I had seen the ethereal figure of a turbaned Sikh, hovering over the bed. He had no legs, just a flowing robe, pink, diaphanous. The shock had been so great that the sense I had of my body was of it levitating a couple of feet and falling back onto the bed. Inexplicable to me then, the memory became significant as I read more of The Mahatmas who were able to appear to Madame Blavatsky in both physical and etheric forms. Another question arises. Who then were the Sikh and the Brahmin who came to my door so unexpectedly all those years ago implanting the first seed of India and pointing to the direction my life would take? Were they what they seemed? It is in a thoughtful mood that I enjoy the family celebrations that follow and immerse myself in studies ready for the Wisdom School adventure.

Madame Blavatsky had left India in stressful circumstances and as I read *The Mahatma Letters* I find myself feeling intense emotion and a strong affinity with this woman with whom I had already discovered another mysterious link. In the early days our Advisors had spoken of a White Brotherhood of Advanced Minds composed of many different groups each with their own specified tasks; one such being named as the Brotherhood of Hahn, under whose guidance we were informed we were working. It had come as a surprise when we were requested to introduce the name of 'Hahn' into our family lineage. Reasons are not given. We are told **reason is not the principle on which Higher Minds**

orchestrate their affairs! Carmella was in the best position to respond. In 1986 she and her partner, changed their surnames by deed poll to B'Hahn, (B = Brotherhood) establishing the name as a branch of the family to be carried by their two sons BenJaya and Asher. It was not until many years later that I discovered Hahn to be Madam Blavatsky's maiden name, her father being Colonel Peter von Hahn. Maybe the sense of affinity is merely through the name. Maybe there are other links, undisclosed. Who knows? With these mysteries in mind and as yet having had no reply at all from India there is nothing for it but to set off into the unknown in search of my Wisdom School.

The Great Imprinters
January 2010

Chennai is a maelstrom of swirling energies. I have no instructions of where to go other than an address 'The Theosophical Society, Adyar'. Guarded gates enclose an estate of two hundred and fifty acres of twisting banyans, towers of tangled trees, tiny temples tucked between secret paths, raucous crows and rainbow flashes of feathered life and a few signs of Hansel and Gretel habitation. What world is this? Leadbetter Chambers, an old colonial building, appears at the end of a winding trail and there I am; a name upon a page allocated not only a bed but four beds swathed in white netting in a cavernous vaulted dormitory with a king size desk.

Describing Adyar is akin to describing a man by his feet, you simply do not see the whole; you know there is a whole but it is elusive. Paths meander; I cannot guess where they will lead. Here there is no show of western opulence; neither does India herself dare to burst through the boundary separating this oasis of stillness from the moving parts that are Chennai. Buildings are symbols of antiquity; the Great Hall of statues saluting Wisdoms found and preserved; pathways are marked by poles bearing the illustrious names of founders long gone yet still present in the Great Stillness. Those that have been before us have built a concentrated energy-field here of some dimensions. It waits. These are the Mahatma Fields; *Mahat* being Universal Consciousness and *Ma* the mind of a realized human. When *ma* resonates to the *Mahat* then one enters a Mahat-ma Field. Each who enters must find their own way through, maybe even adding their own enlivened thoughts to those who hold these vast Mind Fields steady, unassailable and secure.

The first task is to deal with all the many practicalities in order to focus on the Wisdom work. I deal. Rules here are to be obeyed. Arrival is essential promptly at meals in response to the gong. Breakfast at 7am; meditation at 8am; Lectures from 8.30 until lunch at 11.15. 3pm is tea and 6pm dinner; all to be ordered and prepaid. Whatever is on the menu is pot luck. I opt only for breakfast and dinner. There are another eighteen rules listed. I determine to be obedient in all respects though finding that arms and legs need to be kept covered calls for improvisation of my delightfully useless sun dresses. Adyar is an oasis; without snack bars, phones, televisions, bank, or swimming pool. It is time to begin an ashramic life. Adyar demands it. You must change your mind set immediately, let go of life in the fast lane. This is neither main stream nor a minor stream. This is something else.

Who are my fellow students? To begin with we are about thirty, a spectrum of cultures both male and female from Australia, Brazil, Scandinavia, England and America, Switzerland, Belgium and India. India is the largest contingent though there is little chance of dialogue as they reside in a different area of the grounds. There is no communal meeting place indoors and as mosquitoes swarm at mealtimes in the open dining area, dialogue is limited. I learn that mostly students belong to Lodges. I am designated 'unattached', as there are no Lodges in Worcestershire, hence I do not have a ready made sub group. It is known I have only just joined and it is assumed that I am new to theosophy. I am not so sure, but my language base is different so having traversed such a peculiar route to Adyar, it seems prudent to keep quiet and focus on the lectures. There are forty of them, two per day. I attend every one. Our afternoons are free for study.

Our Class Master, Colin Price from UK has chosen to focus for a month on Geoffrey Farthing's book 'Deity, Cosmos and Man'; an outline of esoteric science. The first necessity is to purchase a Theosophical Glossary in order to translate the Sanskrit words used in the text. Often a Sanskrit term contains a key thought enabling a better grasp of the teaching than the word alone expresses. Our course book is divided into twelve segments: The Constitution of Man and Cosmos; Hierarchy; Akasha; Elements; Law; Death and Reincarnation; Origins; Globes, Rounds and Races; Evolution; Spiritualism and Psychism; Spiritual Development; and Religion. The study method is to go over the same segment three times, each time penetrating more deeply. The presenter draws on his background in Aeronautical Engineering and well explored Christian ethics as science, religion and philosophy merge in an exposition of theosophical thought. My notebook fills up rapidly. I am asked by Indian professors for a copy as they cannot speed write in English. I feel good about that as it gives opportunity for contact. Some are going back into their Universities to teach Metaphysics; Psychology or other associated subjects; one is an Atomic Scientist; another is a poet.

I've hired a bicycle so that I can at least reach the gate where transport can be found for forays into Chennai but most often mind free wheels with pen in hand as I contemplate the morning's lectures, address the question of why I am here and pen a mystical tale or two. Our Class Master is clearly building a thought form, a massive structure in which each piece is crafted day after day until they all fit together making a whole; an imprint of gigantic proportions. And that is what, to my mind, Adyar is about. Adyar is holding, at the etheric level, an evolutionary imprint of the Plan for human and planetary evolution and it is this that Madame Blavatsky had been attempting to convey. Such imprints are in place in many and diverse parts of the world in many creative forms. They are indestructible but not necessarily easily accessible. I am here not primarily to make friends and connections but to absorb whatever I am able of this vast imprint; to balance my mystical imagery and sensory perceptions with a more scientific, intellectual apprehension of The Plan. So that is what I do.

There is an extensive book shop where I am drawn to books telling of the real life mystical tale of Madame Blavatsky the woman and her way of being in the world. As she struggled for control of her body and emotions, fighting to break through the dominance of male-minds, the Mahatmas were her Advisors, Informers and a healing force. How she needed their care! In the public domain, holding a perspective of reality that had little credence in the world at large she suffered immeasurably as she held resolutely to her task of paving the way for the Consciousness Revolution that had to come. Is it compassion that I feel so strongly curling through my day as I find myself moved by the indomitable spirit of this Russian woman travelling alone in the East, living with the Mahatmas in a Tibetan hide-away? When I return I determine to bring a thread of her vital essence into Adam House.

There is also a wealth of information to be studied on the creation of Thought Forms, through the illustrative work of Annie Besant and C.W. Leadbeater, which is of particular relevance as the pen is busy informing me: **You work with multiple mind variants to create vehicles for their expression; vehicles through which to manifest thought forms imbued with meaning.** It is indeed in many ways a wisdom school of some proportions.

Chennai too holds prizes and surprises. The city breathes with culture. To explore her is to discover there have been many Masters here. The voice of Krishnamurti still echoes from videos in the tranquillity of the K.M. Foundation; Vivekananda holds his riveting Presence amongst a display of sacred art and words to match portraying the evolution of culture and the relentless Journey of Enlightenment. St. Thomas, intrepid disciple who lived as servant and died as martyr, still calls pilgrims of many faiths to his cave, the Shrine on the Mount and the Great Basilica edging the sweeping sands of the Marina. Where the Great

Imprinters have made their marks, whether they are set upon the page or by virtue of the life, a resonance remains untouched by time, accessible still.

The Essential Mother

Derek is flying in and I am immeasurably glad. He finds it incredulous that I would have wanted to remain in such a strange monastic world. When I tell him I wasn't exactly in it he says 'no wonder' and yet it has been filled with wonder and wisdom and living words. We are heading for Pondicherry where Derek has never been. Travelling down the coast in an auto rickshaw we see the effects of the tsunami on the low lying land. It's a fascinating if rickety ride. We break the journey at Malabalapuram, a half way point, to luxuriate in a hotel with a swimming pool for two days before we move into the Mother's world of Pondicherry. The familiar figure of The Mother, an enchanting Presence, is pictured on street stalls and shop windows, pulling us into her ashram to contemplate the flowered mandala from which the essence of her life pervades all who are drawn into her Presence.

We are children, eating ice creams, quaking as our rickshaw driver hurtles on, a tiny baby on his lap drooping with sleep, flapping balloons tied to his steering wheel. Derek buys me a stuffed bear that says 'Love You'; I buy some of The Mother's books reading him a few snippets and a prized CD of her speaking. Derek looking towards a picture of The Mother on the wall above our bed says: 'I know that woman'. Do I know what he means? Not exactly, neither I suspect does he, but I sense significance in his words that need neither question nor explanation. There are many different ways of knowing.

Madame Blavatsky 1831-1891

The Mother 1878 – 1973

Two Guiding Lights, two women of different characters both Europeans who heard the call of India which drew them to the same coast to unfold their missions; both knowing their tasks which they undertook to the letter; both determined in their life long efforts to further the development of Supramental Consciousness.

They sit in their photo frames on my wall at home still inspiring; holding a steady gaze; two archetypes; two activators.

I am loath to leave Derek to return to Goa without me but there's work to do at home. Sandra and Clive are leaving Adam House in a few months, returning to their home in North Wales. For Sandra the Work and Family is the pivot of her life as they are mine. These months ahead are precious. There are programmes to develop that will bring a new vitality to our work in the light of recent experiences; keys to be found that will unlock more of the Treasury of Wisdom such as the influences of *The Great Solar Rays* that have become the an intrinsic part of our lives.

I am beginning to foresee for the first time ever, a winter alone in Adam House … well not **exactly** alone.

51. Distilling the Essence

The vapour of an ascendant mind is Pure Thought
The vapour of transcendent emotions is Divine Love
The vapour of vibrant matter is the Body of Light
The vapour of the Moving Spirit is the Essence of All Being

The Wedding of the Snow Queen

There is no way that I would have missed the wedding of my grand-daughter Amy, Sandra's youngest child. It will take place on 19th December 2010. Derek is returning once again alone to India in November leaving me to dance for two.

At the Three Kings Christmas gathering of the previous year the fairy story of the Snow Queen had been one of the themes depicted. In the veranda a

life size figure of the Snow Queen had stood equally regally in her white mosquito netting palace a-waiting the telling of the Hans Andersons tale. *The Snow Queen* is an allegorical story telling of the shattering of The Great Mirror leaving shards of tiny distorting fragments so that the World could no longer be seen as a whole. Only by the reunion of a boy, who The Queen had captured, and a girl, whose ever-lasting love for him is symbolised by the Rose, can the Snow Queen restore the mirror to wholeness.

Unaware of my Christmas snow scene Amy had spent the year planning her own. The wedding is to be whiter than white; not just the dress but the world at large. Just in case the world doesn't co-operate a snow machine is hired. On the wedding eve six inches of snow fall in the night leaving roads to Bristol impassable. The groom's relatives in Birmingham have to turn back. It is Charlotte in her Land Rover who forces a way through for us, beating the clock by a hairs breadth. The bride arrives, a cloud of white satin and fur. A band of reindeer-hatted musicians appear to perform, gathering unsuspecting witnesses to a union that has levels of significance beyond the ordinary. How can you ever know who will be called upon to play a star role? Amy and Jon are the boy and girl complete with abundant roses in button holes and bouquets. I am finding it surreal.

Ceremony over, we move to another magical scene of fairy lights and fairy cakes; gospel choir and whirling dervishes. They are all here, my four children, seven grandchildren and Isla, Sandra's tiny grand daughter, first fragment of the next generation; all a living part of me as I am of them. A family whole.

Wave after wave of music is having a revitalising effect pulling me into the changing rhythms, and Clive's brother is pulling me out onto the dance floor. Those legs that once dared to fail, have a life of their own and are dancing with the vitality of a spinning Shivic Tandava; the dance of transformation. I am dancing not just for two but for however many are in need of a surrogate dancer! It is exhilarating. Invisible fetters that I did not know were there are falling, freeing both body and mind.

The Essential Truth

The sense of freedom remained and with it came a sense of recognition that my life journey has been about freedom. In all these long years I have been seeking freedom for others; freedom from webs of prejudice; from damaged minds and the unhallowed past; from the poverty trap and the dwarf of ignorance; and from outmoded patterns, traditions and beliefs whilst ensuring freedom for my family to become whoever they truly are. In that seeking it seems possible that I have at last found my own and with it comes a freedom for the pen that was not a craving but a necessity, if I am to attempt to write and speak in truth as I perceive life to be, and lay my own upon the line. It is time to close the door to Adam House to find a sense of exhilaration by dancing with the pen from which I doubt if I will ever be free.

Now why do I say that? It is because in Welsh for 'pen' means 'head'. Words are such jesters! There is a meridian between the head and the hand. Whatever comes into the head has a ready made channel of expression through the movement of the hand. The pen is an instrument without any investment in the source of that which it conveys. Yet it is an imprinter within its own domain. And it is the servant of Mind ... the Great Mahat. All that the pen has written has been a product of Mind; **whose** mind is irrelevant if it carries the ring of truth that reverberates in the heart. No longer do I feel any need to distinguish between 'my' words and those of any other Întelligence.

The whole truth and nothing but the truth, is pledged every day in the Courts of Law. Truth that must be discovered, extracted from the webs of deceit and falsehood, recognised and recorded. Consciousness is bound by the same pledge, to seek and find those threads that will construct a web of truth that will hold together the fragments of every splintered life or shattered dream. Realizations that have resulted from these experiential years have implications beyond the personal as the whole of society, cultures, traditions, life styles and governments find themselves in the cauldron of change.

So what of wisdom? Wisdom is always present. It is human consciousness that is not always tuned in on the wisdom wavelengths. In a whimsical moment one might say that Wisdom is a goddess who holds truth written on the palm of her hand; the Mother who imparts truth in a glance if you can but read it; the Essential Being, the Self, sitting in its monastery, its balcony, its brave new world contemplating Light … or shadow.

Perhaps it is more pertinent to say in a straightforward manner that there exists a Divine Plan for the furtherance of Humankind; set within the Planetary Scheme of Evolution. The Plan is well in hand, only the methods of its implementation will change according to the response of humanity. Intelligences, seen and unseen, are at work, shaping designs; shifting paradigms; activating programmes; imprinting imagery of a Solar Race that knows no positioning by colour, status, age, culture or gender; a Race based, not on intellect but on the intelligent apprehension of the Life Force and obedience to Natural Law.

That is how truth has fashioned itself into the whole that over-lights my days.

The Elixir

The Spirit of the Law, in whatever form that phrase conveys has, as promised, been ever present on my journey, doing its best to expose me to experiences from which learning will ensue. Alchemy is the Science of Spiritual Experience and the cauldron is the vessel of transformation. The golden particles that remain after the brew has been poured are spiritual gold, an evolved form of consciousness, the Elixir, for which there is no communal recipe. No-one may see within the cauldron of another; no-one may covet another's gold nor seek to measure its purity, for each must tend the fires beneath their own vessel according to the heat that they can bear and select the ingredients that best befit that life. What remains will determine what comes next, and for me I sense there is a next. India is calling. I do not need to answer. She knows that I will come.

Freedoms Gates

The child had grown quietly observant of the world she did not understand. Questions teetered on the edge of her tongue, sometimes tumbling on the check-clothed days of passing years. Occasionally Father would examine a question and pop it in the sugar bowl smiling the words:

'What a sweet notion'.

Another day he might slip a shy question between the creases in his whiter than white handkerchief, folding carefully as he mused:

'You never know when you might need a good question'.

Answers were minimal really until a sudden day when she dropped a boulder of a question too substantial to be scooped up or folded away.

'Father, what is FREEDOM?'

The question sat there staring straight at Father. Slowly he stood to attention; gaze locked into her Mother's shining eyes.

'It is a world that lies beyond the Gates' Father replied, still holding his gaze as if he saw that world within her Mother's eyes.

'Shall we go there one day Father?'

'Yes' his voice held certainty. *'When you have eaten many dinners and when The Law is engraved on your heart'.*

'That sounds a bit painful Father'.

'That's as may be, but it will be worth it child.'

'Do you have to pay to go inside?' asked the child shaking her silver purse.

'Oh yes, but money doesn't buy the ticket. We pay with our lives'.

Contacts

Mhaletta Taylor
Meta Foundation for Human Potential
Adam House, Adams Hill,
Clent,
West Midlands DY9 9PS
UK
email: metafoundation@yahoo.com

Sandra Casey
Hafan, 2 Moelfre Terrace,
Llanbedr, Gwynedd LL45 2LE
North Wales
email: sandracasey@live.co.uk

Carmella B'Hahn
Heartwood
Bowden House Community
Totnes, Devon TQ9 7PW
UK
www.solacealchemy.com
email: carmella@solacealchemy.com